Defining Islamic Statehood

Also by Imam Feisal Abdul Rauf

ISLAM: A Sacred Law
ISLAM: A Search for Meaning
MOVING THE MOUNTAIN: A New Vision of Islam in America
QURAN FOR CHILDREN
WHAT'S RIGHT WITH ISLAM IS WHAT'S RIGHT WITH AMERICA

Defining Islamic Statehood

Measuring and Indexing Contemporary Muslim States

Imam Feisal Abdul Rauf
Founder and Chairman, The Cordoba Initiative, USA

To Roger & Deborah,

with much love,

Y. A. Rauf

January 14, 2016

First published 2015 by
PALGRAVE MACMILLAN

Palgrave Macmillan in the UK is an imprint of Macmillan Publishers Limited, registered in England, company number 785998, of Houndmills, Basingstoke, Hampshire RG21 6XS.

Palgrave Macmillan in the US is a division of St Martin's Press LLC, 175 Fifth Avenue, New York, NY 10010.

Palgrave Macmillan is the global academic imprint of the above companies and has companies and representatives throughout the world.

Palgrave® and Macmillan® are registered trademarks in the United States, the United Kingdom, Europe and other countries.

ISBN: 978–1–137–44680–0 Hardback
ISBN: 978–1–137–44681–7 Paperback

This book is printed on paper suitable for recycling and made from fully managed and sustained forest sources. Logging, pulping and manufacturing processes are expected to conform to the environmental regulations of the country of origin.

A catalogue record for this book is available from the British Library.

Library of Congress Cataloging-in-Publication Data

Abdul Rauf, Feisal, 1948-
    Defining Islamic statehood : measuring and indexing contemporary Muslim states / Imam Feisal Abdul Rauf.
      pages cm
      ISBN 978–1–137–44680–0 (hardback)
      1. Islam and state. 2. State, The. I. Title.

JC49.A238 2015
320.55'7—dc23   2015018878

To our patrons, former Malaysian Prime Minister Abdullah Ahmad Badawi and current Prime Minister Najib Abdul Razak. The two have displayed a remarkable and sincere commitment to promoting and championing an understanding of Islam as a moderate, nonviolent religion, and in implementing such an understanding towards laying the foundations for a modern Islamic State. This book is also dedicated to all the scholars who participated in this project. If not for them, this project would not have been possible.

Contents

List of Illustrations

Figures

Tables

Acknowledgments

Defining Islamic Statehood is the result of a dozen years of work to attain consensus (*ijma'*) among a working group of Muslim scholars and practitioners of Islamic law. This book defines the foundations for a modern Islamic State, and measures and indexes contemporary Muslim countries against this definition.

This project was initially conceived in the course of a discussion I had with Professor Muhammad Hashim Kamali. It gained traction with the help of the late Professor Mahmood Ghazi, who proposed that we convene a small working group of scholars to discuss modern Islamic governance. As the reader will certainly notice, Professor Ghazi's extraordinary scholarship on Islamic law and his political insights permeate the pages of this book. May God bless his soul with His mercy and compassion and grant him the highest reward in Paradise.

The collective wisdom of all of the scholars who participated in this project and their lifetime of study, reflection, struggle, and engagement with their faith shaped the juristic content of this work. In particular, their varied experiences in the diverse Muslim communities all over the world were invaluable in defining the broad foundations of modern Islamic statehood.

Creating a viable index was a vexing and convoluted journey that could not have been achieved without the immense help of numerous individuals and organizations. We are indebted to Zaiton Hassan of Capital Intelligence Advisors, Yeah Kim Leng and Julie Ng of the Rating Agency Malaysia, and Robert Rotberg of the Mo Ibrahim Index of African nations. We owe special thanks to Gallup, especially John and Jonathan Clifton, for educating us on the challenges of polling, developing an index, and ensuring that the juristic definition of each concept in the index correlates with measurable proxies.

Dr Kamel Jedidi, the John A. Howard Professor of Business, and Dr Asim Ansari, the William T. Dillard Professor of Marketing at Columbia University, advised on the statistical analysis and algorithms behind the quantitative narrative of this book. The authors extend appreciation to these two statistical experts for their technical counsel and guidance. Any indexing errors that may arise in this publication are solely the responsibility of the authors.

This book would not have been possible without the dedication and work of the many Cordoba Initiative staff, interns, and employees. We thank Shafiq Walji, Courtney Erwin, James King, Josh Martin, Caity Bolton, Adrienne Johnson, and Ali Karjooravary.

We were exceptionally fortunate to have our editor Eleanor Davey Corrigan, whose guidance at Palgrave Macmillan made this work see the light of day.

As this book also emanates from my life journey, my final thanks are to my late father, Dr Muhammad Abdul Rauf, through whom I met many of my truest teachers, colleagues, students, and friends. I have learned so much from all of them. And, it is this learning that I have sought to share in these pages. May God shower blessings on them all.

The Participants

Convener

Imam Feisal Abdul Rauf is the founder and chairman of the Cordoba Initiative, a nonprofit organization dedicated to improving Muslim–West relations and promoting moderation. For over 25 years he was the imam of Masjid al-Farah in New York City. He is the author of *What's Right with Islam Is What's Right with America* and *Moving the Mountain: Beyond Ground Zero to a New Vision for Islam in America*. In 2010, he was ranked among the "100 Most Influential People of the World" by *Time Magazine*, "Top 100 Global Thinkers" by *Foreign Policy*, and "Top 50 Arabs" by the *Middle East Magazine*.

Scholars

Ahmad Abbadi is the Secretary General of the League of Moroccan `Ulama'` (Islamic religious scholars) and recently retired as director of the Moroccan Ministry of Islamic Affairs. He has been Professor of Islamic Thought at Qadi Ayyad University in Marrakesh, Morocco, and at DePaul University in Chicago, Illinois, where he was a Fulbright Fellow.

Jasser Auda is the executive director of the Maqasid Institute, a global think tank based in London and a visiting professor at Carleton University in Canada. Prior to that he was Associate Professor and Deputy Director of the Center of Islamic Legislation and Ethics at the Qatar Foundation. He is a member of the executive board and also a founding member of the International Union of Muslim Scholars, and is one of the world's foremost experts on the objectives of Shariah. His book *Maqasid al-shari`ah as Philosophy of Islamic Law: A Systems Approach* is used as a central text in graduate programs in Islamic studies around the world.

Dato' Osman Bakar is Chairman, Professor and Director of the Sultan Omar Ali Saifuddien Centre for Islamic Studies in Brunei Darussalam. He was previously the deputy CEO of the International Institute of Advanced Islamic Studies in Kuala Lumpur, as well as the Emeritus

Professor of Philosophy at the University of Malaya. He is a specialist in contemporary Islamic thought and has written books on the relationship between Islam and science, which have been translated into ten different languages. He has worked as Malaysia Chair of Islam in Southeast Asia at Georgetown University's Center for Muslim–Christian Understanding, and in 1994 was awarded the royal award of "Dato" by the Sultan of Pahang and by the King of Malaysia in 2000.

Anies Baswedan is President of Paramadina, a university in Jakarta as well as the Chairman of *Indonesia Mengajar* (Teaching Indonesia). He was named one of the "Top 100 Public Intellectuals in the World" by *Foreign Policy* in 2008 and was named among the "500 Most Influential Muslims in the World" by the Royal Islamic Strategic Studies Center in Jordan. He was also elected to serve as moderator for Indonesia's historic first presidential election.

Mahmood Ahmed Ghazi, who passed away in 2010, is the former president of the International Islamic University in Islamabad. He also served as a judge on the Federal Shariat Court of Pakistan and as Pakistani minister of *Awqaf* (Islamic religious trusts). He translated the works of Muhammad Iqbal, a Pakistani national hero, into Arabic.

Khanjar Hamieh was the director of the Islamic Legal Institute in Beirut. Since 2007, he has been Professor of Philosophy at the Lebanese University in Beirut. He has published extensively on Islamic law and philosophy, Shi'ism, and Sufism.

Mohammad Hashim Kamali is Professor of Law at the International Islamic University of Malaysia. In addition to his professorial duties, he is Chairman and CEO of the International Institute of Advanced Islamic Studies in Kuala Lumpur, Shariah advisor with the Securities Commission of Malaysia, and Chairman of Shariah Board at Stanlib Corporation of South Africa. In 1995 as well as in 1997, Kamali was awarded the Isma'il al-Faruqi Award for Academic Excellence twice. He has served on constitutional review committees in Afghanistan, Iraq, and the Maldives and has been called the most widely read living author on Islamic law in the English language.

Mohammad Javad Larijani is President of the Human Rights Council in Iran and a top advisor to the Supreme Leader Ayatollah Khamenei; he has previously served as deputy foreign minister of the Islamic Republic and as director of the Institute for the Study of Theoretical Physics and Mathematics in Tehran. While he is closely involved with the Iranian government, he participated in this project in a personal capacity and his comments do not represent the official views of the government of Iran.

Ahmad Syafii Maarif, who studied under the legendary Fazlur Rahman at the University of Chicago, was for many years the Chairman of Muhammadiyah, the second largest Islamic organization in Indonesia. It boasts nearly 30 million members and runs over 14,000 educational institutions, from preschools to universities in that country. He is a senior lecturer in IKIP Yogyakarta and an active spokesperson and writer.

Tahir Mahmood is a leading Professor of Law in India and the author of numerous books. He has been a part of the law faculty at Delhi University and has held various prestigious positions in the government of India. His widely acclaimed writings discuss Islamic law and the progressive interpretation of religion-legal matters, which have been cited by the Supreme Court of India and many state high courts in more than 20 judgments.

Tun Abdul Hamid Mohamad is the retired chief justice of Malaysia, with "Tun" being the highest royal award to a civilian for meritorious service to the country. He is now chairman of the Law Harmonizing Committee of Bank Negara (Central Bank) of Malaysia, a member of the Shari'ah Advisory Council of Bank Negara as well as of the Securities Commission, a member of the Judicial Appointments Commission, and a member of the Shari'ah and Civil Law Harmonizing Committee of Brunei Darussalam. Previously, he was a member of the Court of Appeal of Malaysia and judicial commissioner of the state of Penang. His legal career spans 40 years in which he wrote 567 judgments of the Superior Courts and encompassed nearly every important post in the Malaysian judicial system. Moreover, he is an adjunct professor of the Universiti Tenaga Nasional Malaysia (UNITEN) and the Universiti Utara Malaysia (UUM).

Recep Şentürk is General Director and Dean of Graduate Studies in the Alliance of Civilizations Institute at the Fatih Sultan Mehmet Vakıf University, Istanbul, Turkey, and the head of the Department of Civilization Studies. He is a sociologist and a scholar of the *hadith*, the traditions of the Prophet Muhammad and his companions, and Islamic law. He has been a visiting scholar at Emory University Law School. He is a member of the editorial board of the Turkish *Encyclopedia of Islam*, the founder and president of the Istanbul Foundation for Research and Education (ISAR) and the Center for Sciences and Arts (ISM) in Istanbul.

Public relations specialists

Humayun Gauhar is a marketing specialist in Islamabad and was a close advisor to former Pakistani President Pervez Musharraf, serving as Musharraf's chief writer and editor. He is the president of an engineering firm and a charitable foundation and the editor of a number of influential publications in the field of business in Pakistan.

Ramzi Khoury is the CEO of Strategy Falcons LLC, an independent strategic communications group registered in Dubai, Amman, and Kuala Lumpur that has been engaged in perception management projects all over the world. Khoury began his career in Granada Television in the early 1980s and has since held many positions, including editor-in-chief of daily newspapers, advisor to prime ministers and presidents, and Senior Arab Region Advisor to the United Nations Alliance of Civilizations. Khoury is a Christian, with a deep understanding of Islamic theology and culture.

Introduction

This book tells the story of the Shariah Index Project, a project that sought to define the term "Islamic statehood" in a measurable way and then rate countries according to that definition. This book chronicles the thoughts, concerns, points of contention, and ultimately the agreement of a group of scholars representing the global spectrum of Islamic legal and political thought. It captures their spirit of open and honest debate, as well as their consensus, as they sought to define the fundamental requirements and parameters of a present day Islamic state. Finally, it recounts their efforts to establish a methodology that measures a state's compliance with that definition, thereby helping concerned authorities to better align their governments with the divine ordinances enshrined in the Qur'an and the Sunnah.

This project was born out of a need to address a piece of the unfinished business of the Muslim world, namely, how to determine the right balance between institutions of political authority and institutions of religious authority, and to do so within the context of modern day governance. Western societies have addressed this issue by effectively "separating" church and state, and since much of Western progress and development came after this separation, most in the West view this separation as a necessary requirement for good governance. But this view is not widely held in much of the Muslim world. The development and apogee of the Muslim enlightenment was launched with the advent of the Prophet Muhammad. Thus Muslims have difficulty separating religion from political discourse, as religion is an essential part of their existential worldview. Muslims' concept of "the rule of law" cannot be separated from Divine Law. Thus, in 1924, when nation-states were formed from the political breakup of the Ottoman Empire, political movements sprouted throughout the Muslim world seeking to establish

Islamic states. *"Islam is the solution"* and *"The Qur'an is our constitution"* were among the slogans of these twentieth century Islamic political movements.

While it was a rarely used part of the political lexicon for centuries, the term "Islamic state" gained significant momentum at the turn of the twentieth century. In 2011, the aftermath of the Arab uprisings saw renewed interest in the question of Islamic statehood. New governments expressed their commitment to Islamic governance amidst the fears of many that such commitments would lead to the violation of human rights. On 23 October 2011, the Libyan National Transitional Council Chairman Mustafa Abdul Jalil affirmed that, as an Islamic state, Libya would uphold the Shariah as the principal source of legislation. Any law that violated the Shariah would be null and void. Soon after, on 27 October 2011, Tunisia's Islamic party *Ennahda* won the majority of seats in parliament, declaring that Shariah would be the source of the country's legislation, yet assuring foreign news sources that "Tunisia is a society of moderation."

These and other states define themselves as Islamic, but what exactly *is* Islamic statehood? In the desire to see our religion reflected within our political processes, Muslims treat this term as if it were self-evident. And yet there is no consensus about its meaning. Three definitions have been widely used: the first is that an Islamic state is one that has a majority population of Muslims. This demographic definition was used in the creation of the Organization of the Islamic Conference (OIC, now called the Organization of Islamic Cooperation) in 1969.[1] A second definition, which the Afghan Talibani and the Sudan under Omar al-Bashir adopted and which was announced by the Sultan of Brunei in October 2013, focuses on applying the Islamic penal code, specifically punishments known as the *Hudud*, and outlawing "un-Islamic" practices.[2] These states define their Islamicity by forbidding crimes and harshly punishing transgressors. A third definition is that an Islamic state is one that is governed by Shariah, perhaps best described as instituting an "Islamic rule of law," and thereby manifesting the principles of just governance as prescribed in the Qur'an and the Sunnah.

Most Muslim scholars would agree on this third definition. It is not enough to simply have a population with Muslim majority, nor to apply a penal code to define a state "Islamic." If a state is to bear the name of Islam, it must govern according to the positive principles enshrined in the Qur'an and the practice and teachings of the Prophet Muhammad (*Sunnah*). Most scholars would agree on this principle, and several different approaches to governance based on it have been developed over the past millennium.

Nonetheless, there is no consensus on how to accomplish this in practice – especially in the context of the modern nation-state. Furthermore, no attempt has been made to define means to measure a state's compliance with this definition to enable nations to apply the standard in practice.

The conference of scholars

The Shariah Index Project was born out of a desire to fill this gap. Under the aegis of the Cordoba Initiative, an international multi-faith organization working to improve Muslim-West relations that I founded in 2004, we convened a working group of scholars representing the spectrum of Islamic legal and political thought, including Sunni and Shi'i scholars of jurisprudence. Our scholars hail from across the Muslim world, including from Morocco, Egypt, Turkey, Lebanon, Afghanistan, Pakistan, India, Iran, Malaysia, and Indonesia. We met in Kuala Lumpur seven times over the course of six years, supported by the generosity of the former and current Malaysian Prime Ministers Abdullah Ahmad Badawi and Najib Abdul Razak.

The working group was tasked with two goals. The first was to attain consensus on a definition of the Islamic state in a way that reflected the continuity of Islamic thought and tradition. Accordingly, our sources in defining the Islamicity of a state were God's injunctions as stated in the Qur'an and conveyed by the Prophet Muhammad, and the reflections of 14 centuries of Muslim scholars. Muslims continually strive to comprehend the eternal values disclosed through revelation and to implement them in their varied and changing contexts. The second goal of the Project was to create a methodology and an index that would rate nations on their compliance with the definition. While many scholars have attempted to define Islamic governance, the task of rating states' compliance with such a definition has not been undertaken, and this project is thus a much needed contribution to the scholarly discourse.

As can be imagined, our conversations were lively and included impassioned moments of disagreement. While the differences among our scholars mirrored the differences across the Muslim world, their commitment to achieving consensus from the collective pool of their encyclopedic knowledge was an honor and joy to behold. Each scholar brought not only his individual experience and knowledge, but also the collective experience of his community, gleaned from long efforts to bring each society in line with the divine purpose.

After long and thorough deliberations, all of the scholars agreed that the outcomes of governance must accord with the Qur'anic principles of equity and justice for a state to be Islamic. While some scholars felt that these outcomes were the only indicators of a state's Islamicity, other scholars argued that a state's constitutional declarations, its legitimacy, and the religious qualifications of the ruler were also necessary criteria.

These concerns and perspectives, and the resulting degrees of consensus among the scholars are captured in Chapters 2 and 3 of this book, after an introduction to Shariah and the objectives of Islamic law in Chapter 1. The next two address such questions as: Does the Qur'an require Muslims to establish a state? How did the term "Islamic state" arise? Can we prescribe a comprehensive definition of an Islamic state? Is a state Islamic because it declares itself as such, or its political leader has certain qualifications, or is it Islamic because it produces a society based on the principles of the Qur'an and the Sunnah? Quotations from the scholars' conversations provide the basis for the narrative, interspersed with short extracts from our dialogue to give the reader a sense of the diversity of opinions present in our discussions. These chapters reflect the process we went through in reaching consensus on a working definition of Islamic governance, and in using this working definition as a basis for developing a methodology by which we can measure the Islamicity of a state.

Measuring Islamicity

While looking around the room during one of our meetings, one of the scholars, Ahmed Abbadi, remarked that simply gathering such a group and having them work together was a significant accomplishment. While convening the scholars and reaching consensus was challenging, developing a means of measuring compliance proved still more difficult. How are we to quantify the theoretical definition of an Islamic state that the scholars agreed on? The task required us to synthesize the science of Islamic jurisprudence with the indexing methods of the social sciences. What components of a state should be measured in order to determine its Islamicity? Should we engage in polling, or rely upon data that are already available? Our finite financial and human resources forced us to make hard and imperfect choices in developing methods and testing them. But the process through which we developed the measures and the insights we gained in engaging with the challenge is the subject of Chapters 4 and 5.

We do not claim that this index is a perfect measure of a state's Islamicity – achieving that will require many more iterations and more comprehensive and accurate data. We do claim, however, that we have accomplished an important milestone. We have created a powerful tool that can transform the discourse as Muslims seek to bring their societies in line with what they regard as Divine Intent. While, for reasons that will be explained in Chapter 5, we do not consider the index an accurate final measure of state fulfillment of the *Maqasid,* we stand firmly behind our jurisprudence and our methodology. More comprehensive and current data, and further iterations of this initial effort, will continue to improve the quality and accuracy of the index.

This book is divided into three parts. Each part captures the narrative of a necessarily ongoing work in progress. In Part I, we tell the story of accomplishing an initial milestone in achieving consensus among an international group of Muslim scholars on how to define an Islamic state. The story of this project then bifurcates into two tracks. Part II further describes our efforts in seeking to measure this first-step working definition. We briefly skim through our failed efforts and why they failed and describe in greater detail our success in achieving the important milestone of developing a measurement methodology. We emphasize that further iterations and acquisition of reliable and relevant data is necessary to develop an index that will meet the rigorous requirements of this science. In Part III, our contributors relate their stories on how they each understood and sought to apply the principles of their faith in their arenas of work, which fall into three areas: the political and the judiciary – being the main arenas of statehood and governance – and academia, which informs, comments on, and shapes what happens in politics, the judiciary, and governance. In learning about their work, the reader will gain a much deeper understanding of the jurisprudence, the challenges, and the intersection points of law, politics, and governance; the spaces in which statehood is defined and shaped.

We have also, following the "Arab Spring," shared summaries of this work with the Interim Government of Egypt in the hope that this jurisprudence can inform their discourse on what Islamic governance and an Islamic rule of law essentially means and bridge the divide between the Islamic and secular political parties in Egypt, and hopefully in the Muslim world. For if this divide is not successfully bridged, I fear that the Muslim world can see a second political ideological split, akin to the political divide that created the Sunni-Shia split, of global proportions. I say this because over the past century, from Morocco to Indonesia, and in both Sunni and Shia communities and nations, we have witnessed the sprouting of Islamic political parties and political movements – some of which have established "Islamic states" – all of which have this

Islamic-secular divide that to various degrees has deeply fragmented these nations.

And that, of course, is the ongoing and unfinished story of both tracks of this project. It is our hope that this volume, and future indexes that rate nations, will prompt further, dispassionate, and sober discussion about the characteristics and construction of the ideal Islamic state. The insights that leaders, academics, activists, and others can draw from this work will help improve the lives of millions across the globe. We see the project as making an important contribution to ensuring that the governing systems in nations with Muslim majorities and in member nations of the OIC produce the just and principled societies envisioned by God and His Messengers.

Conversation: why is the Shariah index project important?

The scholars highlight some of the key and specific aims of the project:

1. to revitalize Islam and its role in the world
2. to delineate what the Shariah says about the state and governance
3. to benchmark an Islamic state for the twenty-first century
4. to reduce malaise among Muslims who worry that they are not living in an "Islamic" state
5. to clarify for individual Muslims how to better fulfill both their spiritual and temporal obligations
6. to mitigate polarization within the Muslim community
7. to assist current governments in administering according to Islamic principles
8. to reshape perceptions in the West about Islam and Islamic governance

> **Imam Feisal:** Professor Ghazi, how would you describe the primary goals of this project?
>
> **Ghazi:** There's a real and genuine interest among the Muslim masses to have an "Islamic state" and a "revival of the Shariah."[3] In some cases, there are Muslim governments who are sincere in their own understandings and are trying to restore the Shariah. Yet, their perception differs from the masses.

Therefore, first and foremost, there is a need for consensus on what is meant by "Islamic state" or "implementation of the Shariah" in the Muslim world. In addition, Western observers are sensitive about the desire to have an Islamic state. They feel that if Muslim desires are realized, this may have a negative impact on Western culture and civilization; therefore, they oppose it tooth and nail. So, secondly, there is a need to clarify what is denoted by an Islamic state and to illustrate the great contributions that could be gained from the revival of an Islamic state. Thirdly, the perceptions on the principles of an Islamic state differ in various countries with Muslim majorities. I can provide you with an example: Mullah Omar [the then spiritual leader of the Taliban at the time of this meeting] has a genuine and sincere perception of the Islamic state as does Pervez Musharraf [who, at the time of this conversation, was the President of Pakistan], but their ideas of an Islamic state differ in many ways. However, there is always a common set of points on which they can agree. They can accept that this common set of points is the Islamic state and that this is how they can join their hands to reach that objective.

To achieve these three goals, we need to develop an Islamic index whereby we can judge the Islamicity of different states. In order to create such an index, first, we need to create an environment of positive competition in the Islamic states. Second, we need to provide a common basis so all stakeholders can pool their resources to realize a common objective. Finally, we need to reestablish Islam into a unifying force as it was in the past; unfortunately, it has become a dividing force in many Muslim countries. Today, the more you mention Islam in the public and political sphere, the more you contribute to dividing the rank and file of Muslim communities.

Therefore, in order to achieve these goals, we should in this first meeting develop the parameters of a Shariah index for the Islamicity of states by confining ourselves to three basic parameters. First, we should ensure the continuity of the Islamic intellectual tradition by producing new ideas and interpretations that would be accepted by the majority of Muslim scholars and the popularly acknowledged representatives of the Shariah.

Second, we should not lose sight of the requirements of modern times, because we cannot present ourselves as outdated. Of course, we recognize that combining the past with the requirements of the present is a challenging task.

Third, we should not present to the Muslim masses, the West, and Muslim leaders an index that consists of disputes and defensive opinions. We should confine ourselves to what is agreed upon among Muslims, and if there is a disagreement, it should be of the type that can be easily removed without offending the point of view of a certain group. For example, we will say that "such and such an issue" will be judged by the prevalent *madhhab* in the area. This procedure is fair because we can accommodate the different *madhahib*. If this becomes problematic, then we should acknowledge the issue by saying that Muslims differ on this issue.

At the same time, the traditional Islamic *fuqaha'* sitting in the famous Islamic institutions, whether Zaytouna, al-Azhar, Qarawiyyin, Nahdat ul-Ulama of Indonesia, or Nadwat ul-Ulama of India, will feel that this reflects the tradition of Muslims that began from the days of the *sahaba* [the Prophet's Companions] to our time. And hopefully, we will ensure the product will be available in Arabic, English, and other languages, so it will be positively hailed in the Shi'a community of Iran and Lebanon as well as the `*ulama'* of Saudi Arabia, the Indian subcontinent, and elsewhere. Our aim is to provide a realizable first step toward positive transformation in such countries by providing a "roadmap" that would guide leaders in governing according to the principles of Islam.

> **Hamieh:** We're here to understand what the Shariah says about the state, and thus we need to have the sources of Shariah in front of us. In the Glorious Qur'an and sacred Sunnah, the Shariah is very clear about the principles upon which a state should be run if Muslims are ruling. It also talks about the qualities of the ruler in the Islamic state. I think before we propose the principles of the Islamic state and the primary qualifications of the ruler, it's beneficial to understand the Shariah first. The Shariah doesn't ignore these issues. Of course, Sunnis and Shi'is have different views about a state that are both in accordance with the Shariah. In fact, there are even differences within the same school of thought, but there are also issues that they all have agreed upon. Within the revealed text of the Qur'an, Allah has allowed for multiple opinions, due to jurists' multiple understandings of a particular verse or *hadith,* which made many Muslim scholars and jurists agree on some issues and disagree on others. My contention, as Professor Ghazi has just said, is that we should focus on what they have agreed upon.

> **Imam Feisal:** Our basic aim here is *islah* (reform) and to reduce the confusion in the *ummah* about an Islamic state. Our main focus and aim is to clarify what the Shariah says about the state to the interested reader. And it is our hope that those involved in legislation may use these ideas as guidance as they seek to establish laws for their Islamic state.

Larijani: This project was created to address a specific challenge and we should understand this challenge. It's simple: in a number of Muslim communities, the idea of creating an Islamic state has become fashionable. While Muslim intellectuals, youth, and others are speaking about the need for an Islamic state, the harsh response from the Western community is that Islam doesn't have any concept of state. Until 1989, the West said that the only good state was a Communist state or liberal democratic state based on a secular mind-set. They told the world that the best way to live together was by the ideals formulated and diagnosed by Western liberal democracies. After the fall of the Soviet Union, they said that liberal democracies were the *only* way. So Muslims and the Islamic *ummah* are confronted with that powerful claim through the media and propaganda. As a result, Muslims are wondering whether Islam, which we believe is a comprehensive religion, actually addresses issues related to the social life of how to live together. One of the most important aspects of our social life is the creation and the management of a polity. Secular liberals say that Islam is silent in these areas and that Islam is only for the private life and for issues like praying. In matters pertaining to social existence, they argue one should be secular.

In response to this enormous challenge, some have advanced naïve, simple-minded, and even dangerous answers. The emergence of the Taliban and al-Qaeda are examples of this. When we lack a vision for creating an Islamic community, these groups and others are able to pronounce their version of Islam as correct. Our project, therefore, can shed some light for a huge number of Muslims; it can give them guidelines. One of the benefits of our discussion is to find a more rational and reasoned answer that is based on Islam. People are looking for such an answer. The Islamic Revolution in Iran, for example, was one response to this challenge. So this is very important.

Khoury: The question "What is an Islamic state?" is on the mind of every Muslim, as Dr. Larijani noted. And in my opinion, if we were able to read the minds of the majority of Saudis, their answer would be very different from the majority of Pakistanis, Jordanians, or Iranians, for example. At the end of the day, the issue is less whether one is Sunni or Shi`a; rather, it's an issue of perception and what has been created in people's minds. Definitions of an Islamic state are different within a state or even within a movement; for example, within the Muslim Brotherhood movement there are debates and differences of opinion regarding this issue.

The fact is that all Muslim governments have tried to find solutions to this question. Consider the established political systems we have in the Muslim world today. Those that claim to be Islamic all say they derive their legitimacy from the Shariah. So at the end of the day, they are all attempting to find a solution to the problem they are facing. The solution is in the Shariah and this is what we are doing. We are going deep into the Shariah and saying, okay, this is what an Islamic state looks like.

I wish to stress that if this index is not accepted as a product *by Muslims*, then we will fail. This is an Islamic index and it must be accepted by the Muslim world first. In this sense, Professor Larijani's comments are extremely important. We must address the need within the Muslim community and we have to create the necessary elements to make sure this product is acceptable to the vast majority of Muslims. As Dr. Hamieh said, we must source every single thing from the Shariah. This is a detailed and time-consuming process.

We must be clear about our goals. What do we want to achieve with this index? The Shariah index is an Islamic governance index. How do we want it to be used? We must take into consideration the need to influence and positively change perceptions if it is going to be useful.

Imam Feisal: Basically, we want to enhance the discussion on the subject of an "Islamic state." We want to reframe people's understanding of this issue and to raise the level and caliber of the discussion in a manner that's useful for anyone concerned about this subject. The current discourse on the Islamic state is more passionate than coherent, and we want to add coherence. That's a meta-objective of this project. This will reduce polarization within the Muslim *ummah* and the non-Muslim *ummah*. Jamaat Islamiya and other groups like the Taliban or Hamas, which you mentioned, all seek to establish an Islamic state, a *"dawlah islami-yyah."* Yet, there's no coherent understanding among the *ummah* on what this actually means. This is dangerous for the *ummah*. We can change the realities on the ground by dealing with how people use these terms today. So when Hamas, for example, wins an election and says they want an Islamic state; this is a reality on the ground, and our product should be relevant to such situations. We don't want this to be a mere theoretical exercise.

Kamali: I think that once we've identified our set of goals and the essential principles of Islamic statehood, then we can address the existing realities. Yes, we want everyone to listen to our framework, but we cannot take it for granted that everyone will agree with it.

Mahmood: To continue with that thought, I want to point out that there have been several Muslim governments that insist they're already Islamic states. However, their claims are doubted by some Islamic scholars on varying grounds. The Taliban regime in Afghanistan, for example, insisted that it was a true replica of *Khulafa' al-Rashidun*. This claim was doubted by many in the Muslim world. The Saudis also claim that they are a genuine Islamic state, even though this is not endorsed by many genuine Islamic scholars; similarly, the claim of Pakistan that it is a modern Islamic state is also disputed by many Islamic scholars on solid grounds. Undoubtedly, in all these cases, the claim was based on solid grounds but so was the disputation. It's very difficult to dispute the original claim or to dispute the disputation.

Imam Feisal: That's where we come in. We're seeking to build consensus among the scholars on what an Islamic state is. Some groups, for example, define it by the implementation of the *Hudud* penal code only.[4] As I tell people in the United States, that's like saying if you apply the American Penal Code, an American-style democratic state will naturally follow. As a result, another objective is providing a counter position to the misimpression that the Islamic state is driven solely by the application of the penal code within certain quarters of the Muslim *ummah*.

The concept of an Islamic state and Islamic governance has been addressed by many, including most of you who are experts on this topic. One objective of this project, its unique added value, is to extract that information and develop a process by which we can create modern day *ijma`*, or consensus, on it. We're creating a roadmap to establish agreed upon benchmarks for a twenty-first century Islamic state.

Ghazi: The idea is to sell the concept of a model Islamic dispensation that is viable for today's context and realities. If we're concerned with the rising tensions and fissures in the Muslim world, then we should try to bring people together through this project. We all respect and venerate Mawlana Jalaluddin Rumi, and he said, "*Tu barayi vasl kardan amadi, na barayi fasl kardan amadi.*" "You have come to join people; you have not come to divide people." So, we are here for *wasl* (joining) and not *fasl* (separating).

Mahmood: This is true. The purpose of Islam is to unite and this is the message of Rumi's poem. I think our exercise can minimize and mitigate differences on the definitions of an Islamic state; it can create consensus in the Muslim world.

Larijani: Another goal is to nullify the association of Islam with violence and terror. This false perception that doesn't hold water has been impressed upon the Western audience. While our primary focus is to produce an index that is relevant to our current situations in Muslim countries, it should also be understood by the Western community to play a role in cleaning up some of the ambiguities and false impressions about the Islamic world.

Khoury: It's true that the image of Islam in the West is a huge source of divide between the Muslim world and the West today. Of course, this is a perceptual divide. I think the Shariah Index Project can be a fantastic tool to help bridge the divide. One line of action should simply be to establish what is Islamic and what isn't Islamic. If I go back to the Shariah Index Project, for example, I should be able to find that murdering innocent people is not Islamic. This will help.

Hamieh: The misunderstanding in the West concerning Islam, Muslims, and the Islamic state is very dangerous and poses a genuine threat to our communities.

Abbadi: There is also this anxiety among Muslim youngsters and the people of the *ummah* in general about whether they are really living in legitimate states and, if not, then how can they do so.

Imam Feisal: I'm glad that you raised this point, Professor Abbadi, as the issue of governmental legitimacy is of prime concern. My hope is that this project will help clarify for both citizens and political leaders what a government must provide in order to qualify as legitimate in an Islamic sense.

Larijani: Informing Muslims of their Islamic responsibilities – and I'm thinking specifically of Muslims living as minorities – constitutes another objective. To show how a Muslim can base his life and activities, socially and individually, on the teachings of Islam, how he should behave, what he should expect from the community, and so on, is critical, even within a non-Muslim community.

Imam Feisal: Yes, we're seeking to educate Muslims on how they can, within their own realities either as a majority or a minority, fulfill their individual and communal obligations. The issue of harmonization is important in both states with Muslim majorities and states with Muslim minorities. For example, one of the issues being discussed right now in Canada and the United States is in the area of personal status laws, laws pertaining to marriage, divorce, inheritance, etc. The question is whether or not a space can be created for state legal authorities to accept Shariah personal status law for Muslims as legally binding so they can deploy the enforcement mechanisms of the state to enforce these judgments. In the mind of the devout North American Muslim, the more he or she is complying with Allah's will, the more he or she feels satisfied emotionally.

Abbadi: This is true, but I would also say that, in fact, we're *not* living up to our duties as an *ummah*. This is a collective problem. We aren't really connected to each other and we aren't positively participating in shaping our world. In many ways, we've just submitted; we're merely reactive. We must have clear visions to be positive and proactive in shaping history, and we need to be at the international table of consultation. I think that such an index would serve this purpose because it would be a move toward integration and productive engagement.

This project can also provide confidence and a model for change to our contemporary states. We must positively set this index to serve as a motor to promote development, self-confidence, openness, and peace in our countries by saying "look, all of our nations can be Islamic states, but we need to make further efforts to be better." If we can shape this index to promote these positive ideas, then a state of self-confidence and positivity would prevail. This would drive the *ummah* to live up to its duties and aspirations.

Imam Feisal: That's an excellent example of how this project can have a positive impact on empowering Muslims to constructively participate in shaping our world. It reminds me of a conversation I had with a scholar in Bahrain. The question asked was, "Can we arrive at a definition of what makes one a Muslim?" As we all know, for an individual, whoever says the *shahadah* is a Muslim. This is the minimal requirement (*al-hadd al-adna*) for a person to be Muslim, although we also have the maximum or peak requirement (*al-hadd al-āqsa*). Therefore, we have the different *maqām* or levels, from the minimum Muslim to the complete Muslim, each of whom must perform certain things and behave in certain ways.

Akin to this analogy, can we provide a similar answer to states, such that the leaders like Prime Minister Badawi can apply it realistically? We want a product to which they can refer. For example, if a leader inquires, "Can you tell me five or ten things I could do that will increase my state"s Islamicity rating from a three to a seven?" These are the kind of answers we would like to provide. This will give the *ummah* a great deal of confidence and propel it to live up to its duties and aspirations, as Abbadi said.

> **Gauhar:** But it should be clear that the index is not some kind of stick to beat governments and embarrass them so they are compelled to make changes. It should be presented as a tool that can help them govern better.

> **Imam Feisal:** That's right. If we can provide the agreed upon principles for what defines an Islamic state, regardless of how institutions are shaped, then this will give political leaders the opportunity to relate their particular societal programs to these sets of principles. That is one of the objectives of this project.

Part I

Defining an Islamic State and Rule of Law

1
Shariah and the Objectives of Islamic Law

What is Shariah?

The word Shariah in Arabic is a verbal noun stemming from the root *sh.r.'*, meaning to initiate, introduce, or ordain. It refers to the sum total of God's *shar'*, His revealed law and the eternal set of values He ordained for human beings to acknowledge as the basis of their law. Shariah, literally meaning a path leading to water, is figuratively the path trod by all humans to attain God's grace and reward in the hereafter.

In the Qur'an, God does not consider His major commandments to be unique to the Prophet Muhammad and his community.[1] Rather, they are universal commandments revealed throughout history. Thus in its widest and most inclusive sense, the term Shariah refers to the Divine Ordinances, the set of laws ordained by God the Lawgiver (*Shaari'*) for all of humankind, as declared in verse 42:13:

> He [God] has ordained (*shara`a*) for you of religion (*din*) what He commended unto Noah, and that which We have revealed to you (Muhammad), and that which We commended unto Abraham and Moses and Jesus – to establish religion (*an 'aqimu-din*)[2] and not to be divided therein.

The Shariah revealed through the Prophet Muhammad therefore comprises the same essential contents of the message given by God to the other prophets mentioned in this verse, namely Noah, Abraham, Moses, and Jesus. In this sense, it is the common denominator of the whole cluster of laws and guidelines that God revealed to at least these five Messengers. It is that *"eternal Divine Law that carries and embodies the Divine Intent for humankind."*[3] Kamali pointed out that the Shariah by name occurs only once in the Qur'an, in a Meccan sura (45:18), where the text reads: "Thus have We put you on the right way (*shari`atin*) of the Command (*amr*). So follow it and follow not the whimsical desire (*hawa*) of those who have no knowledge." "Because there was no Shariah in existence at that time," he clarifies, "this reference to Shariah can be considered a reference to Islam itself, not to a legal system as such." Despite that, today we think of religion and law as separate entities, the fact that the word *din* in the Qur'an can be translated as both religion and law gives weight to the notion that in reality these are not two separate entities. When we say that there is only one Shariah, and that it is immutable, this immutability belongs to this eternal Divine Intent.

Muslims use the term Shariah – meaning *their shari`ah* – in several ways. In the narrowest sense, Muslims define it as the Divine Intent as crystallized in the rules, ordinances, prescriptions, and prohibitions revealed in the Qur'an and amplified by the teachings of the Prophet Muhammad: the *Hadith* or the *Sunnah*. As Kamali explained, "When Muslims mention Shariah, we basically mean all of the *ayat al-ahkam* [the legislative verses] in the Qur'an – the injunctions – not the history or parables. These *ayat al-ahkam*, around 250 in number, are only about four percent of the entire Qur'an; and in the body of the *Hadith*, it is said that about 1,200 are *ahadith al-ahkam*."

Muslims have also used the term Shariah in a looser sense, where the Shariah refers to everything that is encompassed within the expression "Islamic law." This includes all the laws Muslims have lived under throughout history, ranging from laws derived from non-Islamic sources to laws that were subject to differences of opinion and context. In this sense, when we ask whether the Shariah can evolve we are not asking if the Divine Intent can change. Rather, we are asking whether our understanding of the most fundamental principles of the Shariah, which express the unchanging Divine Intent, can result in different corresponding manifestations based on changing contexts.

What results from this human endeavor to understand the Shariah and translate the Divine Intent into practical law is called *fiqh* (jurisprudence), from the Arabic verb *faqiha*, to understand. *Fiqh* (jurisprudence) is the science that results from human exertion of effort (*ijtihad*) to derive legal rules acquired from four main sources: the Qur'an and the Sunnah, the primary "closed" and finalized sources, and by consensus and analogical deduction, the secondary and "open" sources. Subsidiary sources include government legislation and judicial preference (*istihsan*, the jurist's mandate to find what the best interests are in a given situation) so long as these do not contradict the primary "closed" sources.

Fiqh is the result of human intellectual effort, called *ijtihad*, directed toward attaining this understanding of the Shariah. *Ijtihad*, the method and the process of deducing law from the above sources, is also the action by which laws can be enacted with a particular context in mind. The differing schools of law (*madhhab*, pl. *madhahib*) are differences of *fiqh*, not of Shariah. Thus certain aspects of the Shariah may look different in different times and places, and yet each and all are equally valid and display the impulse of one Shariah. As Ghazi shared, "There will always be diversity in unity. There are no specific requirements from the Shariah that each society must be identical in all respects."

As the conversation among our scholars began, it was clear that the attempt to understand the eternal Divine Intent and its relation to a particular context was not something that simply pertained to scholars of the past, leaving us to create national legislation only from what had been determined through the *ijtihad* of a different time and place. "We cannot think of the Shariah in a simple black-and-white form," Kamali insisted. The Shariah is "not just listed and given to us," he shared. "Rather it is *a vast developed legacy* that has been and *continues to be developed* over time, taking into account the conditions of societies and the people living there." In this light, the task of our group of scholars is to "bring the theory close to current reality and make it understandable to people in light of the contemporary generation's expectations and the world in which we live." He emphasized, "We are not going back to the first century."

Larijani echoed that sentiment, saying that "We need some *ijtihad*... The future is not a Xerox copy of the past, and we must make room for some innovation." Indeed, as Auda said to the group, "To define a contemporary 'Islamic' state will require a great deal of *ijtihad*."

Can Shariah evolve?

Many contemporary Muslims believe that every commandment, no matter how minor, no matter how culturally contextual, is eternally applicable to all contexts. This notion, however, is powerfully contradicted by historical judicial practice.

We know on the authority of the Qur'an itself that God has historically amended His own commandments from one prophet to another, from one era to another. As Jesus says in the Qur'an "(I have come) confirming what was before me of the Torah, and to make lawful for you some of what was forbidden to you."[4] The fundamental spiritual teachings remain constant throughout all of God's revelations to mankind – what

Jesus called the two greatest commandments, to love God and to love your neighbor as yourself (Matthew 22:34-39), upon which, Jesus adds, hang all the law and all the prophets. Islamic jurisprudence and law is built upon these two commandments, with the first commandment referring to what Muslim jurists call `ibadat (laws pertaining to acts of worship) and the second commandment referring to *mu`amalat* (laws pertaining to worldly affairs). It is the practical and social manifestations of those eternal spiritual teachings that change according to the exigencies and requirements of the age.

Not only has God's revelation progressively evolved from era to era, but even within the Islamic religious dispensation, laws have been adjusted according to the needs of the time. In the Qur'an God says that He has abrogated certain verses and replaced them with similar or better ones (2:106), demonstrating on the authority of God that *context plays a central role in the determination of law and the application of commandments.* Indeed the Prophet Muhammad was known to have given different advice for similar questions because the context required different approaches. After the death of the Prophet, we know that his second successor, Caliph Umar al-Khattab (the Prophet's father-in-law), who ruled during ten of the first dozen years after the Prophet's death and established very significant precedents in Muslim history, suspended the Qur'anic mandate of paying people to support their conversion to Islam. (Known as *mu'allafati qulubuhum* – and mentioned in Quran 9:60 – this practice was in many cases meant to compensate them for their losses in leaving behind their homes, property, and livelihoods in Mecca when they joined the Prophet and his faith in Medina). Caliph Umar even suspended the penalty for theft in a time of famine because, he decided, the need to feed oneself in order to survive trumped the sin of theft.

Muslim jurists regard it as possible to revise or reverse precedent based on legal argument or to interpret the context of a Qur'anic or prophetic ruling to determine applicability to modern times, and even to permanently suspend a Qur'anic ruling as Caliph Umar did. That we may do. But no Muslim can argue that the Qur'an or the *Hadith* was mistaken and therefore needs revision. As divine revelation, Muslims will never tamper with the Qur'an or change any part of it. But from the very earliest times Muslim jurists recognized the importance of context in interpreting, applying, or temporarily or even indefinitely suspending a Qur'anic commandment. This provides us with a powerful rationale to reconsider punishments of the Sharia penal code, certainly in the West where Muslims have to abide by Western law, but also in societies with Muslim majorities.[5]

So, are all earlier prescriptions of Shariah valid for today? Our predecessors delved into Divine Intent; they recognized justice as the supreme
objective of Shariah and interpreted laws in that light. The challenge
for our scholars today is to do what our predecessors did in their era,
namely to produce a juristic understanding of Islamic law that is relevant to the modern day context.

Islamic law: any law that is not un-Islamic

Just as law for a contemporary Islamic state cannot just be a mere
replica of past legislation, it likewise does not need to be limited to
the kind of laws one finds in classical books of Islamic jurisprudence,
since new concerns have arisen in modern times. Some Muslims deem
laws not mentioned within the Islamic legal tradition as "not Shariah,"
and therefore as "*necessarily un-Islamic.*" The extension of this thinking,
observed Tun Abdul Hamid, is the "tendency to treat all laws made by
parliament, as well as whatever common law is developed by courts,
as 'secular' and therefore de facto 'un-Islamic.' This means that they
should not be allowed to exist in an Islamic state."

Rather than continuing such distinctions based on sources of law,
Tun Abdul Hamid advocated for an approach that harmonizes traditional Islamic law with secular or civil law. In this light, Tun Abdul
Hamid defines Islamic law as "*any law that is not un-Islamic.*" Of the
five classifications of behavior within Islamic law, *fard* (obligatory),
mustahabb (recommended), *mubah* (neutral), *makruh* (discouraged),
and *haram* (forbidden), only one of them is forbidden, while the
others are all *halal* (permissible). From this perspective, all things that
are not *haram* are de facto *halal* (permissible), and therefore all law
can be considered Islamic and suitable for Islamic governance as long
as it does not violate the tenets of Islam. This has implications for
issues such as holding elections or having a parliament, which may be
considered Shariah-compliant even though they may not directly flow
from the historical Muslim political or legal tradition.

Can we adopt Western concepts and terms into our tradition?

Ghazi was emphatic that the general criticism against adopting Western
terminology is ill-founded, as "the tradition of Islam has always
responded to new situations and problems" and that "terminologies of
other traditions were accepted," at times given a new meaning in light of

the interpretation from the Qur'an and Sunnah. As an example, he cites al-Ghazali's famous work *al-Mustasfa*, which is on the subject of *usul al-fiqh* (principles of jurisprudence). The work is replete with terminology taken from Greek philosophy and logic to the extent that "one cannot understand al-Ghazali's religious thought if one is not familiar with pure Greek philosophy."[6]

There is also a precedent in the sayings of the Prophet and His companions, as Dr.Hamieh pointed out, where the believers are encouraged to seek knowledge and wisdom from whichever source offers it. As the Prophet is alleged to have said, "Seek knowledge even as far as China,"[7] and "Knowledge is the lost inheritance of the believer; wherever the believer finds it, he should take it,"[8] meaning that wisdom from any source "belongs" to the Muslim community. Likewise Imam 'Ali is recorded as saying, "Take wisdom from whoever gives it, whether the person is a believer or an unbeliever."[9]

The caveat, as Ghazi indicated, is that "if we uncritically open the gates to adopting Western terminology, it may affect the continuity of the Islamic tradition and the pristine character of Muslim civilization and culture." In light of that challenge, we need to be selective in what we adopt. There is no harm in adopting a new idea as long as it is "acceptable to the Islamic framework and adjustable to Shariah as a whole...provided it is interpreted in light of Islamic tradition." For example, the term "freedom of conscience" is undoubtedly Western. But, as Ghazi explained, there is something relevant to freedom of conscience within the Islamic tradition: "The Qur'an condemns those who do not speak their hearts, and it does not approve of those who control others' hearts and minds; therefore, freedom of conscience has a basis in the Islamic tradition. Although the term as such was not used by Muslim jurists in the past, its substantive meaning was; so if the material is used to explain the Muslim position on freedom of conscience today, then there is no harm." As long as a new concept resonates with Islamic principles, is consistent with our tradition, and does not conflict with our religious inheritance, we are correct in deeming it Islamic.

In fact, some of us felt a strong resonance between the principles enshrined in the Qur'an and Sunnah and the contemporary model of the democratic nation-state. As I shared with the group, the narrative of the establishment of states in the West is an expression of the attempt to establish justice. The American and French Revolutions replaced the norm of a king as a life-long absolute ruler with a republic whose government was "of the people, by the people, for the people." Legitimacy of the ruler was based on the permission granted by the ruled, an expression of the Islamic concept of *bay'ah*, or allegiance, which can be withdrawn by the people, analogous to the provision for a recall of the elected ruler in some democratic Western states.

This and other like principles were current in the Muslim world before this moment in Western history, even if some are not practiced today. Mahmood quoted Count Leon Ostrorog who, in a lecture in 1927, referred to classical Muslim jurists as

> Those Eastern thinkers of the ninth century [who] laid down, on the basis of their theology, the principle of the Rights of Man, in those very terms, comprehending the rights of individual liberty, and of inviolability of person and property; described the supreme power in Islam, or Caliphate, as based on a contract [i.e., between the ruler and the ruled], implying conditions of capacity and performance, and subject to cancellation if the conditions under the contract were not fulfilled; elaborated a Law of War of which the humane, chivalrous prescriptions would have put to the blush certain belligerents in World War I; expounded a doctrine of toleration of non-Moslem creeds so liberal that our West had to wait a thousand years before seeing equivalent principles adopted.[10]

Many of the principles of good governance espoused by the West actually have roots within, and were practiced by, our Islamic tradition. Thus, although the nation-state is a product of Western civilization, it can be interpreted in light of the principles enshrined within Islamic tradition and thus be an appropriate vessel for the principles and ideals of Islamic governance.

The following discussion on human rights – a term usually associated with the West – is one example of a concept the basis of which has existed within Islamic law.

Conversation: does the Shariah have a theory of "human rights"?[11]

Şenturk highlights *al-adamiyyah* (the concept that we are all children of Adam) and *huqūq al-ādamiyyin* (the rights of humans) as indigenous Shariah concepts equivalent to "birth/natural rights" or "human rights." According to these principles, which were originally put forth by the Hanafi school of law, people are granted citizenship rights and protections based on their humanity rather than their belief in Islam or their contractual agreements with the Islamic state.

These universalist approaches to citizenship and Islamic law represent important Islamic concepts with historical precedent (e.g., the Hanafis granting of rights to the Hindu and Buddhist minorities in India) that can be drawn upon for today's context.

> Şentürk: The concept of *adamiyyah* should be mentioned. There was a difference of opinion among the *fuqaha'* about the Shariah and whether it is *"adami,"* applied universally to all humans or is specific to the citizens of the Islamic state, which include the Muslims and ahl al-kitab, or the non-Muslim *dhimmis*. Two opinions evolved. According to the Hanafis and some scholars from the Shi'a, Maliki, Hanbali, and other schools, the *adami* or human being is the subject of law to which rights and duties are accorded. In other words, Islamic law is a universal law that applies regardless of one's religion; it's for all human beings, not only Muslims. I call this group the universalists. Alternatively, the other opinion takes the citizens of the Islamic state, Muslims and *dhimmis*, as the subject of law and talks about their rights and duties.

This is a fundamental juridical difference. Once we take the *adami*, or human being, as the subject of law and you talk about *ma lahu wa ma 'alaihi*, this means "one's rights and duties." The Hanafis speak of *al- 'ismah bil-adamiyyah*. *Al- 'ismah* means protection, *hurmah*, and the Islamic state must protect the six *Maqasid* because of your *adamiyyah*. Your citizenship is granted as a human being.

> Imam Feisal: Inherently being human. There is the famous example during the time of the Caliph Umar when the son of Egypt's Muslim governor mistreated and hit one of the Coptic citizens. Umar insisted that the Copt be given the right of retaliation against the governor's son in accord with the laws of retribution, and then famously said: "Why did you enslave people when they were born free?" Moreover, before the creation of any of the schools of law, Imam Ali famously declared to his governor in Egypt that people are "of two kinds: either they are your brothers in religion or your equals in creation." Shouldn't these precedents be considered as foundational to our legal tradition vis-à-vis human rights?
>
> Şentürk: Precisely. There is a citation from Imam Sarakhsi's book *al-Mabsut* which says that all human beings are born with intelligence and *dhimmah* or legal personhood, and as a result, they have the right to *hurriyah* (freedom) and *milkiyyah* (ownership) in order that they can do what God planned for them in this life.[12] In fact,

it says that all humans are born (*yuladu*) with these rights, which is the concept of natural or birth rights.

Imam Feisal: Natural rights meaning God-given and stemming from the Qur'anic verse in which Allah says, *Wa laqad karramna bani 'adam*, or "Verily, We have honored the children of Adam."[13]

Şentürk: Yes. According to the Hanafis, *dhimmah* comes with birth; it's not given. Therefore, the *jizyah* is not given in exchange for protection. It's just another tax, like Muslims pay *zakat*. Protection comes by birth; it's not sellable or an object of sale. Imam Sarakhsi says that in order to achieve the Divine Plan for humanity, human beings must have these rights. You are obliged to protect these rights because they are given by God.

This is the more universalistic approach.

The other opinion is *al- 'ismatu bil-iman aw bi-aman*. In other words, you gain citizenship through *iman* (faith) or *aman* (security). So if you don't have *iman*, the Islamic state is not responsible to protect your rights. *Aman* means two things, either security emanating from *dhimmah* (the contractual agreement to protect a non-Muslim resident) or *isti'man*, meaning security given to a non-Muslim temporary visitor of the Islamic state.

Larijani: It is under this heading that we can cover the *Bahá'is*. The *Bahá'is* are neither a minority *dhimmi* nor are they Muslims, and as a result, Imam Khomeini said that they should be treated under "*aman*." So they are citizens; there is a contract between us and them.

Şentürk: Actually, if you use this *adami* approach, the *Bahá'í* problem in Iran would be automatically solved. Because the Hanafis ruled in India, the Hindus and Buddhists had a place in their legal approach, although they were not traditionally included in the *ahl al-kitab*. With the *adamiyyah* approach, the Hanafis said that because they are *adami*, they have the right to worship as they please, even if some practices appear to go against Islamic standards.

But the dominant view today has become that in order to have rights, you should have *iman* or *aman*. In fact, the *adamiyyah* (universalist) approach was completely forgotten after the collapse of the Ottoman state, and even the Hanafis adopted the other view. We should promote this universalistic approach, that these rights are for the *adamiyyin*, all mankind, for everyone in the world.

Kamali: We have discussed the concepts of *'ismah* and *adamiyyah*. *'Ismah* is the essence of humanity; it is basically human dignity that constitutes the matrix of human rights. And as you have said, under the concept of *adamiyyah*, simply being human in itself is what creates a set of rights.

Hamieh: We can say that *al-ismah bil-adamiyyah* is "human rights from the Islamic perspective."

Şentürk: Yes. It is very important to show the contemporary Muslim intellectual that terms such as *"huquq al-insan,"* or human rights, are simply a translation of the Islamic concepts of *huquq al-ādamiyyin* and *al-'ismah bil-adamiyyah.*

Auda: *Huquq al-ādamiyyin.* That's great.

The rule of Shariah: the Muslim understanding of the rule of law

Another important point that the scholars stressed is that an Islamic state is not a theocracy, but a nomocracy – "nomos" meaning law. The term *nomocracy* signifies the *rule of law*, which for Muslims equates to the *rule of Shariah*. Şentürk explained that this means that "What ultimately rules is Shariah – not the government, not a group of people, and not the *'ulama'*. Governors are rulers over the people; the scholars are rulers over the governors; and the Shariah is ruler over all" (*Al-umara'hukkam `ala al-nas, wa al-'ulama'hukkam `ala al-umara', wa al-shari`ah hakim `ala al-jama `ah*).

An important implication of the Islamic rule of law, as indicated by Ghazi, is that no one is above the law nor can they be exempted from the application of the law on any grounds. "According to the Islamic concept of rule of law, even the Prophet lacks authority to forgive in *Hudud* and *qisas* [retaliatory punishment] cases. The authority to forgive or demand *qisas* is the right of the victim, according to the Qur'an." This also means that the ruler himself is subject to the law, and "the second and fourth caliphs are recorded to have appeared before their own judges, stressing the fact that no one is above the law and even the highest political authorities are subject to judicial review." Ghazi contrasts this with Britain, "where the royal family is exempt from many legal provisions." In Islamic Shariah, however, there is no such exemption for anyone.

The core impetus behind an Islamic state is therefore a desire for the rule of law. Calling for a political order based on the Shariah is, in a sense, a desire for a system wherein everyone, including the rulers, is accountable to an overarching set of principles. Though the Qur'an does not specify the structure of this system, it contains the principles to which all should conform. In our effort to identify these principles, we turned toward a field of *usul al-fiqh* (principles of *fiqh*) called the *Maqasid al-Shar'iah:* the objectives of Islamic law. Since the *Maqasid* were such a prominent feature of our conversations, it is only fit to provide here an introduction to them.

What are the *Maqasid*?

Classical origins

Originally, the *Maqasid* were developed by early Islamic scholars as the positive corollaries to the *Hudud* crimes, blended with the positive commandments of the Qur'an and *Hadith*. The *Hudud Allah* ("limits of God") codify the limits on human behavior and prescribe physical punishments meted out for such misconduct. The six *Hudud* are murder, taking arms up against the community of Muslims (treason), drunkenness, adultery, theft, and slander (bearing false witness.) The correlating *Maqasid* that are protected are life, religion, mind, family, property, and honor. Thus, murder is forbidden because protection of life is a fundamental objective of the Shariah, conspiring against Islam is forbidden because the protection of religion is fundamental to the Shariah, drunkenness is forbidden because the protection of mind and sound judgment is fundamental to the Shariah, adultery is forbidden because the protection of lineage and family is fundamental to the Shariah, theft is forbidden because the protection of property is fundamental to the Shariah, and slander is forbidden because the protection of individual honor and dignity is fundamental to the Shariah.

Kamali indicated that early consensus on the *Maqasid* began with the scholars al-Juwayni and al-Ghazali, who set them at five: *nafs* (life), *din* (religion), *nasl* (family or lineage), *mal* (property or wealth), and *'aql* (mind). Because there is also a *hadd* against slander or bearing false witness, a few centuries later the scholar al-Qarafi added the *maqsad* of *'ird* or *karamah* (honor). Some of our scholars felt that it should not be limited to these six, following Ibn Taymiyyah who opened up the *Maqasid* to wider values, including justice, virtue, constitutional rights, and scientific excellence among others. Other scholars felt that many of these values are embedded within these six *Maqasid* (e.g., constitutional rights under honor and scientific excellence under mind,) and that the ultimate goal of achieving justice is a by-product of the fulfillment of these six objectives. As Ghazi said, "Justice is above the *Maqasid*. In order to ensure that real and full justice is guaranteed to everybody, the *Maqasid* will have to be observed. The *Maqasid* exist to promote justice."

Şentürk proposed that "the Maqasid are those fundamental or axiomatic principles on which all other components of Islamic law are based." They are derived, he explained, "from the idea of the *daruriyyat* (necessities), which epistemologically in Islamic philosophy means axioms, un-debatable principles. In every science or discipline, there are such axioms which are taken as givens without debate and upon which all other theories are built. So we can call the Maqasid the axiomatic principles of Islamic law and set them as requirements for the state."

These axiomatic principles that Islamic scholars have been writing about for centuries, Auda said, have actually been confirmed by modern social science. In 1943, psychologist Abraham Maslow penned a theory of the "Hierarchy of Needs," which listed the five key needs that are essential for human flourishing. First, there are **physiological** needs such as food and shelter, which correspond to the *maqsad* of life. Second, there are **safety** needs, including the security of body, employment, and property, which correspond to the *maqsad* of life and that of property. Thirdly, Maslow speaks of the need for **love and belonging**, such as within a family, which corresponds to the family *maqsad*. Fourthly, he writes about the need for **esteem**, which includes giving and receiving respect, a key part of the *maqsad* of honor. And lastly is the need for **self-actualization**, which entails following one's purpose in life, using creativity, and developing our intellectual powers.[14] This correlates with both religion and mind. It seems no coincidence that what constitute the fundamental purposes of God's law happen to also be the fundamental needs of mankind. Through His Prophet, God has not revealed to us a mere code of laws; rather, what He has revealed are the lamps of His loving providence guiding mankind toward this human flourishing.

It is important to note, as Larijani did, that within the Sunni tradition "the *Maqasid* became paramount. The Shi`a `ulama', on the other hand, did not place this emphasis on the *Maqasid*. For them, governance must be judged by more than results; rather it is judged within the parameters of legitimacy." While both Sunnis and Shi'is agree that a ruler should fulfill the objectives of Islamic law, Shi`a scholars place greater emphasis on the legitimacy of the ruler.

Contemporary approaches to the *Maqasid*

While the classical jurists focused on defining the *Maqasid* in a way that *protects against* the negative elements or behaviors that would harm each *maqsad*, Islamic scholarship in more recent times has increasingly expanded the definition of each *maqsad* in order to include the *promotion* of positive elements or behaviors that advance each *maqsad* within society. As Auda shared, "At a basic level, our understanding of the *Maqasid* has undergone a paradigm shift. Where earlier jurists expressed the *Maqasid* in terms of the punishments meted out for wrongdoing and the protections from harm, more modern thinkers speak in terms of the concomitant rights humans enjoy as a consequence of the Shariah and how those rights contribute to personal and social development." This inclusion of the promotion of the good is a natural extension of earlier thought which focused on punishing wrongdoing, especially as it mirrors the positive aspect of the Qur'anic injunction to command the good (*amr bil-ma'ruf*) in addition to forbidding the wrong (*nahy`an al-munkar*),[15] a doctrine known as *hisbah*.

For example, the "preservation of offspring" (*nasl*) is one of the necessities that Islamic law traditionally aimed to achieve. Auda charted the development of this *maqsad* throughout the history of Islamic scholarship:

> Abu al-Hasan Al-Amiri expressed it, in his early attempt to outline a theory of necessary purposes, in terms of "punishments for breaching decency."[16] Al-Juwayni developed al-Amiri's "theory of punishments" (*mazajir*) into a "theory of protection"…Thus, "punishment for breaching decency" was expressed by al-Juwayni as, "protection for private parts."[17] It was Abu Hamid al-Ghazali who coined the term "preservation of offspring" as a purpose of the Islamic law at the level of necessity[18]…However, in the twentieth century, writers on *Maqasid* significantly developed "preservation of offspring" into a family-oriented theory. Ibn Ashur, for example, made "care for the family" into a *maqsad* in its own right. In his monograph *The Social System in Islam,* Ibn Ashur elaborated on family-related purposes and moral values in the Islamic law.[19] The orientation of the new views is neither al-Amiri's theory of punishment nor al-Ghazali's concept of preservation, but rather the concepts of value and system, to use Ibn Ashur's terminology.

Thus, the contemporary understanding of the *maqsad* of family has expanded to include not only the *preservation* of lineage, but also the *promotion* of family values and strong marriages. This process extends to the other *Maqasid* where, for example, the mind *maqsad* is not only the protection against intoxication but the promotion of education, intellectual development, research and development, and intellectual pursuits. Similarly, the honor *maqsad* is not only the protection against defamed honor due to slander but also the promotion of human dignity and the concomitant human rights that protect and advance human dignity, and the property *maqsad* goes beyond protecting against theft to promoting economic development, and so on.

What is the primary purpose and most important function of an Islamic state?

It does not suffice to simply know that human beings are inviolable in their rights in our tradition, as articulated in the classical and contemporary *Maqasid* scholarship. Our scholars felt it necessary, further, to explore the philosophical grounding for these rights: why should life be inviolable, or property, or mind? How are human rights and basic freedoms grounded in Islamic philosophy and theology?

"According to the classical jurists," Şentürk shared with the group, "the primary mission, and the most important function of the Islamic state, is to create the environment of *ibtila'* [testing or trial]." As indicated in many verses of the Qur'an, God's intent in creating the world and its peoples is to test (*li-yabtaliya* or *li-yabluwa*) human beings. As God says in the Qur'an, "Blessed be He in Whose hands is Dominion; and He over all things has Power; He Who created Death and Life, that He may try *[li-yabluwakum]* which of you is best in deed: and He is the Exalted in Might, Oft-Forgiving."[20] God says further that He could have made all of us believers in one religious community (*ummah wahidah*), but He did not so as to test us: "If God had so willed, He would have made you a single people *[ummatan wahidatan]*, but (His plan is) to test you *[li-yabluwakum]* in what He has given you: so compete with each other in being virtuous."[21]

But we can pass this test only if we choose the straight path of our own accord and without any compulsion. "The purpose of an Islamic state," Şentürk continued, "is *not* to make people Muslim by force, but rather *to create a fair testing environment*. As part of this testing environment, people must be free to either succeed or fail on their own accord. Thus, they need freedom. They need rights. Otherwise, God's purpose in creating humanity will be thwarted." Kamali echoed this point, saying that "in the philosophy of the *Mu`tazila*, they gave this *hurriyah*, freedom of conscience and rationality, so much importance that if you interfere with it you interfere with the whole structure of the Islamic state." If we acknowledge God as sovereign, which our scholars later agreed was the primary basis of an Islamic state, then we must allow for the fulfillment of the Divine Intent. We must ensure and protect these rights and freedoms.

Thus it is not the role of the state to enforce a moral code; rather, it is the role of the state to enforce justice. Within the framework of *ibtila'*, individuals must have the freedom to choose to live in whatever manner they like, as long as they do not directly inflict harm on others. Once an individual's actions directly inflicts harm on another, this becomes an issue of justice and thus within the purview and jurisdiction of the state. As Şentürk said, "You can worship a cow, no problem; worship fire, no problem, but you cannot steal the property of another individual. Then the state intervenes."

We all have the rights and freedoms as outlined in the *Maqasid* because, within the framework of God's test or *ibtila'* for mankind, we can only choose the straight path of our own accord and without compulsion, but we also have those rights because the Prophet extended human inviolability to everyone regardless of time and place. The Prophet's Farewell Sermon, what Mahmood called "a Declaration of the Equality of Mankind," begins: "No doubt, your blood and your properties are sacred to one another like the sanctity of this day of yours, in this month of yours, in this town of yours, till the day you meet your Lord. No doubt! Haven't I conveyed Allah's message to you? They said, 'Yes.' He said, 'O Allah! Be witness.'"[22]

As Şentürk explained, during the pre-Islamic period human inviolability was limited in time and space: "People were inviolable all the time only in the Ka`ba (al-masjid al-haram), and universally during the four haram months when the Arab tribes were forbidden from war so as to engage in pilgrimage and commerce." In his farewell sermon, the Prophet abolished the time and place limitations on human inviolability from the pre-Islamic period and universalized human inviolability to all times and places. Rather than addressing "O ye who believe," a common invocation in the Qur'an, the Prophet spoke to all of mankind. As the modern day stewards of his message, we must champion this message of universal human rights within the context of an Islamic state. If we were to deny these rights and freedoms to anyone, we would be simultaneously abandoning the standard set forth by our Prophet while thwarting the Divine Intent of testing mankind.

Implications of a *Maqasid*-based approach

The *Maqasid*-based approach toward defining and rating Islamic governance has salient implications for how we think of and approach law within an Islamic state, and as Auda pointed out, it represents a "means of renewal for the whole of Islamic thought."

Firstly, as Auda stated, a focus on the *Maqasid* of the Shariah naturally lends itself to focusing more on the *ends* rather than the particular *means* used to achieve the ends. The modern Egyptian scholar "Mohammad al-Ghazali differentiated between 'means' (*al-wasa'il*) and 'ends' (*al-ahdaf*). He allowed the expiry (*intiha'*) of the former and not the latter," Auda explained. As situations change, so do the appropriate means for attaining a particular end. "This perspective is gaining ground in both the Sunni and Shi`a traditions, and it is not limited to any one particular *madhhab*," Auda added. For instance, "Mohammad al-Ghazali mentioned the system of spoils of war, despite the fact that it is mentioned explicitly in the Qur'an, as an example of 'changeable means.'"[23] As modern armies already provide their troops with financial compensation, weapons, and armor, they need not provide them with the spoils of war which in the past consisted of the seized weapons and armor of the opponents. Another example Auda gave was the sighting of the crescent moon to determine the start of Ramadan: despite the injunction within the *Hadith* to begin Ramadan at the sighting of the crescent moon, the European Council for Fatwa and Research has concluded that "pure astronomical calculations, as opposed to visually sighting the moon, shall be the modern day's means of defining the start of the month." From this perspective, the fundamental goal of an action or Qur'anic injunction is paramount, and the changing conditions or capabilities of society may necessitate or warrant an alternative and often better means of achieving that end goal.

Secondly, a *Maqasid*-based approach entails a strong adherence to the spirit or goal of the law. Kamali explained that the Shariah is "goal-oriented," and the *Maqasid* represent the "basic purpose, intention, and rationale of the text." He said that "while the *Maqasid* are certainly rooted in the textual injunctions of the Qur'an and Sunnah, [Muslim] jurists point to the fact that the *Maqasid* also look beyond the text, to the general philosophy and objectives of these injunctions." Because the "objective of a law is always the driving purpose of the law," the *Maqasid* or objectives of the Shariah must "always be honored, even if it means violating the letter of the law or suspending the law in exceptional cases where the law's objective is thwarted."

This wisdom and tact in applying the Shariah is called *siyasah shar`iyyah*. Kamali explained that "the idea behind *siyasah shar`iyyah* is that no state can simply rule by the text. Sometimes you make a decision that is against the specific rules of Shariah, though it is in harmony with the spirit of the Shariah." He gave an example of someone who had claimed to 'Umar ibn al-Khattab that the ruler of Egypt had punished him for no reason. Rather than meting out a punishment of lashes to the ruler, 'Umar meted a financial fine – he realized that it was not sound policy to punish a leading official of state before the public. Within a court of law, the *Hudud* are applied if someone commits theft – but "if this person is a first-time offender, already repentant, and unlikely to commit the crime again, do you really want to apply the same [maximum] penalty to this offender?" The Shariah is not without *hikmah*, or wisdom. This wisdom in applying laws, or *siyasah shari'iyyah*, is an important component of governance because, as Ghazi shared, "Islamic states will always face issues that emerge out of conflict between the dictates of the Shariah and the requirements of the context."

The *Maqasid* and the *Hudud*

It is clear that the state should safeguard the fundamental objectives of the Shariah, those values protected by the *Hudud* punishments, but in the end should the state implement the specified Qur'anic punishments for theft, adultery, and so on?

This was an important conversation, as images of amputations and stonings are often the primary images evoked by the term "Shariah" to those outside our tradition. Even within our tradition, many Muslims adhere to the idea that an Islamic state is one that applies the *Hudud* punishments. As Tun Abdul Hamid pointed out, "In Malaysia, 90 percent of the people who say that their country is not an 'Islamic state' would offer one reason alone: *Hudud* law is not implemented." The perception that implementing *Hudud* automatically guarantees Shariah compliance, Kamali said, creates a *Hudud* state, not an Islamic state.

Ghazi blames the Islamic scholars of the twentieth century for creating the perception that *Hudud* application defines an Islamic state. During this time, several Muslim leaders were prompted to enforce Shariah's laws within their borders – Muammar Qadhafi in Libya, Ja'far Nimeiry in Sudan, and Muhammad Zia al-Haqq in Pakistan. When they invited Islamic scholars to advise them, these scholars simply formulated a penal code from the *Hudud*. "Previously," Ghazi explained, "the common perception or understanding was that the Shariah meant equality, it meant justice, it meant access of the common man to the courts and the rulers." But these rulers and their advisors "conveniently ignored social justice, equality, simplicity and the enhancement of the common man's lot. Justice is at the core of the Shariah, but because it was perhaps difficult for the Islamic scholars to tell these leaders to focus on these areas, they didn't do it."

Rulers see the application of the *Hudud* laws as easy, Ghazi continued. Basically, "It doesn't take anything away from them or cost them anything. If, on the other hand, they focus on executive justice, this will require a class of people to share their wealth, and they won't be ready to do that." Instead of working to make substantive changes to a country, such sitting heads of state simply "arrest the thief and cut off his hand. It doesn't cost them a thing."

Kamali added that this prevalent understanding of the *Hudud* is a juristic construct, and that the word *Hudud* is not used in the sense of mandatory or fixed penalties in the Qur'an. "Because the word *hadd* literally means 'limit,' the *Hudud* penalties should be considered the maximum –*not the mandatory*– penalties." As an example, the Qur'an discusses capital punishment as the maximum penalty for murder. But the "victim's family is encouraged to take monetary compensation instead of seeking it, and it is even better if they forgive the murderer entirely."[24] As seen with the above example of a first-time thief who is repentant, the severity of a punishment depends on a number of factors, and the Qur'an only delineates the maximum *Hudud*, or limits, of what that punishment could be.

Moreover, the precedent that Umar ibn al-Khattab set in the discussion above, where he adjusted the *hadd* punishment to a fine in a certain case, demonstrates that the *Hudud* are subject to *siyasah shari'yyah*, and are not an absolute end but rather a means to an end. A fine instead of corporal punishment may be more appropriate in certain instances, and this is an important consideration when discussing *Hudud* application in a modern Islamic state.

Overall, the scholars felt that it is crucial to define an Islamic state by looking at the Shariah's positive law: what kind of society does the Qur'an envision? How can a government develop their society as a just society? The answer is of course the fulfillment of the *Maqasid* of the Shariah: the protection and preservation of religion, life, family, mind, property, and honor. A *Maqasid*-driven state is in a sense the inverse mirror of a *Hudud*-driven state, by which we mean that it recognizes the *Hudud* by focusing on their positive corollaries, the *Maqasid*. To those such as Tun Abdul Hamid referred to, who cannot see their states as "Islamic" unless they apply the *Hudud* punishments, we must communicate that a *Maqasid*-driven state honors the *Hudud* not by their rigid implementation but by capturing their essence and by promoting the kind of society that represents the ideals enshrined in the Qur'an.

The Qur'an says that "in the law of punishments [*qisas*] there is life for you," pointing out that the purpose of punishment is to preserve and advance life.[25] If there are alternate methods to do this, we would not be violating the *Hudud* by using such methods but rather advancing their underlying objective and honoring their values. As the Qur'an says, if we save a life it is as if we saved all of mankind, and it is accepted within our legal tradition that it is better to forgive or accept the *diyah* (financial compensation due to the victim's heirs) rather than to demand the life of a murderer.[26] The ideal is *not* to reach that limit (*hadd/Hudud*) of punishment, but rather to preserve life and the other objectives of the law in our efforts to establish justice in our communities.

Rather than defining Islamic governance by the implementation of certain penalties, we demand of the state that it focus on human development: its capacity to establish the kind of society envisioned in the Qur'an that enhances these six objectives of the Shariah. For is not a society that does not apply the *Hudud* punishments, but wherein no one commits any of these six *Hudud* sins, a better and more Shariah-compliant society – and a more perfect Islamic state – than a society where *Hudud* punishments are applied and there is a high level of these sins being committed?

2
Islamic State: Foundations

Does the Qur'an require Muslims to establish a state or any political order?

Many Muslims across the world assume that the Qur'an requires Muslims to establish a state. However as Ghazi pointed out, the "main and fundamental requirement of the Qur'an for Muslims is to reform themselves *individually* in terms of Islamic social, cultural, and ethical values and norms." Secondly, he said, "It requires Muslims to organize themselves *collectively* into a community of believers." It is only when that requirement has been achieved and the *ummah* comes into existence that "those Muslims who have political authority are required to organize their state and political matters in such a way that they can implement the Islamic principles which are required of a state." He notes that Qur'anic legal principles, such as a penal code or references to international law, can only be enacted by a state government. However, he stressed, *"The Qur'an never says that a state should be established.* It simply gave rise to the concept that these principles must be implemented if Muslims have political authority somewhere; if they do not have political authority, they are not required to implement those principles."

To support this Ghazi brought up examples of early Muslim communities, some of which existed during the time of the Prophet, such as in Abyssinia (modern Ethiopia), that lived, and continue till this day to live, under the rule of non-Muslims: "These Muslim communities living outside the bounds of the Islamic state were never required by the Prophet or by his successors to implement the Islamic Penal Code, to organize the Hajj, to revolt against their respective political setups, to organize themselves politically, or to convert their respective habitats into Islamic states. They were left on their own. They continued to live as good Muslims individually and continued to train their children in terms of the Islamic ethos; what was required of them was only the social, moral, and cultural code of Islam."

Ghazi likens this conditional injunction toward ruling according to the principles in the Qur'an to the *zakat*, a tax dedicated to charitable purposes and one of the five pillars of the faith. Despite the *zakat's* preeminent importance, only Muslims who fulfill certain conditions are required to pay it. The Muslim in question must be above the poverty line and there must be a treasury or a state functionary that collects the *zakat*. Otherwise, the person will not be obliged to pay it. In the same way, the Qur'an does not require Muslims to establish a state per se, but it contains principles upon which a state should be run if Muslims are ruling.

Furthermore, there is no mention in the Qur'an or the Sunnah of the state, that is, a formal entity in which one may be a citizen and to which one owes allegiance. This concept of the "state" is a recent development, rooted in the political, economic, and social changes of post-Enlightenment Europe. Though one can trace it back to the Peace of Westphalia in 1648, it is more directly linked to the outcomes of the American and French Revolutions of 1776 and 1789. Before this modern notion of a state, borders were porous, and people identified themselves with their family, clan, or tribal identities rather than what we now call a "national" identity based on clearly marked lines of geography. Modern scholarship has sufficiently charted the history and development of the nation-state, but what is most relevant to our discussions is that none of that development arose from Islamic sources or civilization. As Larijani pointed out, " ...because this concept of the state is rather new, this prevents us from finding Islamic roots or ideas which are intrinsic to the nature of this collective agency." Professor Kamali pointed out that a look at the etymology of the contemporary word for "state" in Arabic (*dawlah*)[1] shows that classically it meant a "turn of good fortune," a "mutation," the "present life," or the "life to come" – it even meant in some contexts the "stomach of a bird" – but it did not gain a political connotation until the Ottoman and Mamluk periods.

In fact, our founding texts do not specify any particular types of governmental institutions nor is most of Islamic political history normative. As Ghazi shared, "We must affirm that we honor and value this past, yet the history of Muslim experiences in the formation of political entities after the four Rightly-Guided caliphs, or *Rashidun*, do not constitute any normative value." The caliphate model, as it developed after the *Rashidun*, is not a prescription for ideal Islamic governance. In fact, according to Kamali, there were many departures from Qur'anic principles within the history of caliphal rule. Kamali clarified, "the *bay`ah* [pledge of allegiance] was sidelined, no one paid attention to *shura* [consultation] ... Then came the time when respected scholars like al-Ghazali and others affirmed that 'sixty years of dictatorship is better than one night of chaos.' These are serious departures from Qur'anic principles." Mahmood agreed: "the conduct of past Muslim rulers was not necessarily Islamic." After the reign of the Rightly-Guided Caliphs, the Ummayad and the Abbasid Dynasties ruled in a style deeply influenced by the Byzantine and Persian Empires. By this time, the earlier title *Khalifat Rasulallah*, which meant a vicegerent or successor of God's Messenger, became effectively synonymous with the titles of *malik* and *sultan*, both of which essentially mean "king." Though some of these rulers were exemplary individuals, the prevailing system was far from being in accord with the normative principles of Islamic governance.

While there is no specific model for governance prescribed in the Qur'an and the Sunnah, what we do have is a Qur'anic requirement to commit to a set of principles. Such principles include justice, *ihsan* (excellence in behavior and performing good works), *hisbah* (the promotion of the common good and prevention of evil), *shura* (consultation), *bay`ah* (allegiance to the ruler and the legitimacy of rule), and others. As Kamali emphasized, "We Muslims have put too much emphasis on structures and not on the spirit of moral values. Islam is not about structures – it is about meaning. It is less about means and more about ends. Commitment to a form of leadership that is bound by a set of principles, this is Qur'anic, not whether or not the name of the state demonstrates piety and rectitude." Mahmood added the related point that the Qur'an is not a book of recipes for creating a state or writing a constitution. He drew on his experience in the Indian Subcontinent: "Using the terminology of the Indian and Pakistani constitution, I have been saying it and I will repeat it here, the Qur'an and the Sunnah only provide principles. They do not provide a concrete constitution for the state. They only give directive principles for the policy of the state." It is these foundational and guiding principles that we sought to define as the project progressed.

But there were other fundamental questions that we first needed to address.

How did the term "Islamic State" arise?

Given that the state model of governance is a historically recent phenomenon, it is not a surprise that the term "Islamic state" is not found in our founding texts nor is it prominent in any Muslim literature before the twentieth century. And given that the nation-state model of governance did not arise in an Islamic context, it is clear that the term "Islamic state" (*dawlah islamiyyah*) is also an Islamization of a foreign (nation-state) concept. But before looking at the term itself, our discussions first approached what it means for political authority to be "Islamic."

Have we always called ourselves Muslims and our institutions Islamic?

I shared with the scholars an insight gained from the work of the Canadian scholar of comparative religion Wilfred Cantwell Smith. He points out that the names we use to describe ourselves religiously were often coined by others and only later were they adopted by one's group. The early Christians did not call themselves Christians; the name was given to them by the Romans and was not fully adopted by the Christian community until later.[2] Likewise, Muslims did not initially brand themselves as Muslims, nor did they think of their social institutions as "Islamic." This "branding" emerged by the end of the first century after the Prophet's death as Muslims increasingly interacted with non-Muslims.[3] Among ourselves, we do not talk about the "Islamic" caliphate or the "Islamic" Shariah but rather, the caliphate and the Shariah, for the simple reason that we are all Muslims. The use of this nomenclature itself suggests that we are looking at ourselves through the eyes of non-Muslims, calling ourselves by what outsiders have named us.

I have always been struck by the fact that in the Qur'an, God never addresses the Prophet's followers as *muslimun*, "Muslims," but as *mu'minun*, "believers."[4] It is always *"ya ayyuha lladhina amanu"* or *"qul lil-mu'minina,"* ("O ye who believe" or "Say to the believers") but never *"ya ayyuha lladhina aslamu"* or *"qul lil-muslimina"* ("O ye who submit as Muslims" or "Say to the Muslims"). The first appellation applied by the Prophet's followers to their caliph was `Amir ul-Mu'minin – Commander of the Believers – not `Amir ul-Muslimin. Of course, 100 years after the Prophet's death, it became customary to identify ourselves as Muslim, particularly in order to distinguish ourselves from other "believers in God."[5]

How did the term "Islamic State" become an entrenched concept in contemporary discourse?

Our group of scholars looked into the reasons why twentieth century Muslim activists and politicians adopted such language and how their conception of an Islamic state differed from earlier Muslim ideas of governance. Ghazi shared with the group that the term "Islamic state" was never used by any of the earlier scholars of Islam, but was given currency by the Islamic movements which emerged in the first and second part of the twentieth century, like the *al-Jama`at al-Islamiyya* of the Indian Subcontinent, the *Ikhwan al-Muslimin* (the Muslim Brotherhood) of the Middle East, the Masyumi party of Indonesia, and so forth. "These political movements emerged during a time when Muslims were passing through a very bleak period," he said. "The Ottoman Empire had gone, almost all Muslim countries were occupied by one or another colonial power, and World War I had put an end to whatever Muslim prestige was left." Ghazi continued:

> Observing this situation, some Muslim scholars noted that every ideology and culture had the support of a major political power: Communism was being advanced by the very formidable political authority of Russia, Western culture was being promoted by the British Empire, and so on. Consequently, the Islamic political movements of the twentieth century thought that Islam should have its own state-hood, and they tried to organize political movements to mobilize the Muslim masses to establish what they considered to be an Islamic state. Those were the times when romantic appeals were very market-able to the Muslim masses, and when idealistic approaches were very powerful in Muslim writings. In the [Indian] Subcontinent, for example, the most popular Islamic writers on Islamic themes were the most idealistic. Abul Kalam Azad, Abul `ala' Mawdudi, Muhammad Iqbal, and so on all captured the imagination of the people. They were not all jurists, but their purpose was Islamically motivated, and they wanted the Muslim masses to stand up.

As Ghazi noted above, many of the modern scholars who advanced the need for Islamic statehood were not trained jurists. Their intellectual forebears, who had been trained in traditional Islamic sciences like *hadith, fiqh, tafsir, sirah, kalam* and *adab*, [6] were never concerned with the establishment of an "Islamic" state. It was rather the new generation, who were educated in a Western context and witness to both the technological ascendance of the West and the imposition of colonialism in their homelands, that used Islam to unify and frame their political aims in opposition to foreign oppression. Ghazi suggested that in this context, the twentieth century notion that the revival of Islam would come through the establishment of an Islamic state became "a political agenda rather than an agenda of reform or the moral regeneration of the Muslim masses."

But does it matter whether or not the term "Islamic state" authentically represents our tradition, and that it carries implications that we may not intend? I contend that it does. Language and the terms we use are extremely important because they shape how we think about ourselves and our communities. To say that a particular form of governance is what Islam and the Qur'an require of us – by calling something an *Islamic* state – we commit a dangerous misuse of language. As with our opening question, *"does the Qur'an require Muslims to establish a state,"* this perspective treats concepts as though they were beings who can speak and make demands of us.

To illustrate this point, let us look at the use of language in our scholarly tradition. In it, we witness ontologically real beings speak. For example, God speaks. The Prophet speaks. We say *qala allahu ta`ala fi kitabihi al-karim,* "God the Exalted said in His noble Book," or *qala rasul ullahi fi hadithin sahih,* "the Prophet said in an authentic tradition." We find it odd to say *qal al-Qur'anu,* "the Qur'an said" or *yaqul ul-hadithu,* "the Hadith says." In English, on the other hand, we commonly ask, "what does Islam say about this?" In classical Arabic, we do not say the equivalent phrase: *madha yaqul ul-islamu `an hadha?* Yet now, it is even common for modern Arab speakers to ask *madha fahm hadha fil-islam,* or "What is the understanding of this in Islam?"[7]

The danger of this kind of language is that first, it is not accurate. The Qur'an is the record of God's statements; it is not itself a speaker. And Islam is not an actor – God is, the Prophet is, and we are. The implications are extremely important. This misuse of language leads to the presumption that there is only one right answer to a question, what Şentürk called "freezing what is Islamic, when in reality, it is very dynamic." When you phrase your question as: "What does Islam say about such and such?" you presume that only one right answer exists for all times and contexts. This collides with the historic fact that many different opinions in Islamic jurisprudence are considered valid. On the other hand, if you phrase it as what does God, the Prophet, the caliph, or a particular mufti say about a matter, there is an implicit recognition that these actors may – and did – judge one way in one context and another way in another context. In other words, this allows the space for more than one "right" answer. The Prophet was known to have offered different advice when asked the same question by two different people whose contexts differed. In modern times, as a result of this reified way of thinking, many Muslims have collapsed this space for diverse and nuanced opinion, and thereby regard someone who does not agree with a particular opinion as being "un-Islamic." The gradual loss of this understanding in the modern era, and the rise of the fiction that Islam must state one thing for all people at all times, has led to the unfortunate phenomenon of *takfir*, where someone is considered an apostate for merely holding a different opinion.

Can a state be Muslim?

We have discussed in depth the implications of the adjective "Islamic," but what about the "state" – can a state *have* a religious identity at all? This question came up as we were discussing if it is necessary for a state to declare itself Islamic in order to be so, a discussion recounted in more detail in the following chapter. The reason that it seems conceivable that a state can have a religious identity is the same reason we imagine that a state can "declare" anything at all: we think of a state as a corporate entity, with an identity and "personhood" of its own above and distinct from the human beings who govern and live in it.

The treatment of a political community as a corporation is a recent historical development. Historically in the Muslim world, the sultan or caliph ruled over different communities. This structure created the space for different communities to govern themselves internally under the wider umbrella of the empire. It was a relationship between an *individual* and *groups of individuals*. However, after the American and French Revolutions and the creation of the idea of a republic, the concept of the state began to look more like a corporation. Legally a corporation is treated as if it were an individual, a separate legal entity with rights and liabilities distinct from its shareholders. Citizens within this concept of the state are like the shareholders in a corporation (with land analogous to the stock of a corporation), especially considering that originally in America it was only the landowners who had the right to vote. From then until today the relationship between state and citizen is that of a *corporate entity* and *individual citizens*.

Because we think of a state as a person it is conceivable that a state can declare something about itself, including principles and policies. But can a state hold religious belief, and then declare it? In order for a person to become a Muslim, he or she must declare the *shahadah*. Can a state bear witness that there is no god but God and that Muhammad is His Messenger? If a state can declare itself as a Muslim does, should it not also be obliged to pay *zakat*, go on pilgrimage, pray, and fast during Ramadan?

Tun Hamid related this discussion to a decision passed in Malaysia mandating that companies and corporations pay *zakat*. The justification for this, according to the deciding committee, is the religion of "the human beings behind the company," even if their parent company is not Muslim-owned. But Tun Hamid questioned the committee's decision, asking if anything other than a believing human being can be held responsible for performing religious rites. He asks, "does the Qur'anic phrase *'O You who have believed…'* include other than human beings?" He cited a paper issued by the Majlis ul Ulama of South Africa titled *"The Concept of Limited Liability – Untenable in Shariah"*: "Everyone knows that Zakaat is one of the Arkaan (Fundamentals) of Islam. The obligation of this Fardh injunction devolves on Muslims – Muslim human beings, not on kuffar, least of all on inanimate objects such as wheat and rice."[8] If a government wants to tax companies, Tun Hamid said, then let it tax them but not call it a religious obligation. While the individual Muslims working within the company or corporation may have a religious obligation to offer *zakat*, the company itself does not meet the requirements necessary to offer *zakat*, chief among them being that a company is not a believing free human being.

The same can be said of a state. God will not haul a state to be judged on Judgment Day for its actions, including its performance of religious rites. And a state will not be rewarded with heaven or hell – unlike the individuals who make key decisions within a state who will be called to account for their deeds. While we often speak of a state as we do of an individual person, the fact remains that it is not. And it cannot profess faith, it cannot declare the *shahadah*, any more than a chair or a table can.

Considering these many limitations and implications, the scholars considered: should we use another term instead of "Islamic state"? Perhaps we should say "ideal Islamic governance" or "the ideal state by Muslims in the twenty-first century"? The scholars decided that we should use the term "Islamic state" given that the term has become normatively entrenched in societal speech. At the same time, we must attempt to redefine its meaning through our work in this project.

The nation-state is a political reality of the world today. Rather than attempting to invent a new form of governance or revive an older model for modern-day conditions we should work to best define Islamic governance within the structure of the present-day nation-state. As Mahmood said, "if we are fixated on whether or not the concept of the (Islamic) nation-state is repugnant in Islam, we won't be able to proceed further. Clearly, Muslims today take for granted that there is a concept of the state acceptable to the modern world ... Our task here is to spell out the proper relationship between the ruler and ruled in a state that calls itself Islamic or that answers to the description of an Islamic state." Şentürk echoed this sentiment, saying that although the nation-state concept is a new one, political organization and governance are not new, having been called various names throughout Islamic history: *mulk, wilayah ʿam, dawlah,* and *millah.* Muslim jurists, philosophers, and theologians have grappled with and defined the rights and responsibilities of rulers throughout different historical periods and political systems. In the same manner, we must define governance that accords with Islamic principles within the present-day structure of the nation-state.

At the end of these initial conversations, our group of scholars was clear on a number of issues:

1. While the Qur'an does not require Muslims to establish a state, those communities where Muslims have political power should base their governing policies on the principles enshrined in the Qur'an and the Prophetic tradition.
2. While the term "Islamic state" is imprecise and carries connotations that some political leaders prefer to avoid, it is such a commonplace term that, for the purposes of this project, we will use the term to mean a modern nation-state defined by the principles of good governance set out in the Qur'an and Sunnah.
3. While the concept of the modern nation-state is one that has its origins in the West, we can embrace statehood as long as we can interpret it in light of our tradition, articulating the principles of governance that are the hallmark of the Muslim community.

The task then was to identify the principles that define a modern "Islamic state," and to develop a means of measurement by which to evaluate countries' compliance with those principles.

3
Characteristics of Islamic Governance: The Scholars' Consensus

Can we prescribe a comprehensive definition of an Islamic State?

As we approached the task of defining the features of a present day Islamic state, it quickly became evident that while there are principles that represent the core elements of Islamic governance, there is more than one approach to constructing an Islamic state. Our group of scholars, hailing from different corners of Islamic legal and political thought, was itself representative of that multiplicity of perspectives. As Ghazi shared with the group, among the "various efforts to reinvigorate the role of Islam in communities and nations" are perspectives that emphasize the cultural or civilizational aspects of the Muslim *ummah* (such as Prime Minister Badawi's *Islam Hadhari* in Malaysia), perspectives that emphasize jurisprudence under the leadership of a scholarly class (*wilayat al-faqih* – rule of the jurisprudent – in Iran), and those that emphasize the implementation of the *Hudud* (corporal punishments) as the barometer for instituting Islamic law. There are even perspectives, such as in Ghazi's native Pakistan, which emphasize economic development over jurisprudence or instituting *Hudud* punishments – much to the chagrin of some elements of Pakistani society that would rather see the latter.

Are any of these approaches more correct than the others? The scholars agreed that multiplicity is a hallmark of the Muslim *ummah*. As Şentürk said, "We should allow for the existence of different modalities in a way that will reflect the richness of the Shariah, rather than seeking a single model everywhere in the world." After all, as Ghazi shared, "The Prophet of Islam had a habit of giving *different* advice to *different* people in response to the same questions, depending on their unique situations." We should follow that example by recognizing that context shapes the judgment in a legal case. Larijani emphasized the evolutionary nature of this process, saying that "we should avoid talking about an Islamic government or an Islamic state as a finished or finalized product. The reality is that states are social structures that emerge out of different social contexts, following a specific evolution." Therefore, he continued, "It is quite possible to envisage the emergence of different Islamic structures for governance, depending on unique social realities."

While we therefore cannot prescribe any one perspective as the absolute standard of Islamic governance, we can articulate the minimum of what is agreed upon. Ghazi illustrated this point, saying that "if former Malaysian Prime Minister Ahmed Badawi, who advanced the notion of *Islam Hadhari*, and the spiritual leader of the conservative Pan-Malaysian Islamic Party, Nik Abdul Aziz, agreed to establish an Islamic state, then there would be many points of disagreement. But there would likewise be a minimum upon which they would agree." "That minimum," Ghazi said, "should be our product."

The method of establishing this minimum as the essential foundation for Islamic governance is analogous to saying that whoever declares the *shahada* is a Muslim. For example, there are different interpretations regarding the necessity of wearing the *hijab* and different standards as to what constitutes *halal* food, but all agree that one must declare the *shahada* in order to become a Muslim. By establishing these basic and fundamental principles of Islamic governance, Larijani shared that, "societies can start evolving and create their own Islamic states." In other words, when defining Islamic governance, "We should not fix the end; rather we should fix the beginning."

What makes a state "Islamic"?

It was natural, based on the traditional diversity of opinion in Islamic legal thought, that in our efforts to find consensus, our discussions began with passionate disagreement. What makes a state Islamic? Is it its official declarations? Its laws? The qualifications of its rulers? Its deliverables to its society? Or is it based on the outcomes, meaning that the state structures and laws have created a society that manifests the principles and ideals enshrined in the Qur'an and the Sunnah? The fundamental question underlying our discussions was: is the Islamicity of a state defined by what a government **says** about itself, by what it **does**, or by the **society** that it enables?

From the scholars' conversations, we agreed that a modern nation-state is comprised of four elements: its declarations, the source of the ruler's perceived legitimacy, its institutions, and the outcomes of governance. The declarations, largely articulated in the founding documents and constitution of the state, purport to express the vision and aspirations of the people. For example, in the case of the United States, the Declaration of Independence appeals to God and the "Laws of Nature," declaring that "all men are created equal, that they are endowed by their Creator with certain unalienable Rights, that among these are Life, Liberty and the pursuit of Happiness." The *legitimacy of the ruler* is derived from "the consent of the governed," in this case through elections, and a candidate is qualified based on certain criteria outlined in the Constitution. *Institutions* are formed to deliver the desired outcomes – in the case of the United States, the unalienable rights of the people of "Life, Liberty and the pursuit of Happiness." These describe the declared and desired *outcomes of the system of governance* in the United States.

The question of the importance of theoretical declarations and the ruler's qualifications elicited impassioned conversation among the scholars, as many of us held differing opinions on their relative importance in determining a state's Islamicity. I have highlighted some of these conversations below in order to give the reader a broader picture of the varying perspectives among our scholars.

Is a formal declaration required for a state to be Islamic?

The point of contention between our scholars about formal declarations of Islamicity was related to the nature of the state itself. Those who valued declarative statements upheld that a state has an ontological status equivalent to a person – just as a person can declare faith, so can a state. On the other hand, those who believed that giving a state personhood is arbitrary and not in keeping with the Islamic tradition failed to see utility in declarative statements. In other words, a state is not a living being that can declare belief or anything else about itself.

Ghazi, a supporter of the first view, said that "Islamicity should be decided on the state's relation and submission to the Almighty. Theoretical declarations are highly relevant especially in Islam where the power of declarations is such that it only takes a simple declaration of faith (the *shahadah*) in order to become a Muslim." Abbadi cited a Hadith that emphasized the power of a declaration of faith: a companion of the Prophet killed a man in battle despite the fact that the man had declared the *shahadah* and converted to Islam just before he was killed.

When the companion relayed this to the Prophet, the Prophet asked why he killed the convert, to which he replied that the enemy converted simply to try to protect himself. The Prophet grew angry and asked the companion, "Did you open up his heart to see?"

Auda responded to this discussion by making a distinction between an individual's declaration of faith and a state's: "It is correct that the Prophet says that we should only judge the external rather than the internal of a person. If someone believes and accepts the *shahadah* of Islam, then you are not required to open his or her heart to see whether or not this is sincere." However, he continued, "When we talk about the Islamic state, we're talking about that belief which leads to application, not just the mere belief ... we're discussing how to move from belief in the absolute authority of Allah to the process of application in the Islamic state. Many countries believe in Allah, the One, but practically on the ground, there is nothing of Islam."

The position that the state, within Islamic history, has never been something that declares faith was raised by Kamali: "We can't rely on such declarations or labels. Throughout the history of Islam, many different names have been used to describe an Islamic polity other than an 'Islamic state.'" Tun Abdul Hamid added that "If we refer to the Medina Charter, nothing exists like this ... Nothing mentions an 'Islamic state.'" The Medina Charter was a contract of rights and responsibilities between real individuals. I pointed out that abstract notions – such as a "state" – could never take the place of ontologically real parties in that context. A state cannot declare the *shahadah* because the state is simply not an individual, and it is a legal fiction of an "artificial person" – like a corporation – comprised of individuals who can take actions that are either in line with Islamic practice or not.

Further, a state cannot be defined as Islamic simply because it declares itself as such precisely since the effect of such statements cannot be measured: *can* a state, without sentience or free will of its own, submit to God's will? And if it did, how would we know it or hold it accountable? Thus proponents of the latter view believed that the Islamicity of a state is determined by its actions and effects in society or, as Mahmood said, "A state cannot be a Muslim, though it can advance the practice of Islam," pointing out that "the state is never going to be brought before God on Judgment Day to be held accountable for its deeds and rewarded with heaven or hell – it is the leaders of that state that will stand before God and answer for their actions!"

Tun Abdul Hamid also raised a further point that branding something as Islamic is problematic. For example, Muslims proudly speak of "Islamic medicine." But "If Ibn Sina is seen as a 'Muslim' doctor who developed 'Islamic' medicine, does this mean that Muslims can only apply the medicine up to his time? And since the medicine of modern times was developed by non-Muslims does that mean therefore, that modern medicine is un-Islamic medicine, and Muslim doctors practicing modern medicine are doing something un-Islamic?" Analogously, people speak of "Islamic banking." How is that defined? Is a regular bank (that charges interest) Islamic if its employees or managers are Muslim? Or would a bank run by non-Muslims that does not charge interest qualify to be called an Islamic bank? Calling such a bank a zero-interest bank is perhaps a more technically accurate term, but by calling it Islamic we put our religion on the line. If an Islamic bank fails, has Islam failed? As retired Chief Justice of the UAE Sheikh Ali al-Hashimi once told me in a private conversation, "I don't like the use of the term Islamic bank, because when such a bank fails, as has happened, the news will say that 'such and such Islamic bank failed,' and the presumption is that Islam has failed. But if a particular Islamic bank fails, has Islam failed?" Analogously, is Islam unjust because a particular "Islamic state" may be a failed or unjust state? This relates to my earlier points about the misuse of language when we refer imprecisely to something as "Islamic," which implies that the concept of "Islam" is an ontologically real being that acts and prescribes exactly one way of being. With this project we are seeking a more technically accurate description of the term "Islamic state."

Finally, Tahir Mahmood pointed out that some modern nations maintained their traditional rule as sultanates or emirates without declarations and or constitutions. For example, Saudi Arabia did not declare in its constitution that it was an Islamic state until 1992. Would we have considered Saudi Arabia "un-Islamic" up to that point? Would we have given pre-1992 Saudi Arabia a zero rating on our proposed Shariah Index score because some of our scholars deemed declarations necessary?

Our scholars agreed that legitimacy is crucial to an Islamic state as exemplified in the traditional concept of *bay`ah*, which is the legitimization of a ruler through the consent of the ruled. They also agreed that the function of *bay`ah* is fulfilled in the modern world through elections. Yet the scholars disagreed as to whether the legitimacy of a state's ruler is more important than its competency in fulfilling the outcomes of good governance.

Those who upheld that legitimacy is more important believed that the good of an illegitimate state is cancelled out by the fundamental injustice of its founding. Larijani, who held this position, shared that legitimacy is needed in order to truly progress, because substantial progress is dependent on a healthy relationship between the people and their government. He said that a legitimate government "is important because it creates an environment that facilitates new possibilities." It allows us to "witness the emergence of models of living together that are far superior to our current models." Şentürk added that "we have to factor the political dimension, because we are not simply looking at the (delivered political) goods but also the way they are delivered and the political structures in which they are offered to people." Auda maintained, however, that legitimacy is measured by "how well the government works."

Larijani responded to this by bringing up the example of a general that "leads a *coup d'état* and brings a revolutionary junta to power…. He brings prosperity and applies the Islamic *Maqasid* fully. Is this justice? He's still coming to power through a *coup*. If you ask people whether or not it is a good government, some will call it a disaster and say that they are not legitimate…" Auda responded by pointing out that even if we simply measure results, then "an authoritarian or illegitimate government would eventually fail at the *Maqasid* because the injustice of the regime would eventually do injustice to the people's rights." He further explained that "eventually that kind of power will corrupt, and if there's no way to hold him accountable, someone in his administration will start to usurp wealth."

The scholars who supported measuring competency as opposed to legitimacy argued that the government's job is to work towards the best interests of society. Auda said, "Why do we need an Islamic state? In the end, it's for the *maslahah* [best interests] of the people, for enabling people to live a good life, that is, a good Islamic life according to the Islamic criteria. The *Maqasid* can function as a proxy; that is, by measuring how well a state's deliverables correlate to the *Maqasid* is an approximation to measure how well the society lives from an Islamic point of view." He further asserted that an illegitimate government that better provides for its people is better than a legitimate government that does not. Şentürk nuanced this point: "…legitimacy cannot be regarded as [a] one line item." "Everything here relates to legitimacy…If a government fails to respect the inviolability of life, it loses legitimacy, even if it succeeds in other areas."

Ghazi mediated this discussion by suggesting that "the question of legitimacy has two aspects. One aspect is theoretical, which is very significant and has been elaborated by Larijani. The second part is how to break down the concept of legitimacy into points which can be indexed and rated – for example, how they came to power, if they have the consent of the people, whether they meet the required criteria laid down in the early Islamic sources, and whether they uphold and deliver the *Maqasid* of the Shariah."

So, while the scholars were not unanimous regarding the need for a state to declare itself as Islamic, or on the precise qualifications of the ruler beyond *bay`ah*, or on how the ruler achieved power; there was unanimity among the scholars that the outcomes of governance must be in line with Islamic principles. This is best achieved if the structures, laws, and institutions of the state create a society that manifests the ethical principles and ideals of justice enshrined within the Qur'an and the Sunnah. The scholars agreed that the outcomes of governance should be the manifestation of justice in society, achieved through the six objectives of Islamic law (*Maqasid al-shari`ah*): the protection and preservation of life, religion, mind, property, family, and honor.

If we are primarily focused on the outcomes of governance, could a non-Muslim majority country be called Islamic if it fulfills these criteria? Sharia Index Project (SIP) Scholar Anies Baswedan shared that Muslims in certain Muslim-minority countries may experience more "Islam-friendliness" than in some Muslim-majority countries where, for example, its population enjoys fewer rights. This relates to philosopher Muhammad Abduh's alleged statement upon returning to Egypt from Europe: "In Paris, I saw Islam but no Muslims; in Egypt I see Muslims, but no Islam." Auda suggested that Muhammad Abduh was using the objectives of Islamic law (*Maqasid al-shari`ah*) as his measurement, where France may not have been a "believing state," but it nonetheless honored and advanced the protection of life, property, honor, religion, family, and the mind in an exemplary way. Mahmood suggested that, in this light, what we are looking at is the "Islamicity, instead of the Islamic-ness of a government. Just like if someone does a charitable good deed, a Christian in normal parlance will say, 'That is very Christian of you,' even if that person is a Buddhist." In like manner, if a non-Muslim majority country is characterized by justice, good governance, and the principles enshrined in the Qur'an and the Sunnah such as the objectives of Islamic law, we might say "That is very Islamic of you." Should not Islam be known and branded by these attributes anyway? And shouldn't this be how we rate countries? Should we not then rate all countries in our Index according to these principles, whether they have a Muslim majority or not, and whether they are ruled by Muslims or not?

What are the features of Shariah-compliant governance?

In discussing how the principles of the Qur'an and the Sunnah relate to the four elements of a state (declarations, qualifications/legitimacy of ruler, institutions, and outcomes of governance), we strove to outline the most important components of Islamic governance. In order to reach agreement on the defining requirements of an Islamic state, we first compiled a document that included every component that every one of our scholars insisted was a necessary element in defining Islamic governance – even if not all of the scholars agreed that each line item was essential and necessary to our final definition. Included below is the full list, after which we will discuss the process by which the scholars were able to narrow down these items to reach agreement on the defining requirements of an Islamic state.

1 *Foundation of the State*
  - The *rationale* of the state in light of Divine Guidance is the recognition of the sovereignty and supreme authority of God.
    a. If formally declared, it is either by recognizing the Shariah as the supreme source of guidance and lawmaking or by recognizing Islam as the state religion.

  - Basis of *legitimacy* of authority
    1. **Qualifications of the Leader**—the person of highest authority (i.e., the chief executive) should be well qualified in terms of *taqwa* (piety), *hikmah* and `*ilm* (wisdom and knowledge) and `*adalah* (justice); from a Sunni perspective, the most important of these is `*adalah,* justice.
    2. **Consent**—Legitimacy rests upon the consent of the people, or *bay`ah* (consent *and* allegiance), as understood and implemented by the *ummah* ("nation"); *bay`ah* is the locus of political authority.

  - *Functionality* of government
    1. Decision-making should be based on:
       - knowledge and expertise
       - consultation or *shura* by using democratic means and methods, such as parliament
       - general social consensus (*ijma`*) mechanisms (referendums, trade unions, civil society, etc.)
    2. Practical mechanisms to ensure that all laws and policies are in accordance with the Shariah, including maintenance of the *arkan al Islam* (the pillars of Islam – i.e. the declaration of faith, prayer, charity, fasting during Ramadan, pilgrimage)

- *Justice and Equality:* Elimination of hardship and causing harm (*la darar wa la dirar fil-Islam*)
  - Legal/political justice:
    - Corrective justice, including the recognition of:
      - *Qisas* (compensatory punishments)
      - *Hudud* (punishments described in the Qur'an)[1]
      - Capital punishment
    - Distributive justice
    - Political justice
    - International justice: The Islamic state should be in the forefront of every effort towards advancing global socio-economic and political justice, fair play, and cooperation. In the present day this is manifested by, for example:
      - Honoring and recognizing international commitments, treaties, and obligations (such as the Universal Declaration of Human Rights, Geneva Convention, and other international instruments) insofar as these international obligations do not conflict with the principles of Islam
      - Providing support to the oppressed (*al-mustad`afina fil-ard*) within and outside the Islamic State, subject to such limitations as imposed by international treaties and obligations
      - Working towards eliminating Weapons of Mass Destruction globally
  - Equality
    - Equality before the law
      - No crime and no punishment without a legal text to declare them as such
      - Head of state has limited power of clemency
      - No exemption from the law
  - Equality in the courts of justice and other forms of conflict resolution, such as alternative decision-making institutions (i.e., *Jirga* and *Panchayat*)
  - Equality in rights and opportunities (economic, educational, and employment)
  - Equality in burdens and obligations
  - Non-discrimination on the basis of caste, color, race, domicile, gender, and religion
  - Equality in selection and appointment to public offices
- Independence of the judiciary, separation of powers, limited government, checks and balances

- Individual and collective freedoms:
  - Speech and expression
  - Movement and travel
  - Assembly and association
  - Religion and worship
  - Press
  - Preservation of local cultures, languages, and scripts
- *Hisbah* (the institutionalization of the Qur'anic command *amr bil ma`ruf wan nahy `an al-munkar*). In contemporary times, *hisbah* may be expressed via various internal and external regulatory bodies in the following fields:
  - Economy (*hisbah* agencies such as central banks for banking and finance, securities and exchange commissions, etc.)
    - Integrity of the market and business transactions
    - Prevention of fraud, misrepresentation, and false advertisement
  - Governance (*hisbah* agencies such as Federal Aviation Agencies to regulated the airlines sector, ombudsman, vigilance commissions, and anti-corruption commissions)
    - Prevention of corruption in government departments and private institutions (e.g., bribery, nepotism, and delaying tactics)
    - Prevention of hardship (*raf' al-haraj*), such as unnecessarily long queues in government departments, traffic congestion, etc.
    - Accountability of the rulers (*muhasabat al-hukkam*) and transparency
- Judiciary/Law (*hisbah* agencies such as law commissions, judicial accountability commissions)
  - Fair trial and speedy disposal of court cases
  - Prevention of corruption
- Moderation (*i`tidal, wasatiyyah* – avoidance of extremism)
- Promotion of peace and security and prevention of violence and terrorism in all forms, including state terrorism

2   *Goals and Objectives of an Islamic State*

All institutions of governance should at least strive to achieve, protect and promote the Maqasid al-Shari`ah ("the core objectives of Islamic law") and enforce the laws of the land that are not in conflict with the Shariah.

Protection and promotion of the following:

- Life
  - Right to life and personal liberty (freedom from arbitrary arrest, torture, etc.)
  - National security (internal and external) and defense capability
  - Provision of food, shelter, and clothing
  - Opportunities for work/employment
  - Healthcare; its quality, availability, and affordability
  - Protection of environment, including flora and fauna
- Mind
  - Promotion of rationality (as opposed to populism, cultism, and superstition), respect for general consensus, and tolerance of differences
  - Access to quality education (religious and contemporary, compulsory child education)
  - Promotion of science, technology, research, and development
  - Control the undesirable elements of drugs, narcotics, and intoxicants
  - Free dissemination of knowledge
  - Freedom of speech and expression
  - Access to information of governmental activity
- Religion
  - Protection and promotion of the moral and spiritual values of Islam
  - Facilitation of the realization of *amr bil-ma`ruf wan nahy `an al-munkar*, which literally means "commanding the good and forbidding the evil"
    - The objective of *amr bil-ma`ruf* is to promote and protect the moral fabric of society and prevent evil
  - Freedom of *ijtihad* (independent legal reasoning) by competent, qualified, and knowledgeable individuals
  - Furtherance of the capacity of the community to fulfill its religious obligations, including but not limited to the following
    - Availability of mosques, *hajj* affairs, distribution of *zakah*, and observing the sanctity of *Ramadan*
    - *Waqf* (religious endowment)
  - Promoting harmony and good relations among followers of all religious beliefs and religious schools of law (*madhahib*)
  - Protection of religious freedom and other belief systems
  - Prohibition of the desecration of religions and religious symbols

- Family/Lineage
  - Promotion of family as a unit in society
  - Promotion of family values
  - Protection of the institution of marriage with a view toward fulfilling its proper objectives, including procreation, companionship, and sexual gratification
  - Protection of clarity of lineage
  - Provision of child benefits and special benefits for orphans, elderly, and the disabled
  - Education of youth about *adab al nikah* (marriage and gender relationships)
  - Gender and juvenile justice
- Property/Wealth
  - Property:
    - Protection of the sanctity of private ownership, including nonmaterial property such as intellectual property and trademarks
    - Protection of public property
- Trade and commerce:
  - Integrity and stability of trade and transactions
  - Prohibition of trade in unlawful substances and human organs
- Economic justice:
  - Labor rights, fair wages, and equal and fair treatment of domestic and foreign labor
  - Control the undesirable elements of unlawful gain, such as hoarding, exploitative practices, profiteering, *riba* (usury), gambling, and bribery
  - Promotion of equity in material well-being and equitable distribution of wealth
  - Promotion of economic development and sustainability of the individual
  - Insurance of a fair and balanced price regime of essential commodities, if necessary, through subsidies
- Honor/Personal Dignity
  - Government protection of personal dignity and reputation against slander/libel
    - NOTE: "Honor Killing" has no purpose in this objective and is a violation of the sanctity of human life
  - Protection of right to privacy
  - Prevention of misuse of public office to slander and dishonor individuals, families, groups, and organizations

Seeking agreement on the characteristics of an Islamic State

There was no unanimity amongst the scholars that all of these elements were of equal and vital importance in defining Islamic governance. In fact, we had sincere, passionate discussions and disagreements on certain issues when trying to narrow down the above list to the minimum fundamentals.

In order to bridge the differences among the scholars, and get their agreement on our minimum, I was inspired by James Surowiecki's book, *The Wisdom of Crowds*. In this book he shows how "under the right circumstances, groups are remarkably intelligent, and are often smarter than the smartest people in them."[2] Whether drawing upon trends in stock market trades, a motley group of experts to solve a technical problem, or the crowd at a fair ground guessing the weight of the prize ox; Surowiecki shows that the average of the answers given by a wide range of individuals has consistently been the most accurate answer – even more accurate than any one individual's contribution. It seems that a wide and diverse group of people can actually pinpoint the truth better than any single one of us. This piece of evidence resonates with the Prophet's *Hadith* that "My community will not agree on an error." It further supports the reason consensus (*ijma'*) is a primary method of determining the right judgment in Islamic law and provides a strong argument for the idea of the collective vicegerency (*khilafah*) of the community.

There are key conditions for a crowd to be wise rather than a crowd with the mindless and hasty decisions associated with a mob mentality. For a crowd to be wise, there must be diversity and independence of opinion (which we certainly had in our group of Shariah Index scholars!) and some aggregating mechanism to tally the divergent opinions and capture the collective decision of the group. To create such a mechanism, we turned the above list into a voting ballot, where each of the scholars independently gave percentage scores to each line item according to their personal understanding of its relative importance to the final definition of Islamic good governance. All of the items in our original list were also grouped under one of three broader categories: normative declarations, qualifications and legitimacy of leaders, and outcomes of governance. We asked each scholar to allocate a percentage according to the relative importance of these broader categories, such that they together amount to 100%. Those who felt that declarations and the leader's qualifications were of prime importance gave each of those items a percentage score on a scale of 0 to 100, while perhaps giving a lower score to the outcomes of governance. For those who felt that the outcomes of governance were all that mattered, they entered "0%" for declarations, qualifications and legitimacy, while writing in "100%" under outcomes.

These ballots are a testament to the diversity of our opinions and backgrounds, as the values ascribed to each of the line items ran the gamut of opinions. All of the opinions of the scholars were vital and important to this project, and we wanted to be sure that no individual opinion was ignored in the collective decision. This method, drawing upon the insights in Surowiecki's book, allowed us to factor the collective decision of the group in such a way that all opinions were measured. It also left the door open for future voting among a larger group of scholars, rather than fixing this percentage for all time.

While we had divergent opinions, there *was* a category of items that emerged as the most important across the board when we tallied up the scores (Table 3.1). When we tallied up the group's final scores, we found that the *outcomes of governance* were consistently given a high score, while governmental structure was only of prime importance to some of our scholars. Clearly we still held different views with regards to the importance of issues such as formal declarations and the ruler's qualifications and legitimacy, but nonetheless we had found the minimum upon which we all agreed: the **outcomes of governance**. These include the principles of governance (justice, equality, *hisbah, bay`ah, shura*, and *ijma`*) and the fulfillment of the *Maqasid* (protection and preservation of life, mind, religion, family, property, and honor).

This method allowed us to reach a consensus about the minimum requirements of an Islamic state – as analogous to the *shahada* in the individual Muslim – but it also allowed us to continue this project as a

Table 3.1   The scholars' opinions on important criteria for an Islamic State

Categories	Relative Importance to Definition of Islamic State, Allocate 0% – 100%
Normative Declarations	5%
Qualifications & Legitimacy of Leaders	8%
Outcomes of Governance Subtotal:	87%
Principles (justice, *shura, 'ijma', bay`ah*)	35%
Maqasid (Inviolability of Life, Mind, Religion, Family, Property, and Honor)	52%
TOTAL	100%

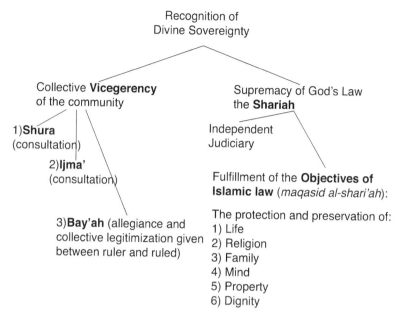

Figure 3.1 Figure of Recognition of Divine Sovereignty

live project. We hope that in the future, a larger group of scholars will participate in such a measure so that – as time goes on – we can measure the collective opinion of a wider scope of scholars in the expectation of a trend line that converges towards a steady answer.

The essential features of Islamic governance: defining an Islamic State

With this in mind, together with Dr. Ghazi, I crafted the following summary that captured the essential aspects of our scholars' discussion and collective decision (Figure 3.1).

The fundamental principle of Islamic governance is divine sovereignty, the recognition that ultimate authority rests with God. The terms *mulk* (kingship or ownership)[3], *hukm* (authority to decide or decision),[4] and *'amr* (command)[5] are the terms used in the Qur'an in regards to authority. Within these verses it is clear that *hukm*, *'amr*, and *mulk* are the ultimate prerogatives of God. No one has the authority to decide, issue an order, or lay down a commandment that contradicts the Divine Command. No legislative body may enact a law that is contradictory to God's Law.

The first mechanism through which divine sovereignty is tangibly expressed is the collective viceregency (*khilafah*) of the community. God says in the Qur'an, "I will make a *khalifah* (vicegerent) on earth,"[6] which was said just before the creation of man. The terms *hukm, mulk,* and *'amr,* the prerogative of God, have been used in the context of communities in the Qur'an.[7] In traditional Islamic thought, the collective viceregency of the community is in turn manifested through three mechanisms: *shura* (consultation) among the community, the *ijma`* (consensus) of the community, and thirdly, the *bay`ah* (allegiance and collective legitimization) that the community can give to or withdraw from the ruler. In modern day democracies, *shura* and *ijma`* are accomplished through parliamentary and congressional processes, and *bay`ah* is manifested via democratic elections.

The second mechanism through which divine sovereignty is expressed on the ground is through the supremacy of God's Law, the Shariah. The supremacy of God's Law is manifested through the mechanism of an independent judiciary and the fulfillment of the objectives of Islamic law (*Maqasid al-shari`ah.*)

The judiciary is the most important institution in Islamic governance, and throughout the majority of Muslim history it has been independent of the ruling body. The second and fourth caliphs are recorded to have appeared before their own judges, stressing the fact that no one is above the law and even the highest political authorities are subject to judicial review. The independence of courts and judges from the political authority ensures the realization of justice, which is the primary function of Islamic governance according to the express provisions of the Qur'an.[8]

Secondly, the supremacy of God's Law is secured by the fulfillment of the objectives of Islamic law, *Maqasid al-shari`ah.* The six objectives of Islamic law are the protection and preservation of life (*nafs*), religion (*din*), mind (*`aql*), property (*mal*), family/progeny (*nasl*), and honor (*'ird/karamah*).

Achieving this consensus amongst our group of scholars, who themselves represent the whole and wide spectrum of Islamic legal and political thought, constituted a significant milestone in defining Islamic governance in the modern day. The protection and preservation of **life** is secured by peace (lack of war), national security, clean environment (potable water, air), and healthcare. That of **religion** is secured by protecting the freedom of religion, facilitating religious observance, and furthering religious understanding and spiritual development. The protection and preservation of **family** is secured by the protection of the family unit as the basis of society and preserving clarity of lineage. Developing the mind through education and protecting it from that which compromises it, including substance abuse, accomplishes the protection and preservation of the **mind**. The protection and preservation of **property** occurs when the people are able to earn sufficient funds to provide for food, clothing, and shelter and all other needs. And lastly, the protection and preservation of **honor** is attained via the preservation and furthering of fundamental human rights.

We hope that the above statement on Islamic governance will prove to be a useful tool as communities across the Muslim world seek to understand the practical application of the term Islamic state and further bring their states into alignment with the Divine Intent. We see this scholarly consensus on the fundamental features of Islamic governance as our first contribution to this effort, especially considering the many competing voices within the *ummah* regarding the issue of Islam and the state.

4
Defining the Maqasid for Measurement

As we began to think about developing an index, it was clear that rating leaders on their qualifications was going to be difficult, and rating them on their legitimacy would be problematic. This difficulty would not help our project's objective of helping countries with Muslim majorities and countries that are committed to Islam and are members of the OIC (Organization of Islamic Cooperation) govern better, but might be seen as an attack on their leaders. We therefore focused on what our scholars unanimously agreed on – and what they determined to represent nearly 90 percent of what defines a state as Islamic – and sought to index countries on how well they performed on the outcomes of governance.

As our discussions turned to trying to find practical ways of measuring theoretical concepts such as justice, we discovered that we could measure and define the *Maqasid* in a way that would also measure the principles of governance, including justice and equality. For example, we might measure justice in part through the independence of the judiciary under the *maqsad* of honor, considering that access to a fair and unbiased trial is central to preserving the honor and fundamental rights of each person. We might measure equality by looking at income disparity under the *maqsad* of property, or by looking at equal access to healthcare under the *maqsad* of life. By embedding these principles of governance within a measurement based on the *Maqasid*, we could ensure we included all of the outcomes of governance that we had agreed constituted the core definition of good Islamic governance. This is how we arrived at the decision to create a *Maqasid* index as a first step to measuring the Islamicity of states. What follows is an in-depth look at each of the six *Maqasid* in turn, recounting our scholars' discussions about the purpose and meaning of each *maqsad* and the indicators by which we can measure them.

Maqsad of religion

The *maqsad* of religion (*din*) originated as the "protected value" behind the injunction toward *jihad* and the value that makes apostasy with conspiracy to harm the religion of Islam a crime. While all the scholars agreed that apostasy is a sin punishable by God in the hereafter, apostasy is not a crime that can be prosecuted by other human beings within the jurisdiction of Shariah or other courts. As some of our scholars pointed out, the Qur'an does not prescribe an earthly punishment for apostasy. Meanwhile, the *Hadith* prescribing death for apostasy was revealed within the context of religious war, where a defection among the followers of the Prophet meant treason and joining the enemy camp. As Şentürk shared, "The verse in the Qur'an on apostasy was revealed after a group of conspirators entered Islam as a group and then left it soon after to persuade others that they couldn't find what they were looking for in Islam."[1] Every instance of apostasy that was punished by the Prophet was apostasy accompanied by treason, an act that threatened what we call today "national security." Treason in all societies was considered a capital offense. Ghazi echoed the statement that apostasy in of itself is not punishable; it is only one of the *Hudud* when it is an act of treason. This is supported by the fact that during the Peace of Hudaybiya, the Prophet agreed that any Muslim who renounced his religion would be allowed to freely return to Mecca. In so doing, the Prophet showed that the Shariah protects freedom of conscience. This is why Professor Kamali held that *jihad* is the root of this *maqsad*, not apostasy. *Jihad* is what we now call "national security" as well as generally protecting religion and all religious communities existing in the state from harm and threat.

The scholars also discussed how the promotion of ethical values and the facilitation of religious practice are at the core of this *maqsad*. Similarly, they discussed how this *maqsad* relates to religious freedom among Muslims and non-Muslims and the promotion of intra- and interfaith harmony. The scholars agreed that this *maqsad* prescribes the promotion of Islamic ethical values, freedom of religious choice, and the facilitation of religious practice to those who have made this choice. It is the state's duty to encourage and promote the positive with regards to religious practice, rather than to prevent what one religion or religious interpretation deems negative. Mahmood indicated that giving state authorities the power to "decide what is heresy and innovation and what is true Islam" can be problematic. It would enable a government to impose its own particular *madhhab* or interpretation of Islam, thereby violating the Qur'anic principle of religious freedom: "There shall be no compulsion in religion."[2] Rather than focusing directly on preventing the negative, Ghazi said that "the prevention of negatives should be done through positive promotion of the faith."

Ignorance of the law is not grounds for punishment in Islamic law; one must know what is right and wrong before being judged. Educating people and speaking to their higher selves is more effective in personally transforming them than is punishing them, and this was the *Sunnah* of the Prophet. Good governance involves a process of elevating people and treating them with dignity. While the Islamic state should promote ethical values, such as proper business conduct, and facilitate the practice of religion by supporting mosques and other religious institutions, the Qur'anic principle of religious freedom means that the state should not use compulsion with regard to individuals' personal beliefs or religious practice, both toward the Muslim community and toward non-Muslim populations residing within its borders. Within the Muslim community, the principle of religious freedom is preserved when the state does not force adherence to a particular *madhhab* or interpretation of Islam. As Ghazi shared, this also means that "the government must respect the authority and freedom of the mosque" by not imposing a particular message and targeting imams who think differently than government officials. In addition, there must exist freedom of *ijtihad* by competent, qualified, and knowledgeable individuals – with competency here defined by Tun Abdul Hamid as "Shariah proficiency."

Dr. Hamieh clarified that "everything regarding freedom has limits in Islam" and makes the distinction between *huriyyah* (freedom) and *infilat* ("uncontrolled and irresponsible freedom") that directly harms others. With regards to an imam's freedom to give a speech in a mosque, one firm limit is that "he cannot attack others, even if they are not Muslims." The limit with regards to *ijtihad* is first that the *mujtahid* must be proficient in Shariah, and second that it cannot cause "strife and *fitna*," as Gauhar shared. Larijani said that we should "promote hundreds of *mujtahid*s. Let them speak about issues, and even against one another." But while the tolerance of reasonable differences is acceptable, Kamali clarified that "when a particular *ijtihad* reaches the level of consensus, there is a requirement that the state should step in and eliminate too much *'ikhtilaf* or differences of opinion," in line with the legal maxim, "*Hukm al-hakim yarfa'ul khilaf*," meaning "The ruler's decision removes difference of opinion."[3]

This principle of religious freedom also applies to the non-Muslim populations residing within an Islamic state. Maarif shared that "the state must also protect the non-Muslim population. In the Islamic state, the non-Muslim is permitted to drink wine, for example; his property is protected and if anyone attacks it, they must be judged." Şentürk echoed this statement, saying that "a state by Muslims isn't only for the Muslim *ummah*, it's for the non-Muslim communities as well." This entails, in part, support for their houses of worship and religious schools, a support that may even be financial. But primarily, religious freedom for the non-Muslim populations within an Islamic state means protecting and supporting their right to believe and practice freely, without compulsion, as individuals and groups. This even extends, shared Maarif, to atheists: "There is a verse in the Qur'an, *wa law shaa'a rabbuka la aamana man fil-ardi kulluhum jami 'an; 'afa anta tukrihu-nnasa hatta yakunu mu'minin?'* 'Had God willed all on earth would have believed; will *you* then coerce people to believe?'[4] So in an Islamic state, there is even a place for atheists. We must protect them." While an Islamic state should in no way promote atheism, as Ghazi indicated, it should protect everyone's right to exercise their God-given free will in matters of belief. As the Qur'anic verse continues, "Let there be no compulsion in religion: truth (*rushd*) stands out clear from error." Rather than trying to compel anyone to believe precisely as we believe, we should focus on improving our own *rushd*, or integrity of conduct, and the divine origin of this integrity will be clear.

In addition to championing religious freedom both within the Muslim community and without, the scholars indicated that the state should also promote intra- and interfaith harmony. This entails working toward harmony between "the *madhahib* and between Shi`a and Sunni," as Şentürk shared, and also between a state's Muslim and non-Muslim populations. As Ghazi said, "Intra-Muslim harmony and harmony between Muslims and other communities are both critical."

In light of the above conversations and in consultation with the *fiqhi* literature, the scholars agreed upon the following responsibilities of an Islamic state within the *maqsad* of religion:

- Protection and promotion of the moral and spiritual values of Islam
- Freedom of *ijtihad* (independent legal reasoning) by competent, qualified, and knowledgeable individuals
- Furthering the capacity of the community to fulfill its religious obligations, including but not limited to:
  - Availability of mosques, *hajj* affairs, distribution of *zakat*, observing the sanctity of *Ramadan*
  - *Waqf* (religious endowment)
- Promoting harmony and good relations among followers of all religious beliefs and religious schools (*madhahib*)

- Protection of religious freedom for both the Muslim and non-Muslim populations
- Prohibition of the desecration of religions and religious symbols
- Positive image building of Islam

Hisbah: does it fall solely in the *Maqsad* of religion or does it run throughout all of the *Maqasid*?

The principle of governance called *hisbah* or "accounting" is derived from the Qur'anic injunction to command the good (*amr bil-ma`ruf*) and prevent the negative (*nahy`an al-munkar*).[5] *Hisbah* is the Islamic idea of the "common good" that defines the "ideal society," as God says in the Qur'an: "You are the best of nations (*kuntum khayra ummatin*) selected for mankind, commanding the good and forbidding the negative," thus defining a good community (*khayra ummatin*) as one that performs *hisbah*.[6] The jurisprudential mechanics of the concept of *hisbah* refer to the various mechanisms in society by which this common good is maintained and strengthened, including checks and balances across all areas of life such as banking control and regulation, food regulation, policing, and the judicial system.

Kamali pointed out that historically within Islamic societies, *hisbah* was enforced by the *muhtasib,* the public regulator who supervised public offices and the marketplace to ensure that vendors used a common system of weights and measurements. He cited an example in medieval Baghdad where "the *muhtasib* passed by a Shariah court in the middle of the day, and there was a very long queue and people were crowding in front of the courthouse. The *muhtasib* came and sent a message to the judge: 'either you give these people a separate time to come or speed up the decision-making, because people are suffering outside your court.'" This is what *hisbah* can mean, Kamali clarified, "the prevention of hardships like long queues at ministries, immigration offices, and so on." Thus, we found that we could measure the principle of *hisbah* as it relates to the economy and the market under the *maqsad* of property, testing the efficacy of regulatory bodies by measuring corruption, income distribution, and property rights. As the mere presence of a regulatory body does not automatically ensure that regulation is effective, we found that we could create a measuring tool that more accurately reflects the reality on the ground by measuring its outcomes within the framework of the *Maqasid*.

In the scholars' discussion on *hisbah*, we found that the main goal of *hisbah* is ensuring justice within society and furthering the common good or *maslahah* (best interests) of the people, as illustrated in the above example. Despite this historical precedence, many hold the view that *hisbah* relates only to the *maqsad* of religion, considering that this principle is cited in the present day as a justification for religious police in some countries. While some of our scholars affirmed that the state does have a role in curbing certain immoral behaviors (such as gambling and prostitution), the scholars agreed that the state should not be involved with enforcing a particular practice of religion, thereby encroaching on the privacy and personal freedom of religion. We generally agreed that in the *maqsad* of religion the prevention of negatives is best done and achieved through promoting the positive, with clear limitations so that the state cannot infringe on private religious practice.

Rather than being confined to the religion *maqsad*, our scholars concurred that *al-amr bi'l-ma `ruf wa al-nahy `an al-munkar* runs through all six of the *Maqasid*, not just the *maqsad* of religion. Because all of the *Maqasid* together define the common good, *hisbah* in of itself represents a general guideline for defining and providing a check-and-balance mechanism for the *Maqasid* and for good governance in general – as long as it does not infringe on individuals' rights and privacy. Thus, as we continued to define the remaining *Maqasid* for measurement, we were mindful to include elements that both promote the positive and prevent the negative.

Maqsad of life

The *maqsad* of life (*nafs*) originated as the "protected value" that makes murder a crime. The "preservation of life" refers generally to the protection of physical life, provision of basic physical needs, and the prevention of harm to the body.

The scholars' discussion regarding the preservation of life centered on issues such as national security, whether the state's duty to protect life is restricted only to its citizens, and the preservation of the environment.

On the issue of national security, the scholars pointed out that this has classically been a fundamental duty of political leadership. Kamali noted that the early Islamic scholar al-Mawardi lists defense of the homeland among the top ten duties of the Caliph, and Şentürk shared that national security is included as a major function of the state within classical books of *kalam*, (scholastic theology). Mahmood made the distinction within this *maqsad* between the *individual* right to life and personal security and liberty, and the *group* right to national security.

Related to national security are those issues regarding international security and responsibilities. The scholars agreed that an Islamic state should honor international commitments, treaties, obligations and recognized rules of international behavior (such as the Geneva

Conventions, Universal Declaration of Human Rights, the provisions of international laws, etc.) insofar as they promote the principles of Islam.

The scholars then turned to the question of international obligations with regards to the *maqsad* of life. Şentürk asked "whether or not the state is responsible for the inviolability of human life just within the state, or alternatively, if the lives of human beings who aren't citizens are violated, is the Islamic state required to protect them?" Kamali answered by saying that "in Islam, the protection of life is a human right" not restricted to citizenship, and that "only the life of the *harbi*, who has declared war, is not protected." Ghazi said that "one of the goals and functions of the Islamic state is to provide support and help to the persecuted and down-trodden on earth," described in the Qur'an as "*al-mustad`afina fil-ard*." God says in the Qur'an, "And why should you not fight in the cause of Allah and of those who, being weak, are oppressed – men, women, and children, whose cry is: 'Our Lord! Rescue us from this town, whose people are oppressors; and raise for us from thee one who will protect; and raise for us from thee one who will help!'"[7] Ghazi continued, saying that "if there is a minority or people being persecuted and you have the capacity to help them, you are obliged to do so." The scholars agreed that an Islamic state has an obligation to assist the *mustad'afina fil-`ard*, the weak or oppressed on earth, wherever or whomever they may be.

Regarding the *maqsad*'s stipulation to preserve the environment, Auda noted that the "environment is related to life because it affects all areas of human life on earth." Not only is this related to the protection of the environment against pollution, but also to "preserving natural resources and sustainability," as Gauhar shared. Larijani reflected that "the way we live and consume goods requires some serious rethinking ... we cannot be *musrif*, wasteful, or extravagant in our habits and mass consumption of goods." All should be done in moderation, he said, including the consumption of meat.[8]

In light of the above conversations, consultation with the *fiqhi* literature, and the necessity to include both those elements that promote the positive (*`amr bil-ma`ruf*) and protect against the negative (*nahy `an al-munkar*), the scholars agreed upon the following responsibilities of an Islamic state within the *maqsad* of life:

- Right to life and personal liberty (freedom from arbitrary arrest, torture, etc.)
- National security (internal and external) and defense capability
- Provision of food, shelter, and clothing to those who cannot afford them

- Opportunities for work/employment
- Healthcare: its quality, availability, and affordability
- Protection of the environment, including flora and fauna

Maqsad of family

The *maqsad* of family or lineage (*nasl*) originated as the "protected value" that makes adultery (*zina*) a crime. The classical jurists originally defined it as protecting lineage under the assumption that a child must know his biological parents to determine inheritance, and this concept was expanded in later centuries to include promoting the well-being of the family as the basic unit of society.

The scholars' conversations regarding this *maqsad* centered around the promotion of the well-being of the family unit, including a focus on a healthy marriage and children. As Kamali shared, the Shariah promotes "lawful marriage that creates a life-long commitment and firm bond (*mithaqan ghalidh*),[9] as well as through a series of legal consequences for the spouses, their offspring, families, and future generations." The primary (*asli*) goal of marriage "is procreation (*tanasul*), and the Qur'an also designates decent cohabitation (*mu'asharah bil-ma'ruf*)[10] that nurtures tranquility, friendship, and kindness (*sukun, mawaddah* and *rahmah*)[11] as the cardinal objectives of marriage." The subsidiary (*tabi'i*) goals of marriage include "sexual gratification, avoidance of promiscuity and disease, and building a comfortable and functional home."

The scholars discussed that this ideal can be attained in part through the provision of pre-marriage counseling and education, *adab al-nikah*, as well as marriage and divorce counseling. Khoury mentioned a law in the United Arab Emirates "which stipulates that anyone seeking a divorce cannot obtain one unless they first go through counselling;" and Mahmood shared a similar example in Pakistan, where at the first pronouncement of divorce the couple must "notify the District Collector, who will institute and chair an Arbitration Council. There will be a nominee of the wife and a nominee of the husband, and for three months, they will try to reconcile. Only when they testify after three months that there is no chance of reconciliation will the divorce become effective." These are examples of measures that a state can take in order to safeguard the institution of marriage.

The scholars also recognized the rights of children, including as Kamali shared, the "right to education, the right to *nafaqah*, or maintenance." Reciprocally, "Parents are entitled to obedience; honoring one's parents is an Islamic imperative."

In light of the above conversations, consultation with the *fiqhi* literature, and the necessity to include both those elements that promote
the positive (`amr bil-ma`ruf) and protect against the negative (*nahy`an
al-munkar*), the scholars agreed upon the following responsibilities of an
Islamic state within the *maqsad* of family:

- Promotion of the family as a unit in society
- Promotion of family values
- Protection of the institution of marriage with a view toward fulfilling
  its proper objectives: procreation, companionship, sexual gratifica-
  tion, etc.
- Provision of child benefits and special benefits for orphans, elderly,
  and the disabled
- Education of youth about *adab al-nikah* (marriage and gender
  relationships)
- Gender and juvenile justice
- Protection of clarity of lineage (such as preventing closed adoption)[12]

Maqsad of mind

The *maqsad* of the mind or intellect (`aql`) originated as the "protected
value" that prohibits drinking alcohol. While classical jurists defined
this *maqsad* mainly as prohibiting the consumption of alcohol and
other intoxicants that compromise the mind and judgment, later jurists
expanded this definition to include the promotion of the mind through
quality education and encouraging scientific pursuits.

The discussion among the scholars centered on the promotion of the
intellect through education and scientific innovation, as well as the
protection of the intellect by promoting sobriety and protecting against
intoxicants. As Şentürk expressed, an "Islamic state should promote
equal access to quality education" for all men, women, and children.
Kamali emphasized that this requirement applies to both spiritual
and secular education. Kamali cited the well-known *Hadith* about the
compulsory nature of education: "*Al- `ilmu faridatun `ala kulli muslimin
wa muslimah*," (acquiring knowledge is obligatory for every Muslim, male
and female.) He continued, "If you read the jurists, they say it's the obligation of the parents to facilitate the child's education in the religious
arkan, or pillars, of the faith. It is an obligation and compulsory."[13]

Ghazi nuanced Professor Kamali's point by adding that obligatory
education is of two levels: *fard 'ayn* and *fard kifayah*. The first, *fard `ayn*,
is at an "individual compulsory level for each and every citizen of the

state," which represents whatever knowledge is required for someone to carry out his or her profession, including literacy and a basic knowledge of the sciences and arts. The second level, *fard kifayah*, represents those specializations that not everyone needs to be proficient in, but in which at least some members of society must be specialized. An example of this would be chemistry: "Obviously, it isn't obligatory for every person within a society to be educated in the specialization of chemistry. However, all societies must have some members who are well-educated and specialists in this field, in order to advance medicine, scientific inventions, and other areas that improve the society."

In addition to the provision of quality education to all members of society, the state must "promote innovation, particularly research and development in technology and the sciences," as Tun Abdul Hamid said. Ghazi gave the example of Iran, which is at the top of the Muslim countries in producing scientific literature. Larijani explained that although many countries with Muslim majorities have fantastic scholars, "the environment isn't good for intellectual productivity." In contrast, he added, the Iranian government spends large amounts of money on science; and publishing research in scientific journals is so highly prized that "if someone publishes a paper, and over the course of the next two or three years, he gets over a hundred citations for instance, he's given a fantastic prize of about $10,000 – averaging $100 a citation!" Along with supporting the sciences, the scholars noted that central to a nation's intellectual development is robust support for "freedom of speech and expression," as Şentürk said. "The state should promote diversity of opinions and tolerance of different views." These are examples of the ways in which a state might promote and encourage scientific and intellectual development, an important component of the *maqsad* of the mind.

While promoting universal education and scientific advancement, the state also has a role in encouraging sobriety and rationality. In this light, the scholars discussed whether a state must legally prohibit alcohol for its Muslim citizens and other intoxicants for all citizens. As Ghazi shared, "The prohibition of liquor and intoxicants has been a policy in Islamic states throughout history. It was banned by the Prophet of Islam, and it continued to be banned throughout all the ages." Other scholars questioned the correlation between the presence of a law and people's behavior and suggested that the state should focus on encouraging the development of a rational foundation that would naturally inhibit one from wanting to partake of intoxicants. As Larijani shared, "The state must invest in deepening the people's beliefs and allowing this rationality to grow."[14]

This kind of rationality relates to a wider conception of sobriety, which includes a presence of mind, an awareness and a rational process of thought. As Abbadi mentioned, when we talk about "rationality, *al- `aqlaniyyah* in Arabic, we don't mean Greek logic, *al-mantiq*. We're talking about the universal reasoning or rationality as identified by al-Shatibi, for example, that is in union with the universe." The scholars related this to the importance of developing *basirah*, meaning spiritual perception or discernment. As Larijani said, "The first priority of `aql is to enrich our faith by *basirah*. This is the essence of Islam. It is *basirah* centered. It means rationality is supreme." Hamieh emphasized that *basirah* is above the intellect because it is not only about knowledge but also understanding and wisdom; we must "know everything from our own wisdom and understanding, not from others."

In light of the above conversations, consultation with the *fiqhi* literature, and the necessity to include both those elements that promote the positive (`amr bil-ma`ruf) and protect against the negative (*nahy `an al-munkar*), the scholars agreed upon the following responsibilities of an Islamic state within the *maqsad* of intellect or the mind:

- Promotion of rationality (as opposed to populism, cultism, superstition), respect for general consensus, and tolerance of differences
- Access to quality education (religious and contemporary, compulsory childhood education)
- Promotion of science, technology, research, and development
- Control the undesirable elements of drugs, narcotics, and intoxicants
- Free dissemination of knowledge
- Freedom of speech and expression
- Access to information on governmental activity

Maqsad of property

The *maqsad* of property or wealth (*mal*) originated as the "protected value" from the prohibition of theft. Later scholars expanded this definition to include not only the protection of public and private property, but also the integrity of trade and prohibition of all types of unlawful gain.

The conversations among the scholars on this *maqsad* dealt with the issues of *riba* (usury) and other forms of unlawful economic gain such as fraud. The discussions also centered on the need for good governance focusing on positive economic development, the integrity of the market through regulation, and just labor laws.

The scholars noted that it is clear that usury is forbidden in the Qur'an: "*Wa ahalla Allahu al-bay `a wa harrama al-riba* – Allah has permitted trade and forbidden usury."[15] For this reason, some communities have developed interest-free banking (a term we prefer over "Islamic banking" for reasons discussed in Chapter 2). Yet Gauhar introduced a debate regarding usury based on the economic distinction between usury and interest. As compared to a common understanding that assumes that all interest is by definition usury (*riba*), Gauhar pointed out that the economic definition of usury is "any amount of interest charged which is two percent above the rate of inflation." In other words, usury is "lending money at an exorbitant rate of interest." I agreed with Gauhar, sharing that I define *riba* not just as any material return on a loan but rather as the "predatory use of capital" to unjustly make a gain. While an exorbitant rate of interest is clearly prohibited by the Qur'an, we chose to sidestep the impossible attempt – for our group of scholars at present in the context of this project – to determine whether or not all interest constitutes *riba* and is thus also prohibited.

The scholars also discussed the "protection of economic development and sustainability of the individual," as Şentürk expressed it. Economic development essentially means, as Larijani said, that "the government will combat poverty by helping its people attain property and wealth." The state should encourage the economic development of its citizens, and support and not punish them in times of economic recession or depression. In support of this requirement, we spoke about how the Caliph Umar al-Khattab suspended the theft penalty for a man guilty of stealing during a famine. We also discussed how the notion of welfare in which a state provides adequate assistance to those who are unemployed or unable to provide for their basic needs, fits this requirement.

Lastly, the scholars discussed the importance of economic regulation as a modern expression of *hisbah*. In early Islamic societies, the *muhtasib* supervised markets and other public spaces to ensure the regulation of prices and weights; general public safety and cleanliness; and that medical, craft, and building standards were enforced. As Gauhar argued, at present, the state should ensure this function of *hisbah* by providing for the "integrity of the market through autonomous regulatory bodies, which are independent of the government, and through internal regulatory bodies or self-governing mechanisms." Examples of these include central banks and bodies that determine the price of petroleum, regulate advertisement, and misrepresentation, and mechanisms that prevent corruption and fraud. Such bodies should ensure that general utilities such as electricity, fuel and water, are not owned by individuals, but should be collectively owned and regulated by the government. According to one *Hadith*, the Prophet said, "Three things cannot be denied to anyone: water, pasture, and fire."[16] These items were the most necessary items for living in the desert, but other things could be added for our time, considering that Imam al-Shafi'i added underground resources like oil and sulfur. The state must ensure the equitable distribution of wealth and natural resources by overseeing the price of key commodities such as water, gasoline, and electricity with the caveat that government ownership or regulation of natural resources does not fall under unlawful monopoly.

In light of the above conversations, consultation with the *fiqhi* literature, and the necessity to include both those elements that promote the positive (`amr bil-ma`ruf*) and protect against the negative (*nahy `an al-munkar*), the scholars agreed upon the following responsibilities of an Islamic state within the *maqsad* of wealth or property:

- Property:
  - Protection of the sanctity of private ownership, including nonmaterial property such as intellectual property and trademarks
  - Protection of public property
- Trade and Commerce:
  - Integrity and stability of trade and transactions
  - Prohibition of trade in unlawful substances and human organs
- Economic Justice:
  - Labor rights, fair wages, and equal and fair treatment of domestic and foreign labor
  - Control the undesirable elements of unlawful gain, such as hoarding, exploitative practices, profiteering, *riba* (usury), gambling, and bribery
  - Promotion of equity in material well-being and equitable distribution of wealth
  - Promotion of economic development and sustainability of the individual
  - Ensuring a fair and balanced price regime of essential commodities, if necessary through subsidies

Maqsad of honor

The *maqsad* of honor or dignity ('*ird* or *karamah*) originated as the "protected value" from the prohibition of slander (*qadhf*). This *maqsad* was originally included under family, as the crime of slander was associated with falsely accusing someone of adultery (*zina*). Later it evolved to be its own *maqsad* that considered the *hadd* crime of *qadhf* as distinct from *zina*. Contemporary scholars have broadened this *maqsad* and have recognized human rights as intrinsic to the notion of human dignity and honor.

Our discussion evolved around a classical notion of human rights within Islamic legal thought that recognizes the fundamental rights and liberties of all based on their simply being human, or *adami*, rather than based on citizenship or religion (*aman* or *iman*). As Şentürk maintained, this notion recognizes legal personhood at birth, rather than "based on citizenship in the Islamic state, which is gained by membership in the Muslim faith or by a treaty with the Islamic state as one of the People of the Book." The scholars agreed that the term *huquq al-adamiyyin* ("the rights of human beings") is the term in the Islamic legal tradition that expressed the notion of "human rights" and preceded the more commonly known contemporary term, *huquq al-insan*.[17]

Among the rights discussed that protect the honor of all are the right to due process; protection from torture, arbitrary arrest, and detention; protection of privacy (including privacy of the home and personal correspondence); protection from discrimination based on race, religion, and gender; and protection against public slander or libel. The scholars were also emphatic that the cultural practice of "honor killing" is a false and wrongful application of this *maqsad* and is a flagrant violation of the sanctity of human life and its clear *maqsad*.

In light of the above conversations, consultation with the *fiqhi* literature, and the necessity to include both those elements that promote the positive (`amr bil-ma`ruf) and protect against the negative (*nahy`an al-munkar*), the scholars agreed upon the following responsibilities of an Islamic state within the *maqsad* of honor or dignity:

- Protection of personal dignity and reputations against slander/libel
- Protection of the right to privacy
- Prevention of misuse of public office to slander and dishonor individuals, families, groups, and organizations
- Protection from discrimination based on race, religion, and gender
- Protection and furthering of human rights

Conversation: what makes this index a measure of "Islamicity" rather than simply a development index?

After the decision was made to use the *Maqasid al-shari`ah* as the basis for our measurement, a number of our scholars expressed concern as to how well this index can be clearly labeled "Islamic." Kamali contended that a broader, values-oriented approach would enable the project to apply universal values to the individual histories and orientations of different countries. However, in the exchange below, along with Şentürk and Larijani, he underlined that the project must convey the unique element of Islamicity as well. Ghazi noted that focusing exclusively on the *Maqasid* could lead to the ironic result of the Caliphate of Umar and Ali scoring as less "Islamic" than pre-Islamic Rome or Persia, since the latter offered a higher quality of life and had more material riches.

Auda and Kamali contend that indicators within the *Maqasid* do actually reflect the Islamic dimension, especially under the *maqsad* of religion, which can be potentially given a higher overall weight. Imam Feisal says that even some indicators under the *maqsad* of religion can be considered common to numerous traditions. Both Kamali and Larijani asserted that measuring more holistically can come at a later date.

> **Kamali:** I am aware that we made a deliberate decision to narrow the project, to make our index values-driven, and based on the *Maqasid*. In this way, it is basically a utilitarian project looking at pragmatic concepts. However, my question is: does this change our philosophical approach from religious to secular? It is critical that this be driven by Islamic principles or the Islamic idea of the *Maqasid* – not materialist philosophy, secularism, or enlightenment concepts. Under the *maqsad* of the mind, for example, is there any measurement of whether the education system offers Islamic teachings or religious values? In my opinion, we have not made a sufficient distinction between this and a materialist approach to education. In the *Maqasid al-shari`ah*, we talk of education and enlightenment of the mind, but this must include the awareness that it originates from a different philosophy.

> **Imam Feisal:** We need to be able to identify the "Islamic DNA" of this project, that is, what makes this project flow from the Islamic legal tradition and existential worldview. Our task is to make this distinction clear. Professor Abbadi pointed out that the idea of `aql* in the *maqsad* of `aql* refers to more than just Greek logic, *al-mantiq*, or intellectual capacity. It also refers to a "universal thinking" that is "in union with the universe," a type of spiritual intellection or discernment, what we have denoted as *basirah* in Arabic. This spiritual discernment is inherited from the Prophetic tradition and is part of what must distinguish and characterize Islamic governance. But nonetheless, if we are measuring education but are unable at present to measure *basirah* due to data limitations,

does that make our measure not Islamic? Is secular education not Islamic? Of course educating a population in the sciences and arts is a significant part of the mandate of an Islamic state, but it may not be the whole picture.

Larijani: Conceptually, we should differentiate between those items that do not exactly fit under the specification of "Islamicity" and those that fit under the specification of any government's competence, whether Christian, Jewish, or secular. So while the government may be weak in Islamicity, it might be strong in terms of general competence, or the reverse. In other words, our index should differentiate between a good competent government and an Islamic one. And I am concerned that in our current approach, a good number of the points are related to the general competence of any government. Why then are we calling it Islamic?

Gauhar: Isn't good governance part of Islamicity?

Larijani: This is a separate issue. Good governance can be Islamic or non-Islamic. But our index aims to measure "Islamicity," so we should make this distinction. Even if competence is considered a part of Islamicity, it should not overshadow it. For the purposes of the Shariah Index Project, we should emphasize the special nature of an Islamic state; later, we can produce another index which measures those themes common to any state. If the flavor of Islam is missing from a state, then it's less Islamic in that sense and would receive a lower mark.

Şentürk: Can I clarify your points? Let's apply these principles to Canada. It will get one hundred points, even though Canada is not an Islamic state.

Imam Feisal: This is the core of my question. What does "Islamic" mean? If you mean the `ibadat* aspect...

Kamali: No, this falls under religion. It will determine the spiritual-religious dimension of government, and that is a separate point.

Ghazi: It seems to me that a number of us feel that because moral and spiritual considerations are difficult to measure, they should not be considered for the index. On the other hand, something which is concrete, like the delivery of goods, is much easier to measure. However, if that is the approach, I take you to the seventh century. Suppose we are judging the Islamicity of the states in the middle of the seventh century. You compare the states of Umar al-Khattab in Medina and Ali bin Abi Talib in Kufa with the Roman Empire, the Persian Empire, and other leading states. In fact, all economic indicators and other products of the

> *Maqasid al-shari`ah* will be very high in the states outside of Kufa
> and Medina, where the people did not have adequate food and
> lacked the necessary animals to ride. Even the caliph lived in a
> substandard way, far below the poverty line. In some cases, he was
> forced to beg for his household items. For Umar, upon entering
> Jerusalem as a victorious head of state, he finds that the people
> have food, are getting whatever they want. All the Maqasid – the
> protection of life, property, everything is there.

Suppose we index this situation. We give all 30 marks to Ali and Umar
on the *Maqasid* of religion and the rest will be zero. For the other states,
they will get the 70 marks for the other *Maqasid* and zero for religion.
Do you mean to say that the Roman or Persian Empire of that time
was 70 percent Islamic and the government of Ali and Umar was only
30 percent Islamic? We have to think about it. What are we going to
judge? Are we going to judge the material well-being of a society? Islam
promotes these, yes. But providing food, security, and health facilities,
for example, to me, these are done by the people themselves. Religion
does not come to educate people on how to heal physical illness. That is
based on human reason and experience, and Islam has come for something different: spiritual and moral growth and to invite each and every
institution to that spirituality and morality. If economic well-being
is achieved within that moral environment, great, it is Islamic. But
economic well-being was achieved before Islam, yet still, the need for
Islam was felt.

> **Auda:** I would disagree that people in Jerusalem were living fine, "in
> the 70 percent," before Islam. Before the Muslims took it over, it
> didn't have justice or rights. Perhaps it was developed in a material
> sense, but it would not score 70 percent. It would score much less
> than that.

What we are really measuring is the *maslahah*, the welfare of the people,
and the *maslahah* is more than just those elements that are directly
theological. *Maslahat al- `ibadi fi-ddunya wal-akhirah* ("the interests of
human beings in the world and hereafter") is the overriding meta-objective (or meta-*maqsad)* of the Shariah, and the *Maqasid al-shari`ah* unpack
or unbundle this meta-*maqsad*. *Maqasid al-shari`ah* serves to fulfill and
advance the *maslahah* of the people, so in measuring the *Maqasid* we are
measuring the *maslahah* of the people.

We should also mention that we are employing *ijtihad* here. We cannot simply copy the World Bank and call it *maslahah*, because this does not completely map the *maslahah*. It maps only part of it. So considering that we are employing *ijtihad* and using data within our own framework of the *Maqasid*, I am comfortable saying that we are measuring *maslahah*. Islam is about health; the Qu'ran critiques those who pray but do not feed the poor, about education and justice. Islamic teachings are adamant about such specific things that will amount to much more than 30 percent of the index. It would easily take it to the 70 percent level.

> **Kamali:** I agree. To say that our index is unrelated to Islamicity is not true. First, it is based on the *Maqasid*, which is a central *shar`i* approach. Second, we have included religion as a category of measurement, and we can put as many value points on it as we want. But as you point out, the Islamic nature of a state is not only within the *maqsad* of religion – it relates to justice and equality, and in general to the *maslahah* of the people.

I do, however, agree with everyone that this cannot be considered complete. As we go on, we will add other metrics that will measure more comprehensively.

> **Imam Feisal:** We need to make it clear that this is just a first iteration of the index, and that we will continue to improve it and strive to capture those elements of the *Maqasid* that we have not yet been able to measure. Perhaps we can call this first iteration of the index "Shariah Index 1.0" so that it is clear that this will be an ongoing work-in-progress, and that we intend to release a "Shariah Index 2.0" in the future.
>
> **Larijani:** We should also score each line item separately, and avoid giving a total score. We don't want to just sum them up. Each line item should be represented in its own index since each is not simply an issue of arithmetic. I think this is a better indicator. Rather than just scoring a country, we should develop a matrix for each with three, four, or six elements.
>
> **Auda:** I agree with what has been said. Those elements that are measured under *hifz al-din* constitute a whole one-sixth or more of the index. And states with a non-Muslim majority would score less in this category, because it is all about *din, `ibadah, sha `a'ir, arkan al-iman*, and so forth. Also, elements of *`ibadah* are imbedded in

every other *maqsad*: *hifz al-nafs, hifz al-nasl, hifz al-mal, hifz al-ʿaql,* and *hifz al-ʿird*. There's an Islamic element under each *maqsad*, so I think that the uniquely Islamic components might constitute up to 30 percent of the overall score. States might score a full 70 percent of the index but fail in the remaining 30 percent, and I think that's fair enough. And states which are Islamic in name only but score nothing on human rights will score 30 percent in the Shariah compliance, which is also fair.

Imam Feisal: As Professor Auda suggested, a key part of the Islamicity of a state is under the *maqsad* of religion. But even here, many elements of "Islamicity" are shared with states with non-Muslim majorities. For example, part of *hifz al-din* is the protection of the rights of non-Muslims. From the time of the Prophet and the rightly guided caliphs, the leaders of our tradition guaranteed the religious rights of people, just as they also supported the building of mosques and so forth. But the guarantee of religious freedom and the protection of religious minorities are common to all good governments – they don't merely reflect the teachings and history of Islam. So I'm even averse to using the term Islamicity, because it assumes a kind of uniqueness that isn't always there. I would rather say something like "adherence or compliance with the objectives of the Shariah" or "thriving according to Islamic values," which I think is more accurate.

When we define what it means to further religion, we must remember what God says in the surah of *maʿun*, "Have you seen the one who lives a religious lie (*yukadhibu bid-din*)? That is the person who drives away the orphan, and does not encourage the feeding of the poor? Woe to those who pray; who are heedless of their prayer, those who strive to be seen [who love to show off their religiosity] but who withhold assistance (*maʿun*)."[18] According to this surah, *din* (religion) includes both acts of worship (*ʿibadat*) and providing assistance (*maʿun*) to the poor and needy. The requirement to provide assistance (*maʿun*) is so central to the point that if acts of worship are performed without concern for the welfare of others, that religiosity is a *lie*. If we read this surah within the context of state policy, it is clear that furthering religion means feeding the poor and providing *maʿun* to the needy, what state policy makers call "human development." If an Islamic state ignores policies that advance human development, then it is living a religious lie no matter how well it may support *hajj, zakat,* or other acts of piety.

The Prophet makes it clear that we can perform our prayers and be spiritually bankrupt: The poor of my Umma would be he who would come on the Day of Resurrection with prayers and fasts and zakat but (he would find himself bankrupt on that day as he would have exhausted his funds of virtues) since he hurled abuses upon others, brought calumny against others and unlawfully consumed the wealth of others and shed the blood of others and beat others, and his virtues would be credited to the account of one (who suffered at his hand). And if his good deeds fall short to clear the account, then his sins would be entered in (his account) and he would be thrown in the Hell-Fire.[19]

In God's eyes, one can pray and perform *`ibadat*, but if he is unjust then his final score is a negative one. In my judgment, the Islamicity of a state does not rely solely upon the *`ibadat*. The *mu`amalat* are equally important, and some may argue even more important. Justice, eradicating poverty – all of these are Islamically *moral* imperatives. Therefore, I am comfortable calling a state that emphasizes human development apart from what is commonly called "religious" as scoring highly on our index as an *Islamic* index.

Part II

Developing an Index of Measuring Nations

5

Indexing the *Maqasid*

Now that our group of SIP scholars had accomplished the essential work of *ijtihad* in order to define the classical understanding of each *maqsad* in a way that could be measured in the modern world, we had to figure out how to create our measurement tool. For this, we needed to draw on the expertise of specialists engaged in indexing.

For the fourth conference of scholars, we invited specialists to initiate our discussions regarding our measurement tool. At first, we tried the approach taken by the Mo Ibrahim Index of African Governance.[1] This index defines governance as the delivery of political goods to citizens. Good governance is divided into five categories: Safety and Security, Rule of Law/Transparency/Lack of Corruption, Participation and Human Rights, Sustainable Economic Development, and Human Development. In order to measure safety and security, this index uses proxy indicators such as the number of refugees, armed conflicts and homicides, and the ease of access to arms. We tried to mirror that approach by considering the *Maqasid* as "political goods," and listing proxy indicators under each *maqsad* in a similar fashion. So, for example, the *maqsad* of life would be subdivided into four key categories including safety and security, standard of living, health, and the environment. Then each category would be measured by a handful of key indicators. For instance, safety and security would be measured by the following: the number of armed conflicts; the intensity of conflicts; the number of refugees, asylum seekers and internally displaced persons; ease of access to arms; and the number of homicides and other violent crimes. This kind of approach relies upon data that is already available in the public sphere, gathered by global agencies such as the United Nations.

Another option was to gather our own data. To do so, we needed to poll individuals. We partnered with Gallup, an internationally recognized polling agency that conducts an annual world poll, and worked with them for several months to see if we could obtain the data that we needed through a combination of their current polling questions and some of our own. However, statistical analysis revealed that Gallup's component questions for any given *maqsad* were not actually measuring the same concept ("life" or "mind"). It became clear that we needed to go through an intermediate step in the process of experimenting with data through what analysts call "factor analysis" in order to be confident that these subcategories and indicators are indeed part of one coherent concept that constitutes the *maqsad* of life, or mind, and so on – a process that will be described in detail below.

In order to complete the initial step of the factor analysis and subsequently create an index the elements of which are internally coherent, we enlisted the help of two experts in the area of statistics and measurement. While, for reasons that will be explained, we do not consider the index as an accurate final measure of a state's fulfillment of the *Maqasid*, the process of bringing contemporary scientific and statistical methods to bear on classical *fiqhi* concepts opened up new avenues of thinking about Islamic jurisprudence.

As a student of physics, I am well accustomed to the iterative process by which scientists develop a theory, test it through experimentation, and finally rework the theory based on the feedback and results of that experimentation. As we investigated the *Maqasid* concepts through the lens of real world data, I saw that we were in effect testing the *Maqasid* theory and generating results that forced us to refine, deepen, and nuance our understanding of the objectives of Islamic law. This chapter looks first at what we learned from this process via a close exploration of the methodology and the results from measuring the *maqsad* of life. Secondly, we look at some of the key concerns we had with our final product, while inviting others to participate in developing an increasingly accurate tool to measure how well contemporary Muslim states fulfill the objectives of Islamic law.

Measuring the *Maqsad* of life

The first step in constructing our measurement tool was, what our measurement consultants called, *conceptual mapping* (see Figure 5.1). The purpose of this step was to create a map that linked the conceptual definition of a *maqsad* (as defined by our jurists) and various publicly available socioeconomic, educational, and other measures that are relevant for the *maqsad*. For example, within the *maqsad* of life the scholars

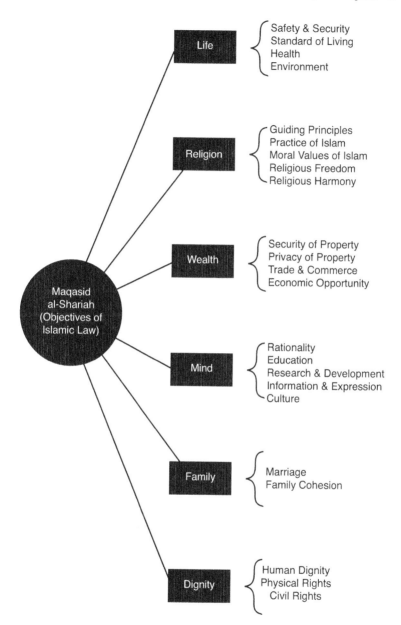

Figure 5.1   Figure of *Maqasid al-Shariah*

included the provision of "opportunities for work and employment." While we could not find a measure that charted a government's efforts to increase job opportunities for its citizens, we could easily find a measure of unemployment rates for each country. This step was essentially a translation process: how did the scholars' definitions conceptually map onto the definitions and measures current within the economic, political, and legal social sciences? The goal of conceptual mapping was to gather a set of component measures and indicators that collectively span the conceptual scope of the *maqsad* as defined by our jurists.

A key decision we had to make to ensure the validity of our results was: in selecting component measures do we include "input" measures, or rely only on "output" measures? For example, in the *maqsad* of life, input measures reflect the efforts made by governments to provide quality and affordable healthcare, including measures such as the number of doctors or hospital beds, or the amount of money spent per 1,000 people. While such measures may indicate the presence of governmental policies or programs in support of the health of a population, they do not accurately indicate the results of such policies, namely how healthy people are. Measuring the results or "outputs" of government policies and efforts allows us to better gauge their effectiveness. We found one key output measure that seemed to indicate the health of a population on a larger scale: life expectancy. If people are dying young in a given country, further analysis could inform us if this is from disease and the unavailability of healthcare, from security threats like war, or from environmental pollution. However, the fact that they are dying at a young age is indicative of the extent to which the *maqsad* of life is protected within that country.

Regarding the other components that our scholars included within the *maqsad* of life, we found that the poverty rate is a proxy measure for what our scholars called the "provision of food, shelter, and clothing." If a large portion of a population lives beneath the poverty line, they are clearly unable to find the means by which to provide food, clothing, and shelter to themselves and their families. "Opportunities for work and employment" was measured by the unemployment rates for each country. To measure the "national security" of a population, we utilized data from the Global Peace Index, which measures ongoing domestic and international conflicts, safety and security, and defense capability across the globe. To capture the "protection of the environment," we used Yale's Environmental Performance Index, which tracks performance indicators covering both environmental public health and ecosystem vitality. These indicators provide a gauge at a national government scale of how close countries are to established environmental policy goals. We were able to measure what the SIP scholars called the "right to life and personal liberty, including freedom from arbitrary arrest and torture" by means of the Physical Integrity Index. This index gives a score for each country based on the prevalence of torture, extrajudicial killing, political imprisonment, and disappearances.

Ijtihad by factor analysis

After collecting the data for each country for all of the above mentioned component measures of the *maqsad* of life, we used statistical methods to analyze and validate the conceptual structure of each *maqsad*. This helped us assess whether the components that were chosen for a specific *maqsad* were indeed internally consistent. Essentially, we wanted to see: Are we measuring one thing, namely the *maqsad* of life, or are we measuring the *maqsad* of honor? Do each of the component measures correlate highly enough to one another to indicate that they are all part of the same underlying concept?

In explaining this process to those of us who were not statisticians, our professors related it to common college academic achievement tests that test students on both a verbal score and a quantitative score. Suppose we did not yet have a differentiated concept of verbal/communication and quantitative/mathematical skills, and we tested students on the following subjects: arithmetic, spelling, algebra, geometry, reading comprehension, vocabulary, calculus, and writing skill. What we find is that those who score highly in algebra will tend to score well in arithmetic, calculus, and geometry. And those who score well in reading tend to score well in spelling, vocabulary, and writing. From the high correlation between algebra, arithmetic, geometry, and calculus, we therefore can conclude that these collectively "stick together" and belong to, and are part of the definition of, a concept we can call quantitative or mathematical skill. And from the high correlation between those who scored well in reading, spelling, vocabulary, and writing, we can again conclude that these also "stick together" and define a concept we can call verbal or communication skill. If we tested, for example, "understanding of poetry" alongside these quantitative skills, we would find that it does not correlate as highly and therefore does not "stick" so well with the mathematical skills; rather, it would correlate more highly with the verbal skill, alongside spelling, reading comprehension, and writing. This is not always an absolute zero or perfect correlation; as in these examples, one must have a threshold reading comprehension in order to read, understand, and solve mathematical problems. However, when looking at the correlations it is clear that reading comprehension nonetheless correlates higher with the other verbal skills. This is how we determine via statistical analysis if the various data we measure "stick together," belong to and help define – and in our case help measure – the specific *maqsad* we are seeking to measure.

Factor analysis is the term used by statisticians to describe the above process, where *observed variables* (the many verbal and quantitative skills) are summarized in terms of a smaller number of *latent unobserved constructs* ("verbal" intelligence as compared to "quantitative" intelligence), which are called *factors*. These factors are "unobserved" because we cannot measure verbal or quantitative intelligence directly; rather, we must measure them by measuring observable manifestations or proxies of them (spelling, arithmetic, etc). Analogously, we tested the data we collected for the *maqsad* of life to see if all of the component measures (life expectancy, poverty rate, unemployment rate, national security, etc) actually cohered together to form one latent concept, allowing us to weed out those components of the *maqsad* of life that did not cohere with the others. With the factor analysis we were effectively testing the *Maqasid* theory to see if there is an underlying concept such as the "*maqsad* of life," and if so, which components are part of that concept.

When we examined the data through the factor analysis, we found that certain elements of the *maqsad* of life as defined by our legal scholars did not statistically cohere with the underlying concept of the preservation of life. Life expectancy, poverty rate, environmental protection, and national security comprised the core components of the *maqsad* of life. Unemployment rate, however, cohered to a greater extent with the *maqsad* of property, which also utilized other indicators of the health of an economy. The "right to life and personal liberty, including freedom from arbitrary arrest and torture" as measured by the Physical Integrity Index correlated poorly with the other measures in the *maqsad* of life, but had a high correlation with the *maqsad* of dignity. This suggests that arbitrary arrest, torture, and political imprisonment primarily result in the loss of human dignity or of a subset of a human right, rather than the loss of life. And finally, the consumption of alcohol, the prohibition of which is a key element of the preservation of the mind, had a stronger negative correlation with the *maqsad* of life than with that of the mind. This came as a surprise, considering that some jurists consider the *maqsad* of the mind to have originated from the prohibition against intoxication.

Key concerns with our approach

That the consumption of alcohol did not cohere with the other measures in the *maqsad* of the mind provoked us to ask ourselves: Is the concept that we have measured actually the same Islamic legal concept as defined by Muslim jurists? If we are to accept the Islamic legal definition of the *maqsad* of the mind, which invariably includes a prohibition on the consumption of alcohol as many jurists consider that to be the genesis of the *maqsad* of the mind, then this means that intoxication has an effect on a kind of mental capacity that is not measured by other indicators of the *maqsad*, such as education and innovation. This is similar to the example of math and verbal skills, which are both intellectual skills yet relate to different aspects of intellectual capacity – and thus are measured differently. The consumption of alcohol certainly relates to the *maqsad* of the mind, but the intellectual capacity that it affects (namely, judgment, self-control, and *basira*) is not one that is measured by formal education and innovation. There are many aspects of `aql indicated by God in the Qur'an,[2] and to fully measure the Islamicity of a state with regards to this *maqsad*, we must include them all within our index.

But where can we find data that measures a population's strength of judgment, self-control, and *basira*? This brings up our other key concern with the measurement tool: the limits of the data that is presently available. This can be divided into two issues. The first issue is the lack of available data. While we were able to find data for much of the component measures for each *maqsad*, there were certain elements of our index that are simply not measured at present. For example, where does one find accurate global data regarding the number of children born out of wedlock, trade in unlawful substances, the extent of bribery, or mosque attendance? These elements are not measured in part because there is no agency in the Islamic world that gathers these data on the ground. Neither do the data, on adoption, for example, make a distinction between open adoption (the child knows the names of his biological parents) and closed adoption (the child does not know his biological lineage) – the key distinction for legal adoption within Islam. The second issue is the accuracy of the available data. Since we used data from existing indexes to create our index, we were forced to face their shortcomings. On various occasions, the available data was not up to date. For instance, the data regarding poverty levels in Tunisia is from 2005. In addition to the fact that this data is almost ten years old, it comes from the pre-Arab Spring period. This raises questions regarding its veracity since it was collected during the authoritarian Ben Ali period. These key concerns (the ability to measure relevant data, the extent to which the data is up to date, and the veracity of the data) were the reasons why we do not consider this index a final and perfectly accurate measure of a state's fulfillment of the *Maqasid*, but a first order 1.0 version.

An invitation

The process of bringing contemporary scientific and statistical methods to bear on classical *fiqhi* concepts, of testing the *Maqasid* theory by using real world data, was a fruitful one. It enabled us to refine our understanding of the objectives of Islamic law in light of statistical feedback, as we discovered through factor analysis what components constitute the underlying construct of each *maqsad*. Having put forward the key insights from our seven conferences of SIP scholars, along with the lessons learned in our initial attempt at measurement, we would like to open up this project and invite the participation of others in our efforts to measure the Islamicity of states along the benchmark of fulfillment of the *Maqasid*.

What follows is an index of Islamic good governance based on the fulfillment of the *Maqasid*. We hope that as more accurate and missing data are gathered and become available we will be able to draw upon the scholarship and insights of this effort to improve our method of measuring a state's fulfillment of the objectives of Islamic law.[3]

6
The *Maqasid* Index

This chapter describes the methodology for constructing the indices for the six *Maqasid* of life, mind, property, dignity, family, and religion. It also describes the statistical methods that were used to check the internal consistency and reliability of the measures that form the indices. Definitions are provided for all the component measures of the six *Maqasid* indices, and the final scores for the 2014 index are given.

Together with our measurement consultants, we utilized the following multistep process to construct the index:

1. Conceptual mapping between the scholars' definition of a *maqsad* and its proxy component measures
2. Data collection on component measures
3. Statistical analysis of the component scores
4. Computation of the final index score

The first three steps were iterated several times to ensure that our proxies and definitions devised and measured the concepts accurately. We used statistical analysis to ensure that the proxy component measures did in fact measure the latent concept of the *maqsad*. When they did not, we repeated the iteration by dropping those measures that did not cohere. When we were satisfied with the statistical analysis, we then compiled a final Shariah Index score for the initial purposes of this project.

Conceptual mapping

The first step in constructing an index score for each *maqsad* was *conceptual mapping*. The purpose of this step was to create a map that would plot out the conceptual definition of a *maqsad* as defined by the SIP scholars in relation to various publicly available socioeconomic, educational, technological, and political measures that are relevant for the *maqsad*. This step produced a set of component measures that spanned the conceptual scope of each *maqsad*.

Data collection

After identifying the main indicators that we would use, the next step was to collect the data. The data was collected from publicly available sources such as the World Health Organization, the World Bank, various agencies of the UN, as well as from other relevant publically available indices and governmental and nongovernmental data sources. In the case that current data were not available for a component for a particular country, then the most recent data were used. Given the broad scope of each *maqsad*, and the diversity of the sources that were employed, data were missing on some components for some of the countries. In many such instances, the missing values were imputed based on the correlation structure of the component measures by using a regression analysis.

Some of the component measures that are used are indices consisting of multiple measures. For example, the SIP scholars consider the protection of the environment (including flora and fauna) as one of the facets of the *maqsad* of life. No single measure can adequately capture all of the components of this facet, as a measure of water purity would not capture other elements of environmental protection such as air quality or pesticide regulation. We considered using a composite of a small number of measures, but a small subset of measures may likewise not be sufficient for capturing the richness of the environmental facet. Hence, we reasoned that it would be more reliable to use the entire Environmental Performance Index (EPI), which is a comprehensive index based on 25 measures that have been validated empirically.

Another decision we had to make to ensure the validity of our results was: Do we include, in selecting component measures, "input" measures, or rely only on "output" measures? For example, in measuring the *maqsad* of life, input measures reflect the efforts made by governments to provide quality and affordable healthcare, including measures such as the number of doctors or hospital beds, or the amount of money spent per 1,000 people. In contrast, output measures focus on the outcomes of such investments, in this case how healthy people are as measured by, for example, life expectancy. The use of output measures also offers parsimony (i.e., the use of fewer measures) and greater comparability across countries. Finally, redundancy was minimized. For instance, healthcare as a facet of the *maqsad* of life could be measured using life expectancy at birth, adult mortality, and infant mortality. However on inspection of the correlation between these variables, we found that the mortality measures have correlations exceeding 0.95 with life expectancy, and thus these mortality measures were dropped to minimize redundancy. If we can measure something with one indicator, why measure it with three? In such a case, adding additional indicators does not add any more information.

During this process we did, however, come up against a key concern that must be mentioned at the beginning: the lack of relevant data for some components of the index. While we were able to find data for much of the component measures for each *maqsad,* there are certain elements of our index that are simply not measured at present. For example, we could not find accurate global data regarding the number of children born out of wedlock, trade in unlawful substances, the extent of bribery, or mosque attendance. These elements are not measured in part because there is no agency in the Islamic world gathering these data. Neither do the data, on adoption, for example, make a distinction between open adoption (the child knows the names of his biological parents) and closed adoption (the child does not know his biological lineage) – the key distinction for legal adoption within Islam. If, in the future, these data become available, we will be able to more completely measure each *maqsad* as defined by the SIP jurists.

Another important concern with missing data is that certain data are not updated regularly and so do not reflect key changes from recent events such as the revolutions and subsequent violence in the Arab countries. For example, Syria has scored relatively high within the *maqsad* of life, and to understand this we must look at the component measures. While it understandably scored quite poorly on the Global Peace Index, which measures the level of war in a country, it scored well in life expectancy and having a low percentage of the population living under the poverty line – two measures that are not updated frequently, but which are severely and negatively affected by war. This must be taken into consideration when interpreting data and scores.

Statistical analysis

After gathering the data, we used statistical methods to analyze and validate the conceptual structure of each *maqsad*. This helped us assess whether the components that were chosen for a specific *maqsad* were indeed internally consistent. We used two measures to establish the internal consistency and reliability of the measures: Cronbach's alpha and factor analysis.

Cronbach's alpha is a measure of the reliability or internal consistency of an index score that is composed from a set of components. It indicates the extent to which a set of index components measures a single unidimensional concept (or a latent construct). The high Cronbach's alpha values for each of the *Maqasid* (above 0.80), indicate that the chosen components for each *maqsad* are internally consistent and represent in each case a single unidimensional concept.

The factor analysis of the component scores for each of the *Maqasid* was also performed to gain further insights about the correlational structure of the components, to assess whether a single factor is retained in the analysis, and to obtain the factor scores for each country. The factor analysis is a statistical technique that is used to summarize the variability among observed variables (components of an index) in terms of a smaller number of latent (unobserved) constructs (the *Maqasid*), which are called factors. For example, the theory underlying the *Maqasid of Shariah,* as interpreted by the SIP scholars, predicts that the variation in the observed variables that measure healthcare, environmental protection, national security, personal liberty, and freedom from poverty could mainly reflect the underlying variation in a single unobserved variable that captures the *maqsad* of life. The factor analysis can be used on indicators of the set of observed variables (i.e., life expectancy, etc.) to statistically confirm whether the data confirms the theoretical expectation of a single factor for life.

The factor analysis results for each of the *Maqasid* yielded a single factor solution, which corroborates the evidence from the Cronbach's alpha that a unidimensional construct underlies each *maqsad*. In each case, we found that an index composed of an equal weighting of the component scores was virtually identical to one based on the final scores for each *maqsad* as a whole, with a correlation between the two indices being greater than 0.999 for each *maqsad*.

These high scores representing internal validity and coherence are representative of the final set of component measures for each *maqsad*, as we had to go through multiple iterations of each *maqsad* in order to find the component measures that best cohered with one another in measuring the underlying concept. Thus, for some of the *Maqasid*, we found outlier measures that did not cohere with the other data sets, even though that measure was part of the theoretical definition of the *maqsad* as defined by the SIP scholars. In summarizing each *maqsad* below, we have indicated if there are components in the scholars' definition that were removed from the final measurement according to what we learned during this stage of statistical analysis.

Computation of the index score

Finally, after deciding which component measures to include within each *maqsad* in light of the statistical analysis, a final score was calculated. An equal weighting of all of the component scores was used to construct the overall index score of a country for each *maqsad*, such that if there were four component measures in one *maqsad* measurement, each would be given a weight of 25 percent in the final score calculation. Before combining the component measures, the raw scores on each measure were transformed to be aligned in the same direction (as for some measures like life expectancy a higher number is desirable, while for others like corruption the lower number is desirable) and were then normalized so that the scores on each component measure were charted on the same scale from zero to one. When we had final scores for each of the countries, those final scores were normalized to a scale of zero to one to facilitate the ease of comparison. Thus, a score of one does not necessarily mean that a country has attained the highest possible level in fulfilling a *maqsad*, but rather that it is the best of all of the countries indexed. Likewise, a score of zero does not mean that, for example, life is not protected to any extent in a particular country, but rather that the country provides the least protection in comparison to the other countries that were indexed.

For the present index, we included countries that are either OIC member states or the majority of whose population is Muslim. We made this decision in order to include the maximum number of countries. While these two criteria generally conform, there are several countries that do not meet both. For instance, while Guyana is a member state of the OIC, its Muslim population was, as of 2010, approximately 7.2 percent. Kosovo, meanwhile, is not a member of the OIC, but has an overwhelming Muslim majority (in 2010 it was roughly 91.7 percent Muslim). In line with our desire to include the maximum number of countries, we also included Bosnia and Herzegovina. In spite of the fact that it is not officially a member state of the OIC and it does not have a Muslim majority, Bosnia and Herzegovina had a 42.8 percent Muslim population in 2010. Conversely, we decided not to include India, a country with the third largest Muslim population in the world (behind Indonesia and Pakistan), given the fact that its Muslim population is only approximately 10 percent of its overall population. Having said that, in future iterations of the index we are open to reconsidering the criteria upon which we composed our list of countries.[1]

Indexing the *Maqasid*

To facilitate the process of creating this measurement tool, we began with those *Maqasid* that we thought would be easiest to measure with the approach that we have chosen. Thus, in our discussion below regarding measuring each *maqsad*, the *Maqasid* are presented in the order in which they were measured.

After the description of each *maqsad*, we have presented the final scores for that *maqsad* for the 15 highest scoring countries, as well as their scores on the component measures. We have decided to present and share the final scores in this manner because we feel that this will enable our index to be most effective. We highlighted the countries that have performed the best and indicated the areas in which they were particularly successful. This will enable governments and scholars to explain high scores by analyzing the best practices within those top-scoring countries. This will also allow countries that are not within the top 15 to develop policies that will improve their performance in these respective areas.

Although we understand that it is essential to explain the data in an intensive manner in order to develop better policies, we have chosen not to engage in this analysis in the present iteration of the index. In future iterations, we hope to examine fluctuations in yearly data, explain the reasons for these fluctuations, and look for patterns in countries based on their performances across the spectrum of *Maqasid*.

Life

In deciding which data to gather in order to measure health, we chose not to use input measures such as the number of hospital beds per 1,000 people, affordability of healthcare, or the number of doctors within a population. While such measures may indicate the presence of governmental policies or programs in support of the health of a population, they do not accurately indicate the results of such policies, namely how healthy people are. However, we found one measure that seemed to indicate the health of a population on a larger scale: life expectancy. This measure captures if people are dying young in a given country from many issues including disease and the unavailability of healthcare, security threats like war, or environmental pollution to such a magnitude that it affects the wider population in a country. Initially, we also included infant mortality, but we found that this measure correlated so highly with life expectancy that it did not provide any new information to our measure.

Similarly, we found that the poverty rate is a proxy measure for the provision of food, shelter, and clothing as well as employment opportunities, two primary elements of the SIP scholars' definition of this *maqsad*. If a large portion of a population lives beneath the poverty line, they are clearly unable to find the means by which to provide food, clothing, and shelter to themselves, and their families.

To more precisely measure the national security of a population, we utilized the Global Peace Index, which measures ongoing domestic and international conflicts, safety and security, and defense capability across the globe.

To capture the protection of the environment, we used Yale's EPI, which tracks performance indicators covering both environmental public health and ecosystem vitality. These indicators provide a gauge at a national government scale of how close countries are to established environmental policy goals.

We were able to measure what the scholars called right to life and personal liberty, including freedom from arbitrary arrest and torture, by means of the Physical Integrity Index. This index gives a score for each country based on the prevalence of torture, extrajudicial killing, political imprisonment, and disappearances. While this index was an accurate measure for this component of the scholars' definition of the *maqsad* of life, we found that it did not correlate as highly with the other above measures. Later on, when developing the measures for the *maqsad* of honor, we found that this measure correlated very highly with it, and thus was more a measure of the concept of human dignity rather than of the concept of physical life.

After the factor analysis, we have the set of key measures that cohere highly with one another and thus comprise the core of the *maqsad* of life. This means that the correlations both between the individual measures and between the measures and the overall score were statistically significant. Thus, the indicators for the fulfillment of the *maqsad* of life include:

1. Life Expectancy at Birth (Values were World Health Organization, CIA World Factbook, and The World Bank).[2]
2. Poverty Rate (i.e., those living without access to basic human necessities as indicated by a daily monetary amount set by each country

according to local costs of living. Values were taken from the CIA World Factbook.)[3]

3. Environmental Protection (EPI)[4]
4. National Peace & Security (Global Peace Index)[5]

When examining the component measures and scores that constitute the final *maqsad* score (Table 6.1), we can see that Qatar scored the best on life expectancy, Brunei scored best on the Global Peace Index, Malaysia and Tunisia succeeded in having the least poverty, and the UAE scored the best on the Environmental Protection Index. It should be explicitly noted that Tunisia's score on the Poverty Index was based on data from 2005. Due to the Arab Spring, there is not more recent data available from Tunisia. Moreover, it is quite possible that the 2005 data collected from Tunisia was based on government sources, and therefore the validity of this data is questionable.

Mind

There were many aspects of measuring this *maqsad* that were straightforward, including access to education and information, promotion of science, and freedom of expression. Access to quality education was measured via the Human Capital Index, based on data from the UNDP

Table 6.1   Rankings of *Maqsad* of life

Country		Final Score	Life Expectancy	Global Peace Index	Poverty Index	Environmental Protection Index
1	Brunei	1	0.937	1.000	0.834	0.888
2	Qatar	0.997	1.000	0.969	0.854	0.828
3	UAE	0.972	0.925	0.854	0.794	1.000
4	Kuwait	0.963	0.969	0.885	0.846	0.844
5	Maldives	0.952	0.908	0.882	0.840	0.880
6	Malaysia	0.95	0.844	0.894	1.000	0.763
7	Tunisia	0.916	0.900	0.740	1.000	0.758
8	Saudi Arabia	0.895	0.885	0.739	0.816	0.891
9	Albania	0.859	0.905	0.768	0.862	0.683
10	Jordan	0.855	0.837	0.803	0.864	0.702
11	Morocco	0.819	0.827	0.779	0.853	0.634
12	Bahrain	0.816	0.968	0.640	0.843	0.633
13	Oman	0.808	0.887	0.790	0.817	0.562
14	Bosnia and Herzegovina	0.804	0.929	0.784	0.806	0.528
15	Azerbaijan	0.792	0.763	0.577	0.971	0.696

Human Development Report. The index is a composite of the adult literacy rate and the combined primary, secondary, and tertiary gross enrollment ratio. How much of a population can read and write? Are children and young adults enrolled in school?

The free dissemination of knowledge is measured by the Telecommunication Infrastructure Index, which measures the number of computer, internet, and telephone users in a population. Easy access to information about governmental activity could be measured by the Online Service Index (which measures the usability of information provided by the government, particularly on its websites) and the E-Participation Index (which measures the use of the internet to facilitate the provision of information by governments to citizens); however, as these are primarily "input" measures, we decided not to include them in the final index.

The promotion of science, technology, research, and development as articulated by the SIP scholars clearly mapped onto the Innovation Index, which draws data from the World Bank regarding innovation outputs by country, including patents granted, and scientific and technical journal articles published. And finally, the freedom of speech and expression was measured through the Press Freedom Index, which reflects the degree of freedom that journalists and new organizations enjoy in each country, as well as the efforts made by each country to respect and ensure that freedom.

Each of these five measures correlated highly with one another and seemed to cohere to represent the latent concept of the *maqsad* of the mind. We were surprised to find, however, that the prevalence of alcohol consumption – the prohibition of which represents the genesis of this *maqsad* – did not cohere within this concept. In fact, we found that the prevalence of alcohol consumption correlated higher (albeit negatively) with the *maqsad* of life and the *maqsad* of family (also negatively) rather than that of the mind. This means that if the prevalence of alcohol consumption measures the lack of a type of mental capacity as put forth by our SIP scholars, it was not a capacity measured by the factors such as education and innovation.

After factor analysis, we found that the following indicators stuck coherently together to constitute a *maqsad* of the mind:

1. Provision of Quality Education (Human Capital Index)[6]
2. Free Dissemination of Knowledge (Telecommunication Infrastructure Index)[7]

3. Promotion of Science, Technology, Research, and Development (Innovation Index)[8]
4. Press Freedom (Press Freedom Index)[9]

When examining the component measures and scores that constitute the final *maqsad* score (Table 6.2), Kazakhstan scored the best in Education (human capital), Bahrain scored the best in Telecommunications Infrastructure, Malaysia scored the best in Innovation, and Suriname scored the best in Press Freedom.

Property

For this *maqsad*, mapping the scholars' definition onto available measures was a relatively straightforward process. We found that we could measure the promotion of economic development by looking at the Gross Domestic Product Per Capita (GDP), which measures a country's overall economic output and represents the market value of all of the final goods and services made within the borders of a country in a year divided by its population. Economic development is also measured through the Doing Business Index, which measures the ease of starting a business that includes elements such as the number of procedures, time in days, and the cost it takes in order to register and start a business in a given country. We also used the Gini Coefficient, which measures national

Table 6.2 Rankings of *Maqsad* of mind

Country	Final Score	Education	Infrastructure	Innovation	Press Freedom
1 UAE	1	0.772	0.835	0.952	0.715
2 Qatar	0.997	0.774	0.827	0.924	0.743
3 Kuwait	0.97	0.835	0.824	0.739	0.800
4 Suriname	0.947	0.783	0.546	0.810	1.000
5 Malaysia	0.912	0.826	0.617	1.000	0.608
6 Brunei	0.881	0.907	0.505	0.837	0.724
7 Oman	0.876	0.769	0.679	0.841	0.670
8 Maldives	0.859	0.796	0.543	0.815	0.762
9 Bahrain	0.858	0.910	1.000	0.645	0.360
10 Lebanon	0.843	0.856	0.555	0.684	0.781
11 Bosnia and Herzegovina	0.839	0.846	0.550	0.610	0.862
12 Libya	0.809	0.907	0.445	0.782	0.654
13 Kazakhstan	0.8	1.000	0.808	0.546	0.413
14 Turkey	0.778	0.828	0.492	0.833	0.558
15 Kyrgyzstan	0.73	0.860	0.521	0.415	0.792

income inequality, to capture the promotion of an equitable distribution of wealth. We measured access to employment, which promotes the sustainability of the individual, by measuring the unemployment rate within each country. Prohibiting unlawful gain is measured through the Corruption Perceptions Index and the International Property Rights Index, which accounts for issues such as hoarding, exploitative practices, and bribery but does not include gambling or *riba* (usury).[10] The protection of the sanctity of private ownership was measured also through the International Property Rights Index, which measures the significance of physical and intellectual property rights and their protection for economic well-being.

The unavailability of relevant data was a limiting factor in trying to measure the concepts that constituted this *maqsad*. In order to make the index more precise in the future, we will need to find data to measure components such as labor rights and the prohibition of trading unlawful substances.

After the factor analysis, we found that the following indicators constitute the *maqsad* of property:

1. Equitable Distribution of Wealth (Gini Coefficient)[11]
2. Promotion of Economic Development (GDP,[12] Doing Business Index).[13]
3. Access to Employment (Unemployment rate).[14]
4. Prohibiting Unlawful Gain (Corruption Perception Index,[15] International Property Rights Index).[16]

When examining the component measures and scores that constitute the final *maqsad* score (Table 6.3), Kazakhstan scored the best in the equal distribution of wealth (Gini coefficient); Qatar had the highest GDP; the UAE has the least corruption (CPI); Malaysia is the easiest Muslim country in which to start a business (Doing Business Index); Qatar is best in international property rights; and Qatar has the lowest unemployment rate.

Honor

The fundamental question that guided our approach toward finding the appropriate measures for this *maqsad* was, "Are people treated with respect?" And yet, as this is still a general question, we needed to rely on statistical analysis in order to help us determine the boundaries of this concept – especially considering that there is much overlap with the other *Maqasid*. Considering that we could not find data on slander, the

Table 6.3 Rankings of *Maqsad* of property

Country	Final Score	Gini	GDP	Corruption	Doing Business Index	IPR Index	Unemployment
1 UAE	1.000	0.941	0.886	1.000	0.907	0.954	0.973
2 Qatar	0.944	0.655	1.000	0.984	0.770	1.000	1.000
3 Saudi Arabia	0.829	0.912	0.860	0.623	0.891	0.745	0.867
4 Brunei	0.827		0.912	0.852	0.710	0.629	0.970
5 Oman	0.808	0.912	0.831	0.639	0.776	0.838	0.808
6 Malaysia	0.791	0.511	0.748	0.689	1.000	0.815	0.963
7 Bahrain	0.788	0.799	0.853	0.656	0.781	0.815	0.808
8 Kuwait	0.744	0.969	0.899	0.574	0.464	0.653	0.960
9 Turkey	0.681	0.686	0.715	0.689	0.656	0.606	0.883
10 Tunisia	0.656	0.805	0.638	0.541	0.754	0.606	0.780
11 Kazakhstan	0.648	1.000	0.745	0.295	0.760	0.352	0.935
12 Jordan	0.633	0.864	0.646	0.607	0.383	0.699	0.821
13 Azerbaijan	0.589	0.864	0.703	0.328	0.650	0.352	0.926
14 Morocco	0.554	0.661	0.582	0.475	0.557	0.514	0.880
15 Albania	0.542	0.997	0.634	0.377	0.541	0.282	0.784

original reason behind this *maqsad*, we set out to find data about issues such as freedom of speech, human rights, rule of law, discrimination, privacy, and political participation.

We found an important resource called the Rule of Law Index, which was released by the World Justice Project. Their category of measurement called "Fundamental Rights" includes issues such as equal treatment and absence of discrimination, right to life, and security of the person, due process of law and the rights of the accused, freedom of opinion and expression, freedom of belief and religion, right to privacy, freedom of assembly and association, and fundamental labor rights. This category of measurement seemed a very good fit with our understanding of this *maqsad;* however, the sample size was only 66 countries, only 16 of which were among the nations with Muslim majorities! While we could not use the Rule of Law Index due to its limited number of Muslim countries, we found that we could use it to test and affirm the validity of our other measures.

We constructed this *maqsad* out of five measures. In our iterative process, we found that the Physical Integrity Index, which looked at indicators for torture, extrajudicial killing, political imprisonment, and disappearance correlated more highly with this *maqsad* than with that of life. The Empowerment Rights Index, our second measure for this *maqsad*, measured issues such as freedom of movement (domestic and foreign), freedom of speech, freedom of assembly and association, workers' rights, and electoral self-determination. Thirdly, we included an indicator that measures the independence of the judiciary, as our scholars had indicated that this could be measured within this *maqsad*. As we were particularly concerned with the rights of minorities and women, we included the Women's Rights Index, which looks at economic and political rights of women in each country.

There were two additional measures, the School for a Culture of Peace's Human Rights Index and Freedom House's Political and Civil Rights Indices, that correlated highly with the *maqsad* but which we decided not to use in the final score. The first, which measured violations of international law and human rights such as extrajudicial killings, arbitrary arrest, and access to a fair trial, was highly correlated with the Physical Integrity Index; so we excluded it in order to minimize redundancy. The second, Freedom House's Political and Civil Rights Indices, also correlated highly with this *maqsad* but we were concerned about acceptability if we included data from an organization that has been accused by some in the past of having a Western bias.

In comparing the World Justice Project's Rule of Law Index with the results from the *maqsad* of honor, which includes the below four indicators, we found our *maqsad* to be a valid measure of the concept of human honor and dignity.

1. Physical Integrity (incidence of torture, political imprisonment, extrajudicial killing, and disappearance)[17]
2. Fundamental Human Rights and Freedom from Discrimination (Empowerment Rights Index,[18] Women's Rights Index[19])
3. Independence of the Judiciary [20]

When examining the component measures and scores that constitute the final *maqsad* score (Table 6.4), Comoros and Brunei are best in preserving the physical integrity of their citizens; Suriname and Mali are the best in basic human rights; Suriname's judiciary exhibits the most independence; and Kosovo and Mozambique are the best in women's economic and political rights in law and practice.

Family

The *maqsad* of family proved to be our most difficult *maqsad* to measure, simply because data for what our scholars would consider our ideal measures simply do not exist – are children raised in a healthy and supportive context, free from abuse and abandonment? Are marriages strong in society, characterized by fidelity and fulfillment? Do children

Table 6.4 Rankings of *Maqsad* of honor

Country	Final Score	Physical Integrity	Empowerment Rights	Independent Judiciary	Women's Rights
1 Suriname	1.000	0.750	1.000	1.000	0.667
2 Kosovo	0.939	0.875	0.833	0.500	1.000
3 Comoros	0.780	1.000	0.833	0.500	0.333
4 Benin	0.744	0.625	0.750	0.500	0.667
5 Niger	0.720	0.625	0.667	0.500	0.667
6 Guyana	0.707	0.750	0.833	0.500	0.333
7 Bosnia and Herzegovina	0.707	0.750	0.500	0.500	0.667
8 Brunei	0.707	1.000	0.250	0.500	0.667
9 Gabon	0.683	0.750	0.750	0.500	0.333
10 Mozambique	0.646	0.625	0.583	0.000	1.000
11 Burkina Faso	0.646	0.625	0.917	0.000	0.667
12 Sierra Leone	0.634	0.750	0.583	0.500	0.333
13 Albania	0.634	0.750	0.750	0.000	0.667
14 Mali	0.610	0.750	1.000	0.000	0.333
15 Turkey	0.585	0.250	0.583	0.500	0.667

honor their parents? Are adoptions open, meaning that a child knows his or her parents, thus ensuring that their lineage is clear? What is the extent in a society of rape, child marriage, prostitution, or children out of wedlock? These ideal measures, some being primarily qualitative in nature and others simply not reported, are not measures collected by government and international agencies, and thus the required data were not available for our index.

Another complication in measuring these proxies for the family *maqsad*, as discussed with the Cordoba Initiative team, is the sensitivity of family values to differing cultural contexts. It is clear from the Qur'an (4:36) that honoring our parents is a central family value, but how that is actually accomplished might look differently within different cultural contexts. Measuring financial support that adult children give to parents, if such a measure existed, might adequately capture what it means to honor one's parents in a particular society but not in other societies, since giving financial support is not equivalent to honoring our parents in every context.

Originally, we began by looking at four measures: adolescent birth rate (annual number of births to women 15 to 19 years of age per 1,000), child labor (percentage of children 5 to 14 years old involved in child labor at the moment of the survey), divorce rate (annual number of divorces per 1,000 people), and the marriage rate (annual number of marriages per 1,000 people). By examining the data, we found that not all of these measures sufficiently or accurately grasped the concept of this *maqsad.*

By looking at the adolescent birth rate between the ages of 15 and 19, we were hoping to gain a glimpse into the number of teenage pregnancies or children out of wedlock. However, because this measure was so highly correlated with the percent of women aged 15 to 19 currently married, the adolescent birth rate was actually measuring the prevalence of marriage among that age range rather than children out of wedlock.

The issue of cultural differences was a key issue with the child labor measure. A 14-year-old boy who works more than 14 hours a week on his family's farm would be considered, according to this indicator, as participating in child labor. According to the norm of Western society, he should be in school, but is secondary education universally relevant and essential for all societies, urban and rural? Especially if his family could not survive without his labor? Thus this measure seemed to actually be an indicator of the wealth of a family (and thus within the *maqsad* of property), rather than an indicator of family values toward children.

The third factor that we examined was the divorce rate per 1,000 people per year. We chose not to include this measure in the final analysis. Jurisprudentially, divorce is not universally reprehensible nor is it forbidden within Islam. While divorce may be more or less taboo within certain societies, a higher divorce rate does not necessarily indicate that marriage is less valued or of a lesser quality, but simply that people see divorce as a socially viable option when a marriage does not work.

Further, the divorce rate is highly correlated with the marriage rate per 1,000 people per year in a society, the fourth factor that we considered, as people cannot get divorced unless they first get married. It turned out that both the divorce rate and the marriage rate are indicators more of *population distribution* within a society, measuring the amount of people within marriageable age in a population, rather than wider societal values toward marriage. For example, in Yemen the marriage rate was comparatively low, but this does not mean that Yemeni society does not value or encourage marriage. The marriage rate in Yemen was low because a large percentage of the population is under the age of ten and thus not yet ready for marriage. The marriage rate is also related to the economy in many communities such as Egypt, for example, where cultural expectations that determine a financial threshold for marriageability cause delays in marriage when unemployment is high – and so the marriage rate in this instance becomes a measure of unemployment, a factor that measures the economy.

In light of these considerations, we chose to use a different measure of marriage in society: the percent of currently married within the age range of 20 to 49 (Table 6.5). This measure, while not indicating the quality of marriage, does give a sense of how many of those within prime marriageable age are currently married, including those who may have been divorced or widowed previously. Also, at the most basic level, we made the assumption that lineage is clear and protected within the bounds of marriage.[21]

The paucity of available data within this sphere severely limited our ability to accurately measure this *maqsad*, and thus this measure does not fully capture either the more classical notion of this *maqsad*, namely lineage, or the more contemporary expansion of this *maqsad* to include family values and the quality of family life for both spouses and children. The measure of the percentage of currently married within prime marriageable age is a fine measure, and yet we hope that in the coming years we will succeed in finding additional effective proxies to measure this *maqsad*. When examining the scores for this *maqsad*, we must remember the narrow scope of what it measures.

Religion

There are a number of key elements to the SIP scholars' definition of the *maqsad* of religion: furthering the capacity of the community to fulfill its religious obligations, promoting harmony and good relations

Table 6.5 Rankings of *Maqsad* of family

Country	Final Score	Average Marriage
1 Afghanistan	1.000	1.000
2 Mali	0.963	0.963
3 Niger	0.940	0.940
4 Uzbekistan	0.938	0.938
5 Burkina Faso	0.928	0.928
6 Bangladesh	0.917	0.917
7 Chad	0.881	0.881
8 Benin	0.873	0.873
9 Guinea	0.862	0.862
10 Tajikistan	0.848	0.848
11 Western Sahara	0.837	0.837
12 Pakistan	0.835	0.835
13 Turkmenistan	0.835	0.835
14 Guinea-Bissau	0.833	0.833
15 Yemen	0.825	0.825

among followers of all religious beliefs and schools, protecting religious freedom for both the Muslim and non-Muslim populations, and prohibiting the desecration of religions and religious symbols.

We had left the *maqsad* of religion for last because we imagined that it would be the most difficult concept to evaluate. Fortunately, we found two indices that allowed us to effectively measure some key aspects of this *maqsad*. Firstly, we used data from the CIRI Binghamton Human Rights Data Project on religious freedom which measures the "extent to which the freedom of citizens to exercise and practice their religious beliefs is subject to actual government restrictions. Citizens should be able to freely practice and share their religion, as long as that sharing is non-coercive and peaceful."

Secondly, we used an index created by the Association of Religion Data Archives (ARDA). This index was formulated from reports on religion in each country written by their respective United States embassy. Initially, we approached these data with caution, thinking that there may be a bias considering the official government source. However, after examining the nature of the data and comparing it with validation measures (the Freedom House Religious Freedom Index), we found the data to be sound. For example, many of the questions simply indicated a fact rather than a subjective value, for example: "Does the government fund religious education?" "Are people put into prison based on religion?" "Does the report mention cases of vandalism toward religious properties or cemeteries by citizens?" Further, while the way in which the questions were coded represented most Western values toward the separation of church and state, we found that we could code such questions differently in order to accord with the scholars' definition of this *maqsad*. For example, while the index assumed that no funding of religious education was preferable to funding, we reversed the values in computing our score since government facilitation of religious practice is part of the SIP scholars' definition of this *maqsad*.

What we found through the factor analysis on the category of government funding of religion intrigued us. While there were some countries in the world that scored highly on both government funding of religion and the other measures, we were surprised to see an opposite situation for all of the countries that were indexed. This means that higher funding of religion in these countries is correlated with more religious discrimination, less religious freedom, and less social harmony between and within religions. Considering that there are also countries in the world where both funding and social harmony are high, it is clear that the funding of religion is not a cause in and of itself of religious discrimination. The question is: What programs and values does government funding of religion promote? A government may be funding religious police and enforcing a particular religious practice or *madhhab*, which decreases religious freedom and is a cause for religious discrimination. From this data it is clear that if governments financially support religion, it must be done carefully and within certain limits. In the end, we decided not to include the government funding of religion in the final index, because it is an "input" rather than "output" measure.

The factor analysis on the data revealed three main concepts in this *maqsad*, as measured within the two abovementioned indices (CIRI[22] and ARDA): **religious freedom**, which measures government restrictions on religious practice;[23] **religious discrimination**, which measures government bias against any religion;[24] and **social harmony among religious groups**, which includes tolerance and understanding among the adherents of different religions as well as respect for religious properties and symbols.[25]

Considering the available data, the index for this *maqsad* is primarily an index of religious freedom and harmony among religious groups. These are two vitally important elements of the *maqsad* of religion. However, when examining the index scores for this *maqsad*, we must keep in mind that it is not a measure of the religiosity of a population, but rather a measure of a government's effectiveness in fostering an environment characterized by religious freedom, freedom from religious discrimination, and harmony between religious groups. As we are able to get accurate data that measures the other important elements of the *maqsad*, including religious practice within a population, we hope to expand the scope of this measurement so as to capture the entire *maqsad*.

When examining the component measures and scores that constitute the final *maqsad* score (Table 6.6), Senegal, Sierra Leone, Suriname, Togo, Mali, Guinea-Bissau, Guyana, Mozambique, Gambia Benin, Niger, Djibouti, Burkina Faso, Gabon, Cote D'ivoire, Cameroon, and Chad all scored the highest in the CIRI Index for Religious Freedom; Senegal, Sierra Leone, Suriname, Togo, Guinea-Bissau, Mozambique, Benin, and Albania scored the highest in terms of Freedom of Religion (based on the ARDA Index); Gambia and Kyrgyzstan exhibited the least religious discrimination (based on the ARDA Index); and Senegal, Sierra Leone, Suriname, Togo, Mali, Niger, Gabon, Albania, and Uganda scored the highest in the extent to which they exhibited social harmony (once again, based on the ARDA Index).

Table 6.6   Rankings of *Maqsad* of religion

Country		Final Score	CIRI Index	Freedom of Religion	Discrimination	Social Harmony
1	Senegal	1.000	1.000	1.000	0.600	1.000
2	Sierra Leone	1.000	1.000	1.000	0.600	1.000
3	Suriname	1.000	1.000	1.000	0.600	1.000
4	Togo	1.000	1.000	1.000	0.600	1.000
5	Mali	0.989	1.000	0.966	0.600	1.000
6	Guinea-Bissau	0.977	1.000	1.000	0.600	0.930
7	Guyana	0.970	1.000	0.990	0.600	0.918
8	Mozambique	0.969	1.000	1.000	0.600	0.906
9	Gambia	0.959	1.000	0.932	1.000	0.544
10	Benin	0.954	1.000	1.000	0.600	0.860
11	Niger	0.929	1.000	0.784	0.600	1.000
12	Djibouti	0.898	1.000	0.969	0.800	0.520
13	Burkina Faso	0.874	1.000	0.898	0.600	0.719
14	Gabon	0.868	1.000	0.799	0.400	1.000
15	Cote D'ivoire	0.859	1.000	0.888	0.600	0.684

SIP 1.0

This index, which represents over two years of working with consultants, represents a revolutionary first step in trying to quantify and measure Muslim majority countries' fulfillment of the objectives of Islamic law. *The key and important breakthrough here is in developing this methodology.*

However, our two chief concerns with the above index are:

1. The lack of available data on a number of key elements in the SIP scholars' definition of Islamic good governance, including certain measures related to morality and spirituality especially within the *Maqasid* of religion, mind, and family.
2. The data that we culled and created the Index from is not current. Ratings for Syria, Egypt, Libya and other countries affected by the "Arab Spring" are not reflected in this Index.

Our intention in offering this initial effort on the jurisprudence and the methodology in creating this index, which we offer as a SIP 1.0, is to advance the discourse among political leaders, academics, and jurists, working in and with the Muslim world around the issues of contemporary Islamic governance, while highlighting the need in the Islamic world to collect some of its own data so as to better measure its own performance. As additional data become available, we hope to be better able to systematically give concrete meaning to the term "Islamic state" through the use of this measurement tool.

We also hope to advance these efforts through the creation of a Shariah Index Institute, which would work with governments, leaders, and organizations around the world to further the global Muslim community's aspirations for an Islamic state. The Shariah Index Institute would use the principles agreed upon by our scholars and the indicators of these principles for the purposes of measurement as well as development.

The work of the Shariah Index Institution would help reveal the challenges and needs that we should address in our methodology, making it of value in refining the applicability and accuracy of our analysis and conclusions.

The work has just begun, and SIP 1.0 is an urgently needed start. If we build upon our efforts here, promote the principles agreed upon by legal scholars from all schools of thought, and continue to refine our data, we can provide solid common ground on which all Muslims – and any state defining itself as Islamic – can stand.

Part III

Sharia Index Project Scholars Speak on Key Challenges in Islamic Governance

7
Practical Applications of Islamic Law in Government and the Judiciary

In this chapter and the subsequent two chapters, which we have crafted as interview-style discussions, the scholars describe their work, the issues they grappled with, and how they each contributed in their respective countries and fields to improving our understanding of the relationship between Islam and the state. Since Islam is a religion of law and since the scholars are devout Muslims, they each strove to integrate their understanding of Islam into their fields of expertise. In particular, they sought to introduce Islam into politics, law, and academia – key spaces in which Islam and state intersect.

In the first interview, former Malaysian **Prime Minister Abdullah Ahmed Badawi** reflects on his *Islam Hadhari* (Civilizational Islam) Initiative. During his term in office, he sought to apply Islamic principles in governing the multicultural and multi-religious Malaysian society. He describes and charts his work promoting interfaith harmony and finding common ground among all Malaysians within an Islamic worldview.

Staying within the Malaysian context, the next interview is with retired chief justice of Malaysia **Tun Abdul Hamid Mohamed**. Since 2010, Tun Hamid has chaired the Law Harmonisation Committee (LHC) of the Central Bank of Malaysia (Bank Negara). Collaborating with representatives from the Bank Negara, Securities Commission, Attorney General's Chambers, practicing lawyers, ISRA, and the Association of Islamic Banking Institutions Malaysia (AIBIM), he has worked to create a legal system that facilitates and supports the development of the Islamic finance industry. Defining Islamic law as "any law that is not un-Islamic," Tun Hamid shares his experience harmonizing Islamic law and civil law in Malaysia and shows how much of common law is actually Shariah-compliant. In light of the 22 October 2013, decision by the Sultan of Brunei to institute *Hudud* punishments in Brunei, he also comments on the legal challenges in implementing *Hudud* in the Malaysian and Bruneian contexts.

The third contributor, **Ahmad Syafii Maarif**, shares his experience as the head of one of the largest Muslim organizations in the world, the Muhammadiyyah of Indonesia. Founded well before Indonesia's independence, the Muhammadiyah played two crucial roles in Indonesia. First, it advanced the independence movement from colonial rule. Second, it laid the foundations for Indonesian democracy and civil society. He describes the role that Islam played in promoting democracy and anti-authoritarian political systems in Indonesia. In so doing, he contributes to the discussion of the Islamic roots for democratic governance.

The fourth interview is with **Mohammad Javad Larijani** who speaks about his experience involved in nation-building in Iran. Acknowledging that an Islamic state – in the modern sense of a nation-state – is a relatively new experiment, he asserts that it must be a polity constructed from an Islamic sphere of rationality. Here he speaks about the Islamic rationality or worldview that must first be defined before seeking to define the structures of an Islamic state and the importance of legitimacy in governance.

Islamic principles in government: the *Islam Hadhari* initiative in Malaysia (Tun Abdullah Ahmad Badawi)

> **Imam Feisal:** Prime Minister Badawi, on behalf of all the Shariah Index Project scholars, I can't thank you enough for being the first patron of the Shariah Index Project, for your initial and continued support that has made this Shariah Index Project possible, and for your keen interest in the progress of this project. When you began your tenure as prime minister of Malaysia in 2003, you launched the Islam Hadhari initiative. Would you describe for our readers your thoughts, and what went through your mind surrounding this initiative?
>
> **Tun Badawi:** Since before Malaysia's independence in 1957, and continuing until now, there have been robust debates as to whether Malaysia is – or should be – an Islamic state. And if it is so, on what basis can we define the nature of the Islam, or Islam-ness, of our Islamic state?

Certainly not on the basis of our demographics: for if we look at Malaysia, Muslims are only 60 percent of the population. That means that 40 percent of the population, a large percentage, is not Muslim. Among them we have Buddhists, Christians, Hindus, Sikhs, Taoists, and the native religions of our indigenous populations of Sabah and Sarawak. Managing such religious diversity on top of our cultural and ethnic diversity is a challenge, though praise be to God, we have successfully managed this diversity.

Also, when I became prime minister in 2003, Malaysia chaired the OIC (Organization of Islamic Conference). I felt that we in Malaysia should make a statement relevant to the specific problems facing the Islamic world. Ever since the non-Western nations broke away from colonial servitude, some have managed to perform well. Oil has been a blessing to some countries, enabling them to attain living standards that they would not otherwise have been able to enjoy. Some also instituted pragmatic political, economic, social, and educational reforms. But despite some post-colonial successes in some parts of the Muslim world, there is also much cause for dismay. The sheer weight of the problems the Muslim world faced, and still does, is tremendous. Many Muslim countries have high rates of poverty, illiteracy, and malnutrition. Some stand out because of oppression, tyranny, and injustice. The Arab Spring and violence we see in several Muslim countries today is testimony to these problems.

Moreover the problems that confront Muslim societies today are not the problems of the sixth century. Political institutions, economic systems, and societal structures are different from what existed during the time of the Prophet Muhammad, peace be upon him, during the times of the pious caliphs and the great imams and scholars of Islam. People are organized under nation-states today and not alliances of tribes. The world economic system has increased in depth, breadth, and complexity and is increasingly interlinked. Science is constantly pushing the boundaries of human achievement. Islamic thought can no longer be isolated from these developments.

So upon becoming prime minister, and recognizing that I was prime minister of all Malaysians, and not only the Malaysian Muslims, and also chair of the OIC, I sought to find ideological common ground between the Muslims and the non-Muslims who make up our religious and cultural diversity in our country, and internationally.

The common ground is the *manhaj* (program) of Islam Hadhari that promotes good governance acceptable to Muslims and non-Muslims.

Imam Feisal: And what does "good governance from an Islamic perspective" mean to you?

Tun Badawi: That was the question I sought to answer. In my judgment, the values that answered this question of Islamic good governance, and also provided an ideological common ground for all Malaysians, were in the academic discourse on those values that led to the heyday of Islamic civilization, known in Arabic as *al-islam al-hadari*, or *civilizational Islam*.

Imam Feisal: Would you explain your understanding of the term *hadari*?

Tun Badawi: The word *hadari* in Arabic is an adjective from the word *hadarah*, which means to be living a settled communal city life instead of a nomadic existence. The term *al-islam al-hadari* refers to the study of what it was in our faith that catalyzed the development of Islamic civilization. What was it that led the Muslims to develop the greatest civilization on earth in the 150 years after the Prophet's death? If we can answer this question, then by recreating that program or roadmap – a *manhaj* in Arabic – we should be able to recreate an Islamic renaissance and contribute to a global human renaissance.

Muslims regard the Prophet as the perfected human (*insan kamil*), his rule as the exemplary rule, and his community in Medina that he forged as representing the model community. Well, why is that? Certainly it has to be found in what he personally represented and accomplished as Prophet and ruler, and the principles he ruled by.

Imam Feisal: What, in your judgment, were the principles he taught and ruled by?

Tun Badawi: First and foremost, as a Prophet he was a religious and spiritual teacher, teaching his people to have perfect faith in God and to acknowledge Him as Creator. From his role as Prophet and teacher, we get the two principles of *faith and piety in Allah*, and *cultural and moral integrity*.

Next, the Prophet said that the superiority of the learned over the mere ritual observer is like his superiority over the least of us. And since we regard the Prophet as the perfected human (*insan kamil*), the difference between a society that is learned over a society that is ignorant is like the difference between the Prophet and an ignorant person. So if our objective is to build a perfected society, it must be knowledge based. The

Prophet is known to have urged his followers to seek knowledge – even as far as China.

And this is what the Muslims did. During the time of the Caliph Ma'mun, all the books from all over the world were translated into Arabic, and knowledge from Greece, India, and China were brought to the capital city Baghdad. It was a cosmopolitan city, benefiting from the wisdom of all the different peoples in it. Just as here in Malaysia, our Chinese and Indian brothers and sisters who have come to Malaysia have enriched us with their knowledge, wisdom, and hard work.

In our attempt to recreate such a renaissance, it is clear that knowledge, learning, and wisdom from all societies and from all over the world must be the basis for our progress in this world and the next. That is why *a vigorous pursuit and mastery of knowledge* is very high among the principles of the Islam Hadhari platform.

Third, from the Prophet Muhammad as military commander we get the principle of *a strong national defense capability*; from his role or *sunna* as lawgiver and judge, the principle of *a just and trustworthy government* and the rule of law; from his *sunna* as administrator who had a particular concern for the poor and underprivileged, we derived the three principles of *a balanced and comprehensive economic development, safeguarding the natural resources and the environment*, so as to provide *a good quality of life for the people*. Together with his role as Prophet and teacher, from which (as we mentioned before) we get the two principles of *faith and piety in Allah*, and *cultural and moral integrity*; and combined altogether, we can then obtain the final and tenth principle, *a free and independent people* living harmoniously with each other.

> **Imam Feisal:** Would you please repeat these ten principles of Islam Hadhari for our readers?
>
> **Tun Badawi:** The *manhaj* Islam Hadhari posits ten fundamental principles – or substantive outcomes and values – of *iman* (faith or piety) and `*amal salih* (good actions) which Muslims individually and societally – therefore countries – must demonstrate as a Divine commandment: the first principle fulfills the idea of *iman*, and the other nine unbundle the meaning of and constitutes `*amal salih*:

1. Faith and piety in Allah
2. A just and trustworthy government
3. A free and independent people
4. A vigorous pursuit and mastery of knowledge

5. A Balanced and comprehensive economic development
6. A good quality of life for the people
7. Protection of the rights of minority groups and women
8. Cultural and moral integrity
9. Safeguarding natural resources and the environment
10. Strong defense capabilities

But key to our Islam Hadhari approach were that it expressed three things:

> First, that it valued ethical values and substance over form. Values are eternal, and because values are shared by people of all faith traditions, when values are emphasized it tends to unite society.

Therefore, while we recognize that rituals are important, that the written word of the Qur'an is sacred, we also believe that as Muslims we must understand the spirit and ultimate objectives of our religion. Rituals alone will not make us good Muslims. The Quran repeatedly commands us to "perform *salah* **and give** *zakah*," and describes the Prophet's true followers as those who "believe **and do good deeds** (*alladhina amanu wa `amilu-ssalihat*) proving that rituals are incomplete without charity, that faith is incomplete without wilful deliberative action that leads to social justice. As much as we are to focus on our worship of God, we have to equally focus on building social welfare and cohesion – which translates into good governance.

Second, it is an approach that commits us to the righteous path of religious moderation, a value highly emphasized by both God and the Prophet. God describes Muslims as a moderate people (*ummatan wasatan*) in the very middle verse of the second chapter of the Qur'an.[1] This is a divine reminder for Muslims to observe and practice moderation, and to avoid extremism. Extremism results in injustice and in denying the rights of people, especially minorities and women, which is why *justice* and *protection of minorities and women* were another two of the ten principles of the Islam Hadhari program.

Third, this approach is to make Muslims understand that what Islam enjoins of progress, which many equate with many aspects of modernity, is firmly rooted in the noble values and injunctions of our faith; and to our non-Muslim brothers and sisters, that these values are shared and part of their faith as well.

Imam Feisal: Did you face resistance to the Islam Hadhari platform from non-Muslims or Muslims?

Tun Badawi: Yes, to the Muslims I had to convince them that this was neither a new religion nor a new *madhhab*, but rather a substantive program of action (*manhaj*). To the non-Muslims I had to show them that these principles were not values that were against any religion, whether Christianity, Buddhism, or Hinduism, but rather are values common to all religions and faiths, especially and including their own.

While I believed that this platform was in fact acceptable to everyone, the process of gaining this acceptance involved heated discussions with different political parties that lasted hours.

Imam Feisal: How did you rally these groups?

Tun Badawi: I engaged the non-Muslims through their political parties and enumerated the principles to them. For example, I was asked to meet the Malaysian Chinese Association (MCA), the second largest political party in Malaysia. I went and explained to them each principle, one by one. I began with saying that I am a Malay, president of UMNO (United Malays National Organization), and a Muslim. Most of you are Chinese and non-Muslim. But let's be fair to each other because I am the prime minister of all Malaysians, and we are talking about the future of this country. I have a responsibility and you have a responsibility. We have common wishes, common desires, and common aspirations that we want to achieve. When I described Islam Hadhari, they asked, "Why Islam? Do you want to impose Islam upon us?" I said, "No, if we are talking about Islam Hadhari, the first principle is to acknowledge our Creator, God, called Allah by Muslims. We all recognize that we are accountable to a Higher Power, by whatever name we call Him. So the first principle of Islam Hadhari wasn't a cause for division.

And then I went through the other nine principles and asked them, "Tell me, which of these principles goes against your religion?" I insisted that they voice any opposition. I didn't want any reservations to remain unaddressed, because the issue was too important.

It was then that they pointed out that, to them, justice was most important. "If you are the leader, just make sure that you are just and fair to us," they said. Since then I always declare that my responsibility – not only to the government but also to God – was to be just and fair to all, not only to my Muslim brothers. I have to be. It is my responsibility in the name of Allah to be fair and just to all. And they gave a thunderous round of applause. That is what they wanted to hear.

Justice is prominent to the Islamic idea of good governance. Any Muslim leader assuming power in their country should be reminded of the Qur'anic verse in 4:58 "Allah commands you to render back your trusts to those to whom they are due; and when you judge between people, that you judge with justice." Because of this, it is pivotal to good governance that concepts such as "equality before the law" and "the rule of law," due process, and an independent judiciary were given so much importance in early Islamic jurisprudence.

> **Imam Feisal:** And it is no accident that the Shariah Index scholars also pointed out that the fundamental definition of an Islamic state is justice (`adalah)
>
> **Tun Badawi:** Yes, I agree.
>
> **Imam Feisal:** How was Islam Hadhari received by the Muslims?
>
> **Tun Badawi:** We Malays are devout Muslims, and as Muslims the term "Islamic" is a very powerful motivator, which is why the Islamic political party has a following. And so that wasn't much of a problem. Some were confused about the nomenclature, and I had to repeatedly emphasize that Islam Hadhari is neither a new religion, nor a new teaching, nor a madhhab. It is an effort to bring the *ummah* back to the basics of Islam, back to the fundamentals as prescribed in the Qur'an and the *hadith*, and recreates the historical formula which built Islamic civilization.

But sometimes, when you want to accomplish certain things, the use of the word Islamic causes opposition. The discourse degenerates into a game of politics and can certainly be very frustrating. So, we have to find common ground between all of us. This is why I decided that focusing on substance, on civilizational Islam – Islam Hadhari – was better. I wanted to see to what extent I'd find support and acceptance. I didn't use any specifically Islamic technical terms, just Islam Hadhari; otherwise, I thought, other groups would not trust us. When drafting these principles, we made sure that they met the needs of Malaysia and Malaysians, so that by following them everyone would benefit. But of course we first had to gain their acceptance.

To me, therefore, Islam Hadhari refers to this kind of an understanding of Islam, an understanding that focuses on the elements of community building and social cohesion, and the progress that any Muslim society needs to make to develop such cohesion, all of which describe the Islamic commitment to good governance as clearly stipulated in the Qur'an.

Imam Feisal: What role did the *Maqasid* play in the development of Islam Hadhari? Did you see Islam Hadhari as an act of contemporary *ijtihad*?

Tun Badawi: I have repeatedly called for the relevance of contemporary *ijtihad* from the sources of the Shariah. And in fact the ten principles of Islam Hadhari do flow from *ijtihad* with reference to good governance, and also from the *Maqasid al-Shariah*. The objectives of the Shariah, what is meant by *Maqasid al-shari`ah*, are about our responsibility to protect and further the values of life, religion, mind, property, family, and dignity.

Imam Feisal: Would you please walk us through this?

Tun Badawi: Religion is what the first principle of faith and piety in Allah is about. Life is described by all other *Maqasid*, but in particular the principle of a strong defense capability. If people don't feel safe, the *maqsad* of life is not protected. The vigorous pursuit and mastery of knowledge describes the maqsid of the mind or `aql. The maqsid of property is expressed in the two principles of a balanced and comprehensive economic development, and safeguarding natural resources and the environment. The *maqsid* of family is expressed in providing a good quality of life for the people, and in cultural and moral integrity. And the *maqsid* of dignity is expressed in the two principles of a free and independent people, and in protecting the rights of minorities and women.

But while we can directly relate the principles of Islam Hadhari to the *Maqasid*, I veered away from using Islamic technical terms in advancing the principles of Islam Hadhari, as I believed they would make it more difficult for people to understand. I preferred to speak in terms of general principles common to all, principles accepted by all as meaningful and relevant to Malaysia's governance.

But I did draw upon key guidance within our tradition regarding Islamic good governance, guidance which emphasizes the centrality of moral leadership and justice. According to the Shariah, moral leadership has always been one of the essential requirements of a government that upholds Islamic principles and values such as honesty and integrity, a passion for justice and a sense of fairness, a love of the people, especially the poor, a willingness to listen to their grievances, and a readiness to seek counsel from the wise and the learned.

Imam Feisal: How did you specifically apply these principles of Islam Hadhari to governance during your administration?

Tun Badawi: This is a very important question, Feisal. We all have seen governments make wonderful declarations about human freedom and development, yet fail to accomplish those objectives.

The biggest challenge every political leader faces is that of implementation. Partly this is because no leader rules in a vacuum but in a political, cultural, and economic context. It is not enough to say that the government should be just and trustworthy, and have credible and independent government institutions. This is why I made a special effort during my administration to combat corruption, against which I took a hard line. I ordered an extensive reform program for the police force and other enforcement agencies. And I committed myself to re-establish the strength, credibility, and independence of our judiciary and our courts. And I hope that the Malaysian people will agree with me that these were vital measures for me to undertake.

I embarked on balancing the budget and redirecting government spending on socioeconomic programs that would help the needy. I emphasized the need to develop the agricultural sector so that the rural areas – which are predominantly Muslim – would not be left behind. Otherwise what would it mean to say that we sought a balanced and comprehensive economic development and provide a good quality of life for the people – two of the Islam Hadhari objectives?

And while we still have a ways to go, I encouraged people to speak up by giving greater space for political and democratic discourse.

So for me, these were not just principles to talk about; they were principles I lived and governed by.

Imam Feisal: Is your approach something that can be implemented by other Muslim-majority nations, and do you see Malaysia as a model to be emulated by the rest of the Muslim world?

Tun Badawi: While I do not pretend that Malaysia has all the solutions to the many challenges of the Muslim world, I do believe that Malaysia can serve as an example of what it is to be a successful, modern Muslim country. We have demonstrated in Malaysia how to live successfully with ethnic and religious diversity, and we have consistently improved governance for the people. So yes, I believe Malaysia's success offers a working model of renewal, reform and, God willing, renaissance for the Muslim world.

At the same time, I am also aware that different countries need different solutions to their problems, and we must respect the sovereignty and independence of each country. We cannot presume to go to another country and tell them what to do! A nation's form of governance must be determined by its people.

However, just as in Malaysia, many Muslim countries are increasingly becoming multi-religious and multiracial. Just look at how the Gulf nations' populations have evolved in the last few decades. Good governance will benefit *all* people living in the Muslim world regardless of their religious or racial identities, and if you analyze what it is that our brothers and sisters are clamoring for in the Arab countries, it is for several line items of the Islam Hadhari manhaj.

Imam Feisal: Would you please walk us through that?

Tun Badawi: Surely. In Tunisia, it was triggered by the desire for a just government, balanced and comprehensive economic development, and a good quality of life for *all* the people. These are line items 2, 5, and 6 of the Islam Hadhari manhaj. In Bahrain, it was triggered by the desire for a just government, and for protection of the rights of the (Shia) minority group. These are line items 2 and 7 of the Islam Hadhari manhaj.

Imam Feisal: I get it Pak Lah. In Egypt, it was the same as in Tunisia, triggered by the desire for a just government, economic development that provides a good quality of life for all the people, which are again line items 2, 5, and 7 of the Islam Hadhari manhaj. And in Libya, it was additionally triggered by the same three as in Egypt plus two more: the desire of the people to feel free and independent, and the rights of tribal minorities, which makes for a total of line items 2, 3, 5, 6, and 7 of the Islam Hadhari manhaj.

Tun Badawi: You've got it Feisal! So, if instead of thinking of the name "Islam Hadhari," and I ask Muslims to think of the substantive principles of what Muslims historically did to build a world-class civilization, I'm sure that they will come up with these principles, whether expressed in these words or other words: the meaning will be the same. These principles will clearly work with any system of government, whether a monarchy or a republic, whether democratic or not, because it is about the substantive principles that guide our rule. Baghdad a thousand years ago was a prosperous, multi-ethnic, multi-religious city, arguably the center of the civilized world. Today Baghdad is plagued with suicide bombings committed by Muslims killing each other. How can you build a happy society, let alone a developed civilization, when people cannot feel safe walking the streets?

For Muslims: rulers and subjects, it is a reminder to the Muslims to treat their non-Muslim fellow citizens well and fairly in all their dealings. I have always stated that this approach is what has brought excellence, distinction, and glory to all Malaysians, Muslims and non-Muslims alike. It is the only authentic way in which the government can administer the well-being of the country and the welfare of its multiracial and multi-religious population.

> **Imam Feisal:** What is the significance of Islam Hadhari to the world at large?
>
> **Tun Badawi:** We have demonstrated that we can roll back the extremists, not by engaging in a "holier-than-thou" contest, but by addressing the root causes of anger and frustration. I believe that the issues that we have addressed in Malaysia are similar to those in many other Muslim countries; but by tackling these issues in a democratic and just manner, making everyone a stakeholder in the society, we prevent people from becoming extremists.

But the world also needs a more conducive environment to enable an internal order that is more just and equitable. There is unease and tension throughout the world resulting from the belief that a single country dominates all military, economic, political, and cultural dimensions of power. The world would be a more peaceful and prosperous place if wealth was distributed more equally. This is possible if the threat of political, military, economic, and trade sanctions are made obsolete. World trade must be conducted more fairly. Wealth must be used to develop education, healthcare, and welfare for the world community. We want a world that provides justice for the weak, opportunities for the needy, and hope for the poor that they may improve their socioeconomic status. We must strive to narrow or close the gap between rich nations and the developing world. A world at peace will provide comfort to the developed nations when there is equality from a socioeconomic perspective. The world should not be divided into the rich and the poor, North and South, East and West, Muslim and-non-Muslim. Neither is the world a shooting gallery for the display of instruments of war and to test the potency of weapons. Allah did not create the world for it to be destroyed by man, but for man to protect, guard, and develop.

The so-called "clash of civilizations" need not be, and is not, inevitable. The higher, true values of Islam are values adhered to by many. No one should judge Muslims on the basis of the extreme deeds committed by the few. Muslims believe that if you have good intentions, God Almighty is always there to lend you a helping hand and assist you in your quest to do good. Differences in opinion must be accepted and tolerated. We must not cease to appreciate the differences that exist between peoples. The Qur'an states that God created the universe and caused it to be inhabited by men and women and people and tribes—*whose ethnicities, languages and cultures He Himself diversified*—so that they may know each other. We must proactively seek peace between cultures and religions by deliberately seeking nonviolent adjustments, dialogue, and negotiations. Above all, we must not fear differences. The Prophet Muhammad said, "Difference of opinion in my community is a sign of the bounty of God." Accepting such differences therefore means accepting God's bounty; while rejecting such differences means rejecting God's bounty!

Imam Feisal: Any last thoughts Tun?

Tun Badawi: First, I am happy to endorse my successor PM Najib's Global Movement of Moderates platform. I believe this is a powerful platform that can rally people of all faiths behind the principle of faith in God and doing good deeds. It follows the tradition of all the Prophets and great religious leaders, all of whom have emphasized moderation. We need moderation today, especially after what we have been seeing of the Arab Spring. It pains me to see Muslims killing fellow Muslims and fellow human beings from Tunisia to Bahrain, and especially in Libya, Egypt, and now – even innocent children – in Syria. We must find ways to strengthen the voices of moderation.

Second, I hope that the principles I have enumerated, by whatever name people want to call it, can become a program of action that the Muslim world adopts. The Muslim world needs a renaissance, and to the extent that our experience in Malaysia can help others see their way, I will work with the powers that be to help see that happen. I hope what I have done as prime minister, and what I hope to do in the remaining years of my life work, will have been to support and enhance these principles in Malaysia and especially the Muslim World.

And from now until that day, I pray that Islam will flourish once again in the way we have just been talking about, and that the Islam of the twenty-first century will do justice to the authentic teachings of our faith. I pray that it will be a civilizational Islam, one that focuses on substance and values, and not on superficial things like appearances. Just like wearing a white coat doesn't make you a real doctor, wearing a particular kind of beard and Arab-style headdress and clothes don't make us authentic Muslims. I pray that the Muslim world and the West will overcome this turbulent period together, that we find courage in ourselves to make the necessary changes to our policies and within our societies. Let the future not speak of bloody borders, but of equal alliances, fair trade, and scientific collaboration between us, and of one humanity under God.

Imam Feisal: Thank you, Prime Minister Badawi.

Harmonizing Islamic law and common law in Malaysia (Tun Abdul Hamid Mohamad)

> **Imam Feisal:** As the former chief justice of Malaysia and having served as an officer in the Judicial and Legal Service and as a judge in all courts in the country, from the lowest to the highest, you have spent much of your lifetime dealing with the intersections of Islamic and civil or secular law. How would you delineate these points of intersection within the Malaysian context?
>
> **Tun Abdul Hamid:** I'll begin with a story. One afternoon in 2002, a doctoral student from the University of Istanbul visited me in my office to interview me for his thesis. He said that his professor had asked him to see me while he was in Malaysia. I welcomed the young man, and the first question he asked was, "What is your definition of Islamic law?" Almost without thinking, I replied, "Any law that is not un-Islamic." This means that any law that doesn't violate the principle of Shariah should be considered as Islamic. After he had returned to Istanbul, he sent me an email in which he said, "How I wish that all of the `ulama` were as broad-minded as you."
>
> **Imam Feisal:** And I recall you re-telling this story to one of our SIP scholars, Professor Tahir Mahmood. What was his reaction, Tun?
>
> **Tun Abdul Hamid:** Yes, I told this story to a group of scholars of Islamic law from more than ten countries in both the East and the West. Everyone laughed. But after a while, Professor Mahmood came to me and said, "Your definition is not a joke, you know. There is a lot of truth in it."

I have come to believe that this is what Islamic law should be. We should look to the sources, including the *Maqasid al-Shariah*, for the principles while the details should be determined by surrounding circumstances.

Imam Feisal: How does this play out in the context of Malaysia? How do people in Malaysia perceive the differences between "Islamic" and "secular" laws?

Tun Abdul Hamid: If you were to ask anyone in Malaysia, including an Islamic religious teacher, for a definition of Islamic law, the most likely answer they would give is "the laws of Allah," "God-made laws," or "the laws as found in the Qur'an and Sunnah of the Holy Prophet." If you showed them the Acts of Parliament, they would immediately describe these laws as "secular" or "man-made." In fact, depending on the political party to which they belong, some might even call them "the laws of the unbelievers."

It is interesting to note that in the Federal Constitution of Malaysia the authoritative English text uses the term "Islamic law," while the official Malay language version uses the term *Hukum Syarak*, meaning Shariah Law. No distinction is made between Shariah (God's ordinances in the Qur'an and Sunnah) and *fiqh* (later human understanding of these ordinances, including legislation that isn't mentioned in the Qur'an and Sunnah but aren't antithetical to the Shariah). Take for example, the civil and criminal procedural laws that are now being used in the "Shariah courts," which is the term used for the "religious courts." A large part of it is taken from the procedural laws in use in the "secular courts." But when they are incorporated in the procedural laws for use in the Shariah courts, with necessary modifications, they become known as "Shariah Civil Procedure Enactment" and the "Shariah Criminal Procedure Enactment," and so on.

Imam Feisal: In other words, laws that were simply *shar'i*, or compliant with the Shariah, were – over time – considered to be the Shariah itself. As a result, this perspective makes no distinction between the Divine law and our human attempts to interpret and promulgate laws based on that Divine law.

Tun Abdul Hamid: That's right. And those making this God-made/man-made distinction look at the law's source, not its content, in order to determine if a law is a "Shariah" or a secular law. As long as a particular view on the issue can be traced to a *kitab*, it is deemed "Shariah." In the Malay language, the word *"kitab"* means an Islamic religious book a few centuries old, usually written in the Arabic script but also including those written in the Malay language. So the result of this is the tendency to treat all laws made by Parliament, as well as whatever common law is developed by the courts, as secular and un-Islamic. This means, according to this perspective that such laws should not be allowed to exist in an Islamic state.

Imam Feisal: What's your opinion of this situation, Tun Hamid?

Tun Abdul Hamid: My opinion is that such misconceptions should be corrected. As lawmakers, our focus should be on the sources *and* the content. This is especially true when the traditional source on a particular law is unavailable, like with some more modern issues.

Imam Feisal: And how do you determine whether or not a particular man-made law is acceptable?

Tun Abdul Hamid: The test is whether or not a law contravenes established Shariah principles – to use the common term, whether it's Shariah-compliant.

Imam Feisal: Can you give our readers an example of why it is wrong to automatically regard a law which doesn't directly emanate from the Islamic sources as necessarily un-Islamic?

Tun Abdul Hamid: Of course. Suppose that there were cars during the time of the Abbasid caliph Harun al-Rashid (d. 193 AH/809 CE). Let's assume that Harun had commissioned a scholar like Abu Yusuf to draft regulations on how cars should be driven on the roads. I am quite sure that today those regulations would be known as the Shariah, or Islamic, traffic laws. And had a speed limit been fixed, it might even be known today as the "Shariah speed limit" or "Islamic speed limit"; and likely, different schools of law would have different speed limits! But because cars are a modern invention of the non-Muslim West – as are the regulatory laws that followed, even though Muslim-majority countries have adopted them – these laws would be considered "secular" or even "un-Islamic" according to this logic. That approach, though perhaps unintentional is, in my view, flawed and therefore should be corrected.

If we sift through the body of existing laws in Muslim-majority countries using the Shariah-compliance test, I believe that a large majority of these laws now in force which are commonly referred to as "common law" or "civil law" are, in fact, already Islamic.

Imam Feisal: That's a very clear illustration of your point that laws cannot be deemed un-Islamic or opposed to the Shariah simply because they originated from a legal system or context that is from outside the Islamic tradition. One could also consider a more contentious issue like holding elections or having a parliament. These are political systems that came out of the West, yet, in my opinion, they can be adopted by Muslims today because they don't conflict with any principles of the Shariah and they benefit society.

Tun Abdul Hamid: True, and one could also argue that we can enact laws today which are actually better and more Islamic than those at the time of the Holy Prophet.

Imam Feisal: Better and more Islamic?

Tun Abdul Hamid: I know that may sound preposterous, but consider this. We agree that no one in history did more to improve the lives and rights of slaves than the Prophet Muhammad. Yet the reality is that slavery was not prohibited during his life. This is understandable considering the circumstances at that time. Today, however, slavery is outlawed, and would anyone contend that outlawing slavery is un-Islamic? Would anyone say that a modern Islamic state must reintroduce slavery to be Islamic or more Islamic?

Imam Feisal: And what has been the response to these questions among the scholars you asked?

Tun Abdul Hamid: So far, no one has answered "yes" to either.

In fact, I would go further and say that outlawing slavery is *more Islamic* than tolerating it, no matter how improved slaves' lives are. The Qur'an teaches us that freeing slaves is a great virtue: "And what will convey unto you what the Ascent is! It is setting free a slave."[2] Also according to the Qur'an, one of the ways to spend *zakah* is on the freedom of slaves.[3] Therefore, the intent and ultimate goal of the Qur'an and Prophet's injunctions on freeing slaves and treating them well is about *eliminating slavery* and achieving the ideal of all human beings' equality. I believe that we have better achieved this clear Divine intent today than in the past. During the time of the Prophet, eliminating slavery couldn't be fully accomplished; however, it can be – and in most places, has been – done today. This shows that our contemporary laws can be more Islamic than the laws at the time of the Prophet.

The big picture point here, is that, by understanding the intent and objectives of Allah's commandments, we can continually strive to achieve them more efficiently and as perfectly as we can. This is also why I endorse the Maqasid al-Shariah approach, because it focuses our attention and efforts on how we can maximally attain Allah's intentions for us.

Imam Feisal: Let's turn to your own work dealing with these issues in Malaysia. I'm wondering how the state of Malaysia has attempted to harmonize Islamic law and modern legislation. How has your definition of Shariah compliance, or Islamic law/common law compatibility, been applied? How does a contemporary nation-state develop laws that are both faithful to the Shariah and appropriate to their specific contexts?

Tun Abdul Hamid: The process of harmonizing Islamic law with contemporary common or civil law has been going on in Malaysia for the past three decades. After Malaysian independence in 1957, the federal and state constitutions provided for establishing Shariah courts. This meant that codified substantive and procedural laws that were Shariah compliant had to be drafted. But we had problems. The Islamic scholars and Shariah court judges were unable to produce a draft that could be enacted as law by parliament and the state legislative assemblies.

Imam Feisal: Why couldn't they do so?

Tun Abdul Hamid: Well, they lacked the expertise and experience in drafting bills; in addition, they didn't know the relevant contemporary laws that had already been legislated by parliament or developed by the courts, out of necessity, to achieve greater justice. The other issue is that they didn't have a ready-made code from within the Islamic sources to work on. The principles of governance were scattered throughout the Qur'an, *hadith* collections, and works of traditional scholars.

Imam Feisal: In other words, the Shariah scholars and judges faced a dual problem. First, they lacked expertise in modern lawmaking and legislation. And second, they didn't have a clear code of law from the Islamic legal tradition to draw upon. What happened?

Tun Abdul Hamid: They worked with common law lawyers, who already had ready-made codes to refer to for criminal and civil procedure. So these lawyers – led by the late Professor Ahmad Ibrahim, who was trained at Cambridge – sat down with the Shariah court judges to draft the laws. I was a state legal advisor (state attorney general) at that time and was involved in this process. We decided to take the laws that were currently in use in the common law courts as the basis from which to work.

Imam Feisal: In other words, the existing secular court's laws were your starting point. Was there any sort of process for reconciling, or harmonizing, these civil laws with the Shariah? I would imagine that there were times when there was conflict.

Tun Abdul Hamid: Yes, and in these cases, we removed or substituted for the objectionable sections. We also added missing sections and placed the laws within a Shariah framework. After all of that, we had them enacted as laws: the Shariah Criminal Procedure Act/ Enactment[4], the Shariah Civil Procedure Act/Enactment, the Shariah Evidence Act/Enactment, the Islamic Family Law Act/ Enactment, and so on. These laws have become "Shariah," while similar provisions in the common law or civil courts paradoxically continue to be perceived as secular or un-Islamic!

Imam Feisal: Can you give us a specific example from your committee meetings of how a civil or criminal law was incorporated into these hybrid Acts or Enactments?

Tun Abdul Hamid: At one of my early meetings with the other committee members, I asked them whether they could produce an Islamic or Shariah criminal procedure code to work from. When I was told "no," I said that we had to start somewhere. Since a criminal procedure code was already being applied in the civil courts, I suggested that we use it as a basis on which to build. I read the laws section by section, translating them from English to Malay and explaining what each meant.

When we came to the section on charging criminals, I went over all of the relevant legal provisions. I described how the charge must contain the details of the accused person and his alleged offence, including date, time, place, and the act he was alleged to have committed, as well as the provision of the law that made the act an offence and the section of the law under which he would be punished, if convicted. Finally, I described how the charge must be read and explained to the accused person, who must be asked whether or not he understood the charge before he pleaded guilty or not guilty. I then asked the Deputy Mufti of the state where I worked whether he had any Shariah objection to it. Thinking for a moment, he approvingly replied: "That is good." I understood him as saying that even though he couldn't think of a Shariah precedent for such a criminal procedure, this section of the existing criminal code was good for attaining justice and it wasn't objectionable to the Shariah. The section was accepted.

That's just one example of how Islamic law developed in Malaysia by adopting provisions from the common law jurisdiction.

Imam Feisal: What about the other areas of law? How did the harmonization of common and Shariah law expand? I assume that other areas underwent a similar process.

Tun Abdul Hamid: Initially, harmonization was carried out in lawmaking, particularly procedural laws, for use in a hearing in the Shariah courts. And this was primarily for family law cases. But harmonization has now taken a greater dimension. It's happening globally, even in the non-Muslim West, Far East, and Australia, with subjects like Islamic banking, Islamic finance, and *takaful*.

Imam Feisal: Can you define *takaful* for our readers?

Tun Abdul Hamid: *Takaful* means "guaranteeing each other" or "joint guarantee." It refers to the concept of "Islamic insurance," and it includes a number of ideas. It is meant to eliminate practices forbidden by the Shariah like *al-gharar* (uncertainty) and *riba* (usury), while promoting such Islamic notions as cooperation amongst policyholders. Its fundamentals are based on Qur'anic verses like "Help one another in goodness and piety, and do not help one another in sin and aggression"[5] or *Hadith* such as "One true believer and another true believer are just like a building whereby every part in it strengthens the other part."

Imam Feisal: Thank you, Tun Hamid. I know that you've been involved in a number of bodies that work in the areas of Islamic banking and *takaful*. Can you tell us a bit about your experiences?

Tun Abdul Hamid: Yes, I've had the good fortune of serving as a member of the Shariah Advisory Council of the Malaysian Central Bank, as well as on the Securities Commission of Malaysia. In this capacity, I've observed how Shariah-compliant products were created. This process was quite similar to the making of "Shariah laws" I was describing earlier. Officers that specialized in conventional banking and trade worked hand-in-hand with the Shariah-trained officers. They would take a modern, conventional product which should be introduced into the Islamic banks, and they would identify the Shariah issues, if any, and look for a Shariah or *fiqh* principle that could be applied to validate the Shariah compliance of the product. At times, different principles were applied at different stages, and the factual matrix was modified by creating a third company between the two contracting parties in order to make the product Shariah compliant.

Imam Feisal: Do you mind elaborating on that, Tun Hamid?

Tun Abdul Hamid: Well, an analogy for how this process worked would be to identify the alcohol in champagne (the Shariah repugnant item), remove it, and then arrive at sparkling grape juice (the Shariah-compliant product)! Through this process, we now have savings accounts, checking accounts, credit cards, Shariah-compliant insurance, and *sukuk*, or Shariah-compliant bonds.

Imam Feisal: These are all financial products that originated outside the Islamic legal framework but that are now commonly practiced or used in countries like Malaysia and throughout the Muslim World. Nevertheless, I can imagine that there was some pushback on this process. Do you ever receive criticism?

Tun Abdul Hamid: We are occasionally criticized. The criticism is that we're only creating Shariah-*compliant* products, as opposed to Shariah-*based* products. Still, I've yet to see anyone, even our critics, come up with a Shariah-based product that is different from a Shariah-compliant product.

Imam Feisal: Can you expand on this point?

Tun Abdul Hamid: I am not a Shariah scholar, but I don't really see a difference between the two. I once asked a Malaysian Shariah scholar who sits on many Shariah Committees all over the world about the difference. He said, "I ask the critics to define 'Shariah compliance' and 'Shariah-based' and show me the difference. They could not do it." The only difference is the source of the product. For example, *sukuk* (bonds) and credit cards are all products which are similar to the conventional products, although modified to make them Shariah compliant. Since it is an adaptation from the conventional product, to such critics it is not Shariah based. On the other hand, Professor Hashim Kamali, a well-known authority of Islamic law, pointed out to me that there are so many products in the market which are based on the principles of *"mudarabah," "musharakah," "murabahah"*[6] and others. Those products are recognized as Shariah based, despite the fact that these Islamic financing practices have themselves been adapted from conventional banking practices in order to render them Shariah compliant. I think he has answered my question.

Imam Feisal: You mentioned that a major challenge was bridging the different levels of expertise amongst the Shariah scholars and common law lawyers to facilitate their working together towards the goal of creating a coherent and effective system of law for Malaysia.

Tun Abdul Hamid: This was definitely our greatest hindrance at the beginning of the harmonization process. The lawyers who knew common law didn't know Islamic law, and those who knew Islamic law didn't know common law.

Imam Feisal: Why was this disconnect so great?

Tun Abdul Hamid: It stemmed from historical and social causes. In Malaysia, common law lawyers and Islamic scholars rarely came into contact with one another. Common law lawyers were often British or other non-Muslims. They were trained in England, spoke English, and even if they were not Englishmen, they were very English in their way of life. On the other hand, the Islamic scholars were Malays, usually from the villages, who had pursued their education in Malaysian Islamic schools and then continued their Islamic studies in Egypt or some other Middle Eastern country. In addition to Malay, they spoke Arabic, dressed differently, ate different foods, and ate it differently too. While the common law lawyers would frequent the clubs and bars, the Islamic scholars wouldn't enter a club or even a bank!

As a result, the separation and mutually-held prejudices, including against the other's profession and the laws they dealt with, developed. This isn't surprising.

Imam Feisal: And what led to the change?

Tun Abdul Hamid: Things began to change with independence. The sons and daughters of these same Islamic scholars became common law lawyers, even though their basic knowledge of – and even love for – Islamic law remained. Also, they were friends and relatives with the new generation of Islamic scholars, leading to contact and mutual respect. These were the people who sat together to produce the Shariah-compliant laws mentioned earlier.

Imam Feisal: In addition to integrating Shariah law with modern methods of lawmaking, what else developed from this partnership?

Tun Abdul Hamid: Well, there was a growing need to establish Islamic banks and Islamic insurance operations. And at that point, a growing partnership between Shariah experts and conventional bankers, insurance operators, actuaries, and accountants became indispensable to producing Shariah-compliant products in these areas. While the Islamic scholars could cite authorities on Shariah concepts like *riba* or *gharar*, this wouldn't create a Shariah-compliant savings account, a Shariah-compliant credit card, or a Shariah-compliant insurance scheme. Therefore, it was those who had studied modern banking or insurance and other "secular" subjects and who worked in the "un-Islamic" conventional banks and insurance companies who provided the expertise! Without them, I doubt that the Islamic scholars, on their own, could have produced Shariah-compliant financial products.

Imam Feisal: So because of the requirement of Shariah-compliant financial products, new interdisciplinary fields have developed.

Tun Abdul Hamid: Indeed, Imam. With the development of these new fields of Islamic banking, Islamic finance, and *takaful*, there's a burgeoning need for lawyers, judges, accountants, actuaries, and even marketing specialists who know those aspects of Shariah relevant to their respective fields. Lawyers, for example, must now be familiar with the Shariah requirements of a transaction in order to prepare contracts, and they must also know how to argue Shariah issues if they arise in the courts. Similarly, accountants must be familiar with the Shariah to prepare Shariah-compliant financial statements, balance sheets, and income statements. This is particularly true because certain items in classical accounting, like interest payments and accrued income/expenses, may not be allowed. Judges must know the laws of Islamic banking and *takaful* to adjudicate cases that deal with these transactions.

Because such court cases are becoming more and more frequent, the need for adequate and professional knowledge of Shariah relevant to all these disciplines is clear.

Imam Feisal: Given these developments, what's the role of the traditional Shariah scholars in this decidedly new world of Malaysian finance and banking?

Tun Abdul Hamid: The older generation of scholars and *muftis* are finding it difficult to follow the new developments in Islamic law in these areas. And in the last decade, a new group has emerged who are fluent in English and Arabic in addition to their Malay mother-tongue. They hold degrees in both Shariah and common law or in comparative studies. They've studied at Islamic universities which use Arabic as the medium of instruction, as well as from premier Western universities which use English. Many of these specialists are also the product of local universities that offer classes in both common law and Shariah, in conventional and Islamic banking, transactions, and so on. Even those purely Shariah graduates who are fluent in both English and Arabic are seriously pursuing these subjects. Many of them now serve on the Shariah advisory boards of banks and *takaful* companies all over the world. They, together with the new breed of common law lawyers, bankers, auditors, and other industry players are the ones who will bridge the gap.

Imam Feisal: How would you characterize the contemporary Western attitude to the development of these interdisciplinary fields of Islamic financial products?

Tun Abdul Hamid: The winds of change are also blowing from the West. Every time I attend an Islamic banking or *takaful* seminar anywhere in the world, I notice that a large number of the participants, including the speakers, are either Westerners or other non-Muslims. Some of them could even be the descendants of those common law lawyers I mentioned earlier. But unlike their forefathers, they're now discussing Islamic law, Islamic banking and finance, and *takaful*. Many are already experts in these subjects. The East and the West seem to have met!

So the Shariah is spreading to the mainstream of law while absorbing the principles of common law or civil law. We can call that "harmonization" or even "globalization." The result is that just as there's a demand for lawyers and judges with sufficient knowledge of Shariah in their respective fields, there's also a growing global need to have a legal and judicial system that can handle *both* Shariah *and* common law issues. In this context, it's not surprising that even countries with small Muslim populations are already taking steps to prepare themselves for this eventuality. The need isn't driven by the size of the Muslim population; it's driven by the size of the growing market for Islamic financial products.

There's also another level of change that I'd like to mention. The difference between the *madhhabs* is likely going to disintegrate. The differences between the *madhhab*s were likely due to geographical separation and poor communication. But this differentiating factor has now vanished. A ruling made by a Shariah committee in one country is easily transmitted to other committees anywhere in the world within literally seconds. Shariah scholars from different countries and regions often sit on the same committees.

Nor is it any longer possible for a committee to follow any one *madhhab* exclusively to arrive at its decisions, due to the complexity of the issues involved. We might call this a "post-*madhhab* period of history" we're currently living in. Even though the *fiqh* traditions of countries remain strong (like Malaysia and the Shafi'i *madhhab*), their legal systems and people's practices reflect rulings and methodologies from across the traditional schools of law, even other legal traditions. This has led to an important cross-fertilization and intellectual collaboration across the legal schools.

Imam Feisal: This is a very important observation, that as Shariah becomes harmonized and globalized, the differences between the *madhahib* will give way to a more universal understanding of Islam. The geographic separation across the Muslim world is rapidly diminishing, and lawmakers are therefore drawing on and learning from other legal schools and traditions to make law that is applicable more widely. One fruit of this collaboration across the Muslim world has been the development of Islamic finance. How can governments better engage with the intersections of Shariah and conventional banking and the expertise required for both in today's banking and finance world?

Tun Abdul Hamid: The shape of these systems will depend on many local and context-specific factors: the constitutional setup of the country, its existing legal and judicial system, the size and influence of its Muslim population, the wishes of its broader population, local politics, and many other factors. I see three likely scenarios for how governments might deal with the intersections of Shariah banking and conventional banking.

First, in countries with Muslim minorities that offer Islamic banking and *takaful*, it's likely that lawyers and judges will learn those principles of Shariah that relate to Islamic banking, finance, and *takaful*. Lawyers in these countries have done just that, or at least they've hired Shariah scholars to assist them. It's more difficult for judges because they often have to make their decisions alone. So they have no alternative but to learn the subjects themselves. In fact, judges in England are already deciding cases on Islamic banking and *takaful*. While they might struggle at first, I believe that over time, some of them will become experts in this field.

The second alternative is for Shariah scholars who are experts in Islamic banking and *takaful* to sit with the common law judges. This, however, will require legislative intervention.

Imam Feisal: Why will this require legislative intervention?

Tun Abdul Hamid: I am speaking here in the Malaysian context. The Federal Constitution provides for the establishment of the judiciary and also for the appointment of judges to the various courts and specifies the qualifications for their appointment. If a Shariah expert meets these qualifications, he could be appointed as judge. But at present, we do not have such people. So if we want a Shariah scholar, who does not meet these constitutional qualifications, to sit as a judge together with the other judges, amendments would have to be made to the constitution to enable that to be done.

Imam Feisal: What about the third alternative?

Tun Abdul Hamid: The third alternative is to merge the existing common law or civil law courts with the existing Shariah courts, combining the expertise of both. This is an important alternative in countries with Muslim majorities like Malaysia where the Shariah and civil courts are separate, because it can resolve the conflict of jurisdiction between the two courts systems.

However, this will clearly involve legislative intervention on an even larger scale, particularly in Malaysia where the Shariah and civil courts fall under different jurisdictions. In Malaysia, specific matters of Islamic law fall within the jurisdiction of the *states* to legislate because the Islamic Shariah courts are state courts under the jurisdiction of the sultan of each state. According to the Malaysian constitution, the matters that can be heard in these state Shariah courts are limited to those involving "persons professing the religion of Islam."[7] Other matters, including banking, finance, and insurance, all fall within the jurisdiction of the federal legislature, as all civil courts are federal courts under the national government. This can get quite complicated. For example, in cases involving family law, Islamic banking, and *takaful,* one or even both parties may not actually be "persons professing the religion of Islam." One party may be a Christian, Hindu, or Buddhist, or the party may be a bank or an insurance company, and can we really call a limited company[8] "a person professing the religion of Islam"?[9]

Moreover, in a single case there may be issues that fall within the jurisdiction of the common law courts and other issues that fall within the jurisdiction of the Shariah court. So which court has the authority to decide the case? And there may be cases that on the surface fall within the jurisdiction of the Shariah court, but upon closer scrutiny reveal that there are constitutional issues as well. The federal court, not the Shariah court, is the interpreter of the Malaysian Constitution.

Imam Feisal: What are some of the difficulties or inherent challenges in this approach?

Tun Abdul Hamid: I see fewer difficulties in countries with a unitary system, like Brunei. But in countries with a federal system like Malaysia problems might arise. This is because powers and jurisdictions are divided between the federal and state governments, so both governments would have to agree to the arrangement. And politics may stand in the way.

I have been suggesting since 1996 how to solve this problem of conflict of jurisdiction between the civil court and the Shariah court. My solution involves the transfer of jurisdiction of the Shariah courts from the states to the federation, a move that would not be welcomed by those states that are under the opposition parties, as they would likely want to retain independent control of their courts. Because of such political sensitivities, no politician would want to pursue this course of action.[10]

Politicians often avoid getting involved in these issues of jurisdiction and harmonization for political reasons. As a result, they and others not well-versed in the separation of powers look to the courts to solve the problem, failing to realize that this would mean the court rewriting the constitution, which isn't its function. In fact, we should worry just as much when the court interferes with the executive branch as we do when the executive interferes with the function of the judiciary. It cuts both ways.

When there is a problem whose solution is politically sensitive, everybody seems to look to the courts to solve it rather than utilizing other political processes that might be more effective. Hence in a case in 2007 I said: "The trouble is that everybody is looking to the court to solve the problem of the legislature."[11]

> **Imam Feisal:** You have highlighted three possible approaches to solve the problem of conflicts of jurisdiction between the Shariah courts and the common law courts. To briefly summarize, they include:

1. The educational approach, where the state can train judges and lawyers in Shariah principles related to banking and related fields, in order that they're able to adjudicate on such cases.
2. Shariah scholars can sit with the judges and lawyers.
3. The state can merge its Shariah and common law courts.

How would you assess the current level of such harmonization in Malaysia?

> **Tun Abdul Hamid:** We've seen that Shariah courts have adopted principles of common law in procedural matters. Harmonization has also taken place in Islamic banking and *takaful*, where land

law, the law of contracts, commercial law, and companies or corporate law are being used in Islamic banking transactions, at least for the time being. The same principles of common law that are used in conventional insurance claims are being utilized to determine liability and damages in *takaful* claims.

In July 2010 the Central Bank of Malaysia announced the establishment of the Law Harmonisation Committee (LHC), and I have been entrusted to chair it. The Committee consists of representatives from Bank Negara (the Central Bank of Malaysia), Securities Commission, Attorney General's Chambers, practicing lawyers, ISRA, and the Association of Islamic Banking Institutions Malaysia (AIBIM). It is supported by a full-time Secretariat at Bank Negara.

The objectives are:

1. To create a conducive legal system that facilitates and supports the development of Islamic finance industry
2. To achieve certainty and enforceability in the Malaysian laws in regard to Islamic finance contracts
3. To position Malaysia as the reference law for international Islamic finance transactions
4. For Malaysian laws to be the law of choice and the forum for settlement of disputes for cross border Islamic financial transactions

We are in the process of identifying the parts of our law that need to be fine-tuned to make them Shariah-compliant. Our ambition is to make all our laws that are in use in Islamic banking, Islamic finance, and *takaful* fully Shariah compliant, not to just make the products Shariah compliant. Hopefully, we could offer our law to the world as a law of choice for cross-border contracts and our courts as the forum for settlement of disputes in Islamic banking transactions.[12]

> **Imam Feisal:** This would indeed be a major development in favor of Malaysia! It is clear that Malaysia's leadership position in the creation and development of Islamic financing products, as well as in harmonizing Shariah and civil law, positions Malaysia very well to be a court of last resort where disputes in Islamic banking are settled according to your law. Would you say that harmonizing Shariah law with common law is more difficult in some areas than others?

Tun Abdul Hamid: In general, I would say yes. For example, try to harmonize civil criminal law with the *Hudud* and we come to an unbridgeable gap. But the question I would ask is: is *Hudud* really the sole, or primary, determinant of a state's Islamicity?[13] I'm not an Islamic scholar, so I won't answer that question. But the critical point is that when we look for common ground between the Shariah and civil law, for similarities rather than differences, we'll be surprised with the extent of these similarities.

Imam Feisal: I have made the same point myself about the *Hudud*. No sane person would suggest that by punishing criminals the way that Americans do means that we would thereby have a US-style democracy! Analogously, the suggestion that by applying the *Hudud* we would automatically have an Islamic state is likewise absurd. An Islamic state has to be based on positive law and when we compare that positive law with civil law we will find many similarities. What you are saying is that we should start by identifying those areas which are already "harmonious" and say, "look at how much of the Shariah and common law is similar."

Tun Abdul Hamid: Yes, and we should focus on these areas, the lowest-lying fruits in harmonization. A good example is commercial law. Unlike the fixed laws that deal with worship (`*ibadat*) Shariah commercial law is flexible and adaptable.

This is an important point for our leaders to bear in mind, because Islamic commercial law in modern nation-states has become increasingly important. No one could have imagined that towards the end of the twentieth century we would experience a renewed interest in the study and implementation of Islamic law. But this is exactly what has happened.

Imam Feisal: And why has that happened?

Tun Abdul Hamid: I can think of three reasons. First, out of piety, Muslims wanted to establish Shariah courts to implement Islamic family law. They wanted Islamic family law to apply to Muslims. Yet even these courts had to absorb principles of common law to fill the obvious gaps, particularly in procedural law. And this has brought common law lawyers and Islamic scholars into contact and into a working relationship of growing mutual respect towards each other, their professions, and the laws they deal with. I mentioned this before.

Second and even more unexpected was the impact of the introduction and development of Islamic banking, finance, and *takaful*. The driving force in these fields is the money market, and this has led non-Muslims and countries with Muslim minorities to get involved. More non-Muslim professionals and academics are getting involved in the study and implementation of Islamic law relating to commercial transactions and Islamic banking, finance, and *takaful*. I think this will have a great impact on the spread, acceptance, and development of Islamic law globally.

Imam Feisal: Money talks!

Tun Abdul Hamid: Yes it does. And because of this, Islamic law will move into the mainstream, while also enriching itself with those principles of common law or civil law which are Shariah compliant.

Imam Feisal: And what is the final reason?

Tun Abdul Hamid: As I mentioned earlier, due to drastically improved communications and globalization, the differences of opinions between the various *madhahib* are disintegrating. This is leading to a global unification of Islamic law.

Imam Feisal: What wonderful insights, Tun! Do you have any concluding thoughts?

Tun Abdul Hamid: I am of the view that the close of the twentieth century and the beginning of the twenty-first century mark the beginning of a new era in the development and spread of Shariah, in particular *mu`amalat*.[14] And it happens because of Islamic banking, Islamic finance, and *takaful*. The scholars, faced with new realities, are developing the Shariah by accepting the views of all *madhahib* instead of strictly following a particular *madhhab*. At times, they even accept isolated views of traditional scholars as well as the views of contemporary scholars even though such views may differ from the majority view of traditional scholars. They consider the views of other Shariah committees all over the world. They accept the current custom (*'urf*) in financial transactions. All these will make the Shariah more global and current. At the same time, the Shariah is moving into the mainstream and making its appearance in non-Muslim countries, applicable at times even to non-Muslims. The beauty is that it is happening without conquest and without conversion. But ironically, it isn't happening because of piety either, it is happening because of money!

Imam Feisal: Thank you very much, Tun. This has been a highly enlightening discussion. It's been a privilege to hear from you, a man who's been – and continues to be – the leading thinker at the forefront of harmonizing Islamic law and civil law in Malaysia.

The Muhammadiyyah and the roots of Indonesian democracy (Ahmad Syafii Maarif)

> **Imam Feisal:** Thank you for joining us Dr. Maarif. As the former head of one of the largest Muslim organizations in the world, the Muhammadiyah of Indonesia, I would like you to share with us some of the challenges and lessons you have gained in your long career. What role has the Muhammadiyah played in the modern Indonesian state?
>
> **Dr. Maarif:** The Muhammadiyah, founded well before Indonesia's independence, played two crucial roles: first in advancing the movement of independence from colonial rule, and second, laying the foundations for Indonesian democracy and civil society.

To begin, we must understand the context from which the organization developed. Indonesia is the largest Muslim nation in the world. Around 88 percent out of a population of 241 million are Muslims. Though there is debate as to when Islam came to the archipelago, we can say that conversion to Islam en masse occurred through *penetration pacifique* (peaceful penetration) in the seventeenth century.

Another central element of the Indonesian context is colonialism. Indonesia was a Dutch colony until 1942, and this colonial rule and the subsequent nationalist push toward independence were central elements of the context in which the Muhammadiyah developed.

> **Imam Feisal:** What role did nationalism play in Indonesian independence?
>
> **Dr. Maarif:** Well, nationalism as it arose in Europe was new to Indonesia, and it was introduced through colonialism. In spite of its origins, nationalism actually became a prime force in our anti-colonial struggle. While Indonesians did not adopt many of the Western ideological underpinnings of nationalism, they harnessed it as an effective tool to fight Dutch colonial rule. Simultaneously, Indonesians used Islam, which shares the nationalist ideal of freedom from alien domination, as a political, ideological, and militarily liberating force.

Imam Feisal: How did this context influence the mission of the Muhammadiyah?

Dr. Maarif: The Muhammadiyah movement, established in 1912, was one of the most important and influential socio-religious movements involved in this process of liberation. Its educational strategy of enlightening Indonesians has significantly contributed to the independence movement. Likewise, it has imbued spiritual meaning into the future of a free Indonesia. The Muhammadiyah also inherited the spirit of the `ulama's religious resistance to colonialism. Thus the Muhammadiyah's philosophy is that life under foreign or domestic exploitation is not a life of honor and dignity. And for this reason, the freedom of a nation or of an individual is absolutely sacred, and a Muslim should fight to achieve it at any cost.

But as I mentioned, the Muhammadiyah not only helped support the independence movement, but also laid the foundations for Indonesian democracy and civil society.

Indonesia declared its independence on 17 August 1945. Thirty-three years before that, the Muhammadiyah put forth in its first constitution the right of the majority to elect its top leadership, while embarking on an educational program to educate Indonesians who could lead our society.

Since its initial emergence in 1912 in the city of Jogjakarta, the Muhammadiyah has established and fostered around 14,000 schools, from kindergartens to universities, 350 hospitals and clinics, tens of orphanages, and many other humanitarian institutions and services. Indeed, there have been hundreds upon hundreds of Indonesian scholars, generals, politicians, educators, social workers, and civil servants who attended, if not graduated, from Muhammadiyah's school system. This is the way through which the Muhammadiyah has given a substantial meaning to nationalism. This Islamic movement adopted a strategy of keeping out of practical politics, thus enabling its members to actively and creatively concentrate their works towards educating the masses, helping the weak, and offering spiritual values to safeguard and shape the course of modern Indonesian culture. This has enthroned the Muhammadiyah as one of the leading Islamic movements in the world. I would even say that there is no other social and educational Islamic movement in the world comparable to the Muhammadiyah.

Imam Feisal: These are some very impressive successes of the Muhammadiyah.

Dr. Maarif: However, I must also admit that qualitatively, in terms of the moral restoration of our whole nation, Muhammadiyah's goals are far from realized. This country has a Muslim majority, but corruption has become rampant in all sectors of life, from our city centers to remote villages. The lines have blended to such a degree that it would be difficult for us to clearly distinguish between corruptors and recognized leaders, between traitors and heroes. From this perspective, Muhammadiyah's prophetic mission will be harder and harder in the future. There is still a long way to go before restoring the moral life of our people, especially the elite. We are facing serious moral problems.

The real problem of Indonesia since its declaration of independence in 1945, in my view, has been the problem of clean and effective leadership. Unfortunately, for the most part, the Muhammadiyah has not been able to provide the nation with these types of leaders yet. Perhaps the Muhammadiyah has, in fact, from the beginning, not been equipped with the means to give birth to such leaders. But we must note that Indonesia is not alone here. Almost all Muslim nations are facing the same acute moral problems. Translating Islamic moral ideals into the concrete realities of social life remain problematic for the entire Muslim world. The work of Muhammadiyah in this direction will be meaningless unless all sectors of society are ready to share this prophetic mission deliberately and seriously. A nationalism that is not imbued with clear moral vision will no doubt bring a nation into bankruptcy, total or partial.

Imam Feisal: We have spoken in our meetings, and Dr. Mahmood shared in his interview with us, the responsibility of the community to choose a leader and then give him their *bay`ah*, which in the present day is achieved through elections. It is interesting that in Indonesia the people's right to elect their leaders was immediately supported upon independence. What caused Indonesian Muslims to naturally adopt the democratic model?

Dr. Maarif: Indonesian Muslims have, from the very beginning, accepted and defended the political democratic system based on their genuine interpretation and understanding of Islamic teachings. According to Mohammad Hatta, Indonesia's first vice president (1945–1956), there are three sources of democracy in Indonesia: the collectivism upon which Indonesian society is based; Western ideas such as socialism and humanism; and the Islamic teachings on Truth, God's justice, and His injunctions to uphold a universal brotherhood. Combined together in harmony, for *Hatta*, these interdependent ingredients allowed democracy in Indonesia to survive, through ups and downs of contemporary Indonesian history. In fact, in Indonesia, these phenomena remain unchanged even until today.

Imam Feisal: Can you speak more about the Islamic roots of Indonesian democracy?

Dr. Maarif: To understand the Islamic roots of democracy, we should recall that the founder of the Muhammadiyah, Ahmad Dahlan (1868–1923), was never trained in any Western educational system. In fact, Dahlan probably gained the inspiration for the idea of the majority's right after he consulted the Qur'anic doctrine of *shura* (mutual consultation). *Shura* is no doubt compatible with the idea of modern democracy, particularly in dealing with the equal rights of people to actively participate in the decision-making process. This point alone would be more than sufficient to indicate that the practices of democracy in reality have been deep-rooted in Indonesian Islam's political culture.

It has to be made clear that the very nature of Indonesian Islam is democratic, peaceful, and hates authoritarianism. The idea of democracy was not only taken over from Western Europe during the colonial era, but as mentioned before, the Qur'anic injunction of *shura* also played a considerable role in assuring support for democracy among Indonesian Muslims. Because of this Qur'anic justification, the Indonesian Muslims since the early decades of the twentieth century have had no hesitation accepting democracy.

The main streams of Indonesian Islam have shown a welcoming attitude towards these aspects of modern civilization on the condition that they do not conflict with the doctrine of the oneness of God and His intrinsic attributes, such as His compassion, His grace, His eternity, His justice, and His forgiveness. Just as important is the concept that humanity is one. These must be maintained and defended at all costs.

Imam Feisal: And in your opinion, is this the Muhammadiyah's role? How does an organization like the Muhammadiyah affect politics?

Dr. Maarif: Though the Muhammadiyah never became a political party, it indirectly influenced the atmosphere of Indonesian politics greatly. Its concentration on education and social welfare contributed significantly to Indonesian nationalism. For the Muhammadiyah, nationalism is empty if the people remain illiterate, poor, and helpless. Illiteracy, poverty, and helplessness were and still are the true enemy of Islam. The founder of this movement, Ahmad Dahlan, was fully aware of the vital role education plays in the process of enlightening the mind and the heart of the people, from the elite to the ordinary. Because of his radical and revolutionary interpretation of Islam, Dahlan was accused by the conservative `ulama of being dangerous. Some even tried to stop his movement. But Dahlan was firm enough in his faith and conviction that Islam, if its followers wanted to seize the future, should show itself as a moral force that can positively direct the course of social change. Otherwise, Islam was no more than a void ritual and ceremony, a historical remnant of bygone centuries. Dahlan was therefore a true originator in changing the mental backwardness of Indonesian Muslims by educating them with authentic Islamic teachings as taught in the Qur'an.

Dahlan was a true `alim and reformer. He understood that the message of Islam should be brought down to earth. It should be used to deal with and solve problems facing humanity. At that time, this understanding of Islam was almost totally alien to the majority of the `ulama in the Dutch East Indies. Thus, a clash between Dahlan and his foes inevitably occurred. Fortunately, the clash was essentially intellectual in nature, not physical. After 1925, two years after Dahlan's death, the Muhammadiyah's influence had grown out from its roots in Jogjakarta, becoming national in character. Gradually and surely, many of the open-minded `ulama and public figures, all from various ethnic groups, joined to solidify this movement.

Imam Feisal: What were some of the key Islamic teachings that the Muhammadiyah has attempted to share with Indonesian society? What values did it consider essential for the nation as a whole?

Dr. Maarif: The Muhammadiyah focused specifically on the issues of human brotherhood, pluralism, democracy, tolerance, and equality. In the context of our discussion, by pluralism I mean the acceptance of many groups in society or many schools of thought in an intellectual or cultural discipline. If this definition is extended, one must accept the reality of the existence of many different religions, philosophies, ideologies, nations, tribes, ethnicities, and cultural backgrounds as hard facts of history. These differences, according to the Qur'an, are not to divide but to enrich our human vision and understanding of reality. "O mankind! Behold, We have created you from a male and a female, and made you into nations and tribes, so that you might come to know one another."[15] The requirement of knowing one another is both the religious and cultural foundation behind building up a universal human brotherhood and pluralism. This cultural building can only be solid and effective if we are ready to accept the reality of differences with tolerance.

Then comes the concept of equality among men. Without accepting the principle of the equal status of mankind there will be no justice and sincere brotherhood on this planet. In my understanding of the Qur'an, the spirit of brotherhood should not be confined just between believers of different faiths, but it is also possible to create it between believers and non-believers, even atheists, provided no one has a hidden agenda to eliminate and destroy the other. The Qur'an is firm in the defense of religious freedom: "For, if God had not enabled people to defend themselves against one another, all monasteries, churches, synagogues, and mosques – in [all of] which God's name is abundantly extolled – would surely have been destroyed."[16] In this verse, the Qur'an has made it clear that the mention of God's name is not only found in mosques but also in monasteries, churches, and synagogues. But, of course, we must also admit the fact that in and under certain circumstances, the Qur'an is more tolerant than those Muslims who claim to be the only representatives of religion and truth. This is where the culture of intolerance comes from.

> **Imam Feisal:** Speaking of this intolerance, how, as a religious leader with great sway in politics and society, would you respond to those in the world today who claim to be the true representatives of religion and the holders of the true structure of Islamic government?
>
> **Dr. Maarif:** Only those who are simple-minded will come to the view that Islam as a political force should manifest in only one way all over the world. This simplistic conclusion is not only dangerous but is totally unfounded sociologically. Indonesia's neighbor, Malaysia, is a Muslim nation too. It has practiced democracy for decades in a way that, in many ways, is different from other

countries. Like Islam, democracy should not be monolithic either. To impose democracy uniformly goes against the very spirit of democracy. This will not work.

Imam Feisal: Your point highlights that democracy must also be contextualized. It has to take on the peculiarities of a culture, and in this regard, establishing a democracy in any country is both experimental and is a process. How has this process played out in Indonesia, and to what degree has it been successful?

Dr. Maarif: The path to actualizing the universal values of a strong and healthy democracy has met serious obstacles in Indonesia. In other words, it has not been easy for this nation to develop a political elite that is democratic both in theory and practice. In most cases, they are only democratic in theory, whereas in practice their daily behavior has no connection with the spirit of democracy. This is one of the obstacles facing the building up of democracy in Indonesia, although the belief in it remains strong and never dies out.

The democratic impulse is so strong in Indonesian Islam that, under Burhanuddin Harahap's government, the first general elections were held in September and December of 1955, only ten years after the declaration of independence. In fact, originally, the elections were planned six months after independence, but the Dutch, aided by British troops, launched brutal attacks on the new-born state in order to continue their colonial system after the defeat of Japan in August 1945. These attacks were what prevented Indonesia from having elections right after their declaration of independence, as was required by its constitution.

The real and dangerous enemies of democracy in Indonesia in the present era are not the people's lack of belief in the system, but corrupt, irresponsible politicians, and amoral conglomerates whose primary concern is not the welfare of the nation, but their own selfish and hedonistic interests.

Imam Feisal: At the same time, there are some that reject democracy on the grounds that it comes from the West. How do you respond to such attacks?

Dr. Maarif: When we discuss the idea of democracy, heated debates and controversies arise among contemporary Muslims. The fundamentalist groups have totally rejected democracy on the basis that democracy is a man-made political system coming from the West. These groups forget the Qur'anic verse that the "East and West belong to God."[17] A Muslim has freedom to take wisdom from any part of the world, even from those who are hostile against him, for as it says in the *Hadith*, knowledge (*al-'ilm*) is a lost inheritance of the Muslim, when a Muslim finds it, it is his and he should take it. With all of its defects and weaknesses, in my view, democracy is much better than all forms of dynastic and authoritarian political systems that still prevail in many Muslim countries. At least in democracy, all citizens have an equal right to participate in the decision-making process, and men and women are guaranteed enough freedom and space for self-expression.

Though Islamic civilization in the present era lags behind Western technological and materialistic progress, that core – its inner dynamic or élan vital – never dies out. Almost all Muslims believe that they indeed have the future, of course, on the condition that they are ready to correct their past mistakes. This strong faith in God's mercy and justice has prevented them from committing intellectual suicide by giving in to nihilism.

> **Imam Feisal:** You very beautifully point out that, regardless of the origin of the East/West dichotomy, the whole earth ultimately belongs to God. Wherever we see some good, as Muslims, we should accept and encourage it – as God continues in the verse you just quoted, "wherever you turn, there is the face of God."[18] Is this the general attitude that Muslims should have towards the modern world in general?
>
> **Dr. Maarif:** Yes. We must remember that Islamic civilization borrowed liberally from its neighbors throughout its history. As an open religion, Islam was historically quite creative in selectively adopting ideas and aspirations from the Greek, Roman, and Persian legacies and of their civilizations. This interactive process lasted for nearly five centuries. Thus, as I said before, for a thinking Muslim, whether any idea and aspiration is Eastern or Western does not matter. All knowledge, provided it does not undermine faith in the Oneness of God and the unity of humanity, should be embraced by him.

I can assure you that Islam can accept the idea of modernity as long as it does not lead humanity to the brink of nihilism, that is, a framework without the existence of God. The difficulty many Muslims face in accepting the idea of modernity is due to the fact that modernity as developed in the West has, to a great extent, been deeply blurred with a nihilism in which the notion of God is removed from human life, or, in Heidegger's words, "there is nothing left" of Being as such. Muhsin Mahdi, the Iraqi-American scholar, wrote: "Modernity began as, and its main characteristic continues to be, an attempt to dispense with transcendence, whether philosophically or religiously conceived. Its aim is to make man feel at home in this world."[19]

The Indonesian Muslim intellectuals who were educated in Western centers of learning, whether domestic or abroad, were well aware of the danger of this nihilistic modernity. But they have, for sure, no objection to the idea of modernity itself, provided a Transcendent God remains intact in the collective and individual lives of human beings.

Imam Feisal: Could you explain further what you mean by the nihilism of the modern world?

Dr. Maarif: From a nihilistic perspective, what we know as God's moral command becomes irrelevant. On the surface of the American currency there is the phrase "In God we trust," but does that trust in God become apparent in the power play of politics? Is God really in the picture in any meaningful way? I am afraid that this nihilism has become more decisive and dominant in the on-the-ground reality.

In the face of such a reality that publicly denies the presence of God in society, what role can religions play? Not much. This isn't helped by the fact that religions are so preoccupied with complex and unending internal problems that lead to schisms and sectarianism. Dealing with these internal burdens, religious people hardly have time to think creatively, let alone offer fresh ideas to humanity. The stamina and energy of religions has been exhausted for centuries. This is a very serious challenge that we have been facing.

If these problems continue, the role of religions as a lofty source of ethics, morality, and guidance will be in acute trouble. To prevent this, religious leaders and elites need to have the courage to speak out on the principles of universal truth shared by all.

Frankly, if we approach the Qur'an sincerely and comprehensively, we'll find that modern humanistic values are compatible with the values of Islam. But Islam also has more to offer by extending all those values towards a transcendent and spiritual orientation. Modern civilization badly needs an ontological anchor to save itself. Islam and other faith systems, if correctly and authentically understood, have the richness to meet the spiritual thirst of mankind. As the Qur'an states, the Prophet Muhammad was sent "as a grace towards all mankind," (*rahmatan lil-`alamin*).[20] This underscores the fact that the Qur'an always offers clear guidance for peaceful coexistence with those who respect and honor one another, regardless of their background.

> **Imam Feisal:** So in a way, what you are saying is that religions need to step up to the plate because the world needs religion deeply as an active grace and compassionate mercy towards all of mankind. And we can't succeed unless we quiet our internal schisms. Only then can the universal and fundamental values of our tradition be deployed to address the issues facing society.
>
> **Dr. Maarif:** Yes, because it is religion and spirituality alone that can counter the materialistic and nihilistic trends of modern society.

Eric Fromm rightly describes the prevailing philosophy in global society at present, where man is *Homo consumens*. This means that to be human is "to have more and to use more." In this consuming society, man, "as a cog in the production machine, becomes a thing, and ceases to be human."[21] In the modern era, the greed of *homo consumens* is seen everywhere, in both the West and the East. This excessive greed of man has first and foremost hurt the natural world significantly. And there is no society that can escape its imperialistic yoke. But why do religions, Islam included, keep silent, about the damage this greed causes? How and when will religious people rise up to prevent the collective suicide of mankind? Not only are we not tackling the problem head on, but even worse than that, religions in the modern era seem, to a very great extent, to have become a part of the problem. The question then is: can religions still offer principles for a new global ethics that curbs injustice and greed in order to improve the conditions on this planet for all of us? Here lies the existential challenge faced by all religions in our era.

I fully and sincerely believe that religion is a perennial need of mankind. I can't imagine a world, for instance, void of the existence of the Transcendental Supreme Being who created and controls it. Of course, this is not in the realm of "scientific probability," but is rather in the realm of metaphysics. His existence is, you may say, "a metaphysical necessity," as the Catholic philosopher, Étienne Gilson, correctly put it.[22]

> **Imam Feisal:** But not everyone sees reality in this way, as there are many who do not even believe in God. This brings up the issue of

religious freedom, which is also an essential component of both democracy and the Islamic values that you have enumerated. Of course we want to offer the wisdom in our tradition to society at large, but we cannot force it upon others due to fundamental tenets of our faith.

Dr. Maarif: This is very true. For a believer, the creation of the universe without the Creator is absurd and unreasonable. But, on the contrary, for a non-believer or an atheist, belief in God, the Creator, the Unseen, is ridiculous, because it can't be confirmed or proven scientifically. In the Qur'an, the term *kafir* means a rejecter, an unbeliever, or an atheist, depending on its context. I think the existence of these two categories (or three—if we add agnostics to our discussion) of mankind is also a perennial problem that can't satisfactorily be resolved until the end of the world. From this perspective, the Qur'an fully admits the rights of non-believers/ atheists to coexist peacefully as human beings with believers/ theists. The following verse clearly confirms our argument: "And had your Lord willed, those on earth would have believed, all of them together. So will you then think that you could compel people to become believers?"[23] In another brief but condensed phrase, the Qur'an says: "There shall be no coercion in matters of faith."[24] For centuries, throughout Islamic history, Muslim rulers, just or unjust, took the spirit of these verses into effect by not forcing others to follow the faith of Islam. Why? Because from a Muslim perspective, anyone who coerces others to accept his/her religion has lost confidence in *their* own faith. The acceptance of faith through compulsion is no doubt contradictory to the principle of man's free will and free choice, both of which have been ordained by God.

Imam Feisal: Belief through coercion is not true belief, because as you mention it is not a result of the individual's free will. This relates to the concept that our scholars brought up in our meetings, that God has created this life as a test – or *'ibtila'*. In order to use our free will to choose the right path we must have the freedom to also choose the wrong. This is one of the reasons that an Islamic government must champion and uphold freedoms within society.

But nonetheless, as you have shared, there are clear consequences for society when God is removed from the picture *en masse* – either through disbelief or other trends in society.

Dr. Maarif: Yes: from the Qur'anic point of view, once man loses God, he will automatically lose his own self. We read the translation: "And be not like those who forget God, and whom He has therefore caused to forget their own selves. It is they who are defiantly disobedient."[25] In one sense, this verse highlights that we can become our true and highest selves only in our search after God, and it follows that society as well can reach its highest potential only in its pursuit of the divine. But this verse also indicates that we have the capacity and freedom both to remember God *and* to be disobedient.

It is this free will, and therefore the capacity for disobedience, that actually marks the fundamental difference between man and nature, since nature has no free will and no free choice but to obey God's command. "Hence what is natural command in nature becomes moral command in man," writes Fazlur Rahman.[26] The role of religions, from this angle, is to advise man to follow God's moral command for his own interest and goodness in life.

Imam Feisal: And as you have stressed, this role of religion can only really be played out through the acts of individuals, whose imperative it is to live just and virtuous lives, always striving to increase our own humility and kindness rather than judge the virtue or piety of any other. When the beautiful philosophies and guidance in our faith are translated into day to day realities between individuals, the light of God's Message will illumine our societies. This is the inner core of Islam: that personal piety, performed only before God.

Dr. Maarif: Exactly. Religion as the source of the highest principles of humanity can only last as long as they are functional in human life concretely. Otherwise, religions will be left as empty rituals and ceremonies, void of their perennial significance and meaning. We do not want this to happen, and thus, we must continue to exert ourselves.

But while this concrete manifestation of our principles begins with the daily interactions between people, it must ultimately manifest on a wider scale – in our governments and nations. At this level, it is imperative that we be devoted to justice, for only justice can save humanity from the destruction of civilization.

That is why the major trends of Indonesian Islam are for democracy and an anti-authoritarian political system. If the present democracy in Indonesia is successful in combating its three powerful enemies, namely corruption, connection, and nepotism, it would be a great example for other Muslim countries to follow in the future.

Imam Feisal: And you have certainly exerted yourself in ensuring that these Islamic – and democratic – principles are advanced in Indonesian society through the Muhammadiyah. Thank you, Dr. Maarif, for your insights and for your work.

Legitimacy and competency in the Islamic State (Mohammad Javad Larijani)

Imam Feisal: Dr. Larijani, based on your personal experience of nation-building in Iran, I would like to discuss in our interview today two interrelated themes that you have introduced within the discussions of our SIP scholars, namely, Islamic rationality and then how that rationality defines the legitimacy of a government. First, could you explain what you mean by an Islamic sphere of rationality?

Dr. Larijani: It basically means the way we make decisions: the reasons, rationale or worldview behind our actions. States are created from and by spheres of rationality. An Islamic state – in the modern sense of a nation-state – is a relatively new experiment, and the specific *structures* that could define it are still being developed. When I speak about an Islamic state, I mean a polity constructed from an Islamic sphere of rationality. Before we can develop an Islamic state, we need to define what this rationality is. Only then will we see what kinds of structures it produces.

The word for "rationale or rationality" in Arabic is `aqlaniyyah; a sphere of rationality that forms the total basis upon which a person acts. For Muslims, this basis must be derived from Islam – either the Qur'an, the *Hadith*, or pillars of deduction like analogy (*qiyas*) and juristic preference (*istihsan*). It also includes ethics, philosophy, and numerous other sciences that spring up from the Qur'an and *Hadith*. These sciences contribute to creating a sphere of Islamic rationale or rationality that guides our actions.

The legacy of Mua'wiya's ascension to the Caliphate was to eradicate the Islamic sphere of rationality in regards to governance. Henceforth, the Caliphate became a hereditary kingship, inherited from Roman and Persian models.

Our task today is to bring this Islamic sphere of rationality back. But as for how modern Islamic social structures will look, I don't think we can know. We have to set the correct conditions and let the structures develop on their own. You see, from the 1960s and onwards, a group of social and political thinkers, chief among them Jürgen Habermas, decided to take an evolutionary approach to government. In this approach, we don't write the ends. Rather, we write the correct context and conditions. From there, we will discover what the ends are without stating them beforehand.

> **Imam Feisal:** Are you suggesting that if we establish the "Islamic context and conditions" the Islamic ends will automatically be realized?
>
> **Dr. Larijani:** In a way, yes. It is more important to establish the Islamic conditions of a government, based on this sphere of rationality, than to philosophize about grandiose goals. Some of the worst political structures in the world have a nice list of ends. Whether they deliver or even if they are capable of delivering these ends is an entirely different issue. Even liberal democracies haven't met most of their ends.
>
> **Imam Feisal:** But if we want to orient our actions, don't we need some general objectives? Without an intention or a goal, how do we frame our actions?
>
> **Dr. Larijani:** Of course, we can speak generally about objectives, and the Islamic sphere of rationality provides these. But governments must be very realistic, transparent and practical when it comes to developing plans to reach those objectives – and this is what I mean by writing the conditions. For example, the *Maqasid* provide clear objectives for governance, but governments cannot simply champion them as political slogans without creating the Islamic context and conditions necessary in order to achieve them. Leaders must, as we have done in this project, concretely lay out the steps toward reaching these goals, measure their success, and then readjust their approach based on that evaluation.

However, I would like to point out that, based on the teachings of the Shi'i Imams, the ultimate goal of the *Maqasid,* and really any of our actions, is to reach human happiness, *sa'adah.* And the happiness of a people is the ultimate test of the health of a society. This isn't a temporary happiness, but rather refers to a lasting felicity, similar to what the Greek philosophers called *eudaimonia*. The Greek understanding of politics also included an emphasis on ethics, which was interpreted as the way people should behave in their private lives and then how they should participate in their public life – in other words, the government. Within the Islamic sphere of rationality, one attains happiness by acquiring wisdom, *hikmah*, and performing good deeds, *al-amal al-salih*. But in order to facilitate an individual's pursuit of happiness, we need to create a social order that protects and assists us in this endeavor.

This *sa'adah*, this lasting happiness, is really the desired objective and state of anyone who realizes the furthest limits of their potential. It isn't just happiness. A more accurate translation might be human flourishing. The greatest purpose of a state, according to this vision, is to encourage the actualization of human potential or, in other words, to encourage human flourishing.

Imam Feisal: This reminds me of the American Declaration of Independence, which asserts that God the Creator endowed Man with certain inalienable rights, among which are life, liberty, and *the pursuit of happiness*. Government is instituted by men to ensure these rights, and specifically, this right to pursue happiness. Liberal democracies certainly strive to provide security, freedom, and assistance, in large part to facilitate their citizens' happiness.

Dr. Larijani: Government legitimacy rests on its ability to bring happiness to the people, as it says in the US Declaration of Independence. However, there is a key difference at the level of vision between Islamic rationality and the rationality of liberal democracy. The difference between an Islamic State and a liberal democratic system is in *how* happiness is defined and realized.

Western states are based on liberal secular rationality. The basic conditions of this society are freedom of speech, democratic means to power, and an equal chance for everyone to gain that power. What we see in the world today is the outcome of an evolutionary process based on ideas and principles established during and after the Enlightenment. Happiness is left to individual taste, and in this context, the state shouldn't subscribe to any specific notion of happiness. Its role in facilitating happiness is to provide security and guarantee individuals the greatest freedom possible to define and work towards their own ideas of happiness. This emphasis on freedom is the result of there being no defined or pre-identified notion of happiness.

An Islamic state is different. It is built on a foundation of Islamic rationality, which means that happiness is already understood as wisdom and good deeds. Liberal democracies leave the meaning of happiness to the individual.

Imam Feisal: I would argue that a government's ability to deliver the *Maqasid* would be constitutive of, and therefore defines, a people's happiness: thus when people enjoy a healthy and secure life, with their dignity protected, enjoy material well-being, a good family life, are able to freely practice their religious beliefs and pursue their intellectual pursuits, they are happy. And this is, in my mind, an Islamic definition of human happiness that can work for all people, Muslims and non-Muslims. And given our history of adopting what works from other traditions, why should Muslims not adopt civil structures that originate from another sphere of rationality? Many of our mechanisms of power come from Western liberalism after all.

Dr. Larijani: Someone once came up to me in Istanbul and said, "The Islamic revolution hasn't brought anything new. Your structures of power, the way power is separated, and the institutions where power is vested are all based on Western models." There is a point to this, but we aren't operating out of thin air. We should make use of these models and see how they would evolve within the framework of an Islamic sphere of rationality. When we were writing the Iranian constitution we put the American and French constitutions in front of us, but we worked through our own parameters. In our opinion, they were lacking in regards to the issue of legitimacy, so we inserted the concept of *wilayat al-faqih*. But they did a fantastic job in regards to consent. Based on their precedent, we wrote in our constitution that every decision must be based on consent via the mechanism of voting.

Imam Feisal: Tun Abdul Hamid made a good point in regards to this very issue. By defining Islamic law as "any law that is not un-Islamic," we can extend this formula and declare that anything that is not against Islam is de facto "Islamic." I understand this to be the basis of what you are saying, namely, that the approach of an Islamic rationality is to accept the realities of the world and only filter out the specific elements that go against it. Otherwise, everything is – Islamically speaking – acceptable by default. We need to keep our understanding of the legal tradition open to interpretation so as to address the new issues that face us today.

To summarize briefly, you're saying that the *raison d'être* of the Islamic state is to facilitate its citizens' happiness. The definition of this happiness, as well as the conditions we set in order to achieve it, are found in what you call the Islamic sphere of rationality. We can adopt structures or laws developed from within another sphere of rationality as long as they are not inconsistent with or contravene an Islamic rationality. However, is it possible that we would disregard any of our own traditional laws, for example certain punishments, if we felt that they no longer served the purposes of this rationality in the present day context?

Dr. Larijani: Yes, and to do this we need to re-engage the laws of the Shariah *in regards to their purposes*. This is where a *Maqasid*-based approach is particularly useful – that is, where we look into the objectives, or *maqasid*, of the Islamic penal code. Let's consider the penalty of cutting off the hand of someone who steals. There are people who steal billions of dollars and go unpunished; justice is not served if we cut off the hand of someone who steals from a grocery store. The philosophy and objective (*maqsad*) behind these punishments is deterrence, not vengeance. The Qur'an always insists that forgiveness is greater. Now if we look at stoning for example; stoning a couple in the middle of Tehran hardly deters people from committing adultery. In fact, it generates sympathy for them. If these laws are having the opposite effect, we should suspend or change these laws. Here we need to take into consideration the objective of the law, the effect(s) of implementing such a law upon society in light of its intent, and the *maslahah*, the people's best interests.

We need to admit that the concepts we use have changed over time. In fact, the very nature of life has changed. Some think that to establish an Islamic state we need to regress a few centuries. Then we can move forward. I don't agree. We need to start with where we are now. If this includes using all of the foreign institutions and concepts at our disposal, so be it. We must recognize and not reject the realities of human life.

Imam Feisal: This reminds me of Hamieh's point that we need to read the realities of our situation in concert with the realities found within the Qur'an. It is through the intellect, a God-given faculty, that we are able to read these two realities concurrently and thereby discover guidance specific to our current situation.

Dr. Larijani: Indeed, all laws have a context, and when legislating we need to be sensitive to that context. When reading these two realities together – our own situation and the guidance within our tradition – we must recognize that the Shariah isn't a codified system of law that can simply be applied without a process. There have always been processes to develop laws within Shariah in relation to their contemporary context, and the situation is no different at present. Today Shariah is a source to which we refer, but legislation is a parliamentary process that is done concurrently with a state's development. Judges can only rule based on laws we develop in parliament, which is why we need to rely on our intellect more as we develop laws in this new context.

In fact, in Shi'i jurisprudence the intellect is the first source of law. We need it even to understand the legal tradition. The Qur'an itself constantly urges us to use our intellect in understanding our world. It is up to us to interpret the guidance of the Qur'an in respect to our situation.

This is of prime importance because if context is neglected and the particulars of a specific situation are ignored, we fall into a Taliban-like approach to Islam, an approach that detaches us from the present by applying a rationality that neither fits our time or place nor embraces human reality.

Imam Feisal: That's a great argument Dr. Larijani as to why we must protect and further the *maqsad* of `*aql*, or intellect/mind, within our societies so that the intellectual capacities and knowledge of our tradition are at a level where we are not susceptible to these extremist approaches to our religion that do not relate to the needs of our present situation.

Dr. Larijani: Exactly. And in order to behave according to the specific situation, we need a high degree of political freedom. Part of the *maqsad* of `*aql* is protecting the freedom of expression – and political freedoms in particular. It isn't absolute freedom, because even in the West there are certain sensitive subjects that are never challenged. But if we want to bring about new understandings of Islam, we need political and intellectual or academic freedom. Otherwise, the moment someone says something new, people will call him a *kafir*. That kind of attitude won't get us anywhere.

This is why there must be a constant reorientation towards the sources of the tradition and the sphere of rationality they create. Through that, we regulate and modify our actions for present and real situations, giving us the opportunity to identify ourselves as Muslims of our time, by which I mean we create the circumstances that facilitate the emergence of the *modern* Muslim man and woman, the formation of *modern* Islamic institutions, and the development of *modern* Islamic governance. Islamic rationality gives us these tools.

Imam Feisal: As we are forming these modern Islamic institutions and governments, could that rationality lead us toward forming what the West terms democratic systems of government?

Dr. Larijani: There is a foundation for democracy within the Islamic rationality, and this takes us to the issue of legitimacy. Any government's legitimacy stems from two pillars: first, the people's consent and second, its qualifications to rule; these two pillars undergird the concept of a legitimate "Islamic state." The people's happiness and the functions of a legitimate state are inextricably linked in this regard. This gives us a concept of democracy within Islamic rationality, as the people must give their consent, or *bay'ah,* to the ruler. Traditionally, the *bay'ah* was an oath the people gave by swearing their allegiance and obedience to the ruler. In contemporary society, giving consent is expressed through voting and the broader electoral process, and is more fully developed by harnessing advanced technology for obtaining this consent and confirming the transparency of the vote or *bay`ah.*

Imam Feisal: Let us turn to this issue of legitimacy. Professor Ghazi, in his paper, defined a government's legitimacy also by two things: the consent of the people, and the supremacy of the Shariah. For him, the supremacy of the Shariah is upheld through two means: the independence of the judiciary and when the government fulfils the *Maqasid al-shari`ah,* which from the Islamic sphere of rationality would equate to facilitating human flourishing and the well-being of the citizens.

Before the people give their consent, you said the candidate must have certain prerequisites. These qualifications are the other "pillar" of legitimacy. How do we determine a leader's qualification?

Dr. Larijani: The ruling structure – the personnel or body of government officials – is considered qualified only if it has strong knowledge of this concept of *sa `adah* that we discussed. This is, as we discussed, a basic difference between an Islamic state and a liberal secular democratic state. A ruler must have knowledge of Islam, of the Shariah, including the *Maqasid al-shari`ah*, and of ways to approach new issues based on Islamic rationality. Additionally, he should have basic knowledge of the relevant laws in the areas of providing security and facilitating happiness. This includes those laws he cannot trespass. He must know those parts of the Shariah that pertain to these situations.

Imam Feisal: Sounds similar to Dr. Ghazi's position of upholding the supremacy of the Shariah.

Dr. Larijani: Yes, but we have to be clear that we are not simply upholding the Shariah in the sense of applying laws or *ahkam* without any contemporary *ijtihad*. We can uphold the supremacy of the Shariah by, as we are doing in this project, using the *Maqasid* as a guide for this *ijtihad* and for legislation in general.

Imam Feisal: Could you give us an example to help our readers understand this point?

Dr. Larijani: Phone tapping is an interesting example. The Qur'an explicitly forbids the believer from spying,[27] and further, part of the *maqsad* of honor is protecting an individual's privacy. Yet part of the *maqsad* of life is national security, so we cannot simply apply this Qur'anic injunction against spying without some *ijtihad*. How far is a government allowed to listen in and record the private conversations of individual citizens, even when there's a justifiable, perhaps national security related, cause for doing so? Ideally, a complete set of state-sponsored laws should fully define the limits of this *tajassus*, or spying, in a way that does not violate the sanctity of an individual's private life. However, even if these laws are unclear, a ruler is still not absolved of his responsibilities in an Islamic sense or from a Shariah perspective.

For this reason, he should be capable of figuring out the limits of spying – as well as on other questions – through the practice of *ijtihad*. This is why it is important for a ruler to be well versed in the Shariah, or even to be a *mujtahid* himself.

Imam Feisal: Or at least have a mechanism to ensure that Islamic ethical commandments are factored in the making of laws. In Malaysia, for example, parliament has a Shariah committee that oversees all legislation to ensure that no law contravenes Shariah for this very reason. So it is not necessary that the ruler must be a *mujtahid;* this is a lofty ideal that may not be very practical. How does this play out in Iran?

Dr. Larijani: It's true that not everyone who holds office will be trained in Islamic law. In Iran, for instance, there's a system of checks and balances that incorporates *mujtahids* at various levels. At the highest level, we have the appointment of an ayatollah who's a *mujtahid* and who controls the Iranian president if he or she acts incorrectly. We also have a guardian council which checks parliamentary legislation, the members of which must craft laws that address actual issues without leaving the limits and boundaries of Islam. In Iran, those in the parliament and the Council of Guardians are qualified to do just that. They determine whether a law contravenes either the Iranian Constitution or Islamic Shariah. So the issues of qualifications don't only apply to the ruling head of state, but also to the legislative, judicial, and executive bodies.

Imam Feisal: In speaking of qualifications, some within the Sunni tradition believe that the ruler's legitimacy is primarily measured by his ability to manage the people's affairs well. According to the Shi`a tradition, how would you view a government that gains authority without complete legitimacy but is able to achieve success on the ground? In other words, is it better to have a legitimate government with limited achievements, or an illegitimate government with many achievements?

Dr. Larijani: We cannot blindly count a ruler's achievements irrespective of whether his rule was achieved through legitimate means or whether he has ruled justly. Such an achievement-based evaluation of rulers causes us to ignore the fundamental issues of legitimacy and the method of governance.

To a degree, this is a difference between the Shi`a and Sunnis. Eventually in the Sunni tradition, government wasn't considered a part of the Shariah. It was more an issue of technical or technocratic skill. Some scholars believed that as long as a person is doing their job, it doesn't matter how that person came to power. Some even defined the four ways of gaining power: consent (*bay'ah*), consensus (*ijma`*), succession, or the sword. The Shi`a would disagree. A religion which prescribes even the importance of brushing one's teeth and having a pleasant breath wouldn't remain silent about governance. And it is worth noting that notable Sunni scholars agreed with this position. In fact, Abu Hanifa, *rahimahullah*, was martyred for standing up to an illegitimate caliph.

So to answer your question, following an illegitimate ruler who employs dubious methods of governance for the sake of on-the-ground achievements is unacceptable, even in the short term. Compare Imam 'Ali ibn

Abi Talib and Mu'awiyah ibn Abi Sufyan.[28] Imam Ali's rule was more successful because he was legitimate, competent, and his methods of governance were just. Even if he didn't attain all the objectives of his rule and was eventually assassinated in Kufa, he governed more justly than Mu'awiyah, who imprisoned and killed many people and squandered the money of the *Bayt al-Mal* (the royal treasury). In comparing Imam Ali with Mu'awiyah, the great fourteenth century scholar, Ibn Khaldun, emphasized Mu'awiyah's many achievements in developing parts of the Islamic world. He sometimes noted that he governed better than Imam Ali because of these achievements, disregarding completely the issue of legitimacy and their vastly different methods of governance.

Achievements cannot be the sole standard for measuring a ruler's success, principally because the success of his efforts is often beyond his power, as such success is ultimately influenced by the domestic and global context. But if the ruler is legitimate and governs with justice according to the principles of the Shariah, this best sets up the government for success – but success is granted by God alone. Thus *the success of a ruler is determined more by the way he rules than the extent to which his objectives are achieved.*

> **Imam Feisal**: Many would still say that governments should be measured by their achievements or what they deliver in terms of political goods or outputs, regardless of how they do so, and arguably must be a part of determining legitimacy.
>
> **Dr. Larijani**: The true nature of a state is quickly rendered transparent when we inquire into its legitimacy, which is important for two reasons:

First, the justice that can be delivered from a state which is founded on a fundamental injustice will always be adulterated.

Second, people need a legitimate government in order to feel that they have a stake in their society. When they feel involved "*the*" government becomes "*our*" government, a government of the people, by the people, and for the people. An illegitimate ruler who just keeps his people fed and comfortable isn't doing them a favor. Their livelihood is dependent on him. If he is gone, they will fall apart. A good legitimate government is by the people, and through the people develops a more mature and developed governance; and survives the death of individuals.

However, despite the prime importance of legitimacy, this doesn't at all mean ignoring competency. Clearly, a government may be legitimate but also incompetent and incapable of delivering on its promised duties.

Ultimately a government must be both legitimate and competent, and legitimacy will even help to ensure competency because it rests on the qualifications of the ruler and the will of the people. I simply want to emphasize that a government cannot be measured by outcomes or achievements *alone*.

> **Imam Feisal:** Clearly legitimacy and competency are both necessary and each alone is insufficient. If a head of state or members of the legislative body lack security experience or expertise even before entering office, then they won't be able to provide security when they're in office. Or as you pointed out, if they do not understand the Islamic definition of happiness, then they can't help society achieve it; which in my opinion should be spelled out in the nation's constitution. Considering that both legitimacy and competency are vital for good governance, how would you define or measure competency?
>
> **Dr. Larijani:** Competency deals with the steps a ruler or government should take in order to govern proficiently. The prescription for competency is actually very basic: the ruler must have a realistic picture of where the country lies in the world, a clear and broad vision of where the nation wants to be, a realistic action plan, and then he must utilize the country's natural and human resources efficiently in service of that plan.

The first aspect of a ruler's competency – having a realistic picture of where the country lies in relation to the world – is accomplished by using efficient and knowledge-based methods such as consulting experts. A primary function of the state is to make decisions that it then implements and enforces, so these decisions must be rooted in reality. For a ruler to have a clear and realistic picture of where the country lies, he cannot be egocentric. He must always consider the fallibility of his ideas and be humbled by the knowledge of others. He must rely on the expertise of others.

> **Imam Feisal:** Can you give us a practical example of what you mean here?
>
> **Dr. Larijani:** Yes. Imagine a government full of brilliant rulers who make correct decisions but who are still ignorant of the role of experts. They're still at fault. If a leader surrounds himself with those who simply reaffirm his own opinions, it renders him completely out of touch with the on-the-ground-reality and his people's needs

and desires. This is wrong. Decisions should be based on a realistic picture of the situation in their respective nations, not simply on what they think or wish the situation to be. All of us, and especially rulers, should humbly admit the fallibility of our ideas. We must rely on qualified experts and advisors.

The second aspect of competency is that rulers have a global or broader vision. Rulers lacking such a vision will be bogged down in the day-to-day and the mundane; they will fail.

> **Imam Feisal**: Would you explain what you mean by a "global vision?"
>
> **Dr. Larijani**: Having a global vision means that his big picture agenda is in tune with his citizens' concerns and reality, particularly with respect to security and fostering an environment in which the citizenry can attain happiness. It must not reflect his personal ambitions. If a ruler has an appetite to conquer other nations, he cannot implement that vision as the legitimate vision of the state, nor is it part of his role as head of state. Clearly, a ruler's job is to bring security to the people and foster an environment that leads to the prosperity and happiness of his people. A vision that aligns with these two duties is legitimate. A vision emanating out of personal ambition is not. Thus, this vision should pass through robust checks and balances before it is adopted by the legal mechanisms of the state.

Third, after acquiring a realistic picture of the state's realities and formulating a good vision, the ruler must create a clear action plan for all projects, which will be evaluated and even modified during execution. This is particularly important when we consider the nature of politics itself. Politicians always want their constituents to consider them successful, which means they often prefer to be vague in their goals. In fact, they avoid a clear action plan, and even more importantly, they evade accountability. This is one place where the *Maqasid* system is quite useful. It would provide us with a method to keep rulers and governments accountable toward their people.

Accountability is essential to ensure that the government sufficiently represents the people, but even before governments can be held accountable, its personnel must be carefully chosen. In a *Hadith* of the Prophet, he said to Abu Hurairah: "If trust has been lost, then the Hour of the last day should be imminent. Abu Hurairah then asked: 'How could trust be lost?' The Prophet answered: 'When incompetent people are made in charge of people's affairs.'" The idea behind this *Hadith* gets at the ruler's responsibility to put competent people in charge of the nation's affairs so as to best channel the nation's resources.

And this is related to the fourth aspect of competency: effectively utilizing the material and human resources of the country in service of the government's clear and realistic action plan. A ruler should utilize the resources before him in the wisest and most effective manner. Human resources are the most important resource at his disposal, even before material resources. In Islam, it is absolutely unacceptable for a government to rely primarily on oil, mines, or other material resources while relegating human resources to a secondary position. Unfortunately, this is a chronic issue in the Muslim world today.

> **Imam Feisal**: Please elaborate on this point that contemporary Muslim world governments have failed to utilize the potential of their citizenry.
>
> **Dr. Larijani**: The potential of citizenry is too often ignored because of failing mechanisms still in place. Primarily, nepotism is a major source of mediocrity, and it's a cancer for many governments.

The appointment of ministers, advisors, and other key staff is extremely important because people take direction from and emulate those at the very highest levels of society and government. As a result, those with the best credentials should be appointed to the positions that are best suited for them. The Prophet Muhammad himself recognized this idea. He once exclaimed that he could find no one more pious than Abu Dharr al-Ghafari; yet on another occasion, he cautioned Abu Dharr to never accept any public position because "You cannot rule," meaning that he lacked the requisite technical expertise and qualities to be a leader. This *Hadith* illustrates the Prophet's acumen in identifying the unique capabilities of people. He understood that they must be placed in positions that match their specific skill set. This makes it clear that piety alone is insufficient for ruling or governance, which requires other skills and abilities.

> **Imam Feisal**: Why do governments fail to appoint competent people in key government positions?
>
> **Dr. Larijani**: Well, politicians typically prefer to make appointments based on the candidate's degree of loyalty to them, rather than their competence in their respective fields. Furthermore, highly

competent people are often unaccustomed to simply obeying instructions, which also makes them less attractive to politicians. This short-sightedness can devastate a society. Imam Ali is quoted as saying that *tafdil al-juhal wa taqhir al-afadil* ("preferring ignorant people and marginalizing exceptional people") can destroy governments. This creates a system of mediocrity, which begins at the top and quickly spreads throughout the entire establishment, and in the process corrodes and ultimately destroys society.

Imam Feisal: Great point, Dr. Larijani. You mentioned earlier that the *Maqasid* system would be useful as a methodology in keeping rulers and governments accountable to their people and tests how far a society has come in developing its Islamicity. How do you see the *Maqasid* fitting within this view of governmental competence?

Dr. Larijani: The *Maqasid* are essential to competency. They are how we measure our government. They provide us with benchmarks. This is why we are supporting the *Maqasid* approach of the Shariah Index Project as a first step of measurement and holding governments accountable. We in Iran will welcome it as a means to keep ourselves in check. But we should also take other future steps down the road to also evaluate legitimacy. We need to spark minds and initiate discussions geared at developing Islamic societal and governmental models for the twenty-first century. To do this we need to speak freely and consider all the implications an Islamic sphere of rationality has in regards to the experiment and evolution of an "Islamic state."

Imam Feisal: Thank you, Dr. Larijani, for your insights on the Islamic state, and how the issues of legitimacy and competence pertain to it.

8
Human Rights and Islamic Governance

In the first interview in this chapter, **Dr. Tahir Mahmood** discusses how human rights and good governance were articulated within Islamic legal discourses long before they became standard in the West. He also stresses the need to counter ignorance within the global Muslim community regarding their rights and responsibilities as described within the Qur'an and the *Sunnah*. Thereafter, he discusses different present-day examples of the role that Islam occupies in states with Muslim minorities. Using his native India as an example, he explores the implications of a state that does not recognize any official religion but does allow religious communities to resolve their private affairs according to their own religious law.

In the second interview, **Dr. Recep Şentürk** discusses an authentic Islamic notion of universal rights, based on the inviolability of all by simply being human (or children of Adam: *adamiyyin*). He draws upon lessons learned from the Ottoman Empire's rule over a pluralistic society to provide solutions to the contemporary challenges of Islamic governance. His examples of the *adamiyyah* heritage of the Ottoman Empire represent the synthesis of the Islamic tradition with fully modern conceptions of human rights. He discusses the abolition of the *dhimmi* status, the fact that the first Ottoman parliament contained roughly equal numbers of Muslim and non-Muslim delegates, and the fact that the *Tanzimat* reforms included, what is recognized today, as the first formal declaration of human rights by a state with a Muslim majority. Lamenting the "collective amnesia" among modern Muslims, which has made the advances of the Ottoman Empire nearly forgotten, Senturk asserts that, if these lessons were relearned, they would enhance the human rights status of the citizens in nations with Muslim majorities.

Rights and responsibilities in the Qur'an and Sunnah (Tahir Mahmood)

Imam Feisal: Dr. Tahir, in one of our SIP conferences you shared a quotation from an early twentieth century European lawyer who said that the concepts of human rights and good governance standards that are so central to the modern West were articulated within Islamic legal discourse long before they became standard in the West.

Dr. Mahmood: Yes, the quotation was from Count Leon Ostrorog, who was a legal advisor to the Ottoman government and a professor of Islamic law at the University of London. Though an outsider to our tradition, he recognized that the fundamental principles of human rights and contractual government were enunciated in our sacred texts and embraced by our early societies long before they became Western values. However, the unfortunate reality is that our societies have either forgotten or disregarded this foundation – and now out of ignorance imagine that such principles originate from the West.

Imam Feisal: Some even imagine these principles to be opposed to our tradition – as if the principles of human rights and democracy were imperialist impositions of the West!

Dr. Mahmood: This is why it is so important that we have a firm understanding of the foundational sources of our religion. The evidence and everyday observation of the happenings in the Muslim community lead to a firm conclusion that the law of Islam is being terribly misunderstood in many countries by Muslims and non-Muslims alike for the simple reason that it is being misused, equally terribly, by the Muslims themselves. And the irony is that Muslims misrepresent their law in the sincere belief that what they think they are doing is actually the Islamic imperative or law on the subject. This comes from a deep sense of ignorance.

Imam Feisal: What precisely are we ignorant of?

Dr. Mahmood: Our rights and responsibilities are drawn from the two primary sources of our law: the Qur'an and the Prophet's *Sunnah*. Although these are the foundational texts of our faith, many contemporary Muslim societies have either forgotten or discarded some of their basic principles. To address this issue, it is imperative that we gain a thorough understanding of the rights and responsibilities enumerated in these primary sources of our faith.

The legal verses of the Qur'an do not furnish the comprehensive code of law; the original law of the Qur'an was progressively incorporated into a wider legal fabric by the Prophet and his followers, successors, and the early doctors of Islamic jurisprudence, one after another. But these verses in the Qur'an do constitute the nucleus of our legal system.

Imam Feisal: And what do these sources tell us about our rights and responsibilities in a society purported to be based on Islamic principles?

Dr. Mahmood: Well, first it must be made clear that we are not just talking about rights, but also responsibilities – as there must be reciprocity within the formal relationships of society.

Imam Feisal: This is a very important insight, Dr. Tahir. In fact, it seems to me that responsibilities come first, and rights only come into play when they have been breached. For example, as an employer I know that I have certain responsibilities toward my staff: to care for their health by providing them sick leave and healthcare, to not make them work long hours, to give just salaries, etc. And there are laws in the United States that attempt to ensure that I fulfill these responsibilities. Ideally, my staff should not have to always be conscious of asserting these rights because they should simply be provided for, and this is best ensured when the relationship is one of compassion and respect. If I were to neglect these responsibilities, my staff would become aware that their rights have been breached and claim them from me. This is what I mean when I say that responsibilities come first.

Dr. Mahmood: And your staff also has responsibilities toward you – namely, doing their work. It is interesting to see that the concepts and principles that apply to government and society are mirrored within the microcosms of society, such as family and the workplace. Each player has responsibilities toward others, while also being entitled to certain rights. In a way, a specific right and its correlating responsibility are actually the same thing, but viewed from opposite angles – that of either giving or receiving.

Imam Feisal: What then are the Qur'anic responsibilities of the community toward its government?

Dr. Mahmood: The community has two main responsibilities toward its government: to choose a just leader, and after they have chosen a leader to accord him obedience and support, which in the past was given in the form of the *bay'ah* and is now given today through franchise.

In regard to choosing a leader, God says:

> Let there arise out of you a band of people inviting to all that is good, enjoining what is right, and forbidding what is wrong: They are the ones to attain felicity. Be not like those who are divided amongst themselves and fall into disputations after receiving Clear Signs: For them is a dreadful penalty.[1]

Thus, those who uphold justice should rule, and it is the responsibility of the community to choose just rulers.

Thereafter, the people's responsibility to them is to obey and follow the ruler in justice. God says in the Qur'an:

> O believers! Obey God and obey the Prophet and those charged with authority amongst you; then if you dispute among yourselves about something, refer it to God and the Prophet, if you believe in God and in the Day of Judgment; this is best and a most commendable policy.[2]

> **Imam Feisal:** And what is the ruler's responsibility towards the community?

> **Dr. Mahmood:** The ruler's responsibilities to the community are many. In the most general sense, the ruler's responsibility is to take care of the people, treat them with kindness and consult them on the nation's affairs. As God says in the Qur'an:

> It is out of mercy from God that you deal with people with kindness. If you were unjust and harsh, they would break away from you. So sympathize with them and be kind to them, and consult them in respect of affairs, then decide and have confidence in God, verily God loves those who have faith in Him.[3]

There is no doubt that the ruler is to serve and take care of the needs of people, he is not there to simply issue commands and expect to be obeyed. He is just as responsible as everyone else for the well-being of society.

> **Imam Feisal:** I also read in that verse an injunction towards ruling with justice, as God conditions obedience to the ruler in this verse upon his sense of justice and kindness.

> **Dr. Mahmood:** Precisely. Justice, as we've mentioned during our SIP meetings, is the foundational principle of Islamic governance.

God commands: "When you judge between persons, judge with justice."[4] Of course, there must always be room for mercy and taking into account human fallibility. Thus, the Prophet said, "It is fairer for the judge to err in acquittal than in conviction."

The ruler must implement two clear principles to uphold justice in society: *equality before the law* and the *rule of law*. The Qur'an affords all of humanity equality and equal protection under the law. God says:

> O believers! faithfully apply the law as divinely ordained, even though it may go against yourselves, or your parents and relatives, to both the rich and the poor both of whom God maintains; do not be guided by personal considerations, so as to act against justice; if you distort or withhold equal justice, God knows well what you are doing.[5]

When we are all equal before the law, we all answer to the same authority. This is a natural corollary to Islam's doctrine of equality. In the Islamic state, nobody in the ruling hierarchy would have any rights whatsoever that are superior to those of an ordinary citizen. Rule of law in its real and purest sense would be the order of the day in a truly Islamic society. This is aptly evidenced in early Islamic history; for example, the two cases in which the Caliph Umar warned a judge that he must not discriminate between him and an ordinary citizen contesting against him. The Caliph Ali bin Abu Talib was, under his own instructions, placed in the court on an equal footing with a Christian litigant against him.

> **Imam Feisal:** So to summarize what you have shared so far, the community's responsibility is to choose a just and worthy ruler and then to offer their obedience and allegiance to that ruler. The ruler's responsibility is to take care of the community, to consult them in their affairs, to rule with kindness and to ensure justice, which entails equality before the law and rule of law.

Now, within the society itself, individual members of the community also have responsibilities toward each other, correct?

> **Dr. Mahmood:** That is a very important point, as we are all responsible to contribute to the well-being of society as a whole. The responsibilities of the community revolve around one key point – recognizing and actuating our unity and oneness – and this involves the practice of good deeds toward one another and

promoting reconciliation between disputing people or groups, including the various racial and religious communities.

First, among our responsibilities toward others within the society is to give back in the form of charity. God says in the Qur'an:

> Verily alms are for the poor and the needy, and those who are involved in its administration, and those who must get social security, and those in bondage or in debt, and in the way of God and for the wayfarer; so is ordained by God, and God is full of knowledge and wisdom.[6]

Imam Feisal: But this giving is not just monetary giving, correct?

Dr. Mahmood: Yes, the Prophet said that "everything has a charity tax (*zakat*) and the charity tax on knowledge is teaching it." From this we can infer that everything we gain in this life should also be shared with others. This sharing contributes to both our development and that of our society. This is why spreading mischief and hoarding away the blessings God has gifted us with are forbidden in the Qur'an. God says:

> Woe to every scandal-monger and back-biter, who piles up wealth and lays by it, thinking that his wealth would make him last forever; by no means will this happen; he will be condemned to hell-fire.[7]

Imam Feisal: And the other part of this verse hints at the issue of accountability and justice, both of which are also major themes in the Qur'an. It is clear here that justice is not simply the imperative of the ruler.

Dr. Mahmood: Exactly. Justice is not simply something that the government enforces upon society, as the commandment to judge with justice is addressed to all of humanity. The foundation for a just government is a just people, and we must constantly work to distinguish our own selves by our just actions. As God says:

> O believers! stand out firmly for God as witnesses to fairness, let not the disinclination of another towards you make you swear and depart from justice, be just – that is nearest to piety; and fear God, verily God knows all that you do.[8]

Justice has such an exalted rank that it is nearest to piety!

Imam Feisal: And it has been said that the purpose of justice is the appearance of unity, to connect to your earlier theme. Justice allows for people to come together in concord and peace, rather than as antagonistic parties vying over their respective interests or rights.

Dr. Mahmood: Yes, as Dr. Mahmood Ghazi quoted during one of our meetings, Rumi had said *"Tu bara'i wasl kardan amadi; nai bara'i fasl kardan amadi"* [you were sent to unite, not to separate]. This is a very important theme in the Qur'an. God says:

> If two parties among believers fall into a dispute, effect reconciliation between them; and if any of them commits excesses to the other, be firm until that party complies with the law; and when that party complies, reconcile them with justice and equity, verily God loves those who act with equity.[9]

Before going to the law we must first try to effect reconciliation among disputing parties, as this is most conducive to unity. We are all brothers, as God says in another verse: "Verily believers are brethren; so reconcile between your brethren; and fear God so that you get His mercy."[10]

Imam Feisal: You had mentioned earlier that this Qur'anic injunction toward reconciliation and unity is not simply between disputing individuals, but also between groups and communities.

Dr. Mahmood: Yes, God says in the Qur'an that the diversity of mankind is intentional and reminds us that still we all come from one source: "O mankind! God has created you from one man and one woman, you are divided into nationalities and communities only so that you may recognize one another."[11]Though efforts have, of late, been made to achieve some unity and friendship between the nations of the contemporary world, they are poor substitutes for the Prophet's doctrines of global human unity and universal brotherhood. The very wording of his "Farewell Sermon" carries the message of universal brotherhood and teaches the lesson of absolute humility. He said:

> O mankind! An Arab is not superior to a non-Arab nor vice versa, the white has no superiority over the black nor vice versa, all of you are Adam's progeny, and Adam was made of clay.

This was a forthright declaration, at once, of the twin Islamic doctrines of human equality and "one world for all."

The Islamic teachings on racial equality, cultural pluralism, and "one world for all" did not remain with the Prophet as mere idealism. The Prophet translated his teachings into concrete action. The presence, among his Companions, of the trio of Salman al-Farsi, Suhaib al-Rumi, and Bilal al-Habashi presented a spectacular scenario of transnational and multiracial brotherhood. He also proclaimed that different peoples in different parts of the world had their own Prophets, and that God has not left any people without divine guidance. In his declaration that all of mankind descended from Adam and he, our ancestor, was made of earth, there could be no implication other than humility and absolute equality before God.

> **Imam Feisal:** You bring up the issue of other religions; can you share the Qur'anic foundation for our responsibilities toward others in our communities who are not Muslims?
>
> **Dr. Mahmood:** The Qur'an clearly states that there can be "No compulsion in matters of religion."[12] Further, it recognizes that the Divine Reality is known by many names: "Say! Call upon 'Allah' (God) or 'Rahman' (the Merciful), by whatever name you call Him – for Him are the best of names."[13] This acknowledges that God is called by different names in different languages and religions. Secondly, it is not our responsibility to compel others to believe, when God who is far more powerful than we are has not forced them to believe: "If your God wanted, the whole world would have believed; how can you force people to become believers?"[14] It even gives instructions on what to say to unbelievers:

Say to non-believers! I do not worship what you worship, and you do not worship what I worship; neither shall I worship what you have been worshipping; nor will you worship what I worship; for you [there] is your religion and for me mine.[15]

Herein is an explicit guidance on how to treat adherents of other religions. Furthermore, God clearly states that one must justly respect and support all who glorify and worship Him, even though the manners of their worship and glorification differ. He criticizes those who bar people from doing such: "Who is more unjust than the one who forbids glorification of God in the places of worship; and tries to disturb the same?"[16]

Imam Feisal: What about people who reject religion or do not believe in one God?

Dr. Mahmood: God says in the Qur'an:

Do not insult those whom they worship other than God; they may, in return, insult God in ignorance. God has made good the practices of every community in its sight and all will finally return to their God, they will then know the reality of all that they do.[17]

This clearly shows that all belief systems must be respected no matter what we may think about them. God will judge in the next world; it is not for us to judge others. This is why when the Prophet was at Ta'if and people stoned him he only said: "I can only persuade you to come to truth, if you do not want to hear leave it."

In fact, during the Prophet's age a group of persons of Indian origin (Hindu or Buddhist by faith) lived in Makkah and Madinah. They were greatly respected in the Arab society and the Prophet himself respectfully referred to them as *rijal al-hind* (people of India). Later, there were in Arabia Buddhists (Ahamira), Jats (Zuts,) and Thakurs (Takakira) of India, and none of them were forced to convert.

Also, another example is the Caliph Umar's Christian house-boy who remained a Christian all his life. The Caliph refused to exert any undue influence on him to convert to Islam. It was also during his reign that a governor in the Syrian region had to quit his post as the penalty for rebuking a non-Muslim for his form of worship.

Imam Feisal: I wish that all Muslims would learn about these examples from the Prophet's and Umar's behavior, to see that everyone in an Islamic state has the right to live their life and express their beliefs as they wish, so long as they don't infringe upon others' rights to religious freedom.

Dr. Mahmood: Exactly. I would like to emphasize that *Islamic law is meant to bring ease to people's lives*, so that they can go about their lives peacefully. The laws are meant to ensure justice in society, not to force religion upon anyone. Of course we pray that the individual members of society will live according to a moral code and walk a spiritual path, but Islamic law would not force them to.

Imam Feisal: Are there any rights that are afforded to us in the Qur'an and the *Sunnah* which you think are not even addressed in the world today?

Dr. Mahmood: There is a key issue – also related to the oneness of mankind – and this is freedom of movement, which is a fully protected right in the socio-political doctrines of Islam. Sovereignty of the entire universe rests, according to Islamic principles, in the One Unseen and Supreme Almighty God alone. All lands belong to Him, and on His lands all human beings have an unfettered freedom of movement. The modern concepts of nationality, citizenship, and domicile, in whose name man's freedom of movement is curtailed, have no place in Islam. For administrative purposes the state can regulate the movement of people but it cannot, by any dint of imagination, find a religion-based justification to impose unwarranted restrictions on the movements of any citizen.

Freedom of movement is guaranteed in Islam to such an extent that even mosques are not out of bounds for any person, not even for non-Muslims. Christians, Jews, pagans, and fire-worshippers had free access to the Prophet's mosque during his lifetime, as well as under the Caliphs who succeeded him. Until today any person, irrespective of creed or faith, can freely enter a mosque anywhere. The restrictions on the entry of non-Muslims into Makkah and Medinah had emanated in the distant past partly from the requirement of physical cleanliness of a high standard inside the holy places and partly from security concerns.

Imam Feisal: These rights that you have enumerated paint a portrait of quite an ideal society, but you mentioned earlier that in the Muslim world today Islamic law is misunderstood and misapplied. To what extent are these rights and responsibilities implemented in Muslim society today?

Dr. Mahmood: On the political level, if we look at the constitutional and legal provisions relating to Islam and its law and the State policies and governmental practices in various Muslim-dominated and Muslim-minority countries, one often finds inherent contradictions, conflicts, and a dichotomy between belief and practice.

Looking at the ground realities, we observe that a formal allegiance to Islam and its law through constitutional and legal provisions do not necessarily make a society truly "Islamic." Nor is such a formal allegiance absolutely necessary if a country is to follow Islamic principles of governance in practice. This is why I have argued in our meetings that a formal declaration of Islam as the state religion is not at all necessary in measuring a state's compliance with the ideals that Islam subscribes to.

I'd like to speak about my own experience in India. The great Indian Muslim scholar, Syed Abu'l `Ala Maududi, had lamented:

> Undoubtedly the Muslims of India are the owners of a superb law written in the books of Islamic jurisprudence which is in complete consonance with the true Islamic teachings, culture, and civilization. Unfortunately, however, that law is not in practice and has been replaced with a different legal fabric which in most of its aspects is wholly un-Islamic. The legal system applicable to the Muslims of India today under the banner of "Mohammedan law" is in its letter and spirit very much different from the true Islamic Shari'at. The loopholes of this distorted law have very badly affected the social life of the Muslims. Hardly can we find even a single family in India one or another of which has not awfully suffered in life on account of this distorted law. Over and above, it has caused a grave damage to the reputation of the Muslims.[18]

Imam Feisal: Could you give us a specific example of this distortion?

Dr. Mahmood: In respect to divorce by the husband, for instance, in all sections of the Muslim fraternity of India it is generally believed that the only legal process of dissolving a marriage is to say the word "*talaq*" thrice or to make the so-called "triple pronounce-ment of divorce" in a single breath. The jurisprudential contro-versy regarding the validity and effect of the triple-divorce formula apart, it remains a fact that a predominant majority of Muslims in the country know it as the true "Islamic" process of divorce.

After a deep study of the classical sources and the authentic books on Islamic law, I have arrived at the conclusion that there are in fact no different "forms" of divorce under Islamic law. The so-called "*ahsan,*" "*hasan,*" and "*bid`i*" *talaq*s are surely not three different "forms," "methods" or even "procedures" for divorce under Islamic law. The Shariah furnishes only one simple process of divorce by the husband. A husband may, if he is convinced that his marriage has irretrievably broken down, quietly pronounce one single divorce. Following this pronouncement of divorce, he has the freedom to revoke it within the period of `*iddah* (roughly three months) and is in fact greatly encouraged to do so. If he does not revoke the divorce pronounced by him and the period of `iddah expires, the marriage stands dissolved. After that, in case the husband now finds himself ready to reconcile, the ball will be in the wife's court. If she agrees, there may be a fresh marriage between the parties. And that is all.

As for the woman's right to divorce, Maududi wrote:

> Islamic law affects a beautiful equilibrium between the divorce rights of men and women. It is a great folly that we have practically withdrawn from our women the right of *khul`*; little caring for the fact that denying them this right, on a footing equal to *talaq*, is absolutely un-Islamic. It is indeed a mockery of the Shariah that we regard *khul`* as something depending either on the consent of the husband or on the verdict of the *qadi*. The law of Islam is not responsible for the way Muslim women are being deprived of their right in this respect.[19]

How many in fact among us know that the women's right to *khul`* is, like *talaq*, wholly unconditional?

Also, in India Muslim girls even though no longer minors are being freely given in marriage against their wishes or without their consent. At the same time, instead of actually paying the *mahr* to the wife the Muslim groom now shamelessly looks for the dowry to be paid to him by her parents – a practice which is wholly repugnant to Islamic law.

Imam Feisal: What would you like to say finally about the recognition of human rights in Islamic law and the state of their implementation in Islamic history?

Dr. Mahmood: The human rights today recognized by the United Nations' proclamations were recognized years earlier in the constitutive sources of Islam: the Holy Qur'an and the Traditions of the Prophet (*Sunnah*). These were implemented by the Righteous Caliphs of Islam who, one after another, succeeded the Prophet during the first four decades after his demise. Thereafter Islamic history witnessed the stress and strain of the glory and downfall of various dynasties and empires. Some of the Muslim rulers might have faithfully implemented the Islamic doctrines on human rights; others might have been lukewarm to them. Their policies and practices would not change the sacrosanct principles of Islam regarding the basic human rights.

Imam Feisal: Thank you for you valuable insights, Dr. Tahir.

Human rights and citizenship in an Islamic State (Recep Şentürk)[20]

Imam Feisal: Dr. Şentürk, during our meetings you briefly discussed the historical process in which classical Muslim jurists developed an authentic Islamic approach to universal human rights. Why do you feel that this historical development is currently relevant to the *umma*?

Dr. Şentürk: The contemporary global Muslim community is suffering from, what I call, "collective amnesia" of our history and of the great advances that were made by Islamic societies and states. Contemporary states with Muslim majorities are not effectively building on this great intellectual and juristic legacy. They are generally ignorant of the experiences of past Muslim states, including those of the Ottomans who attempted to address many issues relating to modern Islamic governance. As a result of this amnesia, the Muslim community is forced to ask the exact same questions about Islam, democracy, and human rights that our predecessors tackled.

As I have argued in my work, the Ottoman state developed a modern system of governance and jurisprudence, which respected civic and human rights and was rooted in the Islamic tradition. In this interview, I would like to focus on the system of human rights that the Ottoman Empire developed, which lay at the foundation of its treatment of non-Muslim minorities under its authority.

To get the discussion started, I would like to argue that the Islamic civilization has always been an "open civilization." It has protected communities it conquered and has maintained good relations with others, including Chinese, Christian, Jewish, Hindu, and Buddhist communities.[21] Islamic jurisprudence (*fiqh*) has provided the theological and legal foundations for this worldview promoting the existence of pluralism. As Ibn Khaldun stated, the goal of *fiqh* is to protect human civilization, irrespective of religious and legal differences.[22] In light of this legal and civilizational openness toward other communities, Muslims in the late Ottoman Empire during the second half of the nineteenth century adopted certain structures and institutions: universal citizenship, constitutionalism, and a representative parliamentary system.

Imam Feisal: Backing away momentarily from the Ottomans, would you describe your broader understanding regarding the Islamic viewpoint on human rights?

Dr. Şentürk: Classical Muslim jurists agreed that an Islamic state is predicated upon its fulfillment of `ismah – the inviolability of its subjects. To this end, these scholars determined that the Islamic state had to guarantee a series of basic rights, which are derived from the six objectives of Islamic law that are considered to lay at the root of legal stipulations: life, property, religion, mind, family, and honor. In other words, to ensure the `ismah of its subjects, the Islamic state has to guarantee rights in these six basic domains. Yet, in spite of this consensus, scholars were divided over the issue of the population to whom the state is obliged to provide `ismah. In particular, scholars disagreed about the following question: Is the state obliged to provide `ismah only to citizens or to both citizens and non-citizens? And, relatedly, who can qualify for citizenship in an Islamic state?

Broadly speaking, two schools of thought emerged among Islamic legal scholars on the state's legal relationship with those under its jurisdiction: the universalist approach and the communalist approach. The universalist approach is based on the concept of *adamiyyah* (humanity or personhood). It asserts that because we are all the children of Adam, `ismah and the accompanying six inviolable rights are universal. The communalist approach, on the other hand, is based on the concept of the "People of the Book." Given that the "People of the Book" are listed as Muslims, Christians, and Jews, this approach predicates the granting of rights and `ismah to particular religious affiliations. Whereas scholars adhering to the universalist approach linked `ismah to *adamiyyah*, scholars adopting the communalist approach predicated `ismah on the declaration of the Muslim faith (*iman*) or, if the person is Christian or Jewish, to a negotiated treaty ensuring security (*aman*) under the auspices of the Islamic state.

Imam Feisal: How do these different perspectives affect how the state treats those living within its geographic boundaries?

Dr. Şentürk: Muslim jurists who employed the universalist *adamiyyah* paradigm regarded the Islamic state as responsible for protecting the inviolability (`ismah) of all human beings (*adamiyyin*), regardless of religion. For example, the Syrian jurist Ibn 'Abidin said, "*Al-adami mukarram wa law kafira*," which means "the human being is to be granted (protective) dignity even if an infidel." Another Syrian, al-Maydani said, "*Al-hurr ma`sum bi nafsihi*," or "the free human being is inviolable in his own right."

Thus, according to the universalists, religion is not a barrier to *'ismah* and the six fundamental rights from this perspective. Those who employed the communalist paradigm restricted *'ismah* only to Muslims and the "People of the Book," namely Christians and Jews. In this fashion, they regarded the Islamic state as responsible only for protecting the `*ismah* of Muslims and the Jewish and Christian minorities.[23]

Imam Feisal: Can you provide some more detail on the universalist view of Islamic law, whereby one's basic rights are given and protected simply by virtue of being human?

Dr. Şentürk: In the *Adamiyyah* approach, fundamental human rights are recognized as universal rights, all human beings enjoy these rights on a permanent and equal basis. They possess these rights simply by virtue of being a human. Similarly, the state (or any authority) cannot revoke these rights for any reason whatsoever. The roots of this approach can be said to go back to the foundational period of Islamic history and Imam Ali, who said, "People are of two kinds, either they are your brothers in faith or your equals in creation." That being said, Abu Hanifa and his followers can be seen as the first thinkers to explicitly formulate this approach. Abu Hanifa argued that being a descendent of Adam, whether Muslim or not, serves as the legal ground for possessing basic rights (*al-`ismah bi al-adamiyyah*).

Imam Feisal: Was this view supported by other schools of law?

Dr. Şentürk: The universalist approach transcended the divisions between the *madhahib* and gained followers from all legal schools. In fact, despite the fact that its originator was Abu Hanifa, it would be misleading to take the universal view on human rights as exclusively a Hanafi perspective. Of course, the view had many Hanafi supporters, such as the scholars Sarakhsi, Zayla'i, Dabusi, Marghinani, Ibn Humam, Babarti, Kasani, and Timurtashi. But there were also many non-Hanafi scholars like al-Ghazali from the Shafi'i school; Ibn Taymiyya and Ibn Qayyim al-Jawziyya from the Hanbali school; Ibn Rushd, al-Shatibi, and Ibn al-'Ashur from the Maliki school; and Mughniyya from the Jafari Shi'a school. They all shared this universalist opinion.

Imam Feisal: What are the core arguments the universalists use to defend their doctrine?

Dr. Şentürk: Generally speaking, they put forth six arguments. First, they said that God's intention in creating humanity was producing a "trial" (*ibtila'*). In the Qur'an, God declared: "He who has created life and death that He may try you (by testing you and putting you through trials) to see which of you is best in conduct."[24] In this trial that is our life on earth, we are tested to see if we will choose the straight path when presented with life's many options. According to universalists, we cannot be free to make the right choices nor can we be held responsible *(taklif)* for our actions, unless we are also free to make the wrong choices. Therefore, it is necessary that all humans enjoy freedom in order to endure this trial.

Second, according to the universalists, all humans must be protected since God does not desire His creations to be destroyed. He intends every ease for His creatures and doesn't seek hardship for them. As we read in the Qur'an: "God desires ease for you, and He does not desire for you difficulty." The Prophet also mentioned that God is more merciful to His creatures than a mother – animal or human – is to its children. The basic fact of one's humanity is enough to warrant protection.

Their third argument centers on the notion of disbelief (*kufr*). According to the universalists, while the Qur'an castigates disbelievers, it does so specifically in the context of war. In all other contexts, in which disbelief is not harmful to Muslim society, it must be tolerated. In this sense, the justification for war and *Jihad* is not to eradicate disbelief. Rather, it is to maintain the inviolability of life and to provide security from those who assault others and stir up war. In this sense, *Jihad* is a defensive war and not an offensive one. Therefore, when peace prevails, everyone must enjoy security and protection, and their lives should be inviolable. In the same line of thought, the fourth argument is that the objective of war is not to eradicate enemies, but rather to force them to make peace and pay taxes in return for protection against external aggression.

Fifth, according to the universalists, God and the Prophet Muhammad strictly prohibited assaulting and killing any human being. They even ordered the protection of non-Muslim women, children, and religious scholars during wartime. There are numerous verses that stress this. For example, "Do not take life – which God has made sacred – except for just cause. And if anyone is slain wrongfully, we have given his heir authority (to demand retaliation or to forgive): but let him not exceed the bounds in the matter of taking life; for he is helped (by the Law)."[25] And "O believers, secure justice and be witnesses for God. Do not let detestation for a people move you to not be equitable; be equitable – that is nearer to God-fearing."[26] "... Whoever slays a soul not to retaliate for a soul slain, nor for corruption done in the land, should be as if he had slain humankind altogether."[27]

Finally, the sixth reason justifying the universalist argument is that the Qur'an explicitly prohibits coercing others into religious adherence. To this end, it is famously written in the Qur'an, "Let there be no compulsion in religion ... "[28] This is especially important today in the context of the modern day nation-state. To make either the acquisition of citizenship or basic human rights dependent on one's religion (in the case of the communalist approach, being Muslim, Jewish, or Christian) incentivizes, and even necessitates, conversion. Such a society, according to universalists, would be both thwarting the Divine Intent of testing mankind (*ibtila'*) and using compulsion in religion by making access to basic rights dependent on belief. In contrast, within the universalist approach toward legal personhood, rights and citizenship are afforded to all individuals simply by virtue of being human.

Imam Feisal: I'm struck by the fact that each of these arguments is premised on the recognition of individual human value and his or her responsibilities both towards God and towards humanity.

Dr. Şentürk: Indeed, all of these arguments are all based on the idea of "the universal human" and his place in a global web of social relations. All of these arguments also attempt to lay foundations for peaceful relations between Muslims and non-Muslims and between members of different belief systems. This is because Islamic law considers the protection of the six basic rights to be a foundation for all religions.

Imam Feisal: So the *Maqasid al-Shari'ah* represent the underlying goals of *all* religious systems?

Dr. Şentürk: Right. According to Islamic theologians and jurists, these six principles constitute the unchangeable core of all religions and legal systems. In fact, this is why they are called *daruriyyat* or Axiomatic Rights, Rights of Human Beings (*huquq al-adamiyyin*), the Foundations (*al-usul*), and the "objectives of the law" (*Maqasid al-Shari'ah*). Among Muslims, there is a consensus that while matters of creed (`aqidah*) cannot be altered, the rules in law (the Shariah) can change, and have changed, in response to their social and cultural contexts. Therefore, Muslims believe that, while all of the faiths and underlying principles taught by Prophets of God have been the same, their specific legal structures and contents have changed over time. Most importantly, the main purpose of all faith-based legal systems – the six *Maqasid al-Shari`ah* – have remained unchanged across history.

Imam Feisal: In other words, though specific legal systems, institutions, and laws have evolved across time and location, the core of all religions and legal systems has always been to protect the six *Maqasid al-Shari`ah*. Tying in your previous discussion on *ibtila'*, can you elaborate on how these six *daruriyyat* (Axiomatic Rights) create this environment of testing?

Dr. Şentürk: All of the *daruriyyat* are necessary prerequisites for an individual to both live in peace and exercise his free will. An individual's religious choices must be honored even if they ostensibly contradict Islamic teachings. This individual's life, livelihood, and family must also be protected since this is the only way he can make decisions and respond to the Divine call. Likewise, this individual must be able to employ his freedom of reason so that he can independently make moral choices regarding right and wrong. Finally, an individual's mind must be honored and protected even if he does not adhere to the way the larger collective thinks. Sarakhsi typified this general line of thinking regarding the relationship between the preservation of the *daruriyyat* and the creation of the environment of *ibtila'*:

Upon creating human beings, God graciously bestowed intelligence and the capability to assume responsibilities and rights (personhood). This was to make them ready for duties and rights determined by God. Then He granted them protection (inviolability), freedom, and property to let them continue their lives so that they can perform the duties they have shouldered. The right to assume responsibility and enjoy rights, freedom, and property exists with a human being when he or she is born. The insane, child, and the sane adult are [at] the same [level] concerning these rights. This is how God gave the proper legal personhood to him when he was born, and thus entails his rights and duties thereof. In this regard, everyone is equal whether child or adult, sane or insane.[29]

Imam Feisal: Concerning the practical implications of the *adami-yyah* paradigm, which you described as mandating the Islamic state to protect the six basic *Maqasid* universally, what are some specific ramifications of this approach in terms of how Muslims historically governed and operated their state?

Dr. Şentürk: One consequence of this approach is that Muslims permitted non-Muslim communities under their rule to practice their traditions and laws insofar as they did not infringe on any of these protected basic rights. (In fact, the same held true for Muslims, who were granted individual freedom insofar as it did not obstruct the freedom of others or their basic rights). For instance, according to early Muslim chronicles, when Egypt was conquered in 640, `Amr ibn al-`As permitted indigenous Egyptians to practice their customary laws. The one exception to this was the tradition of sacrificing a girl to the Nile to ensure the annual flood. Another example, this time from India, is based on Muslim reports that discussed how Muslims allowed Hindus to practice all of their customs aside from the *sati* tradition (in which a widow was burned alongside the body of her late husband). In both of these examples Muslim rulers outlawed non-Muslim customs because they violated the right to life.

Imam Feisal: What if someone violates another person's `ismah, for example? Don't they then lose some of their own rights, at least temporarily?

Dr. Şentürk: Yes. They lose the relevant rights for a temporary period. In other words, according to the universalists, an individual who does not respect the rights of others – often a criminal – loses the part of his `ismah that is relevant to the punishment (*mahall al-jaza'*). While this right is temporarily suspended during punishment, the rest of the rights remain intact. Thus, while a thief might be forced to compensate his victim, the rest of the thief's property should still be protected.

Imam Feisal: Let's turn towards the opposite view, the communalist tradition. They believe that the state is *not* responsible to protect the rights of everyone within their domain. You said that according to this communalist tradition, people are afforded their basic rights by virtue of either their Islamic faith or by a treaty of agreement with the state. Can you please elaborate?

Dr. Şentürk: As I said, this competing communalist worldview, which also gained adherents from the different Islamic legal schools, does not see all humans as inherently being possessors of rights. Rather, it predicates the granting or withholding of rights on religious identification. While the believer (*mu'min*), according to the communalists, possesses rights, the disbeliever (*kafir*) lacks them.

Imam Feisal: What are some of the most important arguments that they used?

Dr. Şentürk: Their most important claim is that the Qur'anic injunction on fighting infidels is a general commandment. It is not, according to the communalists, contingent upon the specific context in which it was revealed. Thus, they see the following verse as sweeping and everlasting: "When the sacred months have passed, slay the idolaters wherever you find them, and take them (captive), and besiege them, and prepare for them each ambush. But if they repent and establish worship and pay the poor-due, then leave their way free. Lo! God is Forgiving, Merciful."[30] To this end, this other statement, which is attributed to the Prophet, is also seen as not being confined to a specific context: "I have been ordered to fight the people till they say: None has the right to be worshipped but Allah."[31] As such, the communalists claim that it is not only repugnant to give disbelievers rights, it is also a moral obligation to combat them. Since disbelief (*kufr*) is the gravest sin, it cannot be permitted. In turn, disbelievers do not deserve rights or protection. Meanwhile, according to the communalists, Muslims qualify for `ismah by virtue of their faith (*iman*). Non-Muslims do not qualify for `ismah unless they make a treaty with an Islamic state and secure its protection in exchange for paying taxes. This pact is called *dhimmah*, and the taxes paid for it are called *jizyah*.

Imam Feisal: So I assume that the universalists and the communalists disagree about the importance of the *dhimmah* pact.

Dr. Şentürk: Very much so. According to the universalists, the granting of `ismah to non-Muslims is not contingent upon the pact of *dhimmah*. Rather `ismah is already the right of all humans and is universally present. Meanwhile, *dhimmah* is understood as constituting the foundation for an alliance between the state and the non-Muslim minorities against third parties. On the other hand, according to the communalists, being a non-Muslim is a cause for war. As such, the *dhimmah* is of significant importance since it overrides this basic *casus belli* and grants protection to the non-Muslims who have entered the agreement.

Imam Feisal: What are some of the practical implications of the differences between the universalist and communalist approaches?

Dr. Şentürk: There are numerous political and legal implications. Generally speaking, it has shaped numerous Islamic political and legal debates since these different views on the granting of `ismah has produced divergent political approaches. Similarly, a wide array of judgments emanated from this contest between rival paradigms on human rights as to whether *'ismah* grants universal human rights or restricted rights to specific groups.

Imam Feisal: Can you give us a few examples?

Dr. Şentürk: Certainly. But I will only mention a handful of implications since an exhaustive analysis of the effects of this disagreement would require a painstaking survey of classical Muslim legal literature. Having made that caveat clear, one important issue that emerges from this debate concerns the conventional state of international relations. The universalist approach argues that peace is the *de facto* state of relations between Muslims and non-Muslims. Specific actions or evidence is needed to render these relations antagonistic. In this view "the cause of war is war" and only if non-Muslims initiate war should Muslims engage in a defensive combat. Thus, the universalist approach clearly distinguishes between hostility (*harb*) and infidelity (*kufr*). While all enemies may be infidels, not all infidels are enemies. On the other hand, communalists argue that *war* is the natural state of relations between Muslims and non-Muslims. This is due to the fact that, in their view, infidelity (*kufr*) is the basic cause of war. In turn, non-Muslims are seen as being enemies (*harbi*) by default and without a treaty of peace, they do not possess the right to `ismah.

Imam Feisal: How do these perspectives address the issue of those who have left Islam, or apostates? This is a very sensitive issue in the contemporary Muslim world. In fact, the definition of apostasy has become so broad in various places that some Muslims define individuals who are Muslim but who hold views that are different from the state's religious establishment as apostates.

Dr. Şentürk: The key question in this debate is whether or not apostasy in itself is a crime and why. For the universalists, apostasy is not a punishable crime unless it is combined with tangible efforts to harm other individuals or Islam. In other words, in order for an apostate to be punished, he must perform a harmful act to the Muslim community, and not simply exhibit disbelief in Islam. From this perspective, even if a non-Muslim is an apostate (*murtadd*), he is not an enemy by default per se. Meanwhile, according to the communalist perspective, apostasy in and of itself is a punishable offense. This argument is based on verses from the Qur'an, for example: "Those who believe, then reject faith, then believe (again) and (again) reject faith, and go on increasing in unbelief, God will not forgive them nor guide them on the way.

To the Hypocrites give the glad tidings that there is for them (but) a grievous penalty."[32] "They swear by God that they said nothing (evil), but indeed they uttered blasphemy, and they did it after accepting Islam; and they meditated a plot which they were unable to carry out..."[33] Focusing on these verses (and others), communalists argue that by abandoning his religion, the apostate loses his citizenship and protection. Ultimately, as a non-Muslim, he is considered to be an enemy by default.

Beyond this disagreement, the two approaches differ about the reasons why apostasy is punishable. For the universalists, apostasy is punishable only insofar as it represents a real threat to the community and state. For the communalists, apostasy deserves to be punished given that deviation from the faith is seen as harming the community and the state.

> **Imam Feisal:** I would imagine that the universalist perspective, which emphasizes the universal rights of *all* people, might also provide a significant model for increasing the rights of women. Did the universalist scholars impact debates on women's rights?
>
> **Dr. Şentürk:** Well, the universalist paradigm does not differentiate between men and women in terms of *'ismah* and human rights. Since men and women are human, or *adami,* both are entitled to the same rights. A woman's life, religion, property, mind, family, and honor are all as inviolable as those of men. Yet, in areas that are not viewed within the domains of basic human rights, women are treated differently than men. In the domain of legal rights, such as inheritance and family law, the fact that women were treated differently than men did not mean, in traditional views, that they received unequal treatment. Since notions of equality and gender roles have significantly changed in the modern period, there is currently a heated debate regarding the nature of women's legal rights in the universalist worldview.
>
> **Imam Feisal:** Can you give us a specific example of how the universalists might view a particular legal issue related to women differently than the communalists?
>
> **Dr. Şentürk:** The issue of marriage and women's consent to marriage is a source of difference. According to universalists, a woman (regardless of whether she is a virgin or widow) has the right to agree on her own to marriage. Therefore, an arranged marriage is not binding until the woman consents. Communalists, on the other hand, give the woman's family greater authority in

determining her marriage arrangement. In turn, a virgin cannot accede to marriage without the consent of her guardian. Likewise, the marriage contract is not binding until the woman's family consents to the marriage. Underlying this approach is the belief that the family serves the woman's interest because her guardians are more experienced in the intricacies of marriage, as she is young and inexperienced. Communalists, however, concede that a widow or divorcee has the right to marry herself independently.

Imam Feisal: What about divorce?

Dr. Şentürk: The system for terminating a marriage in Islamic law is very different from that in modern legal systems. Marriage is allowed to be dissolved solely through the consent of the parties involved and without any formal authorization from external (state or religious) authorities. Put briefly, universalists grant equal rights to both the man and the woman in unilaterally dissolving a marriage (*talaq*). Communalists, meanwhile, assert that only the man, and not the woman, is entitled to unilaterally dissolve a marriage. Having said that, communalists agree that the woman is entitled to file a divorce in court, after which the court can mandate a divorce.

Imam Feisal: You have demonstrated how the approach toward defining legal personhood adopted by the state directly affects its social policies. Where in the Muslim world is the universalist approach applied?

Dr. Şentürk: In general, this perspective has been strongly influential in the Indian Subcontinent, Central Asia, Asia Minor, and the Balkans. This was especially the case during the Ottoman period. The Mughals in India also implemented the *adamiyyah* tradition, granting Hindus basic human rights and freedom of religion in spite of the fact that they are not considered to be the "People of the Book."

Going back to the deep impact that universalism had in the Ottoman Empire, we can see how this perspective affected the configuration of state institutions during the nineteenth century. The most pronounced effect was the Ottoman introduction of a parliamentary constitutional regime. Whereas the Ottoman Empire initially possessed the traditional Islamic state structure of the Divan, during the nineteenth century it evolved into a modern state. Implementing the *tanzimat* reforms, the Sublime Ottoman State (Devlet-i `Aliyya-i Uthmaniyya) adopted modern institutions including a constitution, parliament, and multi-party elections. In the first Ottoman parliament (which was convened in 1876), nearly half of its members were non-Muslim. Similarly, the *tanzimat* reforms abolished the *dhimmi* status, the poll tax (*jizyah*) for non-Muslims, and all other restrictions on non-Muslim citizens, effectively instituting equal citizenship in the Ottoman empire.[34]

Imam Feisal: Did this development under the Ottomans flow from Hanafi jurisprudence?

Dr. Şentürk: This is a somewhat tricky question that I cannot claim to fully answer. Though the Ottoman state nominally followed Hanafi jurisprudential approaches, there is not sufficient research to determine the extent to which it actually followed these principles during its nearly 700 year-long existence. Having said that, the Ottomans did give primacy to Hanafi law, at least in the official configuration of the *millet* system.

Imam Feisal: Would you explain the *millet* system?

Dr. Şentürk: The word "*millet*" is derived from the Arabic word *millah* and means religious community or denomination. Under Ottoman rule, there were several officially recognized *millets*:the Orthodox Christian *millet*, the Armenian *millet*, and the Jewish *millet*. In modern Turkish, the word "*millet*" is used to mean "nation." This new meaning is indicative of a shift in defining communities based on their secular nature (rather than exclusively on their religious nature).

Imam Feisal: Could you provide some more detail regarding the configuration of the pluralistic Ottoman system?

Dr. Şentürk: Just to restate an earlier point, the Ottomans are one example among several of a pluralistic society under Muslim rule. Having said that, an important aspect of the Ottoman system involved the Shaykh ul-Islam (Turkish: Şeyhulislam). While the Ottomans did not create the position of the Shaykh ul-Islam, they rendered it into a central and very prestigious one. The post of the Shaykh ul-Islam corresponds in the modern state structure to those of minister of justice, minister of education, minister of religion, and minister of the *awqaf* (Trusts). Under the Ottomans, the sultan appointed the Shaykh ul-Islam. Once appointed, the Shaykh ul-Islam had the power to dethrone the sultan with a *fatwa*. This demonstrates the check-and-balance system in the Ottoman state. Moreover, the Shaykh ul-Islam's duties were both secular and religious. The sultan and the state bureaucrats sought the Shaykh ul-Islam's approval in state actions such as waging wars against other states.

Imam Feisal: That is very interesting. Let's turn our attention to Ottoman reforms and specifically the Tanzimat. In what way does the Tanzimat connect to the universalist/communalist debate? Do these reforms represent Ottoman attempts to implement the *adamiyyah* paradigm within a modern context?

Dr. Şentürk: The Tanzimat reforms are closely related to the broader univeralist/communalist debate. It is essential to remember, that at the time of the Tanzimat, the Ottoman Empire was in dialogue with Western ideological and cultural trends, including those pertaining to the notions of citizenship and rights. The universalist approach to `ismah made it possible for Ottoman reformers to adapt Islamic law to the new discourse on universal citizenship and rights.

Imam Feisal: Dr. Şentürk, can you describe some of the reforms within the Ottoman Empire, as it moved to a more parliamentary style of governance?

Dr. Şentürk: Ottoman constitutional reforms began in the late eighteenth century with the ascent of Selim III to the throne (1789–1807). In the global context, the 1789 French Revolution and the 1776 American Revolution were strongly reverberating in Europe. Responding to and in some ways emulating these revolutions, Sultan Selim initiated a series of reforms to restructure the state. To do this, he invited a wide spectrum of civil, military, and religious dignitaries to submit their views on the possible causes of the weakness of the Ottoman society and state and their proposals for reform. Aside from facilitating structural reform, Selim's consultations expanded the scope of Ottoman civic participation in governmental decision-making processes. Three fundamentally different approaches to reform emerged in these proposals:

1. A conservative approach which advocated reintroducing past Ottoman methods of governance
2. An eclectic approach which sought to reconcile the European system with the existing order
3. A radical approach which sought to completely replace the traditional system with a modern European one

Imam Feisal: How did the sultan respond? Which reform proposal did he choose?

Dr. Şentürk: The sultan adopted the third approach. In 1792 and 1793, he introduced a series of regulations which came to be known as the New Order (*Nizam-i Cedid*). Selim III also created a new corps of regular infantry, which was designed based on a European model. Moreover, he set up the Advisory Assembly (*Meclis-i Meshveret*), reformed the administration, and improved diplomatic relations with numerous European states.

Imam Feisal: And were Selim III's reforms continued by his successors?

Dr. Şentürk: Selim's successor, Mahmud II maintained the reform program. Mahmud II signed the Charter of Alliance (*Sened-i Ittifak*) in 1808, which promoted a constitutional order. As an agreement between the Sultan and his dignitaries, this charter restricted the sultan's exercise of power and delegated authority to the senate body. In so doing, it facilitated an increase in the representation of the people's will and broader political inclusion.[35]

In addition, Mahmud II announced the Tanzimat (literally meaning "reorganization") reforms before his death in 1839. Later that year, Mahmud II's successor, Sultan Abd al-Majid I, issued the "Hatti-i Sharif of Gulhane" (Royal Decree of the Rose Garden), which initiated the actual reforms. As a result of these reforms, Muslims and non-Muslims in the Ottoman Empire received rights protecting their lives, property, honor, and religion. Likewise, the reforms created a more centralized system of taxation, stipulated the mass establishment of secular schools, reorganized the judicial system, and laid out new rules regarding military service. Later, declarations concerning human rights were issued and these resembled decrees (*adalatname* or *kanunname*) made by earlier sultans. The Tanzimat ended under Abdulhamid II's reign, when the ideas for a Turkish constitution and parliament were first implemented and then rejected by the sultan.

Imam Feisal: In what sense did this fairly extensive period of reform promote the *adamiyyah* paradigm and aim to protect the *Maqasid al-Shari`ah*?

Dr. Şentürk: The Ottoman sultans framed the Tanzimat reforms as directly emerging from the Shariah. In this way, they cast the Tanzimat as protecting the *Maqasid al-Shari`ah*. Beyond this, the Hatti-i Sharif implemented the *adamiyyah* worldview by assuring all Ottoman subjects of their basic rights: life, property, freedom of religion, honor, education, employment, and due process.

The sultanic edict (*ferman*) declared: "All Muslim or non-Muslim subjects shall benefit from these rights. Everyone's life, honor, and property are guaranteed by the state according to Shariah laws." The 1875 Imperial Edict on Justice (*ferman-i adalet*) augmented these rights by legally promulgating an independent and protected judiciary. In this way, the Tanzimat reforms were grounded in the universal application of `*ismah*.

Imam Feisal: This was also an important trajectory towards more representative governance, was it not?

Dr. Şentürk: Yes it was. In fact, the 1876 Constitution marked an important stage in the Ottoman state's implementation of a rule of law. While it certainly had shortcomings and was suspended in 1877 by Sultan Abdulhamid II, the first Ottoman constitution inaugurated a parliamentary system. During the second constitutional period, which began in 1908 (when the Young Turks dethroned Abdulhamid II), the 1876 Constitution was reintroduced along with the parliament.

Imam Feisal: So how would you assess the overall success of these reform efforts?

Dr. Şentürk: The Ottoman reforms introduced a parliamentary system composed of representatives who were elected by Ottoman citizens. While this parliamentary system ultimately ended with the British invasion of Istanbul in World War I, it nonetheless demonstrated that an Islamic system of governance can be reconciled with modern European templates of governance.

Imam Feisal: How has the rise of the nation-state, the spread of European colonialism, and the proliferation of global standards of human rights affected Muslims' views on citizenship and human rights?

Dr. Şentürk: The different views on `*ismah* have affected Muslims' reactions to the rise of the modern nation-state and the growing focus on universal human rights. We can see this in the varied Muslim responses to the evolution of human rights in the West and their spread in the Muslim world. Some Muslims supported the United Nations Universal Declaration of Human Rights (UDHR), while others opposed it. Generally speaking, those supporting the UDHR rooted themselves in the Islamic universalistic legal tradition, whereas those opposing it aligned with the communalist approach.

Imam Feisal: Despite the dissolution of the Ottoman state in the early twentieth century, how has the Ottoman experience promoting the *adamiyyah* paradigm impacted the course of the contemporary Middle East?

Dr. Şentürk: The Ottoman experimentation with parliamentary representation was crucial to the rise of parliamentarianism in the succeeding states with Muslim majorities. However, these same states generally disinherited the Ottomans' universalist approach. Instead, most of these states subscribed to the communalistic view of Islamic law.

Imam Feisal: Do you see this "disinheriting," as you call it, a major problem today?

Dr. Şentürk: Yes, this is what I was referring to earlier when I spoke of the "collective amnesia" of the Muslim world regarding advances of earlier Islamic governments. While the Ottoman state answered many questions about modern governance, contemporary actors have forgotten these answers and have found themselves needing to ask the same questions at present.

The interpretation and practice of Islamic law today by the so-called Islamic states is incomparably more punitive than its practice in history. This modern Islamic legal discourse neglects the universalistic tradition and instead uncritically and rigidly accepts the communalist approach. This transformation occurred shortly after the fall of the Ottoman State in 1922. Unfortunately, with this break in the chain of memory, the modern Islamic legal discourse has lost the universalist dimension that characterized the dialectical discourse that dominated in the classical era. In its stead, modern Islamic legal discourse (including the discussions of human rights) exclusively revolves around religiously defined social categories such as Muslim and *kafir* (non-believer). Even when the Turkish and Arabic discourse on rights occasionally utilize the term `ismah (sanctity), they rarely utilize the category *adamiyyah* (humanity). In so doing, they fail to transcend the communalistic approach and they cripple any attempt to philosophically ground human rights in a universal worldview.

It is essential that we recognize that law is a social institution that is inherited from previous generations. In order to constructively engage in contemporary Islamic political and legal thought, it is thus necessary that we reexamine the relatively recent Ottoman past. By studying the post-Tanzimat juristic concepts and state structures, we can recover an example of a constitutional parliamentary system that embodied the universalist interpretation of Islamic law. In so doing, we can learn from this precedent and adapt our current solutions to the present needs of Muslims in an age of globalization and pluralism. By rooting our present efforts in this universalist or *adamiyyah* tradition we can increase the legitimacy of modern and innovative political and legal projects.

Imam Feisal: Thank you very much, Dr. Şentürk, for your enlightening interview. I hope that our readers will see that the universalist approach to Islamic law and the *adamiyyah* paradigm represent important precedents and models for our Shariah Index Project and its attempt to encourage contemporary Islamic states to protect all of their citizens' `ismah and basic rights.

9
The *Maqasid*, Reform and Renewal

In the first interview in this chapter, **Dr. Mohammad Hashim Kamali** provides a thorough history and discussion of *Maqasid al-Shari`ah*. After describing their scriptural origins, Kamali turns to discuss how classical Islamic jurists further developed the theory. He gives a detailed explanation of the development of each *maqsad* and the three levels of necessity within the elements of each. The primary level, which refers to the goals that are central to the survival of society, are the *daruriyyat* (necessities), while *hajiyyat* (needs) are important in making life easier and relieving burdens, and *tahsiniyyat* (refinements) include the goals leading to the perfection and beautification of the social order and of human behavior. He concludes by discussing the contemporary implications of the *Maqasid* theory for governance and public policy.

In the second interview, **Dr. Jasser Auda** traces the evolution of the *Maqasid* theory from classical to contemporary times. Auda shows how the theory has developed to fit modern concerns and understandings and thus provides a foundation for contemporary reform in the Muslim world. He discusses how a *Maqasid*-based approach has the potential to give rise to new directives and lines of action as Muslim societies develop. He champions a process of *ijtihad* towards concrete measures that will improve human development and strengthen human rights. This thorough discussion of the implications for a *Maqasid*-based approach toward governance illuminates its capacity to bridge the divisions within the Muslim world as well as between Muslims and the rest of the global community.

Dr. Khanjar Hamieh, an accomplished Shi'i scholar from Lebanon, articulates in the third interview the clear need in the present-day for a return to a *Maqasid*-based approach toward Islam and Islamic governance.

200

In his view, the *Maqasid* are not just immediate goals derived from legal rulings. Rather, they are the ultimate and eternal goals that reveal God's intention behind the creation of human beings. Hamieh identifies the underlying message and core principle as *tawhid*, the Oneness of God. From this fundamental unity, he argues, two practical implications are derived: human vicegerency (*istikhlaf*) and man's need for self-purification (*tazkiyya*). This understanding of the laws of the Shariah emphasizes the higher goals that they ultimately represent and puts the *Maqasid* within the perspective of the fundamental objectives of all religions.

In the fourth and final interview, **Ramzi Khoury** promotes the Shariah Index as a powerful tool for reform and renewal in the Muslim world. According to Khoury, since the Shariah Index has achieved the consensus of scholars from different schools of thought and political traditions, it has the potential to be deployed in a way that would promote harmony among the Muslim community. Khoury discusses the importance of the fact that the scholars have achieved consensus on the principles of good governance while recognizing that different forms of governance that fulfill these principles are equally valid. The governments in the Muslim world can use the Shariah Index to strengthen their legitimacy and stability by showing how their governance aligns with the sound Islamic principles agreed upon by scholars from all schools of thought. He urges the creation of a Shariah Index Institute that would work with governments, leaders, and organizations to this end. Drawing from his communications expertise, he discusses the radical groups that are harming the image of Islam and how the Shariah Index would challenge erroneous perceptions about Islam.

Goals and purposes of Islamic law (Mohammad Hashim Kamali)

Imam Feisal: Professor Kamali, as you know our working group has decided to use the *Maqasid al-Shari`ah* to measure the Islamicity of a state. Since you are an expert on the *Maqasid al-Shari`ah* I would like to ask you to discuss this topic in this interview. Why have you devoted so much effort to study the *Maqasid*?

Dr. Kamali: In my role as chairman of the International Institute for Advanced Islamic Studies in Kuala Lumpur, Malaysia, I have been privileged to investigate how Islam can serve as a motivating force for civilizational renewal. I have also been involved with drafting the constitutions of a number of Islamic countries, including Iraq, Afghanistan, and the Maldives. Throughout these experiences, I have come to see the *Maqasid* as central to efforts to renew Islam and ensure justice and good governance.

Imam Feisal: We know that the Shariah refers to God's Law as the commandments and prohibitions mentioned in the Qur'an and the teachings of the Prophet. It should therefore be correct to say that the term *"Maqasid al-Shari`ah"* is another way of saying "the objectives behind God's Law." How do we know that the Shariah is in fact a goal-oriented legal system, in which God has specific intentions guiding his commandments? Moreover, does the Qur'an identify these objectives?

Prof Kamali: Broadly speaking, God's law – the Shariah – is rooted in His desire to benefit both the individual and the broader community. As a result, the Shariah's laws are designed to protect these benefits and to facilitate the improvement and perfection of human life on earth. In fact, the Qur'an often expresses the rationale, purpose, and benefit of its laws, so much so that the text can be described as characteristically goal-oriented.

Imam Feisal: Can you give any specific instances of where the Qur'an is goal-oriented?

Dr. Kamali: The Qur'an explicitly states that its *raison d'être* is to bring mercy and serve as a "healing to the (spiritual) ailment of the hearts, guidance, and mercy (*rahmatan*) for the believers."[1] Likewise, it asserts that the most important purpose of Prophet Muhammad's prophethood is to provide mercy: "We have not sent you but as a mercy (*rahmatan*) to the worlds (*li'l-`alamin*)."[2] In its plural form, "worlds" implies that God's mercy is boundless. It extends to the entirety of humanity and even beyond to the animal world and other worlds we may not know. This emphasis on mercy is conveyed explicitly when God declares, "My *rahmah* extends to all things" (*wa rahmati wasi'at kulla shay'*).[3] The central role of mercy is also apparent in the fact that of God's ninety-nine beautiful names (*al-asma' al-husna*), the two names that introduce 113 of the 114 chapters of the Qur'an are al-Rahman (most beneficent) and al-Rahim (most merciful) (the one exception is Chapter 9 where the opening of *basmalah* is absent).

Imam Feisal: You have shown that the Qur'an and its laws aim to bring mercy (in its various manifestations) to human society. Can you provide more specific examples of how the Qur'an explains the goals and purposes of its laws? How do these specific laws of the Shariah engender mercy and improve societies?

Dr. Kamali: We can see that the Qur'an is a goal-oriented text through an examination of its legal verses. This holds true for both verses focusing on civil transactions (*mu`amalat*) and on devotional matters (*`ibadat*). For instance, in describing the rituals of ablution for prayer, the Qur'an declares the following: "God does not intend to inflict hardship on you. He intends cleanliness for you and to accomplish His favor upon you;"[4] and "truly prayer (*salah*) obstructs promiscuity and evil."[5] In other words, the purpose of prayer is to attain spiritual purity. The best way to do this, according to the Qur'an, is to be physically clean. Similarly, the Qur'an proclaims that the purpose of *jihad* is to grant permission to "those who fight because they have been wronged."[6] The goal of legalizing *jihad* is to fight injustice *(zulm)*. Essentially, the Qur'anic legislation is not simply confined to "do's" and "don'ts." Instead, it routinely provides justifications and objectives to its commandments.

Imam Feisal: There are times, however, when the Qur'an and the *Sunnah* do not give the reasoning behind a particular command. The prohibition on pork and certain other foods comes to mind: "Forbidden to you are: dead meat, blood, the flesh of swine, and that on which has been invoked the name of other than Allah."[7] But I understand that this is the exception. Can you provide further examples of when the Qur'an and the *Sunnah* explain why their laws are in place?

Dr. Kamali: Of course. There are many examples of legal stipulations that explicitly discuss the benefits they bring about or the harms they prevent. Take for example the prohibitions on oppression, corruption, and prejudice or, in a more specific context of trade, the prohibitions on exploitation, usury, hoarding, and gambling. The Qur'an terms all of these prohibitions "wrongful appropriation of the property of others" (*akl al-mal bi'l-batil*)[8] It therefore prohibits them to prevent the "wrongful appropriation of the property of others." In fact, the overall aim of nearly all the Shariah's laws is to provide benefit (*maslahah*) to both individuals and to the broader society. In essence, this benefit results from society's realization of the Shariah – the *Maqasid al-Shari`ah*.

Imam Feisal: If the overriding objective of the Shariah is to benefit humankind as an expression of God's mercy, is this not akin to the establishment of justice in society?

Dr. Kamali: It is. A fundamental aim of the Shariah is to implement justice (*`adl* or *qist*) and provide benefits (*masalih*) to humans. As a result, "*maslahah*" can be considered to be synonymous with the *Maqasid*. In fact, Muslim jurists have used the two terms almost interchangeably.

Imam Feisal: How did jurists identify these objectives of the Shariah? Were the *Maqasid* drawn solely from the text or did they derive them through *ijtihad*?

Dr. Kamali: Muslim jurists differed in their approaches to identifying the *Maqasid*. Although some limited the scope of the *Maqasid* to explicit declarations in the texts, the majority of scholars utilized both the actual text and the underlying effective cause and rationale of that text to deduce the *Maqasid*.[9] Since the Shariah is rational and its stipulations derive from specific objectives, scholars considered it generally unacceptable to conform to a law that defies the purposes of the Shariah. So while the *Maqasid* are certainly rooted in the textual injunctions of the Qur'an and the *Sunnah*, these jurists point to the fact that the *Maqasid* also look to the general objectives of these injunctions.

Imam Feisal: Since this is an important point, could you give our readers an example?

Dr. Kamali: In all legal systems – Western, Islamic, and others – a law is enacted for a specific purpose or objective. For example, the purpose of traffic laws is to guarantee the safety of human life and prevent injury. And, yet, it is hard to find scholars who would argue that emergency medical technicians driving ambulances be fined for exceeding speed limits and going through red traffic lights. In spite of the fact that they break the *letter* of the traffic laws by rushing a person suffering a medical emergency to the hospital, we recognize that these emergency vehicles must violate traffic laws to bring the injured or sick to the hospital as quickly as possible. Forcing ambulances to abide by the letter of traffic laws would defeat the purpose of these laws – the safety and protection of human lives.

The objective of a law is the driving purpose in its application. This is generally defined as the reason or operative cause (`*illah*) of a law. The *Maqasid al-Shari`ah* represent a coherent set of the underlying objectives of the laws of the Shariah. As in other legal systems, it is essential to understand these objectives in order to properly apply specific laws. These objectives must always be honored, even if doing so means violating the letter of the law or, in exceptional cases, suspending the law. In this way, the *Maqasid* approach does not lend itself to a strict literalist reading of the text. Instead, it focuses on integrating the Shariah's values into human judgment and legislation.

Imam Feisal: You say that although the *Maqasid* are based on the Qur'an and the *Sunnah*, they are not bounded by a strict textual methodology. If the *Maqasid* theory represents a dynamic approach to the Shariah, why then were some jurists reluctant to rely on it?

Dr. Kamali: I think that this scholarly reticence might be due specifically to the fact that this exercise involves deductive reasoning. Jurists were probably uncomfortable with the fact that rather than have a clear-cut legal code, the *Maqasid* approach often required them to independently identify the purposes of the Lawgiver. While the leading Islamic legal schools did not fully reject the *Maqasid* theory, it remained on the fringes of mainstream juristic thought and practice. Of course, there were differences of orientation and opinion among the legal schools toward the *Maqasid*. But, in general, most jurists did not focus on identifying the Shariah's deeper goals.

Imam Feisal: In other words, some jurists were fearful of saying that they presumed to know the contents of God's mind when He decreed a law, unless He or the Prophet explicitly gave the reason. In contrast, jurists promoting the *Maqasid* doctrine argued that because God gave reasons for many of His laws, the laws can be considered products of rational processes. In turn, these jurists considered it appropriate to put all of His commandments into a rational structure, including those laws where no explicit reason was given in the Qur'an or the *Sunnah*. Would you mind talking more about the different approaches to identifying the *Maqasid*, how theories of the *Maqasid* changed over time, and the earliest attempts to identify them?

Dr. Kamali: Yes, these are all very important questions that I would be happy to discuss. As we have said, the majority of Muslim jurists did not confine the *Maqasid* to explicit texts alone. (One exception to this was the Zahiri legal school, which maintained that the *Maqasid* can only be identified by explicit texts). The Batiniyyah, for example, asserted that the intrinsic objective of textual injunctions could always be found in the text's hidden meaning (i.e., *batin*). In fact, this is how they received their name, the Batiniyyah.[10]

Imam Feisal: Have any contemporary scholars emphasized the text's inner meanings in relation to the *Maqasid*?

Dr. Kamali: There have been a number of contemporary scholars that have substantially developed the *Maqasid* approach. Ibn 'Ashur (d. 1973) seems to have been the first contemporary scholar to assert that the general objectives (*Maqasid 'ammah*) of Shariah are "the deeper meanings (*ma'ani*) and inner wisdom (*hikam*) that the Lawgiver has contemplated in relation to all or most of the Shariah ordinances..."[11] Similarly, 'Allal al-Fasi (d. 1974) defined the *Maqasid* as "the hidden meanings (*asrar*) and wisdom that the Lawgiver has considered in the enactment of all of the Shariah ordinances."[12] These two definitions can be seen to differ on two related accounts. First, according to al-Fasi, all of the Shariah's laws possess a clear purpose. On the other hand, Ibn 'Ashur takes a less definitive approach and recognizes that "all or most of the ordinances of Shariah" have clear purposes. Second, Ibn 'Ashur disagrees with al-Fasi's assertion that the Shariah can have "hidden meanings" (*asrar*). Instead, Ibn 'Ashur argues that the *Maqasid* should be firm, evident, consistent and exclusive (*thabit, zahir, mundabit,* and *muttarid*). The underlying difference between these two scholars is whether it is possible that there are objectively indecipherable *Maqasid*.[13]

Imam Feisal: Could you describe how these scholars methodologically overcome the fact that some *Maqasid* are not explicitly identified in the Qur'an or the *Sunnah*?

Dr. Kamali: In his important work on the Shariah, *al-Muwafaqat fi Usul al-Shari`ah*, the eighth/fourteenth century Andalusian scholar, Abu Ishaq Ibrahim al-Shatibi, affirmed the need to adhere to explicit injunctions. But, he also argued that one should not reify adherence to these texts to the point that the observance of the text is disconnected from its underlying rationale. Such a rigid adherence, stressed al-Shatibi, ran contrary to the objectives (*Maqasid*) of the Lawgiver. In fact, he even asserted that this reification was akin to defying the explicit text itself. In essence, Shatibi argued that the best approach, which is harmonious with the Lawgiver's intentions, is to read and understand the text of the command or prohibition alongside its underlying objective.[14]

Imam Feisal: Would you give us some more background on Shatibi's work?

Dr. Kamali: The broader context of Shatibi's *al-Muwafaqat* is indeed significant. On the one hand, it was fashioned in response to the social and economic realities in fourteenth century Andalusia. On the other hand, it was an attempt to move beyond the predominant deductive approaches to jurisprudence and their limitations. Utilizing an inductive approach, Shatibi focused more on the broader themes of Shariah and showed the flexibility and dynamism of Islamic law.

Imam Feisal: So, according to Shatibi, although the *Maqasid al-Shari`ah* are not explicitly written in the text, these principles can be clearly induced from the Qur'an, the *Sunnah*, and the overall message of the Shariah?

Dr. Kamali: Yes. However, it is essential to note that Shatibi did not list specific *Maqasid*. Instead, he focused on laying out the major themes of the *Maqasid* and the methods by which they can be identified. Even though it is difficult to read into his silence when it came to listing specific *Maqasid*, it is possible that this was a result from the strong meaning of the word *"Maqasid,"* which to a native Arab conveys a self-evident meaning.

Imam Feisal: But jurists were already using the word *"Maqasid"* in different contexts. You gave the example of the objective of *salah*, or prayer, as being a term used.

Dr. Kamali: That's correct. There is a historical process during which the term *"Maqasid al-Shari`ah"* matured into a separate branch of Shariah knowledge. The tenth century scholar, Abu 'Abd Allah al-Tirmidhi al-Hakim (d.320/932), used the term *"Maqasid al-salah."* Izz al-Din 'Abd al-Salam al-Sulami (d.660/1262), described his book *Qawa'id al-Ahkam* as a work on the *"Maqasid al-ahkam."* He wrote that "most of the objectives of the Qur'an are to facilitate benefits (*masalih*) to mankind and the means that secure them and that the realization of benefit also includes the prevention of evil."[15] In other words, Sulami asserted that all of the obligations (*takalif*) laid out in Shariah were intended to provide benefits for people in this world and the next. This understanding that the Shariah is concerned with the benefits of God's creatures is thus the underlying connotation of the term *masalih/Maqasid*.

Imam Feisal: This reminds me of the jurist Ibn al-Qayyim al-Jawziyyah's (d. 751/1350) well-known description of the Shariah's essence.

Dr. Kamali: Yes. He said that the Shariah exists to achieve justice and the *maslahah* of God's creation. As such, any law that does not operate to this end does not belong in the Shariah: "The foundation of the Shariah is wisdom and the safeguarding of people's interests in this world and the next. In its entirety, it is justice, mercy and wisdom. Every rule which transforms justice to tyranny, mercy to its opposite, the good to the evil, and wisdom to triviality does not belong in the Shariah ... "[16] In fact, Sulami further develops this idea. "One who looks into the totality of the Shariah guidelines for the realization of benefit and prevention of harm will reach the unflinching conclusion that it is impermissible to neglect these benefits and impermissible also to allow the harm to inflict itself – even if there is no text, consensus or a ruling of a particular analogy (*qiyas*) to say so."[17] This statement implies that it is not essential that the *Maqasid* be directly tied to a particular text. Rather, it is more important that they be predicated on an overall understanding obtained from reading sources *in toto*. In other words, induction becomes a method of extracting the *ahkam* from the sources of the Shariah in order to attain the broader objectives of public interest and benefit.

Imam Feisal: Could you elaborate on this process of induction? How has induction enriched the *Maqasid*-based approach to law?

Dr. Kamali: According to Shatibi, induction can be applied in cases in which a text refers to a specific subject at various points without ever giving a decisive injunction. Since these passages collectively lend themselves to a specific meaning, we can induce from them an underlying *maqsad*. For instance, there is not a specific declaration in the Qur'an that the Shariah is for the benefit of the people. Yet, this conclusion can certainly be induced from a variety of textual proclamations.[18] Likewise, according to Shatibi, the scope of the benefits (*masalih*) that the Shariah furthers should be taken into account and needs to be understood in a broad sense. It should include benefits pertaining both to this world and the hereafter and include the material, moral, and spiritual benefits of both the individual and the community. Moreover, it should mandate the prevention of harm. Having said that, Shatibi recognizes that the benefits of Shariah cannot always be ascertained by human reason alone. Instead, there are benefits that require divine revelation to be discerned.[19]

Imam Feisal: So Shatibi used the inductive method to define benefits more broadly, a definition which then informed his understanding of the Shariah and its principle aims (*Maqasid*). Can you give us a few examples of his use of induction in the *Maqasid* theory specifically?

Dr. Kamali: Using induction, Shatibi endorsed the division of the *Maqasid* into three categories based on their respective importance – essentials (*daruriyyat*), needs (*hajiyyat*), and refinements or desirables (*tahsiniyyat*). Then, Shatibi argued that the essential category of the *Maqasid* – the *daruriyyat* – can be classified into six categories, each of which the Shariah preserves and promotes: faith, life, mind, property, lineage, and honor. Beyond this, Shatibi did not confine his inductive method to identifying the underlying objectives and values of Shariah. He also extended it to analyze and determine commands and prohibitions, by asserting that they could either be derived from a clear text or inducted from a broader reading of numerous textual proclamations.[20] It is important to note that these conclusions are of great overall importance. They are not open to doubt and their credibility is not a matter of speculative reasoning.[21]

Imam Feisal: You said that Shatibi's inductive conclusions "are not open to doubt."

Dr. Kamali: Yes. In fact, Shatibi goes a step further and argues that because these inductive conclusions are based on the underlying objectives of Shariah, they actually have a higher order of importance than specific rules. Indeed, his claim that induction is a foundational method in Islamic jurisprudential method and that it underlies the *Maqasid* approach to Islamic law is one of his most important and original scholarly contributions.

Imam Feisal: Allow me to take a step back and summarize some of what has already been said. On the one hand, you established that by using induction and extracting from broad themes the *Maqasid al-Shari`ah* can be decisively obtained from the Qur'an and the *Sunnah*. On the other hand, you discussed how many jurists were unwilling to engage in what they deemed to be a speculative use of the Qur'an. You asserted that, consequently, the *Maqasid* approach "remained on the fringes of mainstream juristic thought on the sources of law." So, what was the place of the *Maqasid* doctrine in early Islamic juristic doctrine? And, how did the modern framework of six *Maqasid* and three levels of necessity take shape?

Dr. Kamali: In the early stages of the development of Islamic legal thought, the *Maqasid al-Shariah* were not widely seen as constituting a theme of Shariah in their own right. Only after the consolidation of the Islamic legal schools, did they gain more traction in jurisprudential circles. It was not until the early fourth Islamic century that the term *"Maqasid"* was used in the juristic writings of al-Tirmidhi. Thereafter, the term *Maqasid* received scant attention until Imam al-Haramayn al-Juwayni (d.478/1085) utilized it extensively. Even to this day, many reputable textbooks on the science of the sources of law (*usul al-fiqh*) do not mention the *Maqasid* in their usual list of topics. Similarly, although they are obviously embedded within discussions of *ijtihad*, the *Maqasid* have often not been treated as such in conventional descriptions of the theory of *ijtihad*.

Imam Feisal: I imagine that there is both a historical and ideational narrative to the development of the *Maqasid al-Shariʿah* doctrine. Would you narrate this history and discuss the seminal thinkers who developed the *Maqasid* doctrine?

Dr. Kamali: Al-Juwayni seems to have been the first to classify the *Maqasid* into the three levels in accordance with their respective importance (essentials, needs, and refinements). He also argues that the Companions of the Prophet Muhammad were well aware of the objectives of Shariah and, therefore, "one who did not ponder over the *Maqasid* of commands and prohibitions (*awamir wa nawahi*) did so at one's peril and was likely to lack insight into the Shariah."[22]

Abu Hamid al-Ghazali (d.505/1111), Al-Juwayni pupil, further developed these ideas. In his works *Shifaʾ al-Ghalil* and *al-Mustasfa*, al-Ghazali discussed the relationship between *Maqasid*, public interest (*maslahah*), and ratiocination (*taʿlil*). Al-Ghazali's promotion of the *Maqasid* approach and the *daruriyyat* aligned with his broader attempts to highlight the importance of reason and in turn integrate and bridge the ostensible differences between faith and reason, as well as the theological approach of the *Mutakallimin* and the rationalist approach of the *Ahl al-Raʾy*.[23] Al-Ghazali asserted that the intrinsic values of the Shariah can be discerned using reason. At the same time, al-Ghazali emphasized the role of revelation in the Shariah. He argued that "the most noble of sciences is one wherein reason and revelation are combined such that opinion (*raʾy*) and law (*sharʿ*) accompany one another...so that one's conclusion is not based on pure reason in isolation of the Shariah nor is it founded on an imitation (*taqlid*) that is not endorsed by reason."[24] In this sense, the character of al-Ghazali's reason can be considered an *ijtihad*-oriented reasoning. To this end, al-Ghazali's approval of *maslahah* is especially pronounced when it promotes the *Maqasid* of Shariah.

Imam Feisal: So al-Ghazali used "*ijtihad*-oriented reasoning," which combines human reason, human welfare, and revelation, to define the *daruriyyat*. Can you go into some more detail as to what these essential *Maqasid*, or core objectives of the Shariah, actually are?

Dr. Kamali: Al-Ghazali argued that the Shariah's underlying foundational objectives can be divided into five basic categories: Religion, Life, Mind, Lineage, and Property.[25] Al-Ghazali refers to these five categories as *daruriyyat al-din*, the essentials of Shariah and Islamic law.

It is necessary to clarify that, when we talk in Islamic law about the essentials or *daruriyyat*, we mean one of two things: either the general essentials of Islamic law (the *Maqasid*) or the category of essentials within each *maqsad*. And here we are discussing the first meaning.

Shatibi defined the *daruriyyat* as "values that are indispensable for the proper maintenance of man's welfare in this world and the next; their collapse will cause chaos and corruption in this life and lead to failure and loss in the hereafter."[26] There are two important points in this definition that should be highlighted. First, according to Shatibi, the *daruriyyat* touch upon both the material and religious aspects of human welfare. Second, the specific nature of the *daruriyyat* is rather vague and, most importantly, is not confined to a particular number or subject.

The Hanbali jurist al-Tufi (d. 716/1316), who slightly preceded Shatibi, defined the *daruriyyat* in a similar fashion. "*Daruriyyat* are indispensable for the survival and orderly management of the affairs of this world (*siyasat al-`alam wa baqa'ih*), and they are known by the attention that the Lawgiver has paid to them in the enactment of His laws, such as the five essential interests..."[27] While al-Tufi only referred to affairs of this world, his definition seems to conform with Shatibi's insofar as he includes religion as one of the main headings and, in turn, does not rule out the notion that the *daruriyyat* pertain to afterlife. The important underlying criterion of the *daruriyyat* is that they are *essential* to society and individuals. It is necessary to preserve and promote these *Maqasid* in order to ensure the continued proper functioning of society.

Imam Feisal: That question of how many *Maqasid* there actually are is a disputed albeit an important one. You mentioned that al-Shatibi and al-Ghazali identified five essential objectives of the Shariah. Today, many Muslim jurists and thinkers refer to *six* essential *Maqasid*: religion, life, intellect or mind, lineage or family, property or wealth, and honor. When did this sixth *maqsad* enter the jurisprudence?

Dr. Kamali: Al-Qarafi added this sixth *maqsad* – the protection of honor (*'ird*) – to the five *Maqasid*. Later scholars, including Taj al-Din 'Abd al-Wahhab al-Subki (d.771/1370) and Muhammad ibn 'Ali al-Shawkani (d.1250/1834), reaffirmed this addition.

Imam Feisal: The inclusion of honor (*'ird*), which is at times translated as dignity, as a *maqsad* is still debated today. Can you guide us through the different sides of the debate?

Dr. Kamali: Initially, scholars asserted that the Shariah's stipulation for the protection of honor fell under the purview of the *maqsad* of lineage or family descent (*nasl/nasab*). Proponents of adding a distinct sixth *maqsad* of honor asserted that the division of the *Maqasid* was intended to reflect the Qur'anic *Hudud*. In other words, they argued that each distinct crime that warranted a *hadd* also formed the basis for a *maqsad*. Since the Shariah had stipulated a separate *hadd* for the slanderous accusation of adultery (*qadhf*) as a way of protecting an individual's honor, they called for a sixth *maqsad* that would explicitly focus on protecting honor.[28]

Imam Feisal: This is one of the more interesting aspects of the *Maqasid* theory. The scholars who added honor as a sixth *maqsad* determined, at least in part, that each of the *Hudud* punishments embodied a particular benefit (*maslahah*) or objective (*maqsad*). They determined that the *maqsad* behind the punishment for murder is the sanctity of human life, the objective behind the punishment for adultery is the sanctity of lineage; punishment for theft is intended to ensure the sanctity of property; the objective behind the prohibition against alcohol consumption is the sanctity of the human intellect and sound judgment; the prohibition against the rejection of God, which is the greatest sin, is derived from the sanctity of religion. And as you said, the objective behind the punishment for slander is the sanctity of human honor and dignity. This is a very compelling argument for including honor as a sixth *Maqasid*, is it not?

Dr. Kamali: Yes, I agree. In fact, I would contend that the Shariah mandates the protection of honor based on the *Hadith* from the Farewell Pilgrimage (*hajjat al-wida'*), which is recorded by al-Bukhari and states: "Your blood, property and honor are (sacrosanct) and forbidden to one another" (*inna dima'akum wa amwalakum wa a'radakum `alaykum haram*). In my view, this *Hadith* leaves little doubt that honor should be identified as a *maqsad* in its own right. Having said that, some jurists argued over whether the notion of honor was an essential goal of Shariah that could be clearly differentiated from other goals and positioned as a freestanding *maqsad*.

Imam Feisal: Would I be correct in saying that the jurists' determination of the *Maqasid* from the *hadd* punishments was another application of induction (*istiqra'*)?

Dr. Kamali: Yes, and as I mentioned, Shatibi heavily relies on induction to identify the *Maqasid*. Moreover, he uses this method to categorize the *Maqasid* into primary *Maqasid* (*Maqasid asliyyah*) and secondary *Maqasid* (*Maqasid tab'iyyah*). The former category is composed of the *daruriyyat* which every individual must protect regardless of their personal predilections. Meanwhile, there is more flexibility in respect to upholding the *Maqasid* included in the latter category.

Imam Feisal: I would like to discuss the differences between the *daruriyyat*, *hajiyyat*, and *tahsiniyyat* later in the interview. But for now, a less technical question. We have heard Shatibi's name throughout this interview. How would you characterize his overall contribution to the development of the *Maqasid* theory and its solidification as a legitimate juristic doctrine?

Dr. Kamali: Well, despite their great importance, as I said earlier, the *Maqasid al-Shariah* is a late addition to the juristic thought of Islamic law's leading schools. It has acquired prominence only through the path-breaking contribution of al-Shatibi. In fact, I would say that he is the primary force behind the current prominence of the *Maqasid* approach to Islamic law.

Imam Feisal: He is indeed a seminal figure. Returning to the issue of the number of essential *Maqasid*, we have learned that the early jurists enumerated five and, at times, six *daruriyyat*. But were they limited to these five or six? In other words, given that the *Maqasid* approach uses induction, can we really say that *all* of which the Shariah seeks to protect fits under these categories?

Dr. Kamali: This is a very important question. As I already mentioned, Shatibi himself did not limit the *Maqasid* to a specific number. Similarly, Ibn Taymiyya (d.728/1328) asserted that the *Maqasid* are not confined to a specific number or subject. It is possible to identify throughout the Qur'an and the *Sunnah* a wide range of purposes. To name but a few, the Shariah orders the fulfillment of promises, honesty and trustworthiness, preservation of kinship ties, being good to one's neighbors, and moral purity.[29] In fact, Ibn Taymiyya asserted that even the essential *Maqasid* could not be limited to the basic five categories. He therefore proclaimed that the *Maqasid* approach should embrace a malleable and evolving approach to law.

Imam Feisal: What about contemporary jurists? Do they agree on these five or six essential *Maqasid*? Have any scholars added any more *Maqasid*?

Dr. Kamali: Jurists from across the different legal schools have agreed on the normative validity of the five *Maqasid*. As we have already discussed, however, this normative judgment neither precluded al-Qarafi from adding the sixth *maqsad* nor did it hinder Ibn Taymiyya from asserting that the list could be expanded to include other *Maqasid*.[30] In fact, contemporary commentators generally adopt Ibn Taymiyya's evolutionary approach to the *Maqasid*. Muhammad 'Abduh, Ibn 'Ashur, Muhammad Rashid Rida, Abu'l `Ala Maududi, Ahmad al-Raysuni, and Yusuf al-Qaradawi have all endorsed this position, enriching the *Maqasid* discourse.[31] To give but one example, al-Qaradawi has explicitly included social welfare support (*takaful ijtima'i*), freedom, human dignity, and human fraternity as *Maqasid al-Shariah*.[32]

Imam Feisal: Given Ibn Taymiyya and others' position that the *Maqasid* should not be restricted to a specific set, would *you* add any *Maqasid* to the list?

Dr. Kamali: Yes, I support the expansion of the *Maqasid al-Shariah*. Needless to say, any expansion must be harmonious with the textual guidelines of Shariah and depends on the particular contemporary priorities. For our particular age, I propose to add global peace and security, constitutional rights and liberties, economic development, and progress in science and technology to the structure of *Maqasid*. All of these objectives are so crucial to welfare and the place of Muslims in the global community that, in my humble opinion, they should stand as individual *Maqasid* on their own right.

Imam Feisal: Let's move away from the historical development of the *Maqasid* approach to an overview of its theory. We have touched on a number of these points already, but I think we should quickly recount the theory's main components. For example, how are the *Maqasid* traditionally classified, how should the three levels of necessity be interpreted, and what implications does the *Maqasid* theory have for governance and public policy?

Dr. Kamali: The *Maqasid* have been classified in a number of ways. They have been classified based on their importance, the scope of their application, their origin, and the nature of the textual evidence that supports them.

Imam Feisal: You mentioned that al-Juwayni is often credited as the first jurist to delineate each *maqsad* into essentials (*daruriyyat*), needs (*hajiyyat*), and refinements (*tahsiniyyat*). This is now the most widespread classification. Can you further differentiate between these three classes within the *Maqasid*? Earlier, you quoted Shatibi's definition of the essential *Maqasid* as representing those "values that are indispensable for the proper maintenance of man's welfare in this world and the next; their collapse will cause chaos and corruption in this life and lead to failure and loss in the hereafter."

Dr. Kamali: Allow me to briefly summarize some of what I have already said. We discussed how Muslim jurists classified the entire range of the *masalih*-cum-*Maqasid* into three categories in a descending order of importance (*daruriyyat, hajiyyat, tahsiniyyat*). We also discussed the division of the *Maqasid daruriyyah* into five or six analytic categories: religion, life, lineage, mind, property, and honor. By definition, these *Maqasid* are deemed to be essential objectives of Shariah. In turn, they are protected in both affirmative and prohibitive manners. In an affirmative sense, we ensure their continued fulfillment by strengthening the means that secure them. To affirm the *darurah* of life, the promotion of basic health care within a population is prescribed. In a prohibitive sense, we preemptively inhibit the possible actions that might threaten their continued existence.[33] To preempt the violation of the *darurah* of life, legal penalties against murder are prescribed. This affirmative and prohibitive approach holds true for the remaining *daruriyyat*.

Imam Feisal: I don't want to jump ahead in our discussion, but it seems to me that the ways in which an individual, a society, or a government protects these essentials would evolve over time. Does the *Maqasid* theory allow for this flexibility? And, what is the actual responsibility of these groups to protect the essential *Maqasid*?

Dr. Kamali: First of all, since Shatibi is suggesting a fairly open approach to defining the *Maqasid*, he seems to also be adopting a flexible approach to protecting them. Just as the *Maqasid* are liable to change, so too are the permitted protective actions that individuals, societies, and governments can take.[34] To this end and in response to your second question, we can assume that since these five principal *Maqasid* constitute foundational interests, they must be promoted through all lawfully available means. In fact, under the principle of unrestricted public interest (*maslahah mursalah*), it is the duty of the rulers and high level jurists (*mujtahids*) to ensure their preservation and protection.[35]

Imam Feisal: How do we distinguish the *daruriyyat* from the *hajiyyat*? What makes any given *maqsad* an essential *maqsad* rather than (merely) a needed one?

Dr. Kamali: The *Maqasid hajiyyah* include objectives of the Shariah that are not essential but rather aim to circumvent unnecessary hardship on individuals. So the defining characteristic here is that the *Maqasid hajiyyah* are important but if they are not fulfilled this does not pose a threat to the very survival of normal order. In other words, the *Maqasid hajiyyah* are those interests that remove hardship in individuals' lives, but unlike the *daruriyyat*, they do not prevent societal collapse.

Imam Feisal: Can you give us examples of what is generally seen as a *hajiyyah*?

Dr. Kamali: Many concessions (*rukhas*) in the Shariah, which pertain to either devotional acts (`*ibadat*) or civil transactions (*mu`amalat*), constitute *hajiyyat*. These concessions seek to prevent individual hardship, however they are not fundamentally essential to individuals' and societies' basic functioning. The Shariah has stipulated concessions in almost all areas of devotional acts. Meanwhile, in civil transactions, the Shariah has enabled certain forms of contracts in order to ease business transactions while ensuring that they do not violate fundamental Islamic business ethics. The sale of *salam* and lease and hire (*ijarah*) are two such examples. *Salam* is a kind of forward sale contract whereby money is paid for a product that will be acquired at a later date. Likewise, in family law the Shariah permits divorce in specific situations as a concession intended to remove hardship.

That being said, there is room for overlap between *daruriyyat* and *hajiyyat*. In specific circumstances, *hajiyyat* are seen as *daruriyyat*. For instance, Shatibi argues that hiring a wet nurse for an unprotected infant constitutes a case in which a general *hajiyyah* is elevated to a *daruriyyah*.[36] More generally, when an issue that is perceived as a *hajiyyah* has implications upon society writ large, it becomes a *daruriyyah*.

Imam Feisal: This malleability is fascinating, but it also seems to allude to a tension. Given the fact that different interests can take on different levels of significance, how did jurists handle situations in which protecting one interest came at the expense of another?

Dr. Kamali: This is certainly a central issue of concern for jurists. In general, a *daruriyyah* takes precedent over a *hajiyyah*. However, in situations in which it is not possible to clearly rank the clashing interests, the prevention of harm takes priority over the fulfillment of benefit.[37] This principle is derived from the basic fact that the Shariah is more emphatic when it comes to preventing evil. According to the *Hadith*, the Prophet said: "When I order you to do something, do it to the extent of your ability, but when I forbid you from something, then avoid it [altogether]."[38]

Imam Feisal: Could you describe the third class of the Shariah's interests, the refinements or desirables (*tahsiniyyat*)?

Dr. Kamali: The *tahsiniyyat* are broadly defined as interests that refine people's customs and conduct. In other words, through the *tahsiniyyat* the Shariah provides guidelines to enhance and even perfect human conduct. While the Shariah stresses the fulfillment of a number of basic interests – the *daruriyyat* and *hajiyyat* – it also lays out ways to further refine these fundamental actions. Beyond promulgating the obligation to pray, the Shariah lays out a variety of *tahsiniyyat* pertaining to prayer: it encourages Muslims to ensure that their bodies and clothes are clean when praying, and it discourages consuming raw garlic before congregational prayer. Likewise, the Shariah recommends supererogatory prayers as a *tahsiniyyah*. In customary matters and relations among people, the Shariah also provides a number of *tahsiniyyat* that are intended to further improve human interaction and conduct: it encourages generously giving charity, gentleness (*rifq*), pleasant speech and manner (*husn al-khulq*), and fair dealing (*ihsan*). Similarly, in addition to stipulating the requirement for fair and just rule, the Shariah advises judges and rulers to be patient, especially when they enforce penalties.

Imam Feisal: This idea of a spectrum ranging from the foundational obligations of Muslims to the acts of refinement is very important. In fact, this ranking also applies to the realization of the *Maqasid*. To fulfill the obligations stipulated in the Shariah, a society or state must, at the very least, protect the *daruriyyat*. Meanwhile, though it should certainly strive to practice the *tahsiniyyat*, these elements are, in fact, not as expedient. That being said, did Muslim jurists prioritize the *daruriyyat* themselves?

Dr. Kamali: The conventional ordering of *daruriyyat* prioritizes the *maqsad* of religion (*din*). This prioritization is based on the idea that religion is the bastion of values and is therefore the most fundamental *maqsad*. In fact, according to this prioritization, the *maqsad* of life and its preservation are subservient to the preservation of religion. Ibn Amir al-Hajj took a second and rather exceptional view regarding the relative prioritization of the *daruriyyat*. He asserted that the *maqsad* of religion is of the lowest priority among the essential *Maqasid*. His argument was based on the fact that religion is the Right of God (*haqq Allah*), whereas the other four essentials consist of the Right of Man (*haqq al-adami*), which usually takes priority over the Right of God.[39]

Imam Feisal: An argument that can be furnished in favour of this comes from your assertion that the *hadd* that forms the basis of this maqsad is actually that of treason rather than mere apostasy, meaning an act that threatens the community's national security rather than the mere shift of one individual's personal belief. This would reduce the role of religion as the value protected by making treason a crime, in favour of perhaps a value akin to strengthening community coherence. Having said that, do you agree with Ibn Amir's lower prioritization of religion?

Dr. Kamali: I believe that the logic behind the prioritization of religion is fundamentally valid. Yet, I also find it open-ended and overly vague. In particular, I find the relationship between the *Maqasid* of religion and life to be problematic. The preservation of religion is fundamentally important. But, it assumes a continued and unimpaired existence of life. Without this preservation of life, the preservation of religion is unsustainable. I would therefore contend that the *maqsad* of life (*nafs*) should be the most essential of the *daruriyyat*. Simply put, life is the carrier of all the *Maqasid*. At the same time, however, I would argue that life may be sacrificed not only for the sake of the protection of religion, but also to protect the other *daruriyyat*. But, in general, I believe that any prioritization within the *daruriyyat* is extremely problematic. However, if need be, I propose to view the *maqsad* of life as an essential starting point for the realization of all of the other *Maqasid*.

Imam Feisal: So how would you prioritize the *daruriyyat*?

Dr. Kamali: I would place the *maqsad* of life as the most pertinent of the *daruriyyat*. I would then rank the *Maqasid* in the following order: life, mind, religion, family, and property.

Imam Feisal: Interesting. I would now like to take a look at each *maqsad* in the order that you proposed: life (*nafs*), intellect or mind (`*aql*), religion (*din*), family descent or progeny (*nasl/nasab*), and property (*mal*). How does the Shariah protect and promote the *maqsad* of life?

Dr. Kamali: Numerous unequivocal texts in the Qur'an and *Hadith* affirm the sanctity of human life. For example, the Qur'an explicitly states: "Do not kill the soul which Allah has forbidden except for the requirements of justice" (*Wala taqtulu al-nafsa allati harrama Allahu illa bil haqq*).[40] There are two important aspects that should be highlighted in this verse. First, this verse stipulates the absolute protection of life. The right to life, regardless of differences of age, race, gender, social status, or religion, is an inherent right of every human being. Second, the violation of this right is impermissible unless it is explicitly deemed permissible in the course of the dispensation of justice. Of course, this statement touches a broader question of justice and capital punishment, however, I will not go into this discussion at present.[41]

By designating life as a *maqsad*, the Shariah has validated both affirmative and prohibitive measures that seek to protect and promote it. Numerous of these measures are explicitly laid out in the Shariah. Others fall under the doctrine of judicious policy (*siyasah shar'iyyah*), according to which the head of state and other lawful authorities are granted the power to introduce measures to protect life. Such measures include the provision of an adequate healthcare system and the assurance of safe living environments.[42]

Imam Feisal: Does the *maqsad* of life necessitate any additional requirements beyond the foundational protection of human life?

Dr. Kamali: As I said earlier, the laws of Shariah are particularly concerned with protecting life. Yet, beyond seeking to ensure the basic protection of life, the Shariah is also concerned with the quality of life. To this end, the Shariah lays out rules for the protection of the *maqsad* of life in three different scenarios: first, a scenario of ease and normality (*al-sa'ah wa'l-yusr*), second, a scenario of hardship that is not life-threatening (*haraj*); and third, a scenario of overwhelming necessity (*darurah*).

Imam Feisal: You mentioned that the Shariah protects life in both an affirmative and prohibitive sense. Could you elaborate on this?

Dr. Kamali: In an affirmative fashion, the Shariah protects human life from the moment of conception. The Shariah lays out elaborate rules regarding pregnancy, birth, and childhood, all of which define responsibilities for the maintenance and support of the child's life and protection. The Shariah also protects the life of an abandoned infant whose parents are unknown (the *laqit*), illustrating the importance that the Shariah assigns to human life *in toto*. Moreover, beyond protecting the basic existence of life, the Shariah actively seeks to facilitate people's ability to earn an honorable living through lawful occupation. These measures include ensuring suitable healthcare, provision of adequate food and shelter, family and child support, and so forth. In this way, the *maqsad* of life intersects with the *maqsad* of honor and accords with the dignity which God bestowed on humankind.[43]

In its defensive sense, the Shariah protects life through a series of penal sanctions. For example, the Shariah determines that potentially harmful or lethal acts of aggression against a pregnant woman can be punished in two ways. In cases in which there is no doubt that the act of aggression killed the fetus, the Shariah stipulates just retaliation (*qisas*). In cases in which there is uncertainty regarding the impact of the aggression, the Shariah calls for payment of all or a portion of the blood money (*diyah* or *ghurrah* respectively). In fact, in cases of unjustified self-induced abortion, the Shariah even holds the mother liable for the death of the fetus.

> **Imam Feisal:** Every legal system employs the threat of legal punishment for those who violate it. But these rules must also account for extenuating circumstances and their effect on particular cases. The Shariah is a very practical system, so how does it deal with such circumstances?
>
> **Dr. Kamali:** The Shariah grants legal concessions in a variety of circumstances such as war and peace, self-defense, pregnancy, starvation, and sickness. In fact, in situations of absolute necessity, the Shariah calls for the suspension of normal commands and prohibitions (*al-awamir wa'l-nawahi*). The legal maxim that "necessity makes the unlawful lawful" (*al-darurat tubih al-mahzurat*) specifically addresses this reality.

Underlying the Shariah's approach to governance is the basic prohibition of shedding the blood of a protected individual (*ma'sum al-dam*) in vain (*hadr al-dam*). The Shariah thus seeks to prosecute the aggressor of unlawful aggression.[44] The collection of laws that lay out the punishment for transgressions in these extreme cases are termed the "limits of God" (*Hudud Allah*). According to the Qur'an, "one who transgresses the limits of God truly commits violence against his own soul." Since the Qur'an explicitly states that these actions are serious transgressions, it limits the discretionary powers of judges and rulers in cases involving these actions.[45] Beyond the legal implications of this statement, this verse highlights the fact that Islam designates itself as a religion compatible with human nature (*din al-fitrah*). Not only is the protection of life a right of humans, it is also considered a Right of God (*haqq Allah*). The intrinsic morality of Islam is thus fused with its legal stipulations.

Imam Feisal: This fusion is in fact emblematic of the Islamic moral legal code. Could you talk more about the *Hudud* punishments? You mentioned that judges and rulers have limited discretionary power to determine punishments for violations of these transgression. However, is application of the *Hudud* mandatory in every single case? We often hear from various groups that the *Hudud* are mandatory.

Dr. Kamali: Yes, this is a claim that I also hear from various groups. However, I would actually contend that the *Hudud* can be considered a juristic construct, which has no clear obligatory origin in the Qur'an.[46] The word "*hadd*" literally translates into "limit." The *Hudud* penalties should be considered limits; they are maximal, not mandatory, penalties. For instance, when discussing the punishment for murder the Qur'an encourages the victim's family to unconditionally forgive the murderer. Recognizing the difficulty in doing so, the Qur'an encourages the family to take monetary compensation from the murderer. Only as a last resort does the Qur'an permit the capital punishment of the murderer.[47] This highlights the fact that the *hadd* punishment of capital punishments represents the maximum – and not the mandatory – punishment. This applies similarly to the other *Hudud* punishments.

Imam Feisal: In other words, the severity of the punishment depends on a number of factors like the crime's context, its seriousness, etc. This actually resembles the "degrees" of crimes we have in American law. For instance, for murder there is a range of penalties stipulated by the degree of action. First degree murder is punished more harshly than second degree murder, in part because the former, which often entails premeditation and intent, is deemed more heinous.

Having said that, let's move on to the second *maqsad*, intellect or mind. How do you define the *maqsad* of the mind and why do you deem it to be so important to the Shariah?

> **Dr. Kamali**: Intellect is a unique quality of human beings, which God endowed us with in order to be His vicegerents in this world. By possessing intellect, we are able to utilize the resources of the world for our benefits. Intellect is both our principal tool with which we acquire knowledge, and it is the prerequisite for us to possess our rights and duties (*mukallaf*). We can divide human reason into three categories: (1) sense perception, (2) intellect, and (3) divine revelation. All three of these categories are interlinked and can be depicted as progressively widening circles. Human reason is predicated, to a large extent on the perception of sense. Sense encompasses the perception of observable and experimental data. The second circle, intellect, encompasses the human ability to perceive abstract and unseen phenomena. Finally, the widest of the three circles, divine revelation (*wahy*) refers to the ultimate determination that approves or disapproves the perceptions of the intellect. Divine revelation guides human reason in judging right and wrong, differentiating the permitted from the prohibited (*halal* and *haram*), ascertaining the essence of moral virtue, and attaining the metaphysical knowledge of belief in God and the hereafter.

It is important to note that these components of reason exist in a complicated relationship with one another. On one level, the perception of senses is governed by intellect, and intellect is governed by divine revelation. On another level, neither human senses nor human intellect hold much value without the other. Meanwhile, although divine revelation is a guide to human reason, revelation also depends on human reason insofar as revelation only addresses competent individuals who are capable of understanding the meaning of the revealed message. Ultimately, this intertwined relationship between these different components highlights the complexity and uniqueness of human reason.

> **Imam Feisal**: In other words, the senses, intellect, and revelation all shape a human's ability to act reasonably, and these relationships are mutually dependent and symbiotic. But the intellect is particularly important for the simple reason that it is necessary to understand the message of God. In the Qur'an, we read that only those

who use their minds will benefit from its verses and signs.[48] So, how does the Shariah protect the Intellect?

Dr. Kamali: As I previously discussed, the Shariah lays out both affirmative and prohibitive means of protection. Affirmatively, the Shariah promotes and protects human intellect through education, freedom of thought and expression, and the dissemination of both the religious and human sciences. Prohibitively, the Shariah lays out a variety of measures that protect the integrity of human reason against disease, corruption, superstition, misguidance, and the consumption and abuse of alcohol and drugs.[49]

Imam Feisal: Moving to the next *maqsad*, how does the Shariah define the *maqsad* of religion? All faith systems balance reason and faith, action and belief, acts of personal worship and acts with social implications. How would you characterize these relationships in the Qur'an and the *Sunnah*?

Dr. Kamali: Like all religions, Islam deems belief in a Supreme Being (along with belief in the validity of Muhammad's prophecy and the existence of the Day of Judgment) to be an essential feature. In this sense, the central role of belief cannot be completely rationalized. In Islam, the role of belief is so central that when an individual performs an act of worship while lacking belief, the value of his actions are reduced and merit less pleasure from God. Essentially, faith is an affirmation of the mind, which is articulated through devotional acts. There are five primary devotional acts through which faith is articulated (collectively these are known as the five pillars of Islam). They are, in order of their respective importance: the testimony of faith (*kalimah shahadah*), daily prayer (*salah*), giving alms (*zakah*), fasting during the month of Ramadan, and a once-in-a-lifetime pilgrimage or the Hajj. Each one of these pillars of faith combines devotion and closeness to God with specific benefits for the individual and society. By making individuals aware of the implications of their actions, these pillars of faith are designed to instill spiritual awareness, discipline, punctuality, and moral virtue.

In addition to these five pillars of ritual performances, the Shariah calls for the performance of any act that pleasures God. This can include any act from carrying out justice (*'adl*), treating others positively in both speech and in conduct (*ihsan*), being truthful and trustworthy (*sidq* and *amanah*), carrying out honest work to support oneself and family, helping the poor, to planting a tree and even removing a small obstruction from a public path. Regardless of the ostensible importance of the act, anything that pleasures God is encouraged.

Imam Feisal: Okay, so how does the Shariah protect and promote the *maqsad* of religion?

Dr. Kamali: Promoting the *maqsad* of religion is the collective duty of the Muslim community and its leaders. Doing so entails, among other actions, the following acts: protecting individuals' freedom of religion and freedom of conscience, combating aggression (both internal and external), administering mosques, helping with the payment of alms, facilitating individuals' ability to go on the *hajj*, and fasting during the month of Ramadan. Whereas this list focuses on affirmative means through which to promote the *maqsad* of religion, there are also a variety of prohibitive means that the community can take. For instance, the community must take measures to prevent individuals from disseminating heretical teachings, carrying out major sins, and engaging in superstition and morally degrading practices. While the primary way to do this is through enlightenment and education, when it is necessary the threat of punishment is also permitted.[50]

Imam Feisal: How does the Shariah promote the *maqsad* of progeny and family descent (*nasl* or *nasab*)?

Dr. Kamali: The Shariah protects this *maqsad* in an affirmative fashion by promoting lawful marriage and solidifying marriage through a series of legal stipulations pertaining to the spouses and their offspring. While its primary (*asli*) goal is procreation (*tanasul*), the Qur'an also promotes marriage as a form of decent cohabitation (*mu'asharah bi'l-ma'ruf*)[51] that nurtures tranquility, friendship, and kindness (*sukun, muwaddah* and *rahmah*).[52] This is in addition to the other secondary (*tab'i*) goals of marriage which include sexual gratification, avoidance of promiscuity and disease, and building a comfortable home.

Imam Feisal: If the Shariah protects family in the affirmative sense primarily through marriage, how does it protect it in the defensive sense?

Dr. Kamali: In its defensive sense, the purity of family descent is protected through penal measures against adultery (*zina*) and slander (*qadhf*). Promiscuity and immoral acts that expose a family to corruption and abuse also invoke disciplinary punishment.[53]

Imam Feisal: Finally, we have the *maqsad* of property. I would like you to discuss this *maqsad* in a bit more detail, because I think it clearly demonstrates the remarkable complexity and sophistication of the Shariah, and its systems for protecting and promoting these key objectives.

Dr. Kamali: Well, I should first mention that the *maqsad* of property is not a goal in and of itself, though it is a sustainer of life and a way to attain a variety of other important goals.

Imam Feisal: And what are the specific areas within property that the Shariah seeks to safeguard?

Dr. Kamali: First, the Shariah protects currency and growth (*al-tadawul wa'l-tanmiyah*), especially the availability and exchange of certain necessities in the marketplace. It encourages lawful trade and regulates the due exercise of ownership rights, including transfer, custody, and inheritance of property. Also, it requires that wealth be spread and fairly distributed among the people to avoid concentration in the hands of the rich.

Private ownership is the principal form of property rights known to the Shariah, but it is moderated in a number of ways. For example, the Shariah recognizes collective and community ownership of land, water, pastures, and arguably of fuel; and it permits the government to regulate the exploitation, assignment, and distribution of public assets. Second, the Islamic theory of property rights recognizes the ultimate sovereignty and ownership of God over the heavens and the earth. Finally, the doctrine of vicegerency (*khilafah*) considers private ownership a trust that must be faithfully carried out; in other words, the owner is master of what he or she owns only if this right is not used to inflict harm on others or violate Islamic moral and religious principles.

Imam Feisal: Indeed, private property ownership rights are extremely important to all people as we spend most of our effort seeking wealth. What are the specific regulations that seek to curb the exercise, or manipulation, of private property and its acquisition?

Dr. Kamali: The Shariah lays down numerous prohibitions on such activities as hoarding and profiteering, usury (*riba*), fraud and market manipulation, price distortion, and unlawful gain. It seeks to prevent anything that will disrupt lawful trade and halt the growth of property. The goal is to ensure that property does not become dormant, diminished, and fail to fulfill the people's needs. Any measures that distort these objectives of Shariah and violate its laws must be curbed and, if necessary, punished.

Imam Feisal: Are there any other protections in the areas of acquiring and maintaining wealth and property?

Dr. Kamali: Yes, clarity and removal of doubt (*wuduh*) is another Shariah objective related to the ownership of wealth. This principle seeks to assign responsibility for wealth's custody and upkeep. It serves the purpose of preventing conflict, especially over ownership claims that can arise from ambiguous contracts that regulate the use, transfer, and exchange of property among people. This is also true of the Qur'an's guidelines for documentation and evidence in transactions and contracts that prevent conflict among people. In addition, whoever takes custody and charge of a property or financial assets (i.e., the *amin*, trustee) is responsible for its upkeep; in cases of serious neglect, he or she may have to compensate the owner for any loss or damage to the property in question.

Another objective of the Shariah is equality and justice in acquiring wealth, as well as the system of rights and duties that comes from it. These must be free of discrimination, and everyone must be treated fairly in a number of areas: economic opportunities and participation in lawful trade and industry, sale and purchase of property, and the rules that govern its use, transfer and transaction. The basic norms that define the exchange of goods and services are equivalence and fair exchange. This is because when the rules of equivalence are violated by exploitation, usury, uncertainty, ignorance, gambling, or fraud, the results are distortion and injustice (*zulm*), which the Shariah prohibits. The law further requires honesty and transparency in transactions and contracts, and failure to do so entitles the victim of fraud and misrepresentation to revoke the transaction or demand fair compensation. Also, owners and creditors are advised to be fair and magnanimous in their demands for debt collection and return; and it is recommended that the creditor grant respite to a debtor who is financially constrained until his condition improves.

Imam Feisal: It seems to me that what you described above reflects the protection of property in the affirmative sense. What about the defensive? You have already mentioned legislating against and punishing for the crime of theft.

Dr. Kamali: Yes. On the whole, the Shariah rules are indeed meant to uphold and promote these objectives in the affirmative sense. However, the Shariah also makes the crimes of theft, bribery, usurpation, and the violation of others' property liable to punishment. You already raised some of these issues. Victims are entitled to fair compensation for damages in cases where exorbitant harm (*darar*) was inflicted. The law also forbids abusive exercise of ownership and other rights (*su' isti'mal al-haqq*), and the Qur'an doesn't allow the squandering and wasteful expenditure of property. It makes such reckless individuals liable to the intervention of the courts, which can actually stop the particular action. These rules are in place to prevent the waste and abuse of beneficial assets.[54]

Imam Feisal: Before we move on from property, I would like to mention to our readers a point that struck me as you were giving your detailed analysis. All of what you outlined above is the responsibility of the Islamic state; it must protect a healthy economy and a just system of property and wealth through these measures. Throughout our meetings, we have frequently discussed the need to move beyond the misconception that an Islamic state is *Hudud*-driven, the myth that to apply the *Hudud* punishments is equal to implementing the Shariah. What is more correct is that the *Hudud*'s objectives – the *Maqasid al-Hudud* – must be implemented. We have established the fact that the *Maqasid al-Shariah* are actually based on the objectives embedded in, and derived from, the *Hudud* penalties. As a result, furthering these six objectives of life, intellect/mind, religion, family descent/progeny, property, and dignity is the priority.

Dr. Kamali: Yes, and based on the precedent of the Caliph 'Umar when he suspended the *hadd* punishment for theft in a time of famine, we can conclude that an Islamic state must first satisfy its citizens' *Hudud*-based needs before it applies these penalties. 'Umar felt that an ideal Islamic society isn't one that merely applies the *Hudud*; rather, it is one that satisfies the people's needs for the objectives of the *Hudud*. Therefore, you can not apply the punishment for theft without satisfying people's need that would make them not steal in order to survive. So those who want the state to apply the *Hudud* are not wrong. But, before applying them, the state must first fulfill the *Maqasid al-Hudud*.

Imam Feisal: Dr. Kamali, we have now gone through the historical development of the *Maqasid al-Shariah* theory, as well as delved into the specific *daruriyyat*. Are there any other categories within the *Maqasid* theory that we should be aware of, in addition to the *daruriyyat, hajiyyat,* and *tahsiniyyat*? How can we identify specific measures or policies that will help achieve the *Maqasid*?

Dr. Kamali: Yes, there are. The "accomplishers" (*al-mukammilat*, sing. *mukammil*) is an added category to all other classes of the *Maqasid*, although they cannot exactly be considered a separate category. A *mukammil* is the way or ways and means that help to achieve the intended result of the particular *maqsad* it's attached to, whether an essential, a need, or a refinement. These might serve either as means (*wasa'il*) or as accomplishers (*mukammilat*) side-by-side with the *Maqasid*. The *mukammilat* are an important extension of the *Maqasid*. As the indispensable means to realizing the *Maqasid*, for all intents and purposes, they may take the status of the *maqsad* they serve. This is based on the Islamic legal maxim, "That which is indispensable for the accomplishment of a *wajib* also becomes a *wajib* (*ma la yatimm al-wajibu illa bihi fa-huwa wajib*)."[55]

Imam Feisal: I understand that these *mukammilat* are the means or accomplishers by which the goal of the particular *maqsad* is realized; as such, they are indispensable to, and can even be regarded as extensions of, the *Maqasid*. It would be helpful if you could give us an example of a *mukammil*, perhaps from the essential *maqsad* of property since we've been discussing it.

Dr. Kamali: Of course. The Qur'an commands that a future obligation (*dayn*) or a mortgage (*rahn*) should be documented and reduced into writing.[56] In this case, documentation is not a goal in itself. Rather, it is a means towards the protection and preservation of the essential *maqsad* of property. By way of analogy, this same requirement to document is extended to all contracts and transactions, as well as financial rights and obligations, in order to protect them against possible conflict and doubt.

Similarly, the Qur'an stipulates that marriage is a means to realize and preserve the *maqsad* of lineage or progeny. In other words, it is a *mukammil* of protecting this *maqsad*.

Imam Feisal: The *mukammilat*, or accomplishers, are the means or ways to accomplish a larger goal – for example, the protection and promotion of property. You already provided us a few examples from the essentials (*daruriyyat*). Can you do so from the needs (*hajiyyat*) and refinements or desirables (*tahsiniyyat*) as well?

Dr. Kamali: Actually, the legal details attached to marriage, like a proper contract, dower, maintenance, guardianship, etc. can be considered the *mukammilat* of marriage. Some of these have also been defined by the Qur'an and the *Hadith*.

To further illustrate how the accomplisher of a need or complementary goal (*mukammil al-hajji*) works, consider the contractual options (*al-khiyarat*, sing. *khiyar*) that can be stipulated for a sale, on the authority of the *Hadith*. For instance, after concluding a sale, the purchaser may specify that he or she will confirm the deal in two or three days. Therefore, the permissibility of a sale is a need within the essential of property; and this particular *mukammil*, the allowance of contract options, makes sure that the sale transaction meets its desired purpose, which is to ensure that it is free of fraud, ignorance, and misrepresentation.

Imam Feisal: So a *mukammil* can also function as the means to achieving another *mukammil*. You gave the example of the *mukammilat* for marriage, the means to achieving marriage, which is already a *mukammil* for protecting the *maqsad* of progeny. Can you give any examples of accomplishers of a *tahsini*?

Dr. Kamali: All legitimate means that keep the marketplace clear of transactions of unclean, poisonous, and harmful substances are accomplishers of a *tahsini*, or desirable goal, and those which ensure that the passageways in the market place aren't overcrowded.[57]

Imam Feisal: And are these *mukammilat* always found in the Qur'an and the *Sunnah*?

Dr. Kamali: They are sometimes identified in the text of the Qur'an or the *Sunnah*. This is the case in all of the above examples. And if they aren't found there, they can be identified using rationality and *ijtihad*.

Imam Feisal: This is a key difference between the *Maqasid* and the *mukammilat*. Earlier, we discussed the *Maqasid*'s basis in the Qur'an and the *Sunnah*, though jurists can look beyond the text itself to its larger, big-picture goals. But with the *mukammilat*, you seem to be indicating an even greater role for human reason.

Dr. Kamali: Yes, and this is a difference between the *Maqasid* and the *mukammilat*, as you said. As we already discussed, although the *Maqasid* are generally rooted in the authority of the text, this may or may not be the case with the *mukammilat*. They are *ijtihad*-oriented and rational, and there is greater flexibility and choice available. Certain means and accomplishers are identified in the text due to their importance to certain ends; however, others are known and identified through people's innate dispositions and needs. Examples are food for the protection of life, sexual intercourse for the protection of progeny, and the instinctive impulse to own property for the protection of material wealth. For these types of *mukammilat*, Islamic law intervenes very little; when it does, it's only for the sake of regulation and orderly utilization.[58]

Imam Feisal: I would assume, however, that we must be careful not to mix the *Maqasid* and the *mukammilat*. The *means* cannot be confused with the *ends*.

Dr. Kamali: Very true. It is important that we safeguard the proper relationship between the *Maqasid* and the *mukammilat*. This is to ensure that the *mukammilat* are not allowed to take the *Maqasid*'s place or to suppress or overrule them. For example, we recognize that food is a means to preserve life. However, it cannot be transformed into a *maqsad* such that one *lives to eat* rather than *eating to live*. This example can be extended to other accomplishers like making money or owning a house and means of transport. If people fail to properly associate these means with their ends, as you indicated, the danger is that they become ends in themselves and corrosive to our spiritual objective and moral ethics.[59]

Imam Feisal: This is an important moral observation: the law seeks to safeguard good ethical behavior. Are there any other important rules that determine, or at least regulate, the *mukammilat-Maqasid* relationship?

Dr. Kamali: The *mukammil* cannot exceed or overrule the initial purpose which it seeks to accomplish. Let's take our previous example of options in the sale contract. The purpose of these options – as a *mukammil* – is to prevent uncertainty or risk (i.e., *gharar*) in the sale. However, if one were to exaggerate the *mukammil* and demand total elimination of all uncertainty, this would be difficult to achieve and might even block the sale altogether. Therefore, a slight amount of *gharar* is unavoidable and tolerated in many transactions, including the contract of sale.

Another example is the existence of the counter-values in a contract of exchange. This principle states that in a valid transaction, the value of what I am paying you must be clearly matched by what you are giving me; only something of value can be exchange for something else of equal value. This is desirable, because existence of the value normally accomplishes the purpose of the sale. Yet this cannot be done in certain situations. For example, if it were demanded in a contract of lease (*ijarah*), it would nullify the contract, since only one of the two sides of the contract is usually present in *ijarah*, not both. Thus, to demand the *mukammil* of sale's fulfillment in *ijarah* – as *ijarah* is also a variety of sale – would exceed the characteristics of the *ijarah* contract and may block it.[60]

> **Imam Feisal:** Or I might give a down payment to a contractor to remodel my kitchen, even though the counter-value is not yet there. He has the money, though my kitchen is not done. And as you said, the *mukammil* of counter-values cannot override its initial purpose, which is to ensure that the contract is done fairly.

Moving on, we have discussed the theoretical relationship between the *mukammilat* and the *Maqasid*, as well as some specific examples of how this relationship plays out. But how would you characterize the *mukammilat's* role in bringing justice, practically? What are some of the practical accomplishers of justice in society?

> **Dr. Kamali:** According to the Qur'an and the *Sunnah*, justice is a higher goal and purpose of the Shariah. As a result, all the ways and means that facilitate the administration of justice fall under the category of *wasa'il* and *mukammilat*. This entails a number of practical actions. For example, setting up courts of general and specialized jurisdiction, establishing detention centers and prisons, formulating rules and procedures that regulate arrest and trial proceedings. Some of these might be of higher priority than others, and their prioritization is an entirely rational exercise that may be determined by competent authorities. As long as these measures do not depart from the right purpose they are designed to serve, they would be included in the *mukammilat* of justice.

In addition, one *mukammil* can sometimes be a means to another, as we have discussed, and the versatility in the *mukammilat* structure is relevant here. For example, appointing judges is a means to the administration of justice, but appointing assistant judges and court clerks is a *mukammil* to the first (appointing judges). In fact, a *mukammil* can sometimes become a *maqsad*, albeit, a specific (*khaas* or *juz'i* – i.e., subsidiary) to another *mukammil*.

> **Imam Feisal:** You have demonstrated for us the grounding of the *Maqasid al-Shariah* in the Qur'an and the *Sunnah*. You have also laid out both the historical development of the *Maqasid* theory

and the various, agreed-upon components of that theory. But let's switch gears and zoom out to look at the big picture role of the *Maqasid* in our world today. My first question is how would you characterize the *Maqasid*'s relevance to the definition of an Islamic state, as well as to good governance according to the Shariah? Can the *Maqasid* help us create an Islamic state?

Dr. Kamali: Well, I would first emphasize that the *Maqasid* are not separate from the Shariah itself; indeed, they are an integral part of it. So when we think about the *Maqasid*'s relevance to the definition of an Islamic state, we could also ask: what is the *Shariah's* relevance to the definition of an Islamic state? When the question is posed in this way, I believe that answering it is not so difficult.

Imam Feisal: And how do *you* answer that question?

Dr. Kamali: Taking al-Mawardi's definition of *khilafah* as the "protection of the religion and management of temporal affairs" (*hirasat al-din wa siyasat al-dunya*),[61] we see that the Shariah is essential to both the protection of religion and the management of worldly affairs. This is a very broad view of the Shariah. Yet if we understand Shariah by its positive law component – that is, its practical laws (*ahkam 'amaliyyah*)[62] – then it relates more closely to the management of worldly affairs. This is because theology and the fundamental sources of religion fall outside the realm of *fiqh* and *ahkam 'amaliyyah*; however, law and religion are interconnected in Islam and clear divisions are neither feasible nor purposeful.

The protection of religion is one of the essential *Maqasid*, and the other four or five are concerned with the management of people's lives, properties, families, and intellectual well-beings. This is important because the *Maqasid* relate to both of the two major elements in Mawardi's definition, perhaps even more so to temporal affairs and the substance of good governance.

Imam Feisal: So how would you define good governance according to the Shariah, and what is the relevance of the *Maqasid* to this definition?

Dr. Kamali: Good governance according to the Shariah is governance under the rule of God's law, a system of governance that upholds the essentials of the Islamic existential view as expressed in the Islamic religion. It is a trust (*amanah*) and is thus accountable and committed to consultation, justice, equality, security of the homeland and of people's rights, and welfare.

Here again, we see the relevance of the *Maqasid al-Shariah*, which is a very important part of the Shariah related to good governance. Still, we cannot forget that the Shariah itself is wider in scope than the *Maqasid*. In other words, the *Maqasid* do not entirely encompass all of the attributes of a good government in Islam.

Imam Feisal: To conclude our interview, I am wondering if you could offer any final thoughts you may have on the *Maqasid al-Shariah* theory. As a *Maqasid* expert, where do you see the unique benefits of this theory in terms of Islamic lawmaking?

Dr. Kamali: First, a *Maqasid*-oriented approach to lawmaking has great promise for bringing unity among the leading schools of Islamic law, both Sunni and Shi'a, since they differ very little on the goals and purposes of the Shariah. In addition, at a time when some of the important doctrines of jurisprudence like general consensus (*ijma'*), analogical reasoning (*qiyas*), and even *ijtihad* seem to have become somewhat methodologically over-imposing and difficult to fulfill, the *Maqasid* have become the focus of attention. This is because they tend to provide convenient access to the Shariah. Of course, it is natural to first attempt to understand the broad outlines and objectives of the Shariah before moving on to its more elaborate details.

Imam Feisal: So in a certain sense, the *Maqasid* can be considered the *mukammil* or *wasilah* to achieve Shariah-compliance. And furthermore, it would be interesting to explore how we can use and develop the notion of *mukammilat* as the proxies to measure the states' achievement of the *Maqasid*, their Shariah-compliancy. What about for the student of the Shariah? What are the advantages of learning about the *Maqasid*?

Dr. Kamali: For the student of the Shariah, an adequate knowledge of the *Maqasid* is important because it can equip him or her with insight and provide a theoretical framework that makes the work of gaining detailed knowledge of the Shariah's various doctrines more interesting and meaningful.

Imam Feisal: Thank you very much, Dr. Kamali. I suspect that our readers now will understand better why, in trying to measure compliance of a state or governance with the Shariah, we opted as a first step to measure nations against how well they fulfil the *Maqasid al-Shariah*.

Maqasid al-shari`ah as a means for contemporary reform and renewal (Jasser Auda)

> **Imam Feisal**: Dr. Auda, as one of the world's foremost experts on *Maqasid al-Shari`ah*, your professional career has contributed significantly toward the contemporary understanding of this discipline in Islamic law. Why has this been the focus of your research, and what are the implications – be they social or legal – of a *Maqasid*-based approach toward Islamic law and society?
>
> **Dr. Auda**: The *Maqasid* are among today's most important tools for Islamic reform and renewal, considering that a *Maqasid*-based approach is a methodology from *within* Islamic scholarship that helps us to address our contemporary concerns within an Islamic framework. Within a *Maqasid*-based approach, we focus on the goals and purposes of revelation and read specific verses and laws through the lens of those purposes, seeking to fulfill those essential goals in light of the realities of the present day.

The implications of such an approach are vast, paving the way for better community and global relations while resolving key issues within Islamic jurisprudence. Within the realm of community and global relations, it enables us to better bridge the Sunni-Shia divide, create resonance with our neighbors of other religions, and perhaps most significantly, promote human rights and human development in the Muslim world. Within the realm of jurisprudence, a *Maqasid*-based approach gives us legal tools to create legislation that is appropriate to present day needs and values. It does this by resolving some key issues with which jurists throughout generations have struggled, including issues related to abrogation, differentiating between means and ends, and understanding Divine and Prophetic Intents.

> **Imam Feisal**: Such an approach clearly has far-reaching effects. Would you please expand on each of the implications that you mention, both within community relations and jurisprudence?
>
> **Dr. Auda**: Before going into each of these, I would like to clarify what exactly we mean by the purposes, or *Maqasid*, of revelation in the present day. The key to understanding the contemporary implications of a *Maqasid*-based approach is first to understand the contemporary approach to the *Maqasid*. The *Maqasid* have been reinterpreted throughout history to reflect the needs of the day, although there is a chain of continuity that connects classical

notions of the *Maqasid* with current notions of human rights, development, and reform, as expressed by contemporary Islamic jurists and thinkers.

The primary shift that occurred in scholarship on the *Maqasid* from the classical period until the present-day was the shift in focus from "punishing or preventing the negative" to "promoting the positive," and developing that as a value. For instance, the "preservation of offspring" is one of these *Maqasid* (the *maqsad* of *nasl* that evolved into what we now call "family"). This was originally discussed in terms of "punishments" (*mazajir*) for breaching decency.[63] Other classical jurists developed this into a theory of "protection," meaning the "protection for private parts,"[64] as well as the "preservation of offspring."[65]

But it wasn't until the twentieth century that scholarly discourse about the *maqsad* of *nasl* spoke about *promoting* the family, rather than just preserving offspring and punishing transgressors. Significantly, twentieth-century writers on the *Maqasid* developed "preservation of offspring" into a family-oriented theory. Ibn Ashur, for example, made "care for the family" to be a *maqsad* in its own right.[66] The orientation of the new views is neither a theory of "punishment" nor one of "preservation," but rather the concepts of "value" and "system" that focuses on developing the family and articulating family values.

> **Imam Feisal:** Do you see this as a more complete application of the doctrine of *hisbah*, where in the Qur'an we are commanded both to "urge the positive and eliminate the negative" (*al-amr bil-ma`ruf wa-nnahy `an al-munkar*)? That the earlier jurists focused more on *annahy `an al-munkar*, while modern jurists have balanced that with a focus on the *al-amr bil-ma`ruf* aspect of the *Maqasid*?
>
> **Dr. Auda:** Yes, as contemporary scholarship focuses now on promoting the positive in addition to eliminating the negative. Because the Qur'an starts with commanding the good and only second speaks of eliminating the negative, some have said that emphasizing the good is actually the priority.

The other *Maqasid* were also interpreted in such a way by contemporary scholars. The preservation of mind (`aql), which until recently was restricted to the purpose of the prohibition of intoxicants in Islam, evolved to include propagation of scientific thinking, travelling to seek knowledge, suppressing the herd mentality, and avoiding brain drain.[67]

The preservation of wealth (*mal*), along with "punishments for theft" and "protection of money" has evolved into familiar socioeconomic terminology, such as social assistance and welfare, economic development, flow of money, well-being of society, and diminishing the difference between economic levels.[68] This development enables utilizing *Maqasid al-Shari`ah* to encourage economic growth, which is much needed in most Muslim majority countries.

The preservation of religion (*din*) had its roots classically in "punishment for giving up true faith."[69] Recently, however, the same theory for that purpose of Islamic Law has been re-interpreted to mean "freedom of faiths"[70] or "freedom of belief."[71] Presenters of these views often quote the Qur'anic verse, "No compulsion in matters of religion,"[72] as the fundamental principle, rather than what is popularly called punishment for apostasy (*hadd al-riddah*) that used to be mentioned in traditional references in the context of the preservation of religion.

> **Imam Feisal:** Professors Ghazi, Şentürk and Kamali among many other scholars have pointed out that the real crime associated with apostasy in the time of the Prophet was treason, a capital crime in all societies, and not related to the personal choice of faith of an individual.[73] So perhaps this more contemporary understanding, that urges greater communal cohesiveness and faith to the sense of community, is more faithful to the original Qur'anic intention of this maqsad of belief?
>
> **Dr. Auda:** Yes, and as they also mentioned in our Shariah Index Project meetings, the most important function of an Islamic government is to create the environment of *ibtila'* (testing or trial), where we can only do well in this test on earth if we choose the straight path by our free will and not because of coercion. Protecting the absolute freedom of religion is a central part of what contemporary scholars see as promoting the *maqsad* of religion.

Finally, the preservation of honor (`ird`) and the preservation of life (*nafs*) were at the level of "necessities" in al-Ghazali's and al-Shatibi's terms. However, these expressions were also preceded by al-Amiri's "punishment for breaching honor" and al-Juwayni's "protection of honor." Honor (`ird`) has been a central concept in Arab culture since the pre-Islamic period. Pre-Islamic poetry narrates how Antarah, the famous pre-Islamic poet, fought the Sons of Damdam for "defaming his honor." In the *Hadith*, the Prophet described the "blood, money, and honor of every Muslim" as "sanctuary" (*haram*) that is not to be breached.[74] Recently, however, the expression of "preservation of honor" is gradually evolving in the Islamic law literature into "preservation and advancement of human dignity," and even the "protection and advancement of human rights" as a purpose of the Islamic law in its own right.[75]

> **Imam Feisal:** Some contemporary scholars have also re-classified the *Maqasid* or added *new Maqasid* that were not identified by early Islamic scholars. How have these scholars expanded our understanding of the objectives of the Shariah in these and other ways?

> **Dr. Auda:** Modern scholarship introduced new conceptions and classifications of the *Maqasid* by giving consideration to new dimensions. For one, in order to remedy what some saw as a focus on the individual rather than families and societies, the notion of *Maqasid* has been expanded to include a wider scope of people – the community, nation, or humanity. This expansion of the scope of the *Maqasid* allows them to respond more easily to global issues and concerns and to create practical plans for reform and renewal.

In addition, contemporary scholarship has introduced new universal *Maqasid* that were directly induced from the texts of the Qur'an and the *Hadith*, rather than from the body of the *fiqh* literature in the schools of Islamic law. This approach, significantly, allowed the *Maqasid* to overcome the historicity of the *fiqh* edicts and represent the texts' higher values and principles. Detailed rulings would, then, stem from these universal principles.

> **Imam Feisal:** An example of this is that Hamieh, another of our SIP scholars, stressed the need to rely primarily on the Qur'an rather than on the scholarship and jurisprudence from over the centuries, saying that we must be careful not to elevate these secondary scholarly texts to a position equal to the revealed source of our religion, the Qur'an. Could you give us specific examples of these new formulations of the *Maqasid*?

> **Dr. Auda:** Some scholars such as Rashid Rida introduced *Maqasid* such as "freedom, independence, social, political, and economic reform, and women's rights."[76] Others such as Ibn Ashur and Yusuf al-Qaradawi add "orderliness, equality, freedom, facilitation, and the preservation of pure natural disposition (*fitrah*),"[77] or "preserving true faith, maintaining human dignity and rights, calling people to worship God, purifying the soul, restoring moral

values, building good families, treating women fairly, building a strong Islamic nation, and calling for a cooperative world."[78] Some, such as al-Alwani, even narrowed down the *Maqasid* to only three: "the oneness of God (*tawhid*), purification of the soul (*tazkiah*), and developing civilization on earth (`imran*)."[79]

An example of not elevating scholarly texts to a status equal with the Qur'an is that some of the contemporary scholars introduced objectives that were not mentioned by the early jurists, but which find reference in the Qur'an. For example, the objective of freedom (*hurriyah*), which was proposed by Ibn Ashur and several other contemporary scholars, is different from the purpose of freedom (`itq*), which was mentioned by earlier jurists.[80] *Al-`itq* is freeing a slave, not freedom in the contemporary sense. "Will" (*mashi'ah*), however, is a well-known Islamic term that bears a number of similarities with current conceptions of freedom and free will. For example, freedom of belief is expressed in the Qur'an as the "will to believe or disbelieve."[81] In terms of terminology, freedom (*al-hurriyah*) is a newly coined purpose in the literature of the Shariah. Ibn Ashur, interestingly, accredited his usage of the term *hurriyah* to the "literature of the French revolution, which were translated from French to Arabic in the nineteenth century CE,"[82] even though he elaborated on an Islamic perspective on freedom of thought, belief, expression, and action in the *mashi'ah* sense.[83]

The above twentieth-century views also show that *Maqasid al-Shari`ah* represent each scholar's own approach to reform and development of Muslim societies, despite the fact that all of these *Maqasid* were induced from the primary texts. Extracting from the Qur'an and the *Hadith* is the jurisprudential basis for reforming contemporary Muslim society, and this gives the *Maqasid* special significance: they form the basis for understanding the fundamental purposes of revelation so as to create legislation appropriate to present day needs and values.

> **Imam Feisal:** That is a key point and supports your earlier assertion that the *Maqasid* represent the primary method for reform and renewal in the Muslim world. With this understanding of the contemporary approach to the *Maqasid*, perhaps we can turn now to our original question. You mentioned earlier a few of the implications that a *Maqasid*-based approach has for community and global relations. Can you elaborate on these social implications?
>
> **Dr. Auda:** These implications stem from the fact that the *Maqasid* are universal values, and by focusing on these universal purposes within our own revelation we are better able to overcome differences both

within the Muslim community and between Muslims and other faith communities.

Today, in the beginning of the twenty-first century, sharp scholastic divisions take place between the adherents of different schools of Islamic law. The sharpest and most devastating of these divisions is the Sunni-Shia division. The apparent differences between various Sunni and Shia schools, as people familiar with Islamic law could assert, boil down to their differences over politics rather than their pillars of faith. However, today, deep divisions between Sunni and Shia are constructed through courts, mosques, and social dealings in most countries, developing into violent conflict in a number of countries. These divisions have added to a wide-spread culture of civil intolerance and the inability of coexistence with the "other."

I carried out a survey on the latest studies on the *Maqasid* written by key Sunni and Shia scholars. The survey revealed to me an interesting similarity between both approaches to the *Maqasid*.[84] Both Sunni and Shia scholars speak about the same topics (*ijtihad, qiyas* [analogy], *huquq* [rights], *qiyam* [values], *akhlaq* [morals], and so on), refer to the same jurists and books (al-Juwayni's *Burhan*, Ibn Babawayh's `ilal al-Shara'i`, al-Ghazali's *Mustasfa*, al-Shatibi's *Muwafaqat*, and Ibn Ashur's *Maqasid*), and use the same theoretical classifications (*masalih, daruriyyat, hajiyyat, tahsiniyyat, Maqasid `ammah, Maqasid khassah*, and so on). Most of the juridical differences between Sunni and Shia *fiqhi* schools are due to differences over a few narrations and a handful of practical rulings.

A *Maqasid*-based approach to the *fiqh* is a holistic approach that does not restrict itself to one narration or view, but rather refers to general principles and common ground. Implementing the "higher" purposes of unity and the reconciliation of Muslims has a higher priority over implementing *fiqhi* details. Accordingly, Ayatollah Mahdi Shamsuddin prohibited aggression along Sunni-Shia lines based on "the higher and fundamental purposes of reconciliation, unity, and justice."[85]

A *Maqasid*-based approach takes the issues to a higher philosophical ground and, hence, overcomes differences over the political history of Muslims and encourages a much-needed culture of conciliation and peaceful coexistence.

Imam Feisal: Which extends beyond Muslims also, does it not?

Dr. Auda: Precisely, the *Maqasid* are also essential to fruitful inter-faith dialogue. There is a lot of resonance, for example, between a *Maqasid*-based approach and an approach that Christians call systematic theology. This is an approach to religion that attempts to draw an overall picture. It is an approach that considers all aspects related to that religion or faith, such as history, philosophy, science, and ethics, in order to come up with a holistic philosophical view.

Imam Feisal: Could you define the term "systematic theology" for our readers?

Dr. Auda: Christian systematic theology asks the following question: "what does the whole Bible teach us today about a given topic?"[86] As such, it involves a "process of collecting and synthesizing all the relevant Scriptural passages for various topics,"[87] such as prayers, justice, righteousness, compassion, mercy, unity, diversity, morality, salvation, and a variety of other themes.[88] Thus, systematic theology uses an "inductive method"[89] that results in "grouping, classifying, and integrating disconnected truths," even referred to as "undigested facts," until their interrelations and the underlying "dogmas,"[90] or "coherent summaries" become evident.[91]

Systematic theology, in the above sense, bears a lot of obvious practical similarities with the *Maqasid*-based approach to Islam that the Shariah Index Project has been illustrating all along. Both approaches deploy the concept of re-interpretation to provide bases for dynamism and flexibility to changing worldviews, without compromising the basic reference of believers to their Scripts.

The classical theory of *Maqasid* defines areas of necessities (*daruriyyat*) that are meant to be preserved and protected by the Shariah, such as "the preservation of faith, life, wealth, mind, and offspring."[92] Similarly, systematic theologians write on similar concepts, such as the importance of protecting life and health, protecting souls by "prohibiting drunkenness" (even though the Islamic approach is to prohibit all amounts and forms of intoxicants, as a form of "blocking the means" to drunkenness), the necessity of nurturing the family, and so on.[93]

A holistic *Maqasid*-based view allows theologians to place specific religious teachings and commands within a general framework of their underlying principles and governing objectives, rather than focusing on a piece-meal understanding and, therefore, a literal application of these teachings and commands. Thus, moral values intended by various commands will not be different across the religious spectrum, despite the fact that they take different forms in their specific practical environments.

Hence, I believe that the above purpose-based approach to theology could play a significant role in interfaith dialogue and understanding.

It reveals commonalities that are necessary for such dialogue and understanding.

Imam Feisal: Systematic theology seems to describe very well the inductive process and method that classical Muslim jurists deployed to develop the Maqasid theory from the totality of the Quranic and Prophetic commandments and prohibitions.

Dr. Auda: There is resonance with advances in modern social research, which gives further evidence that the *Maqasid* theory seeks to fulfill fundamental human needs. Maslow identified a "hierarchy of needs"[94] ranging from basic physiological requirements and safety, to love and esteem, to cognitive needs and, finally, what he calls "self-actualization." The overlap between al-Shatibi's theory of the *Maqasid* and Maslow's theory in terms of the levels of goals is telling. It speaks to the basic needs of all human beings – needs and rights that must be protected.

Imam Feisal: This brings to mind Dr. Senturk's points that human rights – as expressing universal human needs – were an integral part of the Islamic tradition showcased in the concept *"huquq al-adamiyyin,"* where all have rights simply by being children of Adam. But not everyone knows this, and many retort that the Islamic discourse on human rights is borrowed from the West, a point that Professors Şentürk and Mahmood strongly contest.

Dr. Auda: The compatibility of human rights and Islam is a topic of a heated debate, both in Islamic and international circles.[95] A Universal Islamic Declaration of Human Rights was announced in 1981 by a large number of scholars who represented various Islamic entities at the United Nations Educational, Scientific and Cultural Organisation (UNESCO). Supported by a number of Islamic scripts mentioned in its references section, the Islamic declaration essentially includes the entire list of basic rights that were mentioned in the Universal Declaration of Human Rights (UDHR), such as rights to life, freedom, equality, justice, fair trial, protection against torture, asylum, freedom of belief and speech, free association, education, and freedom of mobility.[96]

However, some members of the United Nations High Commission for Human Rights (UNHCHR) expressed concerns over the Universal Islamic Declaration of Human Rights because they think that it "gravely threatens the inter-cultural consensus on which the international human rights instruments were based."[97] Other members believe that the declaration "adds new positive dimensions to human rights, since, unlike international instruments, it attributes them to a divine source thereby adding a new moral motivation for complying with them."[98] A *Maqasid*-based approach to the issue of human rights supports the latter opinion, while addressing the concerns of the former, especially if *Maqasid* terminology is to be "contemporarized" as we discussed and made to play a more fundamental role in juridical reasoning.

> **Imam Feisal**: Would you say that human rights is the ultimate goal of the *Maqasid* theory in our day and age?
>
> **Dr. Auda**: I think the ultimate purpose of the *Maqasid* theory is human *development*, which definitely includes – but is much more comprehensive than – human rights. According to the latest United Nations Development Program (UNDP) reports, most countries with a Muslim majority rank lower than the "developed" range of the comprehensive Human Development Index (HDI). This index is calculated using more than 200 indexes, including measures for political participation, literacy, enrolment in education, life expectancy, access to clean water, employment, standard of living, and gender equality. Nevertheless, some countries with a majority of Muslims, especially oil-rich Arab states, show "the worst disparities," the UN Report says, between their levels of national income and measures for gender equality, which includes women's political participation, economic participation, and power over resources.[99]

In addition to Muslim minorities who live in developed countries, a few countries with Muslim majorities were ranked under "high human development," such as Brunei, Qatar, and the United Arab Emirates. However, the above groups collectively represent less than 1 percent of Muslims. The bottom of the HDI list includes Yemen, Nigeria, Mauritania, Djibouti, Gambia, Senegal, Guinea, Ivory Coast, Mali, and Niger (which collectively represent around 10 percent of Muslims).

I suggest "human development" is a prime expression of *maslahah* (public interest) in our time. Fulfilling the *Maqasid al-Shari'ah* ultimately realizes this public interest through the mechanism of Islamic law. Thus, the realization of this *maqsad* could be empirically measured via the UN "human development targets," according to current scientific standards. Similar to the area of human rights, the area of human development requires more research from a *Maqasid* perspective. Nevertheless, the evolution of human development into a purpose of Islamic law gives human development targets a firm base in the Islamic world, instead of presenting them, according to some neo-literalists, as "tools for Western domination."[100]

Imam Feisal: This is a strong argument in favor of "human development" as a key part of the Islamicity of a state. As you said earlier in our SIP meetings, what we are measuring is the *maslahah*, the welfare of the people, and the *maslahah* includes elements that are directly theological, but also those relating to prosperity, the health of the family, education and so on. Islam is a complete way of life, and it does not divide between the secular and the religious. What in the West is called "development" is a vital part of *maslahah*, but for us the concept is much wider and includes spiritual development as well as material development.

Dr. Auda: Precisely, and fulfilling the *Maqasid* is a fundamental requirement towards reaching development goals, both material and spiritual. But the *Maqasid* are not only essential for human development. As we have discussed, the *Maqasid* are one of today's most important intellectual means and methodologies for Islamic reform and renewal. It is a methodology from within Islamic scholarship that addresses the Islamic mind and Islamic concerns. This is why so many contemporary jurists are using such an approach and have developed traditional *Maqasid* terminology in today's language, despite some jurists' rejection of the idea of contemporarization of *Maqasid* terminology.[101] The Shariah Index Project is an excellent step forward. By identifying the specific juridical mechanisms that are vital to this new *ijtihad*, we can measure the "Islamicity" of states based on the degree of their fulfillment of the *Maqasid* of Islamic law. This degree would reflect the pace of genuine reform that a particular state is pursuing.

Imam Feisal: When you speak of the juridical mechanisms necessary for a new *ijtihad* for today – are you referring to the implications of a *Maqasid*-based approach for Islamic jurisprudence that you mentioned earlier?

Dr. Auda: Yes. As we have seen, a *Maqasid*-based approach toward Islamic law has clear implications for community and global relations, but it also resolves some key issues with which jurists throughout generations have struggled. One example is the false dichotomy underlying the issue of abrogation (*naskh*). A *Maqasid*-based approach resolves the dilemma of opposing evidences and extremist interpretations by calling upon us to view these evidences through the lens of the ultimate goals of the text.

Imam Feisal: Please explain.

Dr. Auda: According to traditional exegeses, the principle of abrogation has support from the Qur'an. The main verse says, "And for whatever verse We abrogate or cause to be forgotten, We bring a better or the like of it" (2:106). The interpretations of the related verses are subject to a difference of opinion.[102] The differences are rooted in the question of who has the authority to determine what God has abrogated. God says that He abrogates what He wills, but does that give man the license to decide which verses have been abrogated simply because our limited minds don't understand a seeming contradiction in His vast revelation?

It is also worthy to note that the concept of abrogation does not have supporting evidence from the words attributed to the Prophet in traditional collections of the *Hadith*.[103] The concept of abrogation always appears within the commentaries given by companions or other narrators, commenting on what appears to be in disagreement with their own understanding of the related issues.

Imam Feisal: How does abrogation result from a false dichotomy?

Dr. Auda: Essentially, it results from the assumption that if two verses seem to contradict in the mind of the scholar, then one of them must have been abrogated. In Islamic juridical theory, jurists have differentiated between a fundamental contradiction (*tanaqud/ ta'anud*) of evidences (verses/narrations) and a seeming opposition/ disagreement (*ta'arud/ikhtilaf*).[104] Contradiction is defined as "a clear logical conclusion of truth and falsehood in the same aspect" (*taqasum al-sidqi wal-kadhib*),[105] meaning that two Qur'anic verses or the *Hadith* clearly say diametrically opposite things. On the other hand, conflict or disagreement between evidences is defined as an "*apparent* contradiction between evidences in the mind of the scholar" (*ta'arudun fi dhihn al-mujtahid*).[106] This means that two seemingly disagreeing (*muta'arid*) evidences are not necessarily in definite nonresolvable contradiction. It is only in the *perception of the jurist* that they are in nonresolvable contradiction. This can occur as a result of some missing part of the narration or, more likely, missing information regarding the evidence's timing, place, circumstances, or other conditions.[107]

The problem in the latter situation is that, usually, one of the "opposing" narrations is rendered inaccurate and rejected or cancelled. This method, called "abrogation" or *naskh*, suggests that the later evidence, chronologically speaking, should abrogate the former. This means that when verses seem to disagree, the verse that is revealed last is considered to be an abrogating evidence (*nasikh*) and verses revealed earlier are abrogated (*mansukh*). Similarly, when Prophetic narrations disagree, the narration that has a later date, if dates are known or could be determined, should abrogate all other narrations. Therefore, a large number of evidences are cancelled, one way or another, for no good reason other than that the jurists failed to understand how they could fit in a unified perceptual framework. They thus fall in a false dichotomy!

> **Imam Feisal:** Could you give us an example of this kind of abrogation by jurists?
>
> **Dr. Auda:** A prime example related to politics is verse 9:5 of the Qur'an, which has come to be named "The Verse of the Sword" (*ayat al-saif*). It states: "But when the forbidden months are past, then slay the pagans wherever you find them, and seize them." The historical context of the verse, in the ninth year of *hijrah*, is that of a war between Muslims and the pagans of Mecca. The thematic context of the verse is also that of the same war, which the chapter is addressing. However, the verse was taken out of its thematic and historical contexts and claimed to have defined the ruling between Muslims and non-Muslims in every place, time, and circumstance. Hence, it was perceived to be in disagreement with more than two hundred other verses of the Qur'an, all calling for dialogue, freedom of belief, forgiveness, peace, and even patience. Conciliation between these different evidences, somehow, was not an option. To solve the disagreement, based on the method of abrogation, those exegetes concluded that this verse (9:5), which was revealed towards the end of the Prophet's life, abrogated each and every "contradicting" verse that was revealed before it!

Therefore, the following verses were considered abrogated: "no compulsion in the religion;" "forgive them, for God loves those who do good to people;" "repel evil with that which is best;" "so patiently persevere;" "do not argue with the People of the Book except with means that are best;" and "(say:) You have your religion and I have my religion."[108]

Likewise, a large number of Prophetic traditions that legitimize peace treaties and multicultural coexistence, to use contemporary terms, were also abrogated. One such tradition is "The Scroll of Medina" (*sahifat al-madinah*), in which the Prophet and the Jews of Medina wrote a "covenant" that defined the relationship between Muslims and Jews living in Medina. The scroll stated that, "Muslims and Jews are one nation (*ummah*), with Muslims having their own religion and Jews having their own religion."[109] Some classical and neo-traditional commentators on the *sahifa* render it "abrogated," based on the verse of The Sword and other similar verses.[110] Seeing all the above scripts and narrations in terms of the single dimension of peace versus war might imply a contradiction in which the "final truth" has to "belong" to either peace or war. The result will have to be an unreasonable fixed choice between peace and war, for every place, time, and circumstance.

Imam Feisal: How did the use of abrogation develop throughout history?

Dr. Auda: After the first Islamic century, one notices that jurists from the developing schools of thought began claiming many new cases of abrogation, which were never claimed by the students (*tabi`in*) of the companions. Thus, abrogation became a method of invalidating opinions or narrations endorsed by rival schools of law and hence contributing to a culture of intolerance and narrow mindedness. Abu al-Hassan al-Karkhi (d. 951 CE), for example, writes: "The fundamental rule is: Every Qur'anic verse that is different from the opinion of the jurists in our school is either taken out of context or abrogated."[111] Therefore, it is not unusual in the *fiqhi* literature to find a certain ruling that abrogated (*nasikh*) according to one school and abrogated (*mansukh*) according to another. This arbitrary use of the method of abrogation has exacerbated the problem of a lack of multidimensional interpretations of the evidences.

A *Maqasid*-based approach solves the dilemmas of opposing evidences and extremist views, such as the ones illustrated above, principally by the posture encouraged by this approach: we identify the ultimate purposes of revelation, and then read specific evidences through the lens of those purposes, deploying specific juridical mechanisms related to the *Maqasid*. For instance, the recent scholar, Mohammad al-Ghazali differentiated between "means" (*al-wasa'il*) and "ends" (*al-ahdaf*). He allowed the "expiry" (*intiha'*) of the means and not the ends. These goals or *ahdaf*, like the *Maqasid*, are those eternal objectives of the Divine

Message. The means to reach them, Al-Ghazali recognizes, may change according to context.

Imam Feisal: Could you give an example of when the means to achieving an objective may change according to context?

Dr. Auda: Recently, Yusuf al-Qaradawi and Faisal Mawlawi elaborated on the importance of the "differentiation between means and ends" during the deliberations of the European Council for Fatwa and Research. They both applied the same concept to the visual sighting of the *hilal* (Ramadan new moon) being mere means for knowing the start of the month rather than an end in its own right. Hence, they concluded that astronomical calculations should be today's means of defining the start of the month.[112] Yusuf al-Qaradawi had applied the same concept to Muslim women's garment (*jilbab*), which he viewed as mere means for achieving the objective of modesty. He writes that "clothing is subject to the mores and customs of the country, the environment of its people, and it changes as time changes and varies according to the needs of the people and the requirements of development. Revelation does not forbid this, with the condition that we preserve the fundamental objectives (*Maqasid*) of the law regarding clothing."[113]

Imam Feisal: Thus, if the *jilbab* is not a requirement but dressing modestly according to the cultural norms of fashion in a given country is, then I understand this to mean that women should be able to wear whatever their culture deems modest without having to follow the norms of another culture. To summarize what you have said in relation to jurisprudence: by differentiating between means and ends we focus on the *maqsad* behind a particular ruling. This helps us to overcome false dichotomies because we discover the purpose behind individual commands, and then act based on that purpose in light of the present-day context. Therefore our jurisprudence about key issues such as those relating to women has a deeper sensitivity to specific situations and contexts.

Dr. Auda: Yes, in fact in my view, "differentiating between means and ends" opens a whole lot of possibilities for radically new opinions in Islamic law. For example, Taha al-Alwani proposed a "project for reform" in his book, *Issues in Contemporary Islamic Thought,* in which he elaborated on his version of the method of "differentiation between means and ends." Here is how al-Alwani applied this approach to the issue of gender equality:

The Qur'an transported the people of those times to the realm of faith in absolute gender equality. This single article of faith, perhaps more than any other, represented a revolution no less significant than Islam's condemnation of idolatry... In the case of early Muslim society, given the long established customs, attitudes and mores of pre-Islamic Arabia, it was necessary to implement such changes in stages and to make allowances for society's capacity to adjust itself accordingly... By establishing a role for a woman in the witnessing of transactions, even though at the time of revelation they had little to do with such matters, the Qur'an seeks to give concrete form to the idea of woman as participant... The objective is to end the traditional perception of women by including them, "among such as are acceptable to you as witness," ... the matter of witnessing served merely as a means to an end or as a practical way of establishing the concept of gender equality. In their interpretations of "mistake" and "remind", Qur'anic commentators have approached the issue from a perspective based on the assumption that the division of testimony for women into halves is somehow connected with women's inherent inequality to men. This idea has been shared by classical and modern commentators alike, so that generations of Muslims, guided only by *taqlid* (imitation), have continued to perpetuate this faulty understanding. Certainly, the attitudes engendered by such a misunderstanding have spread far beyond the legal sphere...[114]

In other words, the Qur'anic model for change is gradual. By allowing women to be witnesses in transactions, it brought them a step forward toward gender equality, and quite a dramatic step when viewed in light of historical circumstances. To follow the Qur'an, we should keep taking steps toward this goal. This approach seems to be gaining followers among our current generation of scholars.

Imam Feisal: What I hear in Al-Alwani's argument is that the particular verse or commandment in the Qur'an which establishes two women as witnesses in the place of one man is not in itself the absolute command for all time, but rather is a means to arrive at the ultimate goal of gender equality. Within the context of the extreme inequality at the time, this verse made the – then – radical move of establishing women as those who *can* give witness. And, following Mohammad al-Ghazali's point that the means may expire in favor of the ends, women's testimony as equal to half of a man's may expire in favor of being equal. This relates to Tun

Hamid's point that if the Qur'anic objective is human equality, then abolishing slavery is desirable even though the Prophet was not able to do so in his lifetime. Likewise if gender equality is the Qur'anic objective, then we should work to achieve that, although it wasn't completely achieved in the Prophet's lifetime.

Dr. Auda: Indeed. There are many more examples that make the same point. A similar expression is Ayatollah Mahdi Shamsuddin's recommendation for today's jurists to take a "dynamic" approach to the scripts, and "not to look at every script as absolute and universal legislation, but open their minds to the possibility of 'relative' legislation for specific circumstances, and not to judge narrations with missing contexts as absolute in the dimensions of time, space, situations, and people."[115] He stresses the need for this approach for rulings related to women, financial matters, and jihad.[116] Fathi Osman is another example, he "considered the practical considerations" that rendered a woman's testimony to be less than a man's, as mentioned in verse 2:282, and "re-interpreted" the verse to be a function of these practical considerations, in a way similar to al-Alwani as mentioned above.[117] Hassan al-Turabi holds the same view regarding many rulings related, again, to women, their attire, and the practices of their daily lives.[118] Roger Garaudy's expression of this approach was to "divide the scripts into a section that could be historicized," such as, yet again, "rulings related to women," and another section that "represents the eternal value in the revealed message."[119] Similarly, Abdul-Karim Soroush suggested that the scripts should be "divided into two parts, essentials and accidentals, accidentals being functions of the cultural, social, and historical environment of the delivery of the main message."[120] Other similar views regarding the Prophetic traditions included Mohammad Shahrour's, who argued that some Prophetic traditions in transactional law are "not to be considered Islamic law, but rather a civil law, subject to social circumstances, that the Prophet practiced organizing society in the area of permissibility, in order to build the Arab State and Arab society of the seventh century," and thus, "could never be eternal, even if it were true 100 percent and authentic 100 percent."[121]

Imam Feisal: This is an important point, and a rebuttal to those who would completely reduce the Qur'an, which we believe to be the word of God, to a historic document.

Dr. Auda: There are some researchers and writers who extend the above consideration of historical conditions into what is called the "historicization" of Islamic scripts, thereby abrogating and cancelling their "authority" *in toto*, as you mention. This "historicist" approach suggests that our ideas about texts, cultures, and events are totally a function of their position in their original historical context as well as their later historical developments.[122] Applying this idea, borrowed from literature studies, to the Qur'an entails that the Qur'anic script is a "cultural product" of the culture that produced it, as claimed by some writers.[123]

Therefore, it is claimed, the Qur'an would become a "historic document" that is only helpful in learning about a specific historic community that existed in the Prophetic era.[124] Haida Moghissi, further, claims that "the Shariah is not compatible with the principle of equality of human beings."[125] For her, "no amount of twisting and bending can reconcile the Qur'anic injunctions and instructions about women's rights and obligations with the idea of gender equality."[126] Similarly, Ibn Warraq claims that the Islamic human rights scheme shows "inadequate support for the principle of freedom."[127]

However, I think that rendering the Qur'an "unfair" and "immoral" goes against the very belief in its divine source. Having said that, I also believe that historical events and specific juridical rulings detailed in the Qur'an should be understood within their cultural, geographical, and historical context of the message of Islam. There is a middle ground. The key for this understanding is, again, to differentiate between time and context-dependent means and eternal immutable end principles. Means may "expire," as Mohammad al-Ghazali put it, while ends and principles do not.

> **Imam Feisal:** Dividing the texts between the essentials and the accidentals, as you mentioned before, is a delicate task but evidently a greatly beneficial approach; wherein we recognize the historical specificity of aspects of revelation, yet preserve those essential and fundamental goals of God's Message. However, all of this depends on us being able to discover the purposes behind divine revelation. How do we know if something is a purpose or goal of revelation, and not merely a means to another purpose or goal?
>
> **Dr. Auda:** We must identify and differentiate the Prophetic roles, and the *Maqasid* the Prophet fulfilled in each role he played during his career. For instance, Al-Qarafi differentiated between the Prophet's roles "as a conveyer of the divine message, a judge, and a (political) leader," and suggested that each of these roles

has a different "implication in the law." Ibn Ashur added other types of "Prophetic roles," which is a significant expansion of al-Qarafi's work. By identifying, differentiating and categorizing the Prophetic roles and their implications, we can categorize the kinds of *Hadith* narrations: those that were meant to be followed exactly, all the way to those that simply described the habit of the Prophet and were neither instructive nor binding.

Ibn Ashur categorized these Prophetic roles and mapped them to *Hadith* narrations.[128] According to Ibn Ashur,[129] there are four key Prophetic roles reflected within the *Hadith* literature, each intended to be followed to varying degrees. The *legislative* role is meant to be followed exactly; an example is the Prophet's sermon at the farewell pilgrimage where he tells the believers to learn the pilgrimage rituals by observing him. The *judgeship* role can be used as a guide for judges, however, related verdicts should be up to the judge according to each case; examples are how the Prophet settled disputes, which is not general legislation but the resolution of a particular issue. The *political leadership* role – meaning those traditions related to the social, economic, and political realm – should be understood in terms of their higher purposes of serving public interests; such as the permission to own barren lands that one cultivates, which would serve the purpose of encouraging cultivation. Lastly, the *non-instructive Hadith* are not obligatory for us to follow; examples include the *Hadith* that described the way the Prophet ate, wore his clothes, laid down, walked, mounted his animal, and placed his hands when prostrating in prayer.

Imam Feisal: This relates generally to what jurists have designated as legislative and nonlegislative *Sunnah*, or *sunnah tashri`iyah* and *sunnah ghayr tashri`iyah*. For example, the Prophet's example on how he performed his pilgrimage, as you mention, is legislative and binding, and therefore is *sunnah tashri`iyah*. However, the fact that the Prophet only performed a pilgrimage *once* is not legislative; we are permitted to go on a pilgrimage more than once if we desire. Thus the Prophet's *Sunnah* of having performed the pilgrimage once is not binding, and therefore *sunnah ghayr tashri`iyah*.

Dr. Auda: Exactly. And understanding the purposes behind revelations is vital if we are to understand which elements are essential, and which are accidental or historically specific. Ibn Ashur's "re-interpretation" of the above narrations of *Hadith* raises the level of purposefulness in traditional methods and allows much flexibility in interpreting and applying the scripts. This opens the means for those who want to live according to the Shariah in the present day.

Imam Feisal: "Opening the means" and its corollary "blocking the means" are technical terms related to our discussion. Can you explain them and their role in a *Maqasid*-based approach?

Dr. Auda: Blocking the means (*sadd al-dhara'i*) in Islamic law entails forbidding, or blocking, a lawful action because it could be the means that lead to harmful results.[130] Jurists from various schools of Islamic law agreed that the means should be blocked if their "leading to unlawful actions" should be "more probable than not," but they differed over how to systemize the comparison of probabilities. Jurists divided the "probability" of unlawful actions into four different levels.[131]

A classical example of an action that results in a *certain* harm is digging a well on a public road, which will most certainly harm people. An example of an action that results in a *rare* harm, according to al-Shatibi, is selling grapes, even though a small number of people will use them to make wine. Blocking the means does not apply to such action, jurists agreed, "since the benefit of the action is more than the harm, which happens in rare cases in any case."[132] Harm is *most probable*, jurists argued, when weapons are sold during civil unrest or grapes are sold to a wine-maker.[133] And harm is *probable*, some jurists claimed, when a woman travels by herself, and when people use legally correct contracts with hidden tricks as a means to usury.[134] Malikis and Hanbalis agreed to block these means, while others disagreed because the harm is neither *certain* nor *highly probable*.

The above classical examples show that, again, "means" and "ends" are subject to variations in economic, political, social, and environmental circumstances, and not constant rules. A woman travelling by herself, the selling of weapons, or the selling of grapes could lead to probable harm in some situations, but could definitely be harmless or even beneficial for people in other situations. Therefore, it is inaccurate to rigidly classify actions according to probabilities of harm in hard and fast categories, as shown above.

Imam Feisal: An example of blocking the means that our readers may find relevant to their lives – and mentioned by Dr. Kamali in his article – is speed limits that block the means (speeding) to traffic fatalities. In Western societies, the prohibition on driving while under the influence of alcohol is another example, because it is *highly probable* that there will be an accident if someone drives a car while drunk, although consumption of alcohol in those societies is legal.

Dr. Auda: Exactly. But while "blocking the means" is useful in situations like in preventing traffic accidents, it could also be misused by some pessimistic jurists or politically motivated authorities. Today, blocking the means is a recurring theme in current neo-literalist approaches. It is utilized by some authoritarian regimes for their own ends, especially in the areas of laws related to women. For example, in the name of blocking the means, women are prohibited from driving cars, travelling alone, working in radio or television stations, serving as representatives in government, and even walking on a road.[135]

With reference to Muslim women, *opening the means* for them to learn, drive, and have their independent lives is more appropriate to their situation today. Indeed, some classical jurists proposed "opening the means" (*fat-h al-dhara'i`*) in addition to blocking them (*sadd al-dhara'i`*).[136]

Imam Feisal: Clearly, opening the means is a natural and logical extension of the classical notion of blocking the means. It also mirrors the contemporary transformation of the *Maqasid* to focus on promoting the positive (*amr bil-ma`ruf*), rather than just inhibiting the negative (*nahy `an al-munkar*) which was the focus of many classical jurists.

Dr. Auda: Indeed, and as we spoke about earlier, the Qur'anic injunction to promote the positive and inhibit the negative (*hisbah*) makes it clear that we must also, and perhaps as a priority, promote what is positive. Punishing the negative may prevent people from doing wrong according to the letter of the law, but it does not lead to human development and human flourishing, a point that Dr. Larijani emphasized in our discussions. It is not enough to penalize a population. Governments must work hard to promote human development and flourishing, and only then should they achieve a high score in our Shariah Index.

I trust that readers now see how the *Maqasid*-based approach in jurisprudence provides us with important legal tools: namely, differentiating between the roles the Prophet played and their implications in law; opening the means in addition to barring them; differentiating between means and ends; and resolving the false dichotomy associated with abrogation. These legal tools enable contemporary Muslim societies to engage in contemporary *ijtihad* that reforms and renews present day Muslim society.

This is why I maintain that the *Maqasid* are among today's most important tools for Islamic reform and renewal. If we approach our religion in this way – by looking upon the ultimate purpose of revelation and reading specific laws or verses through the lens of those purposes – we will be better equipped to overcome differences within our own community and with other faith communities across the globe.

> **Imam Feisal:** Thank you for these marvelous insights Dr. Auda. This has been such a fruitful conversation, and you have tied together many of the themes from our SIP conversations while demonstrating in clear terms the importance of a *Maqasid*-based approach toward Islamic law. And thank you for suggesting that the Shariah Index Project furthers such an approach in the global Muslim community, so that we can reap the benefits that we spoke about today and share them with humanity.

A critical reading of the universal Maqasid of religion and Shariah (Dr Khanjar Hamieh)

> **Imam Feisal:** Dr. Hamieh, given your knowledge of the Shia and Sunni tradition and your practical experience as a jurist in Lebanon, what do you see as the need for a *Maqasid*-based approach in solving the problems facing us today?
>
> **Dr. Hamieh:** We are returning to the discussion of the universal objectives (*Maqasid kulliyah*) of religion and the Shariah, after Muslim scholars such as al-Shatibi, al-Juwayni, and al-Ghazali began it ages ago, because of two needs.

First, this is a response to academic and international criticisms of Islamic law. The literature that discusses the *Maqasid* provides a traditional yet coherent view of Islamic law that is global and humanitarian and well-suited for our current world.

Second, the Muslim community has a genuine need to gather and aggregate the disparate legal opinions of jurisprudence from over the centuries across the Muslim world into one system organized under universal objectives and priorities. To create such a system, we need to first achieve a universal understanding of religion based on the objectives, or *Maqasid,* of religion in the widest and most universal sense. This means the shared aspirations and goals of every divine religion, and not just any one particular religion. The Qur'an makes it clear that religion is a universal phenomenon, and the principles that guide it are accessible to all human beings through their intellect.

As God says in the Qur'an, "If God had so willed, He would have made you a single people, but (His plan is) to test you in what He has given you: so race towards being virtuous; for unto God shall you return" (5:48). This verse suggests that virtue is a common and shared denominator among all religions, and provides a basis for an underlying unity. God has given guidance and laws to each community and people, and if He had wanted to make us all one people, He would have. God willed our differences. Rather than telling us to eliminate them, He encourages us to work together in doing good works while keeping our ultimate return in mind. This is a possible outcome of a *Maqasid*-based approach, emphasizing the fundamental goals of religion.

The great jurist Ibn 'Ashur, whom both Dr. Kamali and Dr. Auda referenced, divided the *Maqasid* into legal rulings (*ahkam*), best interests (*masalih*), and benefits (*manafi'*). He stated that these are the ultimate objectives of the law, and he considered it necessary to identify and fathom the *Maqasid* before any further elucidation of the law. The law determines our course of action in life, so every situation requires us to identify the best interests specific to it, all in keeping with our ultimate objective in life, which is living in harmony with the principle of *tawhid*.

The *Maqasid* are universal and rational principles that apply to all recipients of the Divine Law. God says in the Qur'an, "He has ordained for you as religion what He charged Noah with, and what We have revealed to thee, and what We ordained Abraham with, Moses and Jesus: 'Perform the religion, and scatter not regarding it'" (42:13). This includes the People of the Book, even though the details of our law differ. And as Shia and Sunni Muslims we are recipients of the same Law. We clearly share the same objectives and do not differ from our Sunni brothers on this issue. One needs only to look at the foundational generation of Imami [Shia] jurists from the fifth, sixth, and seventh centuries. These jurists made great strides in understanding theology and the principles of jurisprudence (*usul al-fiqh*), drawing out its themes. They took into account issues of interest, harm, and disadvantage. For example, Shaykh al-Tusi, one of the foremost authorities in the Shia tradition, said that the Shariah is based on an intellectual approach to law as it relates to interest and harm: "If the intellect cannot justify a single-source account (*khabar al-wahid*)[137] then its veracity is questionable, based on what the intellect itself prohibits and allows."

Another seminal Shia jurist, Allamah al-Hilli, emphasized in his primer *al-Mabadi'*, "Laws are dependent on interests (*masalih*), therefore it is possible that the existence of obligation (*kawn al-wujub*) is an interest (*maslaha*) in one case and a detriment (*mufsida*) in another." This again illustrates the centrality of an intellectual approach to the law.

> **Imam Feisal**: Do you still see this approach to law, which emphasizes the role of the intellect in determining the goals or interests that form the foundation of law, present today in how Muslims approach the Shariah?
>
> **Dr. Hamieh**: In my opinion, this approach, which was once essential to our tradition, has faded in modern times. It falls upon us to renew it for two reasons. First, legal opinions and interpretations of the Qur'an have diverged to such an extent that the Muslim community has fragmented into sects. Some of these groups claim exclusive access to the Qur'an and the *Sunnah*, declaring their own understanding to be absolute. They consider those who disagree with them to be unbelievers, at times even punishing them with the *Hudud* simply because of their differing opinions.

These groups fail to recognize how diversity of opinion is more in keeping with the Divine Intent, since "He appointed to each of us a law and a way" (5:48). It only enriches the tradition, empowering it with the flexibility needed to deal with the issues facing the Muslim community.

The second reason is because of the challenge posed by the successes of a globalizing secular culture to the Muslim community, particularly in the West. It confronts them while they remain entangled in the small details of the *fiqh* rulings and the interpretation of legal texts and commentaries.

We are engaging these texts in the wrong way. We must actively interpret the texts in light of our contexts. Many fail to recognize the constant interaction between legal texts and actual life. Some even elevate certain key texts from the legal tradition to a position that rivals the Qur'an and the *Hadith* in primacy and sanctity. In addition to dividing the Muslim community, their experience of their own humanity and civilization is fragmented and premature, related to the Qur'an only in the most superficial of ways. A *Maqasid*-based approach can reorient the efforts of the Muslim community toward a correct direction – a much needed and desired objective.

> **Imam Feisal**: This point is extremely relevant to Muslims today. From my own experience as an American imam, Muslim minorities in

Western countries living under another system of laws, norms, and values, constantly feel the weight of this challenge. We need an intelligent and rooted approach towards the legal problems that face us in day-to-day life, whether about issues like interfaith relations and marriage, inheritance, and other such areas of law. Many contemporary approaches seem to reduce Islam to merely a system of rules, failing to see the higher purposes, such as justice, that God emphasizes in the Qur'an. Furthermore, our own traditional societies are confronted by the progress of the West. Many in our societies are attracted to Western systems such as banking or new technological advancements, but don't know how to fit this with our legal tradition.

And as you point out, some react by burying their heads in the details of books and the *fiqh* rulings. But what I hear you saying is that we need an approach that invokes greater ethical principles. In meeting these challenges that face us, the *Maqasid* provide a framework within which we can organize and reorient Islamic jurisprudence.

> **Dr.Hamieh:** Yes, but I would also add that we should not rely solely on the achievements of past scholars and jurists. We cannot simply perpetuate what they saw as priorities in their day and age. We must look at the priorities of our day and age. Outside of the revealed text (Qur'an) and the Prophetic tradition (the *Hadith*), all other texts are secondary. These secondary legal texts, which are the source of many of our rulings, were written by fallible human beings. We must recognize that these writers were operating within the limits of their understanding and contexts.

We must not elevate these secondary texts to a position equal to the revealed source of our religion. In fact, in keeping with the tradition of these scholars, we should make every effort to subject our understanding of the *Maqasid* to constant review and renewal at the levels of legal principles (*usul*), the texts they come from, and even at the level of quality and quantity in order to formulate a response relevant to actual life.

> **Imam Feisal:** How do you suggest we go about undertaking this constant review?
>
> **Dr. Hamieh:** Whenever we deal with the *Maqasid*, whether at the broadest and most universal level or at the level of specific legal decisions (rulings which relate to individuals), we engage in a

process of rational thought (*fikr*). This process seeks to apply the Qur'anic text in a way appropriate to the context of time and place. The key here is that there is always a relationship between the priorities that face us in life and the objectives of the law.

Imam Feisal: Both Dr. Kamali and Dr. Auda also made a case for leaving the *Maqasid* open to enhancement and further interpretation because of this relationship between the priorities of life and the objectives of the Law.

Dr. Hamieh: Understanding this relationship is part and parcel of religion. Taha Jabir al-Alwani, the contemporary Azhari scholar, states that, "understanding the *Maqasid* comes through understanding revelation (the Qur'an), and understanding priorities comes through understanding actual life. Religiosity is the combination of the two."

This is a key point, for right and good religiosity is the combination of understanding both revelation and real life exigencies. So there is a right religiosity (*din al-haqq*) and a wrong religiosity (*din al-batil*). The Qur'an refers to "those whose efforts go astray in the present life, while they think that they are doing good deeds," (18:104) people who think that they are practicing religion but are in fact failing at it. If we don't understand both the revelation and the priorities of our context, we can lose our religion and practice false religion, or use religion to escape from the realities of the world. And this goes against our intellectual and legal tradition. Our tradition is one of harmonizing the realities of our situation with the realities found within the Qur'an. For example, al-Shatibi was among the first to do this in formulating the *Maqasid*. His *Maqasid* wed the intellect with the transmitted tradition. He relied on universal inductions that were not limited by particular individual instances. In doing this, he was able to deal with issues that are purely objects of the intellect in a way that didn't overshadow or sideline the transmitted roots of the discussion. But Al-Shatibi's *Maqasid* are means to greater goals, not ends in of themselves.

For instance, in regards to the *maqsad* of *din*, religion, al-Shatibi doesn't refer to it in itself, since ultimately the *Maqasid* are all branches of religion. Rather he meant issues such as *jihad* in defense of doctrine, as is covered in many jurisprudential texts. But it is also permissible to classify *jihad* under other *Maqasid* such as life or honor, as it is also a means of defending life, or honor, and mobilizing against any threats to life, as well as any other threats against the best interests of the Muslim community. It also could mean removing those obstructions that prevent human beings from living their life in accordance with their own free will.

The rest of the *Maqasid* are issues of preventing the negative also. By `*aql*, the mind, al-Shatibi doesn't mean thought or the cognitive processes of the brain, nor freedom of thought. Rather he means removing the obstructions that keep the mind from working soundly, an example of which is alcohol and intoxication. The *maqsad* of life (*nafs*) is induced from the prohibition of murder. Wealth (*mal*) is a protection of ownership deduced from the prohibition of theft, cheating, and other financial crimes. And honor ('*ird*) is the protection of family and marriage deduced from the prohibition of fornication; basically, it is whatever destroys families. My point is that al-Shatibi's *Maqasid* are immediate goals that are in themselves means to higher and loftier goals. My call to re-evaluate the *Maqasid* is not meant as a criticism of al-Shatibi or al-Juwayni or al-Ghazali. Their efforts were revolutionary and appropriate to their time, but the rapid changes of our current time necessitate a more dynamic and versatile system pertinent to the problems of our age – a system founded upon a universal understanding of religion.

> **Imam Feisal:** Are you suggesting a formula that not only advances the Law's objectives from a prevention of the negative to the promotion of the positive, but goes further into what Dr. Auda calls the *maslaha* [interest] of human development; to regard the *Maqasid* as the *mukamillat* – what Dr. Kamali translates as "the accomplishers" of the highest understanding of human development?
>
> **Dr. Hamieh:** Yes, a human development that is not oriented merely toward this ephemeral world, but also our permanent abode: the next world. A correct orientation towards the next world sets the affairs of this world in place.
>
> **Imam Feisal:** Your comment reminds me of the verse, "had the peoples of the cities believed and been God-fearing, We would have poured upon them blessings from heaven and earth" (7:96).
>
> **Dr. Hamieh:** Yes, surely blessings will come and our societies will improve only if we take up the task of living righteously, and a key factor of this is a correct understanding.

We need to open a wide door of interpretation to the Qur'anic text as our key primary source, using the interpretive literature as an aid toward the eternal principles found within the Qur'an. In other words, the principles of the Qur'an need to be looked for and found in the Qur'an, not in the secondary literature. To do this we need to engage in a process of continuous reorientation towards the principles found within the text of the Qur'an in respect of our continuously changing context. Through such a process we unveil not only the text, but also our own selves.

> Imam Feisal: You again remind me of the Qur'an, wherein God says, "We shall show them Our signs in the horizons and in themselves, till it is clear to them that He is the truth." (41:53). What I hear you describing is this process of engagement whereby, as this verse explains, God reveals Himself through the cosmos and through our own souls just as He reveals Himself to us in the Qur'an.
>
> Dr. Hamieh: And it is through this process that we delineate absolute universals through reading the Qur'an in light of the other signs of God. This is a process of reading the revealed book simultaneously with the book of life (*kawn*), that is, the physical, phenomenal world.
>
> Imam Feisal: Dr. Hamieh, you said earlier that constant review of what constitutes the *Maqasid* of religion can be done through rational thought, guided by this correct understanding, as we apply the Qur'anic text in a way that is appropriate to the exigencies of our time and place. What are the specific steps that need to be taken in order to extract what you call the universal *Maqasid*?
>
> Dr. Hamieh: I would suggest the following six steps as a preliminary roadmap:

1. One must engage in direct and close readings of the Qur'an aimed towards creating a background from which a preliminary hypothetical framework of the *Maqasid* can arise.
2. This leads to a crystallization of thought that contains the different universals that were perceived by the intellect during its preliminary readings.
3. One then returns to the text to verify the accuracy of the hypothetical framework and the universals contained within it.
4. The fourth step is to gather and arrange the different types of derived universals in order to both reveal the relationships between their different aspects and to highlight their differences in regards to knowledge, action, education, and doctrine.
5. One then divides the universals into different fields, building bridges of interaction and integration between them. This is in order to create personal legal mechanisms through which relevant meanings and solutions are derived by each individual obliged by the law (*mukallif.*)

6. The final step is to create a complete theoretical vision that encompasses all of the aforementioned principles and fields, including their historical equivalents (such as al-Shatibi's *Maqasid*). This is in order to bring to fruition the capacities, inner dispositions, and hidden capabilities found within the human soul – an end that is essential to all religion.

Imam Feisal: This intellectual process is how we arrived at the *Maqasid* theory. But would we achieve the same results? How would the *Maqasid* look through such a system?

Dr. Hamieh: Through such an engagement with the Qur'an, we realize that the root of every law, thus every *maqsad* of the law, is *tawhid*. That is, the objective of every *maqsad* is to unite us, as individuals and as a society, with God and His will. The Qur'an and all divine revelations[138] have this unity of God (*tawhid*) – and unity of humankind – as their fundamental point. It is the common spirit and universal root of every divine message.

Tawhid manifests in two practical ways: Vicegerency (*istikhlaf* or *khilafa*) and purification of the self (*tazkiyyah*). Al-Alwani uses the word "civilization" ('imran) instead of Vicegerency. Of course, al-Alwani's wording is synonymous with vicegerency, as promoting civilization is one goal of God's vicegerent, but the Qur'anic language is one of vicegerency, which comes from the fact that God has given man a higher station compared to other creatures. This is alluded to in the Qur'anic narrative of the angels prostrating themselves to Adam. We humans therefore have a purpose in this world that is fundamentally intertwined with our nature as servants of God, a mission devoted to the promotion of good.

The second imperative, self-purification, means that just as man is naturally inclined to be good and just, he also has the opposite desire, and this leads to spiritual pollution. He needs to purify himself and his society from this spiritual pollution. Thus, he suffers from the tendency to remain ignorant and the desire to control, dominate, and overpower others. To overcome this spiritual pollution, he must purify himself.

Imam Feisal: So these two duties, one in reference to the self, another in reference to the world, are in a sense the mechanisms of embodying *tawhid*, which is the utmost goal of any religious way of life. Sufis call unification with God *fanaa fillah* and *baqaa billah*; Buddhists call this enlightenment, an embodied and lived practice of the highest principles of religion, a life in harmony with the Divine Will.

Dr. Hamieh: This is why these together comprise the larger framework of all the *Maqasid*, as they are the worldview in which the other *Maqasid* live and breathe. They are the overarching universal *Maqasid* of religion (*Maqasid al-din al-kulliyah*) about which no Prophet disagrees: The unity of God (*tawhid*), vicegerency (*istikhlaf*), [139] and self-purification (*tazkiyya*). These *Maqasid* are general categories that give birth to a great number of values and around which all of the other universal *Maqasid* take shape. They are all connected to the divine commandments that are expressed in the verses of the Qur'an, whether they are legislative verses (*ayat al-ahkam*) [like the rulings on usury, corporal punishment, blood money, or inheritance] or purely ethical ones.

They are all oriented toward these three overarching *Maqasid*. So for instance, from the *maqsad* of self-purification we have the *Maqasid* of altruism, mercy, beautiful action (*ihsan*), patience, abstinence, God-consciousness and humility. Then, under the *maqsad* of vicegerency we have the *Maqasid* of dignity, justice, freedom, responsibility, and rational thought.

Imam Feisal: Is there any limit to these principles?

Dr. Hamieh: Not at all. There is no limit to the best interests of human beings, so there is no limit to these objectives. Rather, every situation has its own specific objectives. You see, even Shatibi's *Maqasid* are still a part of this. For instance, I explained that the *maqsad* of religion simply refers to *jihad*. In this new system, *jihad* would fit under dignity, freedom, or justice, all of which are higher *Maqasid* of the Shariah. Or take for example the *maqsad* of *nafs*, the preservation of life. There are many Qur'anic verses which forbid murder, yet there are also verses which command *jihad* and fighting in the path of God. It is evident that the protection of life is not sought as an end; rather, it is for the sake of a more important function. This is the *maqsad* of vicegerency. In other words, the taking of a human life is not prohibited merely in order to preserve life but rather, it is prohibited because it robs another individual of the vicegerency endowed to them by God. This vicegerency gave that person the potential to contribute to society and help his or her fellow beings. Murder robs both the victim and society of this potential contribution.

Imam Feisal: This is a beautiful point Dr. Hamieh. In effect, you are calling us to recognize the deepest level of the *Maqasid* and the most profound meanings behind the laws of the Shariah. Murder is prohibited not simply because life is sacred, but because God, in creating that particular individual, has endowed him or her with a purpose known only to Him. This person has a specific contribution to make, whether large or small, and murder prevents him from realizing this potential and keeps all of humanity from his valuable contribution.

Dr. Hamieh: This is precisely what I mean by taking the most universal of the *Maqasid* into consideration. This is the same for all the other *Maqasid*. Behind the *maqsad* of wealth is aspiring to live a life of dignity, stability, and freedom of choice and thought. In this day and age, poverty constricts the capability to live a noble life for many people. This is why the protection of one's property and the promotion of acquiring a *halal* income are sacred. Otherwise, greed and the hoarding of wealth are criticized in the Qur'an, and it is full of warnings as to the dangers of wealth. Thus wealth is neither negative nor positive in itself, but it becomes negative when one is distracted by wealth and greed; when wealth becomes your god instead of a means to approach God. And it becomes positive when, through it, you realize your potential as a vicegerent of God. The *maqsad* of family falls under a similar situation. It promotes vicegerency because such a calling usually rises from someone with a stable and loving family, whose desires are channeled into a blessed relationship, and who thus maintains inner and outer purity.

Imam Feisal: So what you mean by the word *Maqasid* are the ultimate and eternal goals that, in a sense, reveal God's intention behind the creation of human beings, and not the immediate goals that are derived from legal rulings. It is a concern about the ultimate purpose of religion itself in relation to day-to-day life. Just as the practical implication of the Divine Imperative to unite with God's will plays out as vicegerency and the purification of the self, purification plays out practically as both the elimination of the negative and the promotion of the positive. But ultimately, we are talking about what is positive in the most universal sense. The *Maqasid* are a call to all human beings, regardless of what they identify themselves as, to realize their deepest purpose in life, as both servants and vicegerents of God.

Dr. Hamieh: This is the purpose behind revelation itself. God's guidance, embedded in the Qur'an, encompasses both the next life and this life. It is not silent about what the best interests of humanity are in any given situation. We need an approach that identifies these best interests.

Imam Feisal: This relates to Dr. Ghazi and Dr. Larijani's points on the rationale behind an Islamic state. This system you illustrate is how we can develop the rationale of an Islamic state, rooted in the Qur'an and the *Hadith*, in order to find the guiding principles toward which we should orient our actions. As Dr. Ghazi noted, the main difference in an Islamic state is that it is not valueless or value-neutral. It has guiding principles and moral objectives, and it operates on an understanding of the purpose behind the creation of humanity.

Dr. Hamieh: Yes, and it must not merely tell people what to do, but rather provide them with a means of attaining their best interest in accordance with God's will.

What we must aim to do is provide a complete background, and a succinct worldview based on the Qur'an, which allows us to interact with and respond to the challenges of actual life. This worldview and system relates to God's Will as found in the Qur'an, not disparate *fiqh* opinions. We need to realize that legal opinions relate more to the understanding of scholars rather than the understanding of God.

We have to steer away from the illusion of having a monopoly over truth, an illusion that causes us to unjustly limit the freedoms of others who may reach different conclusions. We must admit that what is accomplished by one interpreter is no more than a reflection of his own awareness and the breadth of his comprehension. The interpreter of revelation does not have direct access to the absolute, but rather, is born from life and its experiences. Therefore a good jurist must enable people to reach their own solutions directly, rather than dictate to them what they should or shouldn't do, for we all swim in a way relative to our own situation. When God gave us the capacity to open the doors of our potential, how can our understanding of His Law close those doors? Rather, we must remember that God's Law opens the potential of all humanity, for this is demanded by the all-encompassing mercy of God that embraces every existent thing. Only through such an understanding will we be able to solve the problems that face us today.

Imam Feisal: Thank you for your deep insights, Dr. Hamieh.

Creating harmony and correcting misperceptions on the meaning of an Islamic State (Ramzi Khoury)

> **Imam Feisal:** The Prophet tells us that differences of opinion are a blessing to the community, yet there are many groups today claiming that only their interpretation is the true Islam. How could the Shariah Index help Muslims make sense of these competing and often conflicting claims?
>
> **Khoury:** The best way to confront this is by the delivery of knowledge, and this is what the Shariah Index does: it delivers legitimate knowledge of the first degree.

By summoning the guidance of trusted scholars representing *all* of the main Islamic schools of legal interpretation, the index simplifies the very complicated process and huge undertaking of delving into the Shariah. Because the final product enjoys the *ijma'* of these prominent scholars, the Muslim layperson can trust the Shariah Index's jurisprudence without having to worry about which school endorses it and which rejects it.

Ijma' is a rarity in this world of competing schools, a breath of fresh air! The vast majority of people depend on what they are told by the "authority" they follow and believe is the "legitimate" source of information. When there is *ijma'* over any issue, then it, rather than the *ijtihad* of one authority, is the universal Islamic norm, and therefore its legitimacy is of the highest caliber.

The Index, by showing the true depth of the Shariah, clarifies the true essence of Islam as a religion broadly serving humanity. It is a tool that Muslims can utilize to understand the divine requirements of the Shariah, and to differentiate between the eternal, unchanging divine requirements and the applications of law established by man through *ijtihad*, which are suited to the circumstances of a certain time and place. Some *ijtihad* used today is outdated and is no longer suitable for this day and age, but many Muslims are under the impression that this is Divine Law that cannot be adapted for modern societies. The Shariah Index outlines the underlying principles that can guide us in any age.

An index by its nature makes a lot of content available at a glance. This is a powerful source of information that when made available can be used by all people. Scholars can refer to it, the layperson can use it as a guide, and governments can use it as a tool for development. It took the top scholars six years to develop an index that all people could understand in a glance!

> **Imam Feisal:** What are some of the claims that would be challenged by the Shariah Index's illumination of the "true depth of the Shariah" and "the true essence of Islam"?
>
> **Khoury:** Many of those demanding that the Shariah be the "foundation of rule in a state" are focused on the implementation of *Hudud* as if the Shariah is only concerned with punishment. Another example is the various forms of *ijtihad* that are pushed out there about who the leader is, all of which are purely designed to ensure that *Emir al-Mo'mineen*, the ruler, is the person heading a specific organization by demanding the *bay'ah* even before the state is erected.

Often proclamations of the "one true Islam" are just political demands packaged in a religious outfit. Many political demands made in the name of Islam have no foundation in the Shariah, yet are communicated to give the impression they were the orders of Allah, God the Almighty, and not the politicians who need them to achieve their narrow goals of today. Hardline ideological political groups push principles in the name of Islam that are either unrelated to Islam or are illegal *fatwas* launched for the purpose of achieving narrow political interests.

For example, many voices in the Islamic world are drowned out by the banner of radical forms of "Salafi thought," in other words regressive thought, demanding that society move backward, not forward.

The radical Salafis seek to serve their specific narrow goals without adversely affecting their own operations. So they use the *Sunnah* to reinstate the dress code and the way of life of 1,500 years ago and to declare modernity as *haram,* yet they drive cars, watch television, conduct interviews, and use social media on the Internet to push their versions of what is *haram* and *halal.* By their standards, something is *halal* if it serves their scheme and *haram* if it does not; they do this in order to brand their followers and create a gap between them and the rest of society in the hope that their branded followers will one day become the majority.

These groups fight to win the minds and hearts of people at the expense of reality and the actual interests of the public. They create perceptions of their authority and righteousness in order to remain in power.

Such perceptions were used to promote Osama bin Laden as the true leader of Muslims, the one who represents the true Islam as opposed to every other "flawed" version of the religion.

Al-Qaeda did the same with Ayman Zawahiri and several other people who were given new names and titles to brand them as Islamic leaders. Individuals who were as yet unheard of were designated "Emirs" of specific geographic territories, and since they all followed central command, Bin Laden was by default perceived as the *Emir al-Mo'mineen*, or the Caliph of the Muslim Nation, by youth that lacked knowledge of Islam.

Al-Qaeda branded itself as the only party on earth representing true Islam. And as a result of its violent acts, marketed by powerful communications machines, the organization became recognized on an international level by Muslims and non-Muslims alike. In doing so, Al-Qaeda and other extremist groups acting in the name of Islam have harmed the image of Islam and of Muslims and created a divide both within the global Muslim community and between the Muslim community and the rest of the world.

> **Imam Feisal:** Could you give an example of how the discourse within the Islamic world over the definition of an Islamic state has adversely influenced perceptions in the West?
>
> **Khoury:** The popular political demand for an Islamic state has posed a challenge to governments and the people of many countries due to conceptual variations of what defines an Islamic State. The answer to this question tends to be based on the need of the politicians and not the Shariah. This is a given, because, as the Shariah Index scholars have pointed out, there has never been a Divine Order to establish a state.

Every time a radical group seizes territories and supposedly manages them "under Shariah law," the image of Islam suffers major damage in the West. Territories in Afghanistan managed by the Taliban, for example, became associated in the minds of non-Muslims worldwide with what a "real Islamic State" would be. The Islamic State in Iraq and Syria (ISIS) has rebranded itself several times, starting with the title "Al-Qaeda in Bilad al-Sham" and now with the potent new brand of simply "The Islamic State." The simplicity of the terrorist group's new name is dangerous. The name implies that it is the one and only true Islamic state. This group, previously disregarded as an ultra-radical bunch of hooligans, has now managed to grab territory in both Syria and Iraq, where it has erected its

"Islamic state." The leader of the group, Ibrahim Samara'i, aka Abu Bakr al-Baghdadi, appointed himself "the Caliph of all Muslims," and called upon all other Islamists to give him *bay'ah* or else be put to death.

The minute ISIS launched its anomaly of a state it attacked Christian residents, kicked them out of the state, and stole their homes and belongings. It destroyed an 1800 year old church as well as many Shiite shrines. It declared female circumcision a due "Islamic act," for the first time in the history of Islam, and it killed many Muslims in cold blood. This "Islamic state" is not trying to gain acceptance from the world, or even from the Muslim population who suddenly found itself under ISIS's rule! One would think that these acts in "The Islamic State" are a deliberate design to communicate to the West a terrible image of Islam, a deliberate operation to instill the maximum level of Islamophobia. Even Muslims have the right to fear the erection of an Islamic state if it is founded on the principles of these thugs, who claim to derive their whole doctrine from the Shariah.

The truth is, of course, that rogue anomalies such as theirs that are declared as states are far from Islamic. The challenge is to communicate this truth to the world in the face of the images of carnage and mayhem perpetrated by these enemies of Islam who are committing evil in its name.

> **Imam Feisal:** You have been engaged in several projects to bridge the divide between the Muslim world and the West. How would you evaluate that divide today, and what is fueling it?
>
> **Khoury:** There are flawed perceptions on both sides of the divide. There is a common perception in the West that Islam is a bloody religion that endorses violence and mayhem. The truth is that the Muslims who hold such hostile intentions towards the West are a tiny minority that is as much the enemy of the Muslim world as it is the enemy of the West.

In the Muslim world there is a common perception that the West is out to destroy Islam and that all Western policies and actions toward the Muslim world are part of a "crusade" to achieve that purpose. The truth is that the policies adopted by the West have nothing to do with religion, but rather are motivated solely by the Western states' geopolitical, military or economic interests in a specific region. Those in the West who hold hostile intentions toward Islam and Muslims, some of whom seem to be ready to bring Armageddon through a third world war against the Muslim world, are a tiny minority that is as much the enemy of the West as they are the enemy of the Muslim world.

On both sides, there are those who are working to deliberately exacerbate the divide or to achieve narrow interests at the expense of people's general welfare, and they achieve their goals by utilizing perception management, namely by orchestrating very loud horrific events that rapidly influence people's perception, events that involve bloodshed and mayhem. Those working on the side of the truth, to protect human rights and establish accord among nations, are unable to compete with this by conducting the same kinds of events that would attract worldwide attention. How can promoting the sanctity of life, for example, compete with a massacre on the news?

To combat it, we need perception management on the part of those who have true knowledge and the legitimacy required to promote the truth to the public. We have made considerable strides in communicating the truth on both ends, but we still have a long way to go. To compete, we have to develop and utilize complex tools that require a lot of effort. It took the good scholars engaged with the Shariah Index Project over six years of work to develop an Islamic tool for the benefit of the Muslim world. I say this tool can be used on both sides of the divide in order to bridge it.

> **Imam Feisal:** How do you see the Shariah Index as a perception management tool?
>
> **Khoury:** The Shariah Index would give people a baseline – an understanding of the true essence of Islam – that they can hold up to the claims put forth by those acting in its name. When you clarify the reality of a situation, you can correct erroneous perceptions, and we need to do a lot of this.

If we consider the science of perception management as a weapon used to win a war, then it is a good weapon when used in the service of the truth. Unfortunately, perception management has been associated with the work of intelligence agencies because some of these agencies make use of it to achieve nefarious goals. Moreover, as I said, we have seen Al-Qaeda and the likes utilize perception management to achieve their goals as well. A vehicle can be used to run over innocent people, but that does not change the fact that it is a vital form of transportation used for good purposes, including transferring patients to hospitals to save their lives.

Imam Feisal: How could the Shariah Index change erroneous perceptions in the West and help bridge this divide?

Khoury: Even though the good scholars were not focused on communicating to the West when they were developing the Shariah Index, it is a fantastic tool to show the whole world that the Shariah shares so many values in common with the rest of the world. As such, Islam and its followers cannot be detrimental to accord among nations!

Muslims today are a great source of success stories in business, science, technology, and all facets of life and are contributing a wealth of achievement that has advanced society. The perception that Muslims, due to their religion, pose a danger to the values in the West, for example, is a lie that must be combatted through the delivery of knowledge. No one can expect a Christian, Jewish, Buddhist, or Hindu layperson to go dig into the Shariah to understand it and thereby reach correct conclusions about it. Even a typical Muslim layperson does not do this. The Shariah Index can communicate the true essence of Islam to non-Muslims and clarify all of the issues of importance to them. This is how we can correct the erroneous perceptions about Islam and prevent a clash of civilizations from becoming a reality.

The Shariah Index can also show Muslims how much they have in common with the West. There are those in the Muslim world who reject anything Western as an "infidel value," deeming it *haram* just because it is the norm in the West. Well, many of the norms in the West today, again as pointed out by the Shariah Index scholars, are the Divine Demands of Allah the Almighty in Islam. Just because the West has adopted a value doesn't make it un-Islamic.

Imam Feisal: Could you provide some example of these intersecting values?

Khoury: Most Islamic states have signed and ratified international accords and agreements, such as the Universal Declaration of Human Rights, but in many societies, the religious segment of the public has the perception that such accords are imposed on their governments by the West and are therefore un-Islamic in nature, if not the conspiracy of "infidels" to turn Islamic societies into a copy of the West and impose Western values on the "Muslim Nation." This has led to the prevalent phenomenon of governments signing the accords but not implementing them, either because there is a lack of local demand for their implementation or because they can silence any demands by claiming that these accords are un-Islamic.

But in fact, such accords are not un-Islamic, because the Shariah demands the protection of human rights, as the index clearly shows. The Shariah Index sheds light on the fact that when it comes to human rights, freedom of speech and press, and other supposedly Western values, most of these values are part and parcel of the Shariah, or at least are not in contradiction to the Shariah, and therefore can and should be implemented by Muslim societies for the purpose of serving the public interest. If a value is in contradiction to the Shariah, then it would also be pointed out by the Shariah Index, and it would become a specific exception and not in any way indicative of a norm that Western and Islamic values are fundamentally different.

A great example of one of these values is the environment. The Muslim world is lagging behind the rest of the world when it comes to the environment, despite the fact that the environment is an integral Divine Injunction in Islam. Today the environment is a priority in the West, and the Muslim world regards it, as best, as a *kamaliyat*. An Islamic state, by utilizing the Shariah Index as a guideline for development, would address environmental issues as a priority.

Imam Feisal: How do you think the Shariah Index can be used as a tool, and not just as a reference book, to achieve the aims we've discussed? How can this information actually go beyond the theoretical, beyond changing perceptions, and actually change the facts on the ground?

Khoury: I am an advocate of institutionalizing the index upon completion, and I believe that a Shariah Index Institution should be created for the purpose of development rather than for the purpose of measurement, and this is why:

Most governments in the Islamic world derive their legitimacy from Islam, one way or another. Don't expect them to be happy when we say we want to measure how Islamic their state is, or even how compliant their state is with the Shariah. This becomes an issue of national security, and the project could well be fought tooth and nail by many governments and official religious institutions in the Muslim world.

Implementation of the Shariah in one state greatly differs from another state due to the fact that every state has its own system of governance. This is true even of the Gulf Arab states. The system of governance in Saudi Arabia is very different from that of the United Arab Emirates, Bahrain, or Oman. The political, social, economic, and of course religious realities on the ground, as well as the "needs" of each state, are very different. Every one of these states claims, at least internally, that they have correctly implemented the Shariah, but the majority of parties out there that are demanding a unified Islamic system across the board are working to destabilize these regimes or even topple them. We are not talking about liberal movements looking for democracy, but radical fundamentalist movements, some of which are also violent and wreaking havoc and mayhem in some states today.

The Shariah Index Institution should be dedicated to working hand in hand with public and private sector organizations in every state in order to help the state develop its economy, society, political system, and more, by following the guidelines of the Shariah Index with the same great legitimacy and flexibility that we saw in the good scholars who worked together to develop the Index and achieve *ijma'* over it.

The Institution would therefore not differentiate between Sunni or Shia, because it will be an institution for all Muslims, dedicated to providing all Islamic states with the knowledge they need to progress. The operating and guiding principle of the Shariah Index Institution would be this: Let us help the state serve the people in a way compliant with the Shariah.

Under the direction of good scholars, Sunni and Shia and from all schools of thought, the Institution would provide experts in economics, sociology, environment, and other human sciences, such as communications, that would help states develop their policies as needed. No one would be there to judge, only to help. Their work would be analogous to the religious or spiritual teacher, whose objective is not to punish his students, but rather to educate and develop them to their maximum potential.

Because the scholars represent different schools of thought and hail from countries with different forms of government – monarchies, republics, some avowedly Islamic, some avowedly secular – the consensus of the good scholars leaves the space for more than one interpretation of the Shariah on the form of governance. They have agreed on the deliverables, while allowing space for disagreement on the political forms.

In addition to working at the level of the state, the Shariah Index Institution would work with Islamic organizations to help reach accord between Muslims at the regional and international levels. Who can deny the enmity we see today among Muslims? The enmity has resulted in violence and has dragged the Muslim world backwards, demoting stability and progress in various regions of the world. If our great scholars were able to work together amicably throughout the process, then the Muslim world could achieve harmony despite the cultural, political, or religious differences that have plagued modern Islamic history.

Finally, the Shariah Index Institution would work with global organizations to clarify the true Islamic values and communicate them in the West in an effort to correct the erroneous perceptions about Islam and the values held by its believers.

Because great Muslim scholars of different *madhhabs* developed the Shariah Index, it will have the same credibility in the West as it does in the Muslim world. As a credible tool to understand Islam, the Shariah Index will not only shed light on the truth but will also help dismantle the propaganda campaigns used to tarnish Islam and its followers.

Many of these campaigns utilize partial "truths" to promote a lie. This is why details are vital in eliminating misconceptions, and the Shariah Index provides such details, all of which illuminate the essential common ground that every Muslim can and should agree on: God's law came down for the sake of humankind and to serve the common good.

Imam Feisal: Thank you, Ramzi, for advising us on how to deploy the Shariah Index in a way that could advance harmony among the Muslim community and bring sound Islamic principles, stability, and legitimacy to governments in the Muslim world. And thank you for emphasizing that within the sphere of common agreement and universal consensus that our scholars have sought to define, we can create the space for recognizing that more than one interpretation of the Shariah, especially as it regards governance, should be deemed valid by Muslims.

Glossary

`Adalah Justice

`Alim (pl. `Ulama') A scholar, a learned man, from the root `ilm; a mujtahid or a faqih would be considered a `alim

`Aql Intelligence or mind, one of the six objectives (Maqasid) of Islamic law

*`Ibadat*  Within Islamic law, this refers to those laws that deal with acts of worship and ritual, such as prayer, fasting and pilgrimage. These laws are in contrast to mu`amalat, or laws that pertain to civil obligations or transactions between people, that include personal or family law, commercial law or law of transactions, criminal law, and administrative law, i.e., laws of governance and international law.

*`Illah*  In the science of fiqh, the effective cause; the ascertainment of the reason (or `illah) underlying a legal rule is an essential step in the process of reasoning by analogy (qiyas). A legal principle established by an original case is extended to cover new cases on the ground that they possess a common `illah.

`Imran The developing of civilization on earth, one of al-Alwani's three meta-Maqasid (along with tawhid and tazkiah)

`Ird Honor or dignity, one of the six objectives (Maqasid) of Islamic law

`Ismah Inviolability or protection under the law

`Itq Freedom from slavery, an objective of the law spoken of by early jurists; this notion of freedom is distinct from the more contemporary "hurriyah," meaning freedom in the sense of freedom of religion or speech, and "infilat" meaning uncontrolled or irresponsible freedom that harms the self or others, and leading to chaos.

'Urf Tradition or custom; also a source of law when it does not contradict Shariah

Abu'l `ala' Maududi (d. 1979) A journalist, theologian, Muslim revivalist leader and political philosopher in twentieth century British India, and later Pakistan; he was a political figure in Pakistan and founder of Jamaat-e-Islami, the Islamic revivalist party

Adab al nikah The rules, or ethics, of marriage relationships

Adamiyyah Humanity or personhood, that we are all the children of Adam; this concept is the basis of what Şentürk calls the universalist paradigm of rights within Islamic law, where protection (`ismah) under the law is afforded to all human beings regardless of religious affiliation. This is in contrast to what he calls the communalist approach, which recognizes state protection only to those who are of certain faiths (Muslim, Christian, or Jew) and others who have made an arrangement with the state (see "aman").

Ahadith al-ahkam Those prophetic traditions that contain binding legislative verses that are used as the basis of law

Ahl al-bayt Literally meaning "the people of the house," modern Muslims use this term to refer to the lineal descendants of the Prophet Muhammad. But because the Qur'an also uses this expression to refer to Abraham's family as well, it can and should be applied to the lineal descendants of Abraham.

Al-Ghazali, Abu Hamid (d. 1111/505 H) Renowned Persian theologian, jurist, mystic, and religious reformer, al-Ghazali was one of the major thinkers in developing the Maqasid theory. Considered one of the most influential Muslim thinkers of his time, he is most noted for shifting Islamic discourse away from neo-platonism and bringing Sufi philosophy to closer harmony with Orthodox Islam.

Al-Juwayni, Imam al-Haramayn (d. 1085/478) Persian Shafi`i jurist who was one of the first to articulate the Maqasid theory, classifying them into the three categories of essentials, needs, and refinements. He wrote extensively on Islamic government and was al-Ghazali's teacher.

Al-Qarafi, Ahmad ibn Idris (d. 1285/683 H) Maliki uṣuli jurist who lived in Ayyubid and Mamluk Egypt, whose writings elaborated on the Maqasid theory. He was the first to include the maqsad of `ird/honor to the previously recognized five Maqasid of Islamic law.

Al-Shatibi, Abu Ishaq Ibrahim (d. 1388/790 H) Maliki uṣuli scholar from al-Andalus, whose well-known book on Islamic jurisprudence, "al-Muwafaqat fi Usul al-Shari`ah," elaborated the Maqasid theory.

Aman Security or protection, in Islamic law this signifies a safe conduct or pledge of security by which a non-Muslim's life and property become protected by the sanctions of the law for a limited period. The protection (`ismah) of the rights of citizens by the state, according to the communalist perspective (see Senturk's interview, Part III), is afforded either due to the citizen's faith (iman) or by this pledge of security (aman).

Amir ul-mu'minin "Commander of the Faithful," used as a title for a Caliph, and now used by some rulers (for example, the King of Morocco) to claim legitimacy from a Muslim community.

Asl (pl. Usul)   Literally, "source or root;" technically, the sources of law or the principles of jurisprudence

Basirah   Spiritual perception, discernment, or insight

Bay`ah   Oath of allegiance given by the people to their leader

Bilal al-Habashi   Also known as Bilal ibn Rabah, he was a former slave emancipated by Abu Bakr, and later went on to become a companion of the Prophet. He was known for his beautiful singing voice and was considered the first Muezzin, one who recites the call to prayer.

Daruriyyat   Essentials; within the category of needs that each maqsad should promote, these are the most important and essential benefits. After the daruriyyat in importance are needs (hajiyyat) and refinements (tahsiniyyat).

Dawlah Islamiyyah   Islamic state

Dhimmi   Literally, non-Muslims living under the jurisdiction and protection of traditional Muslim Rulers, most often referring to the Jewish and Christian constituents.

Din   Religion, one of the six objectives (Maqasid) of Islamic law

Faqih   A legal scholar who has studied fiqh

Fard   An action is fard or wajib (obligatory) if it is a religious obligation in Islamic law. This is one of the five qualifications of actions in Islam (obligatory/fard, recommended/mandub, permissible/mubah, disliked/makruh, or forbidden/haram). A fard `ayn is an obligation that falls upon everyone; for example, the five-times daily prayer is a fard `ayn. No one can pray this prayer on another's behalf. A fard kifayah is an obligation upon the whole community that can be fulfilled by one or a few individuals; for example, the funeral prayer upon a deceased Muslim is an obligation that the whole community is responsible for, but a few members of the community can do it on behalf of the whole community.

Fatwa (pl. Fatawa)   A non-binding legal opinion based on a point of Islamic law and pertaining to either civil or religious matters, issued by a mufti

Fiqh   Islamic jurisprudence; literally, "understanding," fiqh refers to the human endeavor to understand the Shariah and translate the Divine Intent into practical law.

Hadd (pl. Hudud)   Literally meaning "hindrance" or "limit," hadd is the technical term for the corporeal punishment for acts deemed forbidden, namely unlawful intercourse (zina), false accusation of unlawful intercourse (qadhf), drinking wine (khamr), theft (sariq), and highway robbery (qat` al-tariq).

Hadith A report, a tradition, usually about the Prophet but also on some of his companions or some other early authority

Hajiyyat One of the three categories in the standard classification of the Maqasid, "needs" refers to elements that are important but not absolutely essential (daruri) in order to fulfill a maqsad.

Halal Lawful or permitted according to Islamic law

Haram An action is haram when it is forbidden according to Islamic law.

Hisbah Literally meaning "accounting," hisbah is a term referring to the Qur'anic injunction to command the good (amr bil-ma'ruf) and forbid the wrong (nahy `an al-munkar). Historically within Islamic societies, hisbah was enforced by the muhtasib, the public regulator who supervised public offices and the marketplace to ensure that vendors used a common system of weights and measurements. The main goal of hisbah is ensuring justice within society and furthering the common good or maslahah (best interests) of the people, and thus this principle runs through all of the Maqasid and represents a general guideline for defining and providing a checks and balances mechanism for the Maqasid and for good governance in general – as long as it does not infringe on the individuals' rights and privacy. See the section in Chapter 4 titled "Hisbah: Does it fall solely in the maqsad of Religion, or does it run throughout all of the Maqasid?"

Hudud See Hadd

Ibtila' Divine test or trial; the purpose of an Islamic state is to facilitate an atmosphere of ibtila', where citizens have the freedom and rights to choose to live in whatever manner they like, as long as they do not directly inflict harm on others. Their decisions, toward either righteous action or folly, will be the basis of their judgment by God upon their passing. However the state should not enforce religious belief or practice to the extent that it thwarts the divine intent of testing mankind.

`Iddah The three-month period of time a woman must observe after a divorce or the death of her spouse before remarrying, which extends to childbirth if she is pregnant.

Ijtihad The effort expended in inferring the rules of the Shariah from the textual sources, or the implementation and applying of these rules towards the formulation of a legal opinion or judgment.

Imarah Emirate, a political territory that is ruled by an emir

Infilat Uncontrolled and irresponsible freedom that may harm the self or others, as opposed to "hurriyah," freedom in the sense of freedom of religion or speech.

Islam Hadhari   Literally, "Civilizational Islam," this refers to an initiative promoted by the Malaysian Prime Minister Abdullah Badawi that calls for government to be based on the principles of Islam and the Qur'an.

Istihsan   Juristic preference or activism; this source of law can be used as a last resort if all other sources of law have been consulted without indicating a clear answer. The legal scholar will choose the course of action that appeals most to the public good ("maslahah").

I'tidal (also Wasatiyyah)   Moderation and avoidance of extreme positions or actions

Jihad   Effort directed towards a determined objective, either a personal spiritual goal or a military action for the expansion or defense of Islam

Jizyah   A tax paid by non-Muslims living in an Islamic state and which guarantees them protection.

Khalifah (also Istikhlaf)   Caliph; rrom Qur'an 2:30, "I will make a khalifah (vicegerent) on earth." This verse was said just before the creation of man and therefore indicates the collective vicegerency of mankind as representatives of God on earth. "Khalifah" was also the title of the leader of the Sunni Islamic caliphate.

La darar wa la dirar   Literally, "do not inflict injury nor repay one injury with another," this hadith is the basis for al-masalih al-mursalah (public interests), a legal principle that says that, in matters for which the Shariah has not made an explicit ruling, laws should be adopted that promote the general well-being of the people and protect them from harm.

Madhhab (pl. Madhahib)   Literally meaning way, path, opinion, or ideology, the madhahib are the schools of Islamic law. The main Sunni madhahib are Hanafi, Hanbali, Maliki, and Shafi`i; while the predominant Shi'i madhhab is the Ja'fari school.

Mal   Wealth or property, one of the six objectives (Maqasid) of Islamic law

Mandub   An action is mandub (recommended) if it is considered praiseworthy but not obligatory in Islamic law. This is one of the five qualifications of actions in Islam (obligatory/fard, recommended/mandub, permissible/mubah, disliked/makruh, or forbidden/haram). This qualification is also known as mustahabb (liked).

Maslaha   The "common good" or "public interest." "Maslahat al-`ibadi fi-ddunya wal-akhirah" ("the interests of human beings in the world and hereafter") is the overriding objective of the Shari`ah as a whole, and thereby the ultimate goal of all of the Maqasid.

Ma`un   Assistance

Millah (or Millet [Turkish])   Meaning "religious community," the millah or millet system in the Ottoman Empire ensured that the various religious communities could be governed by their own religious law and legal courts with regards to personal status law. The millet system was a pre-modern example of religious pluralism, and it offered protection for religious minorities.

Mu`amalat   Within Islamic law, this refers to those laws dealing with the civil obligations or transactions, including commercial, criminal and administrative law, and family law. These laws are in contrast to 'ibadat, or laws that pertain to acts of worship and ritual (including prayer, fasting, and pilgrimage).

Mubah   An action is mubah (permissible/neutral) if it is neither forbidden nor recommended in Islamic law.

Mudarabah   A contract used in Shariah-compliant banking by which one partner provides all of the capital and the other partner provides expertise on how to manage investments made with said capital. What profits or losses generated from this project are shared between the two partners based on a pre-negotiated ratio.

Muhammad Abduh   (d. 1905) Egyptian Islamic jurist, religious scholar, and liberal reformer who was regarded as one of the key founding figures of Islamic Modernism

Muhasabat al-hukkam   Accountability of the rulers

Muhtasib   The muhtasib was one who enforced hisbah (see term above). Historically within Islamic societies, the muhtasib was the public regulator who supervised public offices and the marketplace to ensure that vendors used a common system of weights and measurements.

Mujtahid   an Islamic scholar who is competent to interpret shariah using ijtihad

Mukammil   Literally meaning "accomplishers," these are those means that are needed in order to accomplish a larger goal. For example, marriage is a mukammil or accomplisher of the goal of preserving lineage.

Murabahah   A practice found in Shariah-compliant banking wherein a fixed profit margin is declared at the start of an agreement. This can be in the form of a fixed-income loan, where a lending bank is compensated for the time-value of its money but cannot acquire additional profits outside the terms of the original contract. This declaration of earnings stands as a way to avoid riba. Should the bank take additional moneys in the form of late fees or other penalties, these must be explicated in the original contract and may be required to be donated to charity.

Musharakah   A commonly used practice in Shariah-compliant banking that includes a joint venture, whereby two or more parties invest in a project. While gains will be determined by pre-agreed ratios, loss is strictly proportionate to each party's contribution.

Mutakallimun   Scholars of Kalam (Theology), or the discipline of seeking theological knowledge through debate and reason.

Nafaqah   Adequate maintenance and financial support provided to a wife and child

Nafs   Literally "self," thus the "individual self;" this term is used in the Maqasid theory to refer to life, one of the six objectives (Maqasid) of Islamic law.

Naskh   Abrogation; based on the Quranic verse "And for whatever verse We abrogate or cause to be forgotten, We bring a better or the like of it" (2:106). The principle of abrogation suggests that in the case of two fundamentally contradictory verses, the verse revealed at a later date abrogates the earlier verse. There are differences of opinion, however, regarding what constitutes fundamental contradiction ("tanaqud," as opposed to seeming opposition/"ta`arud" in the mind of the jurist) and who has the authority to determine which verses have been abrogated. Thus, across the legal schools there is no consensus on abrogated verses.

Nasl   Lineage, one of the six objectives (Maqasid) of Islamic law; twentieth century jurists expanded the maqsad of nasl to the maqsad of family.

Qadhf   Literally meaning slander or libel, this hadd offense is the false accusation of adultery (zina). This offense is considered the origin of the maqsad of `ird/honor.

Qiyam (s. Qimah)   Values

Qadi   Judge

Qiyas   Analogy; used in juristic reasoning, it is one of the four sources of law in Sunni jurisprudence

Ra'y   Although sometimes used for an opinion on a specific question of law, ra'y is more often used for the body of such opinions held by a particular jurist (i.e., the ra'y of Abu Ḥanifa) and for the reasoning used to derive such opinions.

Raf' al-haraj   Prevention of hardship

Rashid Rida   (d. 1935) Prominent student of Muhammad Abduh, Rashid Rida was a prolific author on Islamic reform, most notably the concept of Pan-Islamism. Much of his writing can be found in the journal Al-Manaar, which he edited from 1898 until his death.

Riba Usury, which is forbidden in Islam according to Qur'an 2:275: "Allah has permitted trade and forbidden usury." Some understand this to mean that all interest in banking is forbidden, however others argue that what is prohibited is the predatory use of capital.

Sahabah The companions of the Prophet

shahada Declaration of faith in Allah and the Prophet as His messenger

Shura Consultation

*Siyasah Shar`iyyah* Shariah-oriented public policy, where a ruler uses wisdom and tact when applying Shariah. The principle of siyasah shar`iyyah authorizes government leaders to make decisions and conduct affairs in harmony with the spirit and purposes of Islamic law, even at the expense of a temporary departure from specific rules. This is generally seen as an instrument of flexibility and pragmatism.

Sukuk (s. sakk) Islamic bonds. They differ from fixed-income bonds common in the West in that interest is not included.

Sunnah Literally, "trodden path," Sunnah refers to precedent, local custom, or traditional practice. It is usually used to apply to the normative practice of the Prophet. Sunnah is categorized as either sunnah tashri`iyyah (legislative Sunnah, meaning that which has juridical or normative value) or sunnah ghayr tashri`iyyah (non-legislative Sunnah, meaning the habits or example of the Prophet that are not legislatively binding upon Muslims).

Tafsir Quranic exegesis

Tahsiniyyat Refinements or desirables; within the classification of needs that the Maqasid should promote, this is the third category after essentials (daruriyyat) and needs (hajiyyat).

Takaful The method of insurance within Shariah-compliant banking, which is based on the idea of combining the risks of a large group of individuals' major losses through the spreading and sharing of liabilities.

Taklif A term of theological and legal vocabulary, denoting the imposition on the part of God of obligations on his creatures, of subjecting them to a law; the corresponding passive participle mukallaf refers to someone who has achieved physical maturity, is of sound mind, and therefore deemed responsible under the law.

Talaq Divorce

Tanzimat Meaning "organization" in Arabic, it refers to the "reorganization" of the Hanafi school of law in Ottoman Turkey that coincided with a period of reform in the Ottoman Empire in the mid-nineteenth century that was characterized by attempts at modernization, and the evolution from an empire model to the emerging nation-state models of rule. The tanzimat reforms integrated the diverse ethnic groups of the Ottoman Empire – including non-Muslims and non-Turks – more thoroughly into Ottoman society and enhanced their civil liberties and granted them equality throughout the Empire.

Tawhid   The oneness of God, and one of al-Alwani's three meta-Maqasid (along with tazkiah and `imran).

Tazkiah   The purification of the soul, one of al-Alwani's three meta-Maqasid (along with `imran and tawhid).

Ummah   Literally the "nation", "people", or "community" this generally refers to the Muslim collective. In the Qur'an, this often refers to the early community that emerged under the Prophet's leadership.

Usul al-fiqh   Literally the "roots of jurisprudence," this refers to the study of the origins, sources, and principles upon which Islamic jurisprudence is based, including the philosophical rationale of the law and the procedures by which the law is derived from its sources. The four key sources of Sunni jurisprudence are the Qur'an, Sunna, consensus (ijma`), and analogical reason (qiyas).

Wilayat al-faqih   Literally the "rule of the jurisprudent," this refers to a legal-political arrangement that exists in Iran, which emphasizes the juridical and leadership power of the scholarly class.

Zakat   Obligatory payment by Muslims of a determinate portion of specified categories of their lawful property for the benefit of the poor and other enumerated classes, one of the five pillars of Islam

Zina   Unlawful intercourse, one of the six acts punished according to the Hudud

Notes

Introduction

1. This has changed more recently with the inclusion of countries such as Guyana and Suriname, whose populations are predominately non-Muslim.
2. Regarding the Afghan Taliban see Emran Qureshi, "Taliban" in *The Oxford Encyclopedia of the Islamic World* ed. John Esposito (New York: Oxford University Press, 2009). Regarding the Sudan see Carolyn Fluehr-Lobban, "Sudan" in ibid. Regardin g Brunei see BBC "Brunei announces tough new code of Islamic law," 22 October 2013, http://www.bbc.com/news/world-asia-24624166.
3. In 2013, the Pew Research Center surveyed more than 38,000 people in 39 countries and reported that the overwhelming percentages of Muslims in many countries want Shariah to be the official law of the land. More than 8 in 10 Muslims in Pakistan (84%) and Bangladesh (82%) hold this view, and the percentage was nearly as high across the Southeast Asian countries surveyed (86% in Malaysia, 77% in Thailand, and 72% in Indonesia). In sub-Saharan Africa, at least half of Muslims in most countries surveyed said they favor making Shariah the official law of the land, including more than 7 in 10 in Niger (86%), Djibouti (82%), the Democratic Republic of the Congo (74%), and Nigeria (71%). Support is widespread among Muslims in the Middle East-North Africa region, especially in Iraq (91%) and the Palestinian territories (89%). See Pew Research Center's Religion & Public Life Project and Pew-Templeton Global Religious Futures Project, *The World's Muslims: Religious, Political and Social Views* (Washington, D.C.: Pew Research Center, 2013).
4. For example, on 23 October 2013, Sultan Hassanal Bolkiah of Brunei published his plan to implement the Shariah Criminal Code, a three-phase plan that would eventually introduce *hudūd* punishments in Brunei. See note 2. In 1993, the Kelantan State Legislative Assembly of Malaysia passed a law to introduce *hudūd* in the state, but it could not be implemented due to constitutional constraints. See Mohammad Hashim Kamali, "Punishment in Islamic Law: A Critique of the Hudud Bill of Kelantan, Malaysia," *Arab Law Quarterly* (1998), 203–234. However, following the publication of Brunei's Shariah Criminal Code in October 2013, the Kelantan State Government decided to introduce a bill seeking permission from Parliament to let the state implement the law in Kelantan. As of the time of writing, the introduction of the bill has been postponed, pending the study report of a joint committee on the issue.

1 Shariah and the Objectives of Islamic Law

1. Of course, there are specific adjustments to God's laws that factored in the context in which they were revealed.
2. The word *din* can also be translated as "law" as the word *din* is also used in the Qur'an(12:76) in the story of Joseph to refer to the King's Law (*din al-malik*).

This verse (42:13) can also be translatedas "He [God] has ordained (shara`a) for you of the Law (dīn) what He commended unto Noah, and that which We have revealed to you (Muhammad), and that which We commended unto Abraham and Moses and Jesus — to establish the Law (an 'aqīmu-ddīn)and not to be divided therein."

3. Feisal Abdul Rauf, *Islam: A Sacred Law: What Every Muslim Should Know about Shariah* (Brattleboro, VT: Qibla Books, 2000), 136. Italics in the original.

4. Qur'an, 3:50.

5. See Abdul Hamid Mohamad's interview in Part III and his comments on the challenges in attempting to apply *hudud* laws in Malaysia and Brunei, in response to the Sultan of Brunei's decision to implement *hudud* in Brunei.

6. See Abu Hamid Muhammad al-Ghazali, *al-Mustasfa min 'ilm al-Usul* (Cairo: al-Maktabah al-Tijariyyah, 1356, 1937).

7. This widely cited *Hadith* does not have a clear and verified origin. Its content and general message are, however, clearly consistent with other Hadith whose authority is verified.

8. *Jami' al-Tirmidhi*, 41:2687.

9. *Nahjul Balagha*, Saying 79. Taken from *Peak of Eloquence NahjulBalagha: Sermons, Letters, and Saying of Imam Ali ibn AbiTalib* eds. Muhummad ibn al-Husayn Sharif al-Radi and Mohammad AskariJafery (Accra; New York: Islamic Seminary Publications, 1984).

10. Léon Ostrorog, *The Angora Reform: Three Lectures Delivered at the Centenary Celebrations of University College on June 27, 28, & 29, 1927* (London: University of London Press, 1927).

11. For an expanded discussion on these ideas see the interview with Şenturk in Part III.

12. Abi Bakr Muhammad b. Ahmad b. Abi Sahl al-Sarakhsi, *Usul al-Sarakhsi*, Abu al-Wafa al-Afghani ed. (Istanbul: Kahraman yay, 1984), 333–334.

13. Qur'an, 17:70.

14. A. H. Maslow, "A Theory of Human Motivation," *Psychological Review*, 50 (1943), 370–396.

15. See Qur'an, 3:104, 3:110, 7:157, 9:71.

16. Abu al-Hasan Muhammad ibn Yusuf al-Amiri, al-*I'lam bi-manaqib al-Islam* (Cairo: n.p., 1387/1967), 125

17. al-Haramayn al-Juwayni, *al-Burhan fi Usul al-Fiqh* ed. 'Abd al-'Azim al-Dib (Doha: Shaykh Khalifah ibn Hamad 'Ali-Thani, 1399/1980), 747.

18. Abu Hamid Muhammadal-Ghazali, *al-Mustasfa min 'ilm al-Usul* (Cairo: al-Maktabah al-Tijariyyah, 1356, 1937), 258.

19. Mohammad al-Tahir Ibn Ashur, *Usul Al-Nizam Al-Ijtima `i Fil Islam* ed. Mohamed El-Tahir Mesawi (Amman: Dar al-Nafais, 2001), 206.

20. Qur'an, 67:1–2.

21. Qur'an, 5:48.

22. *Sahih al-Bukhari*, 1741. Taken from *The Translation of the Meanings of Sahih Al Bukhari Arabic English* ed. Muhammad Muhsin Khan (Riyadh: Dar-us-Salam Publications, 1996), v. 2, book 26, hadith 797.

23. Abu Hamid Muhammad Al-Ghazali, *Al-Sunnah al-nabawiyahbaynaahl al-fiqhwa-ahl al-hadith* (Beirut: Dar al-Shuruq, 2005), 161.

24. "And therein We prescribed for them: 'A life for a life, an eye for an eye, a nose for a nose, an ear for an ear, a tooth for a tooth, and for wounds

retaliation'; but whosoever forgoes it as a freewill offering, that shall be for him an expiation" (Qur'an, 5:45). Also: "and the recompense of evil is evil the like of it; but whoso pardons and puts things right, his wage falls upon God; surely He loves not the evildoers" (Qur'an, 42:40).

25. Qur'an, 2:179.
26. Qur'an, 5:32.

2 Islamic State: Foundations

1. According to Lane's Lexicon.
2. Wilfred Cantwell Smith, *The Meaning and End of Religion* (Minneapolis, MN: Fortress Press, 1991).
3. See Fred Donner, *Muhammad and the Believers: At the Origins of Islam* (Cambridge: Belknap Press of Harvard University Press, 2010).
4. In Qur'an, 22:78 God says "It is He Who has named you muslims, both before [in former scriptures] and in this [Revelation]." Because "Muslim" is a common title today, many translations of this Qur'anic verse do not translate the word *muslim* in its literal meaning of "one submitting to God." However, God also, in the Qur'an, calls Abraham a Muslim (3:67) and the disciples of Jesus Muslims (5:111). As the believers in God in former revelations were not literally titled Muslims, it is clear that in the Qur'an the term *muslim* is used according to its literal meaning (submitting to God) rather than as a label or title.
5. The Qur'an refers to believers who are of the People of the Book: "And some there are of the People of the Book who believe in God, and what has been sent down unto you, and what has been sent down unto them, men humble to God, not selling the signs of God for a small price; those – their wage is with their Lord; God is swift at the reckoning." Qur'an, 3:199.
6. Hadith, Jurisprudence, Qur'anic Exegesis, Biographical History of the Prophet, Theology, and Literature.
7. See Smith, 76. "Here, then, is a process of institutionalization, of conceptual reification. Concepts, terminology, and attention shift from personal orientation to an ideal, then to an abstraction, finally to an institution." This abstracted and institutionalized entity then speaks and acts like a person, despite its lack of actual personhood.
8. Mujlisul Ulama of South Africa, "The Concept of Limited Liability—Untenable in Shariah," (n.d), 23. http://www.mohrasharif.com/PDFs/limited-liability.pdf.

3 Characteristics of Islamic Governance: The Scholars' Consensus

1. Recognition of the *hudūd* can be achieved via fulfillment of their ultimate objectives, the *maqāsid*. See Chapter 1.
2. James Surowiecki, *The Wisdom of Crowds: Why the Many are Smarter than the Few and how Collective Wisdom Shapes Business, Economies, Societies, and Nations* (New York: Doubleday, 2004), xiii.
3. Qur'an, 2:107; 3:26; 3:26; 3:189; 5:17; 5:18; 5:40; 5:120; 7:158 etc.
4. Qur'an, 6:57; 12:40; 12:67; 28:70; 28:88; etc.

5. Qur'an, 3:154; 7:54; 10:31; 13:31; 30:4 etc.
6. Qur'an, 2:30.
7. Qur'an, 4:54; 45:16.
8. Qur'an, 38:26; 4:135; 4:58.

4 Defining the Maqasid for Measurement

1. Qur'an, 3:72.
2. Qur'an, 2:256.
3. Ahmad ibn Idris al-Qarafi, *Kitab al-Furuq: anwar al-buruq fi anwa' al-furuq* (Cairo: Dar al-Salam, 2001), v. 4, 103.
4. Qur'an, 10:99.
5. Qur'an, 3:104, 3:110, 7:157, 9:71.
6. Qur'an, 3:110.
7. Qur'an, 4:75.
8. *La taj'alu butunakum maqābar al-hayawanat* ("Do not make your bellies the graves of animals") – Imam 'Ali.
9. Qur'an, 4:21.
10. Qur'an, 4:19.
11. Qur'an, 2:187.
12. A closed adoption is an adoption wherein the child's original parents are kept hidden.
13. *Sunan ibn Majah*, 224.
14. As we will see later in the section on measurement, the consumption of intoxicants did not correlate with educational achievements.
15. Qur'an, 2:275.
16. *Sunan Ibn Majah*, 2473.
17. See the discussion on p. 39.
18. Qur'an, 107.
19. *Sahih Muslim*, 2581.

5 Indexing the *Maqasid*

1. See Ibrahim Index of African Governance. http://www.moibrahimfoundation.org/iiag/. Accessed on 3 December 2014.
2. This is evident by the multitude of verbs used to describe intellectual capacity in Qur'an:"*afala ya `qilun?*" (36:68); "*afala yubsirun?*" (32:27); "*ya ulil-albab*" (2:179); "*law kanu yafqahun*" (9:81).
3. We are aware of two different projects that have previously attempted to quantify Islamic practices and values in contemporary countries with Muslim majorities. The first of these is the two-article study by Scheherazade S. Rehman and Hossein Askari, "How Islamic are Islamic Countries?," *Global Economy Journal* 10:21 (2010), 1–37 and "An Economic Islamicity Index (EI²)," *Global Economy Journal* 10:3 (2010), 1–37. The second is Daud Abdul-Fattah Batchelor, "A New Islamic Rating Index of Well-Being For Muslim Countries," *Islam and Civilisational Renewal* 4:2 (April 2013), 188–214. Both of these studies have been extremely helpful in conceptualizing our current

index. That being said, our project is unique and different from these other studies since it both seeks to define Islamic statehood and since it synthesizes this rigorous theoretical conceptualization with a quantitative evaluation of these criteria. In particular, since the *maqasid*-based approach is grounded in scholarly traditions, SIP's quantification is particularly beneficial on two accounts. First, it draws on an extensive tradition of scholarship and can therefore root itself in previous theoretical debates. Second, it can contribute to these debates and make them more relevant for contemporary Islamic governance in Muslim countries.

6 The *Maqasid* Index

1. The final list of countries that we indexed are, in alphabetical order: Afghanistan, Albania, Algeria, Azerbaijan, Bahrain, Bangladesh, Benin, Bosnia and Herzegovina, Brunei, Burkina Faso, Cote D'Ivoire, Cameroon, Chad, Comoros, Djibouti, Egypt, Gabon, Gambia, Guinea, Guinea-Bissau, Guyana, Indonesia, Iran, Iraq, Jordan, Kazakhstan, Kosovo, Kuwait, Kyrgyzstan, Lebanon, Libya, Malaysia, Maldives, Mali, Mauritania, Morocco, Mozambique, Niger, Nigeria, Oman, Pakistan, Palestine, Qatar, Saudi Arabia, Senegal, Sierra Leone, Somalia, Sudan, Suriname, Syria, Tajikistan, Togo, Tunisia, Turkey, Turkmenistan, UAE, Uganda, Uzbekistan, Western Sahara, and Yemen.

2. The average values were taken from the World Health Organization and the CIA Factbook. World Health Organization, *Global Health Observatory Data Repository* (Geneva, Switzerland: World Health Organization, 2013). http:// apps.who.int/gho/data/node.main.688, "Life Expectancy Data by Country," accessed on 28 October 2014; Central Intelligence Agency, *The CIA World Factbook 2014* (New York: Skyhorse Publishing, 2013). https://www.cia. gov/library/publications/the-world-factbook/fields/2102.html#138, "Life Expectancy at Birth," accessed on 28 October 2014. The life expectancy value for Kosovo was taken from The World Bank, *World Development Indicators 2013, GINI Index* (Washington: The World Bank Publications, 2013). https:// data.worldbank.org/country/Kosovo, accessed on 10 November 2014.

3. Central Intelligence Agency, *The CIA World Factbook 2014* (New York: Skyhorse Publishing, 2013). https://www.cia.gov/library/publications/the-world-factbook/fields/2046.html#af, "Population Below Poverty Line," accessed on 28 October 2014. The most recent values were used. The year of the data for each country is as follows: Afghanistan (2008/2009), Albania (2012 est.), Algeria (2006 est.), Azerbaijan (2012 est.), Bahrain (NA), Bangladesh (2010 est.), Benin (2007 est.), Bosnia and Herzegovina (2007 est.), Brunei (NA), Burkina Faso (2009 est.), Cote D'Ivoire (2006 est.), Cameroon (2000 est.), Chad (2001 est.), Comoros (2002 est.), Djibouti (2012 est.), Egypt (2008 est.), Gabon (NA), Gambia (2010 est.), Guinea (2006 est.), Guinea-Bissau (2006 est.), Guyana (2006), Indonesia (2012 est.), Iran (2007 est.), Iraq (2008 est.), Jordan (2002), Kazakhstan (2011 est.), Kosovo (2013 est.), Kuwait (NA), Kyrgyzstan (2011 est.), Lebanon (1999 est.), Libya (NA), Malaysia (2009 est.), Maldives (2008), Mali (2005 est.), Mauritania (2004 est.), Morocco (2007 est.), Mozambique (2009 est.), Niger (1993 est.), Nigeria (2010 est.), Oman

(NA), Pakistan (2005–2006 est.), Palestine (2010 est.), Qatar (NA), Saudi Arabia (NA), Senegal (2001 est.), Sierra Leone (2004), Somalia (NA), Sudan (2009 est.), Suriname (2002 est.), Syria (2006 est.), Tajikistan (2013 est.), Togo (1989 est.), Tunisia (2005 est.), Turkey (2010), Turkmenistan (2004 est.), UAE (2003), Uganda (2009 est.), Uzbekistan (2011 est.), Western Sahara (NA), and Yemen (2003).

Values that were not listed in the index, were imputed based on the Infant Mortality values and the Life Expectancy at Birth values using the following calculation: $v = 1.91608 + 0.00741 * \text{Mort\_inf} - 0.04709 * \text{Life\_Exp}$; poverty_Est=exp(v)/(1+exp(v)). Infant mortality values were taken from Central Intelligence Agency, *The CIA World Factbook 2014* (New York: Skyhorse Publishing, 2013). https://www.cia.gov/library/publications/the-world-factbook/rankorder/2091rank.html "Infant Mortality Rate," accessed on 7 November 2014.

4. Hsu, A., J. Emerson, M. Levy, A. de Sherbinin, L. Johnson, O. Malik, J. Schwartz, and M. Jaiteh, *The 2014 Environmental Performance Index* (New Haven, CT: Yale Center for Environmental Law and Policy, 2014). http://www.epi.yale.edu, accessed on 28 October 2014. Values that were not listed in the index were imputed based on the Life Expectancy values and the Physical Integrity values (in the Honor maqsad) using the following equation: envir protection_Est= $4.11 + 0.759 * \text{Life\_Exp} + 0.69 * \text{Phys\_int}$. Physical Integrity values were taken from David L. Cingranelli, David L. Richards, and K. Chad Clay, *The CIRI Human Rights Dataset (2014)* (Binghamton, N.Y.: State University of Binghamton, 2014). http://www.humanrightsdata.com, accessed on 28 October 2014 (Physical Integrity Index is embedded within the larger dataset).

5. Institute for Economics and Peace, *Global Peace Index 2014.* http://www.visionofhumanity.org/#/page/indexes/global-peace-index, accessed on 28 October 2014. Values that were not listed in the index were imputed based on the Life Expectancy values and the Physical Integrity values (in the Honor maqsad) using the following equation: global peace_Est= $3.3396 - 0.127 * \text{Phys\_int} - 0.01173 * \text{life\_Exp}$.

6. United Nations, *United Nations E-Government Survey 2014: E-Government for the Future We Want* (n.p: United Nations Publications, 2014). http://unpan3.un.org/egovkb/en-us/Data-Center, accessed on 28 October 2014 (Human Capital Index is embedded within the larger dataset).

7. United Nations, *United Nations E-Government Survey 2014: E-Government for the Future We Want* (n.p: United Nations Publications, 2014). http://unpan3.un.org/egovkb/en-us/Data-Center, accessed on 28 October 2014 (Telecommunication Infrastructure Index is embedded within the larger dataset).

8. The World Bank, *Knowledge Economy Index and Knowledge Index* (n.p: The World Bank Group Publications, 2012). http://info.worldbank.org/etools/kam2/KAM_page5.asp?tid=0&year=2002&sortby=Inn&sortorder=ASC&weighted=Y&cid1=s, accessed on 28 October 2014. Values that were not listed in the index, were imputed based on the Human Capital Index and the Telecommunication Infrastructure Index using the following calculation: KIInnovhat= $-0.36359 + 3.87107 * \text{EHumanCap} + 8.6455 * \text{Einfra}$.

9. Reporters Without Borders, *World Press Freedom Index 2014* (Paris: Reporters Without Borders Publications, 2014). http://rsf.org/index2014/en-index2014.php, accessed on 28 October 2014.

10. What is needed to improve the "Islamicity" rating: (1) Amount of gambling in society (2) A definition by scholars as to how *rība* is defined, and then a measure of its extent in society.

11. This was compiled using three sources: The World Bank, *World Development Indicators 2013, GINI Index* (Washington: The World Bank Publications, 2013). http://data.worldbank.org/indicator/SI.POV.GINI/countries?display=default, accessed on 28 October 2014 (Link is to the 2013 GINI Index); Central Intelligence Agency, *The CIA World Factbook 2014* (New York: Skyhorse Publishing, 2013). https://www.cia.gov/library/publications/the-world-factbook/fields/2172.html, "Distribution of Family Income- GINI Index," accessed on 28 October 2014; Institute for Economics and Peace, *Global Peace Index 2014*. http://www.visionofhumanity.org/#/page/indexes/global-peace-index, accessed on 28 October 2014. No index provided up-to-date information on all of the listed countries. The most recent values, regardless of their date and their source, were used for the index. The source and year is as follows for each country: Afghanistan (GPI, 2014), Albania (WB, 2012), Algeria (CIA, 1995), Azerbaijan (CIA, 2008), Bahrain (GPI, 2014), Bangladesh (WB and CIA, 2010), Benin (WB, 2012), Bosnia (CIA, 2007), Brunei (NA), Burkina Faso (CIA, 2007), Cote D'Ivoire (CIA, 2008), Cameroon (CIA, 2001), Chad (WB, 2011) Comoros (WB, 2004), Djibouti (CIA, 2002), Egypt (CIA, 2008), Gabon (WB, 2005), Gambia (CIA, 1998), Guinea (WB, 2012), Guinea-Bissau (GPI, 2014), Guyana (CIA, 2007), Indonesia (WB, 2010), Iran (CIA, 2006), Iraq (WB, 2012), Jordan (WB, 2010), Kazakhstan (CIA, 2011), Kosovo (WB, 2011), Kuwait (GPI, 2014), Kyrgyzstan (CIA, 2007), Lebanon (GPI, 2014), Libya (GPI, 2014), Malaysia (WB and CIA, 2009), Maldives (CIA, 2004), Mali (WB, 2010), Mauritania (CIA, 2000), Morocco (CIA, 2007 est.), Mozambique (CIA, 2008), Niger (WB, 2011), Nigeria (WB, 2010), Oman (GPI, 2014), Pakistan (WB, 2011), Palestine (WB, 2009), Qatar (GPI, 2014), Saudi Arabia (GPI 2014), Senegal (WB, 2011), Sierra Leone (WB, 2011), Somalia (NA), Sudan (WB, 2009), Suriname (WB, 1999), Syria (WB, 2004), Tajikistan (WB, 2009), Togo (WB, 2011), Tunisia (WB, 2010), Turkey (WB, 2011), Turkmenistan (CIA, 1998), UAE (GPI, 2014), Uganda (WB, 2013), Uzbekistan (CIA, 2003), and Yemen (CIA, 2005).

12. The GDP measurements were based on the International Monetary Fund, *The World Economic Outlook Database October 2014* (Washington D.C.: International Monetary Fund, 2014). http://www.imf.org/external/pubs/ft/weo/2014/02/weodata/index.aspx, accessed on 28 October 2014 (Gross Domestic Product based on Purchasing-power-parity per capita value is embedded within the larger dataset). The UN values were used for Palestine (2012), Somalia (2012), and Syria (2012). United Nations, Department of Economic and Social Affairs, Statistics Division, *World Statistics Pocketbook* 2014 ed. (New York: United Nations Secretariat, Department of Economic and Social Affairs Population Division, 2014).

13. World Bank Group, *Doing Business: Measuring Business Regulations* (Washington D.C.: World Bank Group, 2013). http://www.doingbusiness.org/rankings, "Ease of Doing Business Rank," accessed on 28 October 2014.

14. Central Intelligence Agency, *The CIA World Factbook 2014* (New York: Skyhorse Publishing, 2013). https://www.cia.gov/library/publications/the-world-factbook/rankorder/2129rank.html, "Unemployment Rate," accessed on 28 October 2014. Many of the values are from different years and are estimates. The most recent estimates were as follows: Afghanistan (2008 est.), Albania (2013 est.), Algeria (2013 est.), Azerbaijan (2013 est.), Bahrain (2005 est.), Bangladesh (2013 est.), Benin (NA), Bosnia (2013 est.), Brunei (2011), Burkina Faso (2004), Cote D'Ivoire (NA), Cameroon (2001 est.), Chad (NA), Comoros (1996 est.), Djibouti (2007 est.), Egypt (2013 est.), Gabon (2006 est.), Gambia (NA), Guinea (2009 est.), Guinea-Bissau (NA), Guyana (2007), Indonesia (2013 est.), Iran (2013 est.), Iraq (2012 est.), Jordan (2013 est.), Kazakhstan (2013 est.), Kosovo (2013 est.), Kuwait (2011 est.), Kyrgyzstan (2011 est.), Lebanon (NA), Libya (2004 est.), Malaysia (2013 est.), Maldives (2012 est.), Mali (2004 est.), Mauritania (2008 est.), Morocco (2013 est.), Mozambique (2007 est.), Niger (NA), Nigeria (2011 est.), Oman (2004 est.), Pakistan (2013 est.), Palestine (2013 est.), Qatar (2013 est.), Saudi Arabia (2013 est.), Senegal (2007 est.), Sierra Leone (NA), Somalia (NA), Sudan (2012 est.), Suriname (2008), Syria (2013 est.), Tajikistan (2013 est.), Togo (NA), Tunisia (2013 est.), Turkey (2013 est.), Turkmenistan (2004 est.), UAE (2001), Uganda (NA), Uzbekistan (2013 est.), Western Sahara (NA), and Yemen (2003 est.).

15. Transparency International, *Corruption Perception Index* (s.i: Transparency International Publications, 2014). http://www.transparency.org/cpi2013/results, accessed 28 October 2014. © Transparency International. All Rights Reserved. For more information, visit http://www.transparency.org.

16. Francesco Di Lorenzo, *International Property Rights Index 2014* (Washington D.C.: Americans for Tax Reform Foundation/Property Rights Alliance Publications, 2014). http://internationalpropertyrightsindex.org/countries, accessed on 28 October 2014. The 2014 index did not contain values for numerous countries. Missing values were therefore taken from the 2013 Index and the 2012 Index. The following countries' most up to date values were from the 2014 index: Algeria, Bangladesh, Benin, Burkina Faso, Cote D'Ivoire, Cameroon, Chad, Egypt, Guyana, Indonesia, Jordan, Malaysia, Mali, Mauritania, Morocco, Mozambique, Nigeria, Pakistan, Saudi Arabia, Senegal, Turkey, Uganda. The following countries most up to date values were from the 2013 index: Albania, Azerbaijan, Bahrain, Bosnia, Brunei, Gabon, Iran, Kazakhstan, Kuwait, Lebanon, Libya, Oman, Qatar, Sierra Leone, Yemen. The following countries most up to date values were from the 2012 index: Syria, Tunisia, UAE. The remainder of the values that were not listed in the index were imputed based on the Corruption Index using the following calculation: IPRIhat=2.44835 + 0.066724*CPI. (Corruption Index). For 2013 Index see Francesco Di Lorenzo, *International Property Rights Index 2013* (Washington D.C.: Americans for Tax Reform Foundation/Property Rights Alliance Publications, 2013). http://www.propertyrightsalliance.org/userfiles/2013%20International%20Property%20Rights%20Index-PRA.pdf, accessed on 28 October 2014. For the 2012 Index see Gaurav Tiwari, *International Property Rights Index 2012* (Washington D.C.: Americans for Tax Reform Foundation/Property Rights Alliance Publications, 2012).

17. David L. Cingranelli, David L. Richards, and K. Chad Clay, *The CIRI Human Rights Dataset (2014)* (Binghamton, N.Y.: State University of Binghamton,

2014). http://www.humanrightsdata.com, accessed on 28 October 2014 (Physical Integrity Index is embedded within the larger data set).

18. Ibid. (Empowerment Rights Index is embedded within the larger data set). Accessed on 28 October 2014.

19. Ibid. (The Women's Rights Index is the average of Women's Economic Rights and Women's Political Rights. Both values are embedded within the larger data set). Accessed on 28 October 2014.

20. Ibid. (Independence of the Judiciary Index is embedded within the larger data set). Accessed on 28 October 2014.

21. United Nations, Department of Economic and Social Affairs, Population Division, *World Marriage Data 2012* (New York: United Nations Secretariat, Department of Economic and Social Affairs Population Division, 2013). http://www.un.org/en/development/desa/population/publications/dataset/ marriage/wmd2012/MainFrame.html, accessed on 29 October 2014. The data used was from the most recent year in which there was even partial data regardin g either men or women. Since there are years in which data was given for one of the sexes and not the other, this data is used and combined with the most recent data on the other sex. For instance, there is partial data available for marriage rates of men in Afghanistan from 2008, and complete data on women from 2010. These two data sets were used. In turn, many of the values are from different years. The most recent complete data was as follows: Afghanistan (Male 2008; Female 2010), Albania (2011), Algeria (2002), Azerbaijan (2009), Bahrain (2001), Bangladesh (2011), Benin (2006), Bosnia (2004), Brunei (2001), Burkina Faso (2010), Cote D'Ivoire (1998), Cameroon (2011), Chad (2004), Comoros (1996), Djibouti (2002), Egypt (Male 2006; Female 2008), Gabon (2000), Gambia (1993), Guinea (2005), Guinea-Bissau (Female 2006), Guyana (2009), Indonesia (2010), Iran (2011), Iraq (Male 2004; Female 2007), Jordan (Male 2004; Female 2007), Kazakhstan (2009), Kosovo (NA), Kuwait (2005), Kyrgyzstan (2009), Lebanon (2007), Libya (2006), Malaysia (2010), Maldives (Male 2006; Female 2009), Mali (2006), Mauritania (2000), Morocco (2004), Mozambique (2007), Niger (2006), Nigeria (2008), Oman (2003), Pakistan (2007), Plestine (2007), Qatar (2010), Saudi Arabia (2007), Senegal (2010), Sierra Leone (2008), Somalia (Female 2006), Sudan (2008), Suriname (2004), Syria (2001), Tajikistan (2010), Togo (1998), Tunisia (1994), Turkey (Male 2000; Female 2008), Turkmenistan (Male 1989; Female 2009), UAE (2005), Uganda (2011), Uzbekistan (Male 1989; Female 1996), and Yemen (2003).

22. David L. Cingranelli, David L. Richards, and K. Chad Clay, *The CIRI Human Rights Dataset (2014)* (Binghamton, N.Y.: State University of Binghamton, 2014). http://www.humanrightsdata.com, accessed on 28 October 2014 (Freedom of Religion Index is embedded within the larger dataset).

23. The Association of Religion Data Archives, Roger Finke, *International Religious Freedom Data, 2008* http://www.thearda.com/Archive/Files/Descriptions/ IRF2008.asp, accessed on 4 November 2014.
     For Religious Freedom (Government restrictions on religion practice) we measured the summated score of the following questions:
     a. Does the government interfere with an individual's right to worship? (Q39)*
     b. How is freedom of religion described? (Q40)

    c. Does the government generally respect the right to freedom of religion in practice? (Q41)

    d. Does the government policy contribute to the generally free practice of religion? (Q42)

    e. Does the constitution provide for freedom of religion? (Q64)

    f. Are people put into prison based on religion? (Q82)

    g. Has there been any harassment of minority religious groups? (Q88)

    h. Do government or security authorities harass or allow harassment based on religious brand? (Q90)

    i. Were there any reports of forced religious conversion? (Q92)

    j. Is religious literature or broadcasting limited or restricted? (Q75)

24. Ibid. For Religious Discrimination (Government favoritism) we measured the summated score of the following questions:

    a. What is the nature of government or public holidays? (Q73)

    b. Are people, based on religious identity or activity, discriminated against? (Q81)

    c. Are allegations reported of discrimination in education, housing and/or employment based on religion? (Q84)

    d. When a person sells or buys land or property, do laws or practices benefit or discriminate based on religion? (Q85)

25. Ibid. For Social Harmony among religious groups (tolerance and understanding among adherents of different religions; respect for religious properties and symbols) we measured the summated score of the following questions:

    a. Are the relationships among religions in society generally amicable? (Q65)

    b. Societal attitudes toward other or nontraditional religions are reported to be _____. (Q58)

    c. Does the report say the government promotes interfaith understanding? (Q72)

    d. Do people face hassles if they do not belong to the dominant religion of the country? (Q69)

    e. Were there any religiously-related land or property disputes? (Q71)

    f. Are there activities reported that promote tolerance and understanding between adherents of different religions? (Q94)

    g. Are tensions related to religion reported? (Q96)

    h. According to the report, is there an organized interfaith dialog? (Q98)

    i. What are social attitudes towards conversions to other religions? (Q59)

    j. Does the report mention cases of vandalism towards religious properties or cemeteries by citizens? (Q99)

    k. Does the report mention cases of bombing towards religious properties or cemeteries by citizens? (Q100)

    l. Were there reports of derogatory graffiti being put on religious properties? (Q103)

7 Practical Applications of Islamic Law in Government and the Judiciary

1. Qur'an, 2:143
2. Qur'an, 90:12–13.
3. "The alms are only for the poor and the needy, and those who collect them, and those whose hearts are to be reconciled, and to free the captives and the debtors, and for the cause of Allah, and (for) the wayfarer; a duty imposed by Allah." Ibid., 9:60.
4. "Act" for the Federal Territory and "Enactments" for the States.
5. Ibid., 5:2.
6. Islamic financing terms referring to investment partnerships that do not involve interest: *Mudarabah* (profit sharing) is a kind of partnership where one partner (*rabb al-maal*) provides the capital to the other (*mudarib*) for investment in a commercial enterprise. In *musharakah* (joint venture), investment comes from all of the partners, it is managed by all, and all share in the loss or gain. In *murabahah* (cost plus), a seller expressly mentions to the buyer the cost he has incurred on the commodities for sale and sells it with a profit that is known to the buyer.
7. This is provided by Item 1, List II (State List) of the Ninth Schedule of the Federal Constitution.
8. In American terminology, a limited company is a corporation.
9. For additional discussion about the conflict of jurisdiction between Shariah and civil courts see Abdul Hamid Mohamad, "Civil and Syariah Courts in Malaysia: Conflict of Jurisdictions." Institute of Islamic Understanding, International Seminar on Islamic Law in the Contemporary World, Malaysia. 24–25 October 2000; "Conflict of Civil and Shari'ah Law: Issues and Practical Solutions in Malaysia." International Seminar on Shari'ah and Common Law, Kolej Universiti Islam Malaysia, Palace of the Golden Horses, Malaysia, 20–21 September 2006.
10. See Lim Chan Seng v. Pengarah Jabatan Agama Islam Pulau Pinang (1996) 3 CLJ 231. See also see Abdul Hamid Mohamad, "Harmonization of Islamic Law and Civil Law: Is it Possible?" Kulliyah Undang-Undang Ahmad Ibrahim, Universiti Islam Antarabangsa, Malaysia, 24–25 July 2004.
11. Latifah Bte Mat Zin v. Rosmawati Binti Sharibun & Anor (2007) 5 MLJ 101.
12. See Abdul Hamid Mohamad, "The Need for Shariah-Compliant Law of Choice for Islamic Finance Transactions." Conference on Internationalisation of Islamic Finance: Bridging Economies, Global Islamic Finance Forum, Kuala Lumpur, 18–20 September, 2012.
13. For a discussion on *hudud,* see p. 55.
14. Those laws in Shariah that deal with issues pertaining to worldly issues, including commercail and family law, as opposed to the laws pertaining to acts of worship, the *'ibadat.*
15. Qur'an, 49:13
16. Qur'an, 22:40
17. Qur'an, 2:115
18. Qur'an, 2:115

19. Muhsin Mahdi, "Modernity and Islam," *Modern Trends in World Religions* ed. Joseph M. Kitagawa (La Salle, IL: The Open Court Publishing Company, 1959), 5.
20. Qur'an, 21:107.
21. Eric Fromm, *The Revolution of Hope: Toward a Humanized Technology* (New York, Evanston, London: Harper & Row, 1968), 38.
22. See Etienne Gilson, *God and Philosophy* (New Haven: Yale University Press, 1969), 141 n. 20.
23. Qur'an, 10:99.
24. Qur'an, 2:256.
25. Qur'an, 59:19.
26. Fazlur Rahman, *Major Themes of the Qur'an* (Minneapolis, Chicago: Bibliotheca Islamica, 1980), 14.
27. Qur'an, 49:12.
28. Ali, the nephew and son-in-law of the Prophet, on becoming the fourth Caliph, was opposed by the governor of Syria, Mu'awiyah. In 657, Mu'awiyah led a campaign against Ali at the Battle of Siffin, which basically ended without a victor; however, after Ali was assassinated in 661, he assumed the Caliphate, initiating the Umayyad dynasty from his base in Damascus.

8   Human Rights and Islamic Governance

1. Qur'an, 3:104–105.
2. Qur'an, 4:59.
3. Qur'an, 3:159.
4. Qur'an, 4:58.
5. Qur'an, 4:135.
6. Qur'an, 9:60.
7. Qur'an, 104:1–4.
8. Qur'an, 5:9.
9. Qur'an, 49:9.
10. Qur'an, 49:9–10.
11. Qur'an, 49:13.
12. Qur'an, 2:256.
13. Qur'an, 17:110.
14. Qur'an, 10:99.
15. Qur'an, 109:1–5.
16. Qur'an, 2:114.
17. Qur'an, 6:108.
18. Abul `Ala Maududi, *Huquq al-Zawjayn* (Lahore: n.p, 1934).
19. Maududi, *Huquq*.
20. This discussion covers many themes that are discussed in Recep Şentürk's article "Sociology of Rights: 'I am Therefore I Have Rights': Human Rights in Islam between Universalistic and Communalistic Perspectives," *Muslim World Journal of Human Rights* 2:1 (2005), 1–31.
21. See Recep Şentürk, *Açik Medenniyet* (Istanbul: Timaş Yay, 2010). Samuel Huntington lists nine civilizations other than Islam in his well-known book on the clash of civilizations: Western, Latin American, African, Islamic, Chinese, Hindu, Orthodox, Buddhist, and Japanese. Six of these civilizations lived

under Islamic rule wholly or in part: Western, African, Hindu, Orthodox, and Buddhist. Only three of the nine civilizations did not come under the Islamic rule: Latin American, Chinese, and Japanese. See Samuel P. Huntington, *The Clash of Civilizations and the Remaking of World Order* (New York: Simon and Schuster, 1996).

22. 'Abd al-Rahman ibn Muhammad Ibn Khaldun, *al-Muqaddima* (Beirut: Dar al-Qalam, 197–?), v. I, 332–333.

23. See Recep Şentürk, "Sociology of Rights: Inviolability of the Other in Islam between Communalism Universalism," in *Contemporary Islam* (eds) Abdul Aziz Said, Mohammed Abu-Nimer, and Meena Sharify-Funk (New York: Routledge, 2006), 24–49.

24. Qur'an, 67:02.

25. Qur'an, 17:33.

26. Qur'an, 5:8.

27. Qur'an, 5:32.

28. Qur'an, 2:256.

29. Sarakhsi, *Usul al-Sarakhsi*, II, 334.

30. Qur'an, 9:5. Also see 9:12; 8:39.

31. *Sahih al-Bukhari*, 6924–6925.

32. Qur'an, 4:137.

33. Qur'an, 9:74.

34. For a more detailed discussion on these reforms during the late Ottoman period in the area of minority rights, see Recep Şentürk, "Minority Rights in Islam: From Dhimmi to Citizen" in *Islam and Human Rights* (eds) Shireen T. Hunter and Huma Malik (Washington, DC: Center for Strategic & International Studies, 2005), 67–99.

35. For this period, see Stanford Shaw, *Between Old and New, The Ottoman State Under Sultan Selim 1789–1807* (Cambridge, MA: Harvard University Press, 1971). For Sened-i Ittifak see Halil Inalcik, *Sened-i Ittifak ve Gulhane Hatt-i Humayunu:Tanzimat'ın uygulanması ve sosyal tepkileri* (Ankara: Türk tarih kurumu basımev, 1964), 630–662; Rifat Onsoy, "Sened-i Ittifak ve Turk Demokrasi Tarihindeki Yeri," (Ankara: Turkiye'de demokrasi Hareketleri Konferansi 6–8 Kasim 1985 H.U.Edb. Fakultesi Dergisi, c.4, no. 1, 1985). For Mahmud's reforms, see Midhat Sertoglu, "Tanzimata Dogru," (Bildiriler, Istanbul: Sultan ll. Mahmud ve Reformlari Semineri 28–30 Haziran 1989), 1–10; Mehmet Seyitdanlioglu, "Tanzimatin on hazirliklari ve Meclis-i Vala-yi Ahkam-i Adliye'nin Kurulusu 1838–1840," Bildiriler, Istanbul: Sultan ll. Mahmud ve Reformlari Semineri 28–30 Haziran 1989), 107–112. Also see Halil Inalcik, "The Nature of Traditional Society: Turkey," in *Political Modernization in Japan and Turkey* (eds) Robert E. Ward and Dankwart A. Rustow (Princeton, NJ: Princeton University Press, 1964), 13–14.

9 The *Maqasid*, Reform and Renewal

1. Qur'an, 10:57.

2. Qur'an, 21:107.

3. Qur'an, 7:156.

4. Qur'an, 5:6.

5. Qur'an, 29:45.

6. Qur'an, 22:39.
7. Qur'an, 5:3
8. Qur'an, 2:188.
9. Abu Ishaq Ibrahim al-Shatibi, *al-Muwafaqat fi Usul al-Shariah*, 2 ed. (Beirut: Dar al-Ma'rifa, 1395/1975), 2: 393.
10. Ahmad al-Raysuni, *Nazariyyat al-Maqasid 'ind al-Imam al-Shatibi* (Rabat, Morocco: Matba'at al-Najah al-Jadidah, 1411/1991), 149.
11. Muhammad al-Tahir ibn Ashur, *Maqasid al-Shariah al-Islamiyya* (ed.) Muhammad al-Tahir al-Mesawi, (Amman: al-Basa'ir li'l-Intaj al-'Ilmi: 1418/1998), 171. This book was first published in 1946, whereas 'Allal Fasi's book (see note below) was published in 1963.
12. 'Allal Fasi, *Maqasid al-Shariah al-Islamiyya wa Makarimuha* (Casablanca: Maktabat al-Wahdat al-'Arabiyya, n.d), 3.
13. 'Abd al-Rahman Ibrahim Zayd al-Kilani, *Qawa'id al-Maqasid 'ina al-Imam al-Shatibi: 'ardan wa-dirasah wa-tahlilan* (Amman: al-Ma'had al-Alami lil-fikr al-Islami; Damascus: Dar al-Fikr, 2000), 128.
14. al-Shatibi, *al-Muwafaqat*, 2:394.
15. 'Izz al-Din 'Abd al-Salam al-Sulami, *Qawa'id al-Ahkam fi Masalih al-Anam* (ed.) Taha 'Abd al-Ra'uf Sa'd (Cairo: al-Matba'ah al-Husayniyyah, 1351/1932), 1:8. Sulami's disciple, Shihab al-Din al-Qarafi (d. 684/1283), continued his teacher's work and made his own contribution to the subject.
16. Ibn al-Qayyim al-Jawziyyah, *I'lam al-Muwaqqi'in 'an Rabb al-`Alamīn* (ed.) Muhammad Munir al-Dimashqi (Cairo: Idarat al-Tiba'ah al-Muniriyyah, n.d.), vol. III, 1.
17. al-Sulami, *Qawa'id al-Ahkam*, 2: 160.
18. Shatibi, *al-Muwafaqat*, 2:6; see also al-Jawziyyah, vol. 1; Yusuf al-Qaradawi, *Madkhal li-Dirasat al-Shariah al-Islamiyyah* (Cairo: Maktabah Wahbah, 1411/1990) 58.
19. al-Shatibi, *al-Muwafaqat*, 1:243; Qaradawi, *Madkhal*, 64–65.
20. al-Shatibi, *al-Muwafaqat*, 3:148.
21. al-Shatibi, *al-Muwafaqat*, 2:49–51; Abu Ishaq Ibrahim al-Shatibi, *Kitab al-I'tisam* (Makkah al-Mukarramah: al-Maktabah al-Tijariyyah, n.d.), 2:131–135.
22. al-Haramayn al-Juwayni, *al-Burhan fi Usul al-Fiqh* ed. 'Abd al-'Azim al-Dib (Doha: Shaykh Khalifah ibn Hamad 'Ali-Thani, 1399/1980), 2:518.
23. Mutakallimun in this context refers to the Mu'tazilite rationalist school of theological thought who unlike their intellectual counterparts, the Ash'arites, advocated the role of reason much more widely than the Ash'arites. *Ahl al-Ra'y* (partisans of considered opinion), as opposed to the Traditionists (*Ahl al-Hadith*) who were also inclined to recognize a wider scope for human judgment in the determination of the rules of the Shariah.
24. al-Ghazali, *al-Mustasfa* 1:5; also quoted in 'Abd al-Rahman Ibrahim al-Kilani, *Qawa'id al-Maqasid*, 166.
25. al-Kilani, *Qawa'id al-Maqasid*, 1:287.
26. Shatibi, *al-Muwafaqat*, II, 8.
27. Najm al-Din Sulayman al-Tufi, *Sharh Mukhtasar al-Rawdah* (ed.) Abd Allah al-Turki, (Beirut: Mu'assasat al-Risalah, 1407/1987) III, 209; also quoted in al-Kilani, *Qawa'id al-Maqasid*, 166.
28. al-Qaradawi, *Madkhal*, 73.
29. Taqi al-Din Ahmad ibn Taymiyya, *Majmu` Fatawa Shaykh al-Islam Ibn Taymiyya* (Cairo: n.p., 1991), 32:134.

30. al-Kilani, *Qawa'id al-Maqasid*, 168.
31. al-Raysuni, *Nazariyyat al-Maqasid*, 44; Muhammad Khalid Mas'ud, *Islamic Legal Philosophy*, (Islamabad: Islamic Research Institute, 1977), 193–194.
32. Qaradawi, *Madkhal*, 75.
33. Shatibi, *al-Muwafaqat*, 2:277.
34. al-Kilani, *Qawa'id*, 170.
35. For details on *maslahah mursalah* see Mohammad Hashim Kamali, *Principles of Islamic Jurisprudence*, 3 ed. (Cambridge: Islamic Texts Society, 2003), 351–369.
36. Shatibi, *al-Muwafaqat*, II, 12.
37. al-Qaradawi, *al-Madkhal*, 70–71.
38. Ahmad b. 'Ali b. Shu'ayb al-Nasa'i, *Sunan al-Nasa'i* (Cairo: al-Matba'a' al-Misriyyah, 1930).
39. Ibn Amir al-Hajj, *al-Taqrir wa'l-Tahbir* 2 ed. (Beirut: Dar al-Kutub al-'Ilmiyyah, 1403/1983), II, 231.
40. Qur'an, 6:151.
41. For a fuller discussion and review of the Qur'an and the *Hadith* on the sanctity of life and right to personal security, see Mohammad Hashim Kamali, *The Right to Life, Security, Privacy and Ownership in Islam* (Cambridge, UK: Islamic Texts Society, 2008).
42. For details on *siyasah shar'iyyah* see Mohammad Hashim Kamali, "Siyasah Shar'iyyah or the Policies of Islamic Government," *The American Journal of Islamic Social Sciences* 6(1989), 59–81.
43. Qur'an, 17:70.
44. Yusuf Hamid al-'Alim, *al-Maqasid al-'Amma li'l-Shariah al-Islamiyya* (Cairo: Dar al-Hadith; Khortum: al-Dar al-Sudaniyya li'l-Kitab, 1417/1997), 65, 315.
45. al-Shatibi, *al-Muwafaqat*, 2:277.
46. Mohammad Hashim Kamali, *Punishment in Islamic Law: An Inquiry into the Hudūd Bill of Kelantan* (Kuala Lumpur: Ilmiah Publishers, 2000), 45–52.
47. Qur'an, 2:178.
48. Qur'an, 2:164, 38:29.
49. al-'Alim, *Maqasid al-Shariah*, 226.
50. al-'Alim, *Maqasid al-Shariah*, 268–269.
51. Qur'an, 4:19.
52. Qur'an, 21: 30.
53. Abu Hamid Muhammad al-Ghazali, *Ihya' 'Ulum al-Din* 2 ed. (Cairo: Dar al-Fikr, 1400/1980), II, 22; al-Sulami, *Qawa'id al-Ahkam*, I, 53; al-'Alim, *Maqasid al-Shariah*, 412.
54. al-'Alim, *Maqasid al-Shariah*, 521; Kilani, *Qawa'id*, 171. Regarding fair dealing in the work place see Mohammad Hashim Kamali, *Rights to Education, Work and Welfare in Islam* (Cambridge, UK: Islamic Texts Society, 2010).
55. Gamal Eldin Attia, *Towards Realization of the Higher Intents of Islamic Law: Maqasid al-Shari'ah- a Functional approach* tr. Nancy Roberts (London and Washington: the International Institute of Islamic Thought, 2004), 109.
56. Qur'an, 2:282–283.
57. Riyad Mansur al-Khalifi, "al-Maqasid al-shar'iyyah wa atharuha fi fiqh al-mu'āmalāt al-maaliyyah," *Majallah Jami'ah al-Malik 'Abdulaziz al-Iqtisad al-Islami* 17:1(1425/2004), 14.
58. Attia, 111.

59. 'Izz al-Din 'Abd al-Salam, *Qawa'id al-Ahkam fi masalih al-anam* (Beirut: Dar Ibn Hazm, 2008), vol. I, 124–125. Also discussed in Attia, 110.
60. al-Shatibi, *al-Muwafaqat*, II, 13–14; see also al-Khalifi.
61. Abu'l-Hasan al-Mawardi, *Kitab al-Ahkam al-Sultaniyyah* (Cairo: Matba'at al-Sa'adah, 1327/1959), 14.
62. More appropriately known as *fiqh*.
63. al-Amiri, *al-I'lam*, 125.
64. al-Juwayni, *al-Burhan*, v. 2, 747.
65. al-Ghazali, *al-Mustasfa*, 258.
66. Muhammad al-Tahir Ibn 'Ashur, *Usul al-nizam al-ijtima'i fi al-Islam* (Tunis: al-Sharikah al-Tunisiyah lil-Taqzi', 1976), 206.
67. Jasser Auda,*Naqd nazariyat an-nash baht fi fiqh maqasid al-sharia* (Beirut: Al Shabaka al-Arabiya lil-abhath wa-al-nasr, 2013), 20.
68. Quttub Sano, *Qiraat Ma`rifiyah Fi Al-Fikr Al-Usuli* (Kuala Lumpur: Dar al-Tajdeed, 2005), 157.
69. al-Amiri, *Al-I'lam*, 125.
70. Ibn 'Ashur, *Maqasid Al-Shari'ah*, 292.
71. Jamal al-Din 'Atiyah, *Nahwa Taf'il Maqasid Al-Shari`ah* (Beirut: Dar 'Atiyah, 1996), 171; Ahmed Raysuni, Muhammad Mustafa Zuhayli, and Muhammad 'Uthman Shubayr, "*Huquq al-insan: mihwar maqasid al-shariah*," (Doha: Wizarat al-awfaq wa-al-shu'un al-Islamiyah, 2002).
72. Qur'an, 2:256. This is my translation for "lā ikrāha fī al-dīn." I understand it to mean that there is no compulsion in any matter of the religion, rather than merely "in religion," as in other translations (for example, Yusuf Ali's and Pickthall's).
73. See Şentürk's interview and Chapter One in this volume.
74. *Sunan ibn Majah*, 3933.
75. al-Qaradawi, *Madkhal*, 101; Atiyah, *Nahwa*, 170; Raysuni et al.; Mohammad al-'Auwa, *Al-Fiqh Al-Islami Fi Tariq Al-Tajdeed* (Cairo: al-Maktab al-Islami, 1998), 195.
76. Mohammad Rasheed Rida, *Al-Wahy Al-Mohammadi: Thubut Al-Nubuwwah Bil-Qur'an* (Cairo: Mu'asasat Izziddin, n.d), 100.
77. Ibn 'Ashur, *Maqasid Al-Shari'ah*, 183.
78. Yusuf al-Qaradawi, *Kayfa Nata`amal ma`a Al-Qur'an Al-`Azeem* (Cairo: Dar al-Shorouk, 1999).
79. Taha Jabir al-Alwani, *Maqasid Al-Shari'ah* (Beirut: IIIT and Dar al-Hadi, 2001), 25.
80. For example, Kamaluddin al-Siwasi, *Sharh Fath Al-Qadir* 2 ed. (Beirut: Dar al-Fikr, n.d) vol. 4, 513.
81. For example, Qur'an, 18:29.
82. Ibn 'Ashur, *Usul Al-Nizam*, 256, 268.
83. Ibn 'Ashur, *Usul Al-Nizam*, 270–281.
84. For example, Mohammad Mehdi Shamsuddin, "*Maqasid Al-Shariah*," in *Maqasid Al-Shariah* (ed.) Abduljabar al-Rufa`i (Damascus: Dar al-Fikr, 2001); Mohammad Hussain Fadlullah, "*Maqasid Al-Shariah*," in *Maqasid Al-Shariah* ed. Abduljabar al-Rufa`i; Abdulhadi al-Fadli, "*Maqasid Al-Shariah*," in *Maqasid Al-Shariah* (ed.) Abduljabar al-Rufa`i; al-Alwani, "*Maqasid Al-Shari'ah*,"; Qaradawi, *Madkhal*.
85. Shamsuddin, "*Maqasid Al-Shariah*," 26.

86. Wayne Grudem, *Systematic Theology* (Leicester: Inter-Varsity Press; Grand Rapids: Zondervan Publishing House, 1994), 21.
87. Grudem, 22.
88. For example, Gruden, 67, 65, 110, 119, 123, 135, 143, 164, 172, 189, 208.
89. Charles Hodge, *Systematic Theology* abridged by Edward Gross (New Jersey: P & R Publishers, 1997), 26.
90. Louis Berkhof, *Systematic Theology* (Grand Rapids: W.B. Eerdmans, 1996), 15.
91. Roger Olson, *The Mosaic of Christian Beliefs: Twenty Centuries of Unity and Diversity* (Downers Grove: InterVarsity Press; Leicester, UK: Apollos, 2002), 74.
92. al-Ghazali, *Al-Mustasfa*, vol. 1, 172; Muhammad ibn 'Abd Allah ibn al-Arabi, *Al-Mahsoul Fi Usul Al-Fiqh* (eds) Husayn 'Ali Yadari and Sa'id 'Abd al-Latif Fudah (Amman: Dar al-Bayariq, 1999), v. 5, 222; Sayf al-Din al-Amidi, *Al-Ihkam fi usul al-ahkam* (Cairo: Mu'assasat al-Halabi, 1967), v. 4, 287.
93. Grudem, 124, 208, 241, 781, 1009.
94. See Maslow.
95. Mohammed Osman Salih, "Al-Islam Huwa Nizam Shamil Lihimayat Wa Ta'ziz Huqouq Al-Insan" (Khartoum: Unpublished paper presented at the International Conference on Islam and Human Rights, 2006).
96. International Protection of Human Rights (University of Toronto Bora Laskin Law Library, 2004). Available at http://www.law-lib.utoronto.ca/resguide/humrtsgu.htm, accessed on 15 January 2015.
97. United Nations High Commission for Human Rights, Specific Human Rights Issues July, 2003. Available at http://www.unhchr.cAH/Huridocda/Huridoca.nsf/(Symbol)/E.CN.4.Sub.2.2003.NGO.15.En, accessed on 1 February 2005.
98. United Nations High Commission for Human Rights, Specific Human Rights Issues July, 2003.
99. United Nation Development Programme, *Annual Report 2004* Available at http://www.undp.org/annualreports/2004/english, accessed on 5 February 2005.
100. Mohammad Shakir al-Sharif, *Haqiqat Al-Dimuqratiyah* (Riyadh: Dar al-Watan, 1992), 3; Mohammad Ali Mufti, *Naqd Al-Judhur Al-Fiqriyyah Lil-Dimoqratiyyah Al-Gharbiyyah* (Riyadh: al-Muntada al-Islami and Majallat al-Bayan, 2002), 91.
101. For example, Sheikh Ali Jumah, Mufti of Egypt (Cairo, Egypt: Personal communication, December 2005).
102. For example, Fakhr al-Din al-Razi, *Al-Tafsir Al-Kabir* (Riyadh: Markaz al-Turath lil-Barmajiyat, 2013), v. 3, 204; al-Fadl Ibn al-Hussain al-Tubrusi, *Majma' Al-Bayan Fi Tafsir Al-Qur'an* (Beirut: Dar al-'ulum, 2005), v.1, 406; Muhammad Mahmud Nada, *Al-Naskh Fi Al-Qur'an: bayna al-mu'idin wa-al-mu'aridin* (Cairo: Maktabat al-Dar al-Arabiyah lil-Kitab, 1996), 25.
103. Etymologically, abrogation (naskh) is derived from the root n.s.kh. I carried out a survey on this root and all its possible derivations in a large number of today's popular collections of the *Hadith*, including, Al-Bukhari, Muslim, Al-Tirmithi, Al-Nasa'i, Abu Dawud, Ibn Majah, Ahmad, Malik, Al-Darami, Al-Mustadrak, Ibn Hibban, Ibn Khuzaimah, Al-Bayhaqi, Al-Darqutni, Ibn

Abi Shaybah, and Abd al-Razzaq. I found no valid *Hadith* attributed to the Prophet that contains any of these derivations of the root n.s.kh. I found about 40 instances of "abrogations" mentioned in the above collections, which were all based on one of the narrators' opinions or commentaries, rather than any of the texts of the *Hadith*.

104. al-Ghazali, *al-Mustasfa*, 279; al-Shatibi, *al-Muwafaqat*, v. 4, 129; Taqi al-Din Ibn Taymiyah, *Kutub wa-rasa`il wa-Fatawa* (Riyadh: Markaz al-Turath lil-Barmajiyat, 2013), v. 19, 131.

105. Abu Hamid Muhammad al-Ghazali, *Maqasid Al-Filasifah: fi al-mantiq wa-al-hikmat al-ilahiyah wa-al-hikmat al-tabi'iyah* (Cairo: Muhyi al-Din Sabri al-Kurdi, 1912), 62.

106. Ibn Taymiyah, *Kutub wa-rasa`il wa-Fatawa*, v. 19, 131.

107. Abdul-Aziz al-Bukhari, *Kashf Al-Asrar* (Beirut: Dar al-Kutub al-'ilmiyyah, 1997), v. 3, 77.

108. Qur'an, 2:256, 6:13, 23:96, 30:60, 41:46, 109:6, respectively.

109. Burhan Zuraiq, *Al-Sahifah: Mithaq Al-Rasoul* (Damascus: Dar al-Numair and Dar Ma'ad, 1996), 353.

110. Zuraiq, *Al-Sahifah*, 216.

111. Cited in al-Alwani, *Maqasid Al-Shari'ah*, 89.

112. Oral Discussion, Sarajevo, Bosnia, May 2007, 18th regular session for the European Council for Fatwa and Research.

113. Refer to Qaradawi's article in *Maqasid Al-Shariah Al-Islamiya: Dirasat Fi Qadaya Al-Manhaj Wa Majalat Al-Tatbeeq*, eds. Muhammad Salim al-'Auwa and Ahmad Zaki Yamani (London: al-Furqan Islamic Heritage Foundation, al-Maqasid Research Centre, 2006), 117–121.

114. Taha Jabir al-Alwani, *Issues in Contemporary Islamic Thought* (London; Washington: International Institute of Islamic Thought (IIIT), 2005), 164–166.

115. Mohhamed Mehdi Shamsuddin, *Al-Ijtihad wa-al-tajdid fi al-fiqh al-Islami* (Beirut: al-Muasasah lil-Dirasat wa-al-Nashr, 1999), 128. He clarifies that he is "inclined to this understanding but would not base (any rulings) on it for the time being."

116. Shamsuddin, *Al-Ijtihad* 129.

117. Abdel Wahab El-Affendi and Fathi 'Utman eds, *Rethinking Islam and Modernity: Essays in Honour of Fathi Osman* (Leicester: The Islamic Foundation, 2001), 45.

118. Hassan al-Turabi, *Emancipation of Women: An Islamic Perspective* 2 ed. (London: Muslim Information Centre, 2000), 29.

119. Roger Garaudy, *Al-Islam wa-al-qarn al-wahid wa-al 'ishrun: Shurut Nahdat al-Muslimin*, trans. Kamal Jadallah (Cairo: al-Dar al-Alamiyah lil Kutub wal-Nashr, 1999), 70, 119.

120. Abdul-Karim Soroush, "The Evolution and Devolution of Religious Knowledge," in *Liberal Islam: A Source Book* (ed.) Charles Kurzman (New York: Oxford University Press, 1998), 250.

121. Muhammad Shahrur, *Nahwa usul jadidah lil-fiqh al-mar'ah: al-wasiyah, al-irth, al-qiwamah, al-ta'uddudiyah, al-libas* (Damascus: al-Ahali lil-Tiba'ah wa-al Nashr wa-al-Tawzi', 2000), 125.

122. Victor Taylor and Charles Winquist eds, *Encyclopedia of Postmodernism* (London: Routledge, 2001), 178; Friedrich Meinecke, *Historicism: The Rise of a New Historical Outlook*, trans. J.E. Anderson (London: Routledge and Kegan Paul, 1972).

123. Nasr Hamid Abu Zaid, "Divine Attributes in the Qur'an: Some Poetic Aspects," in *Islam and Modernity: Muslim Intellectuals Respond* (eds) John Cooper, Ronald L. Nettler, and Mohamed Mahmoud (London: I.B. Tauris, 1998), 199; Mohammed Arkoun, "Rethinking Islam Today," *Annals of the American Academy of Political and Social Science* 588 (July 2003), 211.

124. Nasr Hamid Abu Zaid, *Al-Imam Al-Shafi'i wa-ta'sis al-idiyolojiyyah al-wasa-tiyyah* (Beirut: al-Markaz al-Thaqafi al-'Arabi, 2007), 209; Ebrahim Moosa, "The Debts and Burdens of Critical Islam," *Progressive Muslims: On Justice, Gender and Pluralism* (ed.) Omid Safi (Oxford: Oneworld, 2003), 114.

125. Haideh Moghissi, *Feminism and Islamic Fundamentalism: The Limits of Postmodern Analysis* (London; New York: Zed Books, 1999), 141.

126. Moghissi, *Feminism and Islamic Fundamentalism*, 140.

127. Ibn Warraq, "Apostasy and Human Rights," in *Free Inquiry* (February/March 2006), 53.

128. Mohammad al-Tahir Ibn Ashur, *Ibn Ashur-Treatise on Maqasid Al-Shariah*, trans. Mohamed El-Tahir El-Mesawi (London-Washington: International Institute of Islamic Thought (IIIT), 2006), chapter 6.

129. Ibn Ashur, chapter 6.

130. Muhammad ibn al-Shawkani, *Irshad Al-Fuhul ila tahqiq al-haqq min 'ilm al-usul* (Amman: 'A. Hamdan, 2003), 246; Muhammad Abu Zahra, *Usul Al-Fiqh* (Cairo: dar al-Fikr al-'Arabi, 1958), 268.

131. Abu Zahra, *Usul Al-Fiqh.*, 271.

132. al-Shatibi, *Al-Muwafaqat* v. 2, 249.

133. Abu Zahra, *Usul Al-Fiqh*, 273.

134. Abu Zahra, *Usul Al-Fiqh*, 273

135. Wajanat 'Abd al-Rahim Maymani, *Qa`idat al-dharai` wa-ahkam al-nisa' al-muta'alliqah bi-ha* (Jeddah: Dar al-Mujtama`, 2000), 608, 22, 32, 50.

136. Ahmad ibn Idris al-Qarafi, *Al-Dhakhirah* (Cairo: Matba'at Kuliyat al-Shariah, 1961), v. 1, 153; Ahmad ibn Idris al-Qarafi, *Kitab al-Furuq : anwar al-buruq fi anwa' al-furuq* (Cairo : Dar al-Salam, 2001), v. 2, 60 ; Burhaneddin Ibn Farhoun, *Tabsirat Al-Hukkam Fi Usul Al-`Aqdiyah Wa Manahij Al-`Ahkam* (ed.) Jamal Mar'ashli (Beirut: Dar al-Kutub al-'ilmiyah, 1995) v. 2, 270.

137. A *khabar al-wahid*, a Hadith which is reported through only one narrator, is called a *hadith ahad* in the Sunni schools of law. The Shafi'i and Hanbali schools give precedence to these *ahadith* over *qiyas*, whereas the Hanafi school gives priority to *qiyas* in matters of law. Imam Malik would follow a *hadith ahad* only if it was backed by the practice of the Companions and the generation after them, otherwise he preferred *qiyas*. This shows that Sunni jurists agree with Shaykh al-Tusi that, if the intellect finds such a *hadith* unacceptable, it is set aside, since *qiyas* is essentially an art of intellection.

138. Heavenly books, i.e., the Bible, the Torah, etc.

139. *istikhlaf* is synonymous with what Dr. Mahmood Ghazi calls *khilafa*.

Bibliography

Indexes

Central Intelligence Agency, *The CIA World Factbook 2014* (New York: Skyhorse Publishing, 2013). https://www.cia.gov/library/publications/the-world-factbook/fields/2102.html#138, "Life Expectancy at Birth," accessed on 28 October 2014.

Central Intelligence Agency, *The CIA World Factbook 2014* (New York: Skyhorse Publishing, 2013). https://www.cia.gov/library/publications/the-world-factbook/fields/2046.html#af, "Population Below Poverty Line," accessed on 28 October 2014.

Central Intelligence Agency, *The CIA World Factbook 2014* (New York: Skyhorse Publishing, 2013). https://www.cia.gov/library/publications/the-world-factbook/rankorder/2091rank.html "Infant Mortality Rate," accessed on 7 November 2014.

Central Intelligence Agency, *The CIA World Factbook 2014* (New York: Skyhorse Publishing, 2013). https://www.cia.gov/library/publications/the-world-factbook/fields/2172.html, "Distribution of Family Income- GINI Index," accessed on 28 October 2014.

Central Intelligence Agency, *The CIA World Factbook 2014* (New York: Skyhorse Publishing, 2013). https://www.cia.gov/library/publications/the-world-factbook/rankorder/2129rank.html, "Unemployment Rate," accessed on 28 October 2014.

Cingranelli, David L., David L. Richards, and K. Chad Clay. *The CIRI Human Rights Dataset (2014)* (Binghamton, NY: State University of Binghamton, 2014). http://www.humanrightsdata.com, accessed on 28 October 2014.

Di Lorenzo, Francesco. *International Property Rights Index 2013* (Washington, DC: Americans for Tax Reform Foundation/Property Rights Alliance Publications, 2013). http://www.propertyrightsalliance.org/userfiles/2013%20International%20Property%20Rights%20Index-PRA.pdf, accessed on 28 October 2014.

Di Lorenzo, Francesco. *International Property Rights Index 2014* (Washington, DC: Americans for Tax Reform Foundation/Property Rights Alliance Publications, 2014). http://internationalpropertyrightsindex.org/countries, accessed on 28 October 2014.

Hsu, A., J. Emerson, M. Levy, A. de Sherbinin, L. Johnson, O. Malik, J. Schwartz, and M. Jaiteh, *The 2014 Environmental Performance Index* (New Haven, CT: Yale Center for Environmental Law and Policy, 2014). http://www.epi.yale.edu, accessed on 28 October 2014.

Ibrahim Index of African Governance. http://www.moibrahimfoundation.org/iiag/, accessed on 3 December 2014.

Institute for Economics and Peace, *Global Peace Index 2014.* http://www.visionof-humanity.org/#/page/indexes/global-peace-index, accessed on 28 October 2014.

International Monetary Fund, *The World Economic Outlook Database October 2014* (Washington, DC: International Monetary Fund, 2014). http://www.imf.org/external/pubs/ft/weo/2014/02/weodata/index.aspx, accessed on 28 October 2014.

Reporters Without Borders, *World Press Freedom Index 2014* (Paris: Reporters Without Borders Publications, 2014). http://rsf.org/index2014/en-index2014.php, accessed on 28 October 2014.

The Association of Religion Data Archives, Roger Finke, *International Religious Freedom Data, 2008.* http://www.thearda.com/Archive/Files/Descriptions/IRF2008.asp, accessed on 4 November 2014.

The World Bank, *Knowledge Economy Index and Knowledge Index* (n.p: The World Bank Group Publications, 2012). http://info.worldbank.org/etools/kam2/KAM_page5.asp?tid=0&year=2002&sortby=Inn&sortorder=ASC&weighted=Y&cid1=s, accessed on 28 October 2014.

The World Bank, *World Development Indicators 2013, GINI Index* (Washington: The World Bank Publications, 2013). https://data.worldbank.org/country, accessed on 10 November 2014.

Tiwari, Gaurav. *International Property Rights Index 2012* (Washington, DC: Americans for Tax Reform Foundation/Property Rights Alliance Publications, 2012). Accessed on 10 November 2014.

Transparency International, *Corruption Perception Index* (s.i: Transparency International Publications, 2014). http://www.transparency.org/cpi2013/results, accessed 28 October 2014.

United Nations, *United Nations E-Government Survey 2014: E-Government for the Future We Want* (n.p: United Nations Publications, 2014). http://unpan3.un.org/egovkb/en-us/Data-Center, accessed on 28 October 2014.

United Nations, Department of Economic and Social Affairs, Population Division. *World Marriage Data 2012* (New York: United Nations Secretariat, Department of Economic and Social Affairs Population Division, 2013). http://www.un.org/en/development/desa/population/publications/dataset/marriage/wmd2012/MainFrame.html, accessed on 29 October 2014.

United Nations, Department of Economic and Social Affairs, Statistics Division. *World Statistics Pocketbook* 2014 ed. (New York: United Nations Secretariat, Department of Economic and Social Affairs Population Division, 2014).

World Bank Group, *Doing Business: Measuring Business Regulations* (Washington, DC: World Bank Group, 2013). http://www.doingbusiness.org/rankings, "Ease of Doing Business Rank," accessed on 28 October 2014.

World Health Organization, *Global Health Observatory Data Repository* (Geneva, Switzerland: World Health Organization, 2013). http://apps.who.int/gho/data/node.main.688, "Life Expectancy Data by Country," accessed on 28 October 2014.

Secondary Literature

Abdul-Fattah Batchelor, Daud. "A New Islamic Rating Index of Well-Being For Muslim Countries," *Islam and Civilisational Renewal* 4(2) (April 2013).

Abdul Rauf, Feisal. *Islam: A Sacred Law: What Every Muslim Should Know about Shariah* (Brattleboro, VT: Qibla Books, 2000).

Abu Zahra, Muhammad. *Usul Al-Fiqh* (Cairo: dar al-Fikr al-'Arabi, 1958).

Abu Zaid, Nasr Hamid. "Divine Attributes in the Qur'an: Some Poetic Aspects," in *Islam and Modernity: Muslim Intellectuals Respond* John Cooper, Ronald L. Nettler, and Mohamed Mahmoud (London: I.B. Tauris, 1998).

Abu Zaid, Nasr Hamid. *Al-Imam Al-Shafi'i wa-ta'sis al-idiyolojiyyah al-wasatiyyah* (Beirut: al-Markaz al-Thaqafi al-'Arabi, 2007).

El-Affendi, Abdel Wahab and Fathi 'Utman (eds) *Rethinking Islam and Modernity: Essays in Honour of Fathi Osman* (Leicester: The Islamic Foundation, 2001).

al-'Alim, Yusuf Hamid. *al-Maqasid al-'Amma li'l-Shariah al-Islamiyya* (Cairo: Dar al-Hadith; Khortum: al-Dar al-Sudaniyya li'l-Kitab, 1417/1997).

al-Alwani, Taha Jabir. *Maqasid Al-Shari'ah* (Beirut: IIIT and Dar al-Hadi, 2001).

al-Alwani, Taha Jabir. *Issues in Contemporary Islamic Thought* (London; Washington: International Institute of Islamic Thought (IIIT), 2005).

al-Amidi, Sayf al-Din. *Al-Ihkam fi usul al-ahkam* (Cairo: Mu'assasat al-Halabi, 1967).

al-Amiri, Abu al-Hasan Muhammad ibn Yusuf. *Al-I'lam bi-manaqib al-Islam* (Cairo: n.p., 1387/1967).

al-Arabi, Muhammad ibn 'Abd Allah. *Al-Mahsoul fi usul al-fiqh* (eds) Husayn 'Ali Yadari and Sa'id 'Abd al-Latif Fudah (Amman: Dar al-Bayariq, 1999).

Arkoun, Mohammed. "Rethinking Islam Today," *Annals of the American Academy of Political and Social Science* 588 (July 2003).

Attia, Gemal Eldin. *Towards Realization of the Higher Intents of Islamic Law: Maqasid al-Shari`ah- a Functional Approach* tr. Nancy Roberts (London and Washington: the International Institute of Islamic Thought, 2004).

'Atiyah, Jamal al-Din. *Nahwa Taf'il Maqasid Al-Shari`ah* (Beirut: Dar 'Atiyah, 1996).

Auda, Jasser. *Naqd nazariyat an-nash baht fi fiqh maqasid al-sharia* (Beirut: Al Shabaka al-Arabiya lil-abhath wa-al-nasr, 2013).

al-'Auwa, Mohammad. *Al-Fiqh Al-Islami Fi Tariq Al-Tajdeed* (Cairo: al-Maktab al-Islami, 1998).

al-'Auwa, Muhammad Salim and Ahmad Zaki Yamani, (eds) *Maqasid Al-Shariah Al-Islamiya: Dirasat Fi Qadaya Al-Manhaj Wa Majalat Al-Tatbeeq* (London: al-Furqan Islamic Heritage Foundation, al-Maqasid Research Centre, 2006).

BBC. "Brunei announces tough new code of Islamic law," 22 October 2013, http://www.bbc.com/news/world-asia-24624166, accessed on 3 January 2014.

Berkhof, Louis. *Systematic Theology* (Grand Rapids: W.B. Eerdmans, 1996).

al-Bukhari, Abdul-Aziz. *Kashf Al-Asrar* (Beirut: Dar al-Kutub al-'ilmiyyah, 1997).

Donner, Fred. *Muhammad and the Believers: At the Origins of Islam* (Cambridge, MA: The Belknap Press of Harvard University Press, 2010).

Eisa, Mohammad. *Jami` At-Tirmidhi.* (Khurasan: 864 A.D.).

al-Fadli, Abdulhadi, "Maqasid Al-Shariah," in *Maqasid Al-Shariah* (ed.) Abduljabar al-Rufa`i (Damascus: Dar al-Fikr, 2001).

Fadlullah, Mohammad Hussain, "Maqasid Al-Shariah," in *Maqasid Al-Shariah* (ed.) Abduljabar al-Rufa`i (Damascus: Dar al-Fikr, 2001).

Fasi, 'Allal. *Maqasid al-Shariah al-Islamiyya wa Makarimuha* (Casablanca: Maktabat al-Wahdat al-'Arabiyya, n.d).

Fluehr-Lobban, Carolyn. "Sudan" in *The Oxford Encyclopedia of the Islamic World* (ed.) John Esposito (New York: Oxford University Press, 2009).

Fromm, Eric. *The Revolution of Hope: Toward a Humanized Technology* (New York, Evanston, London: Harper & Row, 1968).

Garaudy, Roger. *Al-Islam wa-al-qarn al-wahid wa-al 'ishrun: Shurut Nahdat al-Muslimin* trans. Kamal Jadallah (Cairo: al-Dar al-Alamiyah lil Kutub wal-Nashr, 1999).

al-Ghazali, Abu Hamid Muhammad. *Maqasid Al-Filasifah: fi al-mantiq wa-al-hikmat al-ilahiyah wa-al-hikmat al-tabi'iyah* (Cairo: Muhyi al-Din Sabri al-Kurdi, 1912).

al-Ghazali, Abu Hamid Muhammad. *al-Mustasfa min 'ilm al-Usul* (Cairo: al-Maktabah al-Tijariyyah, 1356, 1937).

al-Ghazali, Abu Hamid Muhammad. *Ihya' 'Ulum al-Din* 2 ed. (Cairo: Dar al-Fikr, 1400/1980).

Grudem, Wayne. *Systematic Theology* (Leicester: Inter-Varsity Press; Grand Rapids: Zondervan Publishing House, 1994).

al-Hajj, Ibn Amir. *al-Taqrir wa'l-Tahbir* 2 ed. (Beirut: Dar al-Kutub al-'Ilmiyyah, 1403/1983).

Hodge, Charles. *Systematic Theology* abridged by Edward Gross (New Jersey: P & R Publishers, 1997).

Huntington, Samuel P. *The Clash of Civilizations and the Remaking of World Order* (New York: Simon and Schuster, 1996).

Ibn 'Ashur, Muhammad al-Tahir. *Usul al-nizam al-ijtima'i fi al-Islam* (Tunis: al-Sharikah al-Tunisiyah lil-Taqzi', 1976).

Ibn 'Ashur, al-Tahir Muhammad. *Maqasid al-Shariah al-Islamiyya* (ed.) Muhammad al-Tahir al-Mesawi (Amman: al-Basa'ir li'l-Intaj al-'Ilmi: 1418/1998).

Ibn 'Ashur, Muhammad al-Tahir. *Ibn Ashur-Treatise on Maqasid Al-Shariah* trans. Mohamed El-Tahir El-Mesawi (London-Washington: International Institute of Islamic Thought (IIIT), 2006).

Ibn Khaldun, 'Abd al-Rahman ibn Muhammad. *al-Muqaddima* (Beirut: Dar al-Qalam, 197–?), v. I.

Ibn Taymiyah, Taqi al-Din. *Kutub wa-rasa`il wa-Fatawa* (Riyadh: Markaz al-Turath lil-Barmajiyat, 2013).

Inalcik, Halil. *Sened-i Ittifak ve Gulhane Hatt-i Humayunu: Tanzimat'ın uygulanması ve sosyal tepkileri* (Ankara: Türk tarih kurumu basımev, 1964).

Inalcik, Halil. "The Nature of Traditional Society: Turkey," in *Political Modernization in Japan and Turkey* (eds) Robert E. Ward and Dankwart A. Rustow (Princeton, NJ: Princeton University Press, 1964).

Hashim Kamali, Mohammad. "*Siyasah Shar'iyyah or the Policies of Islamic Government*," *The American Journal of Islamic Social Sciences* 6 (1989), 59–81.

al-Jawziyyah, Ibn al-Qayyim. *I'lam al-Muwaqqi'in 'an Rabb al-`Alamin* (ed.) Muhammad Munir al-Dimashqi (Cairo: Idarat al-Tiba'ah al-Muniriyyah, n.d.).

al-Juwayni, al-Haramayn. *al-Burhan fi Usul al-Fiqh* (ed.) 'Abd al-'Azim al-Dib (Doha: Shaykh Khalifah ibn Hamad 'Ali-Thani, 1399/1980).

Kamali, Mohammad Hashim. "Punishment in Islamic Law: A Critique of the Hudud Bill of Kelantan, Malaysia," *Arab Law Quarterly* (1998), 203–234.

Kamali, Mohammad Hashim. *Punishment in Islamic Law: An Inquiry into the Hudud Bill of Kelantan* (Kuala Lumpur: Ilmiah Publishers, 2000).

Kamali, Mohammad Hashim. *Principles of Islamic Jurisprudence* 3 ed. (Cambridge: Islamic Texts Society, 2003).

Kamali, Mohammad Hashim. *The Right to Life, Security, Privacy and Ownership in Islam* (Cambridge, UK: Islamic Texts Society, 2008).

Kamali, Mohammad Hashim. *Rights to Education, Work and Welfare in Islam* (Cambridge, UK: Islamic Texts Society, 2010).

al-Khalifi, Riyad Mansur. "al-Maqasid al-shar'iyyah wa aathaaruha fi'l-fiqh al-mu`amalat al-maaliyyah," *Majallah Jami'ah al-Malik 'Abdulaziz al-Iqtisad al-Islami* 17:1(1425/2004).

Khan, Muhammad Muhsin ed. *The Translation of the Meanings of Sahih Al Bukhari Arabic English* (Riyadh: Dar-us-Salam Publications, 1996).

al-Kilani, 'Abd al-Rahman Ibrahim Zayd. *Qawa'id al-Maqasid 'ina al-Imam al-Shatibi: 'ardan wa-dirasah wa-tahlilan* (Amman: al-Ma'had al-Alami lil-fikr al-Islami; Damascus: Dar al-Fikr, 2000).

Mahdi, Muhsin. "Modernity and Islam," *Modern Trends in World Religions* (ed.) Joseph M. Kitagawa (La Salle, IL: The Open Court Publishing Company, 1959).

Maslow, A.H. "A Theory of Human Motivation," *Psychological Review* 50 (1943), 370–396.

Mas'ud, Muhammad Khalid. *Islamic Legal Philosophy* (Islamabad: Islamic Research Institute, 1977).

Maududi, Abul `Ala. *Huquq al-Zawjayn* (Lahore: n.p., 1934).

al-Mawardi, Abu'l-Hasan. *Kitab al-Ahkam al-Sultaniyyah* (Cairo: Matba'at al-Sa'adah, 1327/1959).

Maymani, Wajanat 'Abd al-Rahim. *Qa`idat al-dharai` wa-ahkam al-nisa' al-muta'alliqah bi-ha* (Jeddah: Dar al-Mujtama`, 2000).

Meinecke, Friedrich. *Historicism: The Rise of a New Historical Outlook* trans. J.E. Anderson (London: Routledge and Kegan Paul, 1972).

Moghissi, Haideh. *Feminism and Islamic Fundamentalism: The Limits of Postmodern Analysis* (London; New York: Zed Books, 1999).

Mohamad, Abdul Hamid. "The Need for Shariah-Compliant Law of Choice for Islamic Finance Transactions." Conference on Internationalistion of Islamic Finance: Bridging Economies, Global Islamic Finance Forum, Kuala Lumpur, 18–20 September 2012.

Mohamad, Abdul Hamid. "Conflict of Civil and Shari'ah Law: Issues and Practical Solutions in Malaysia." International Seminar on Shari'ah and Common Law, Kolej Universiti Islam Malaysia, Palace of the Golden Horses, Malaysia. 20–21 September 2006.

Mohamad, Abdul Hamid. "Harmonization of Islamic Law and Civil Law: Is it Possible?" Kulliyah Undang-Undang Ahmad Ibrahim, Universiti Islam Antarabangsa, Malaysia, 24–25 July 2004.

Mohamad, Abdul Hamid. "Civil and Syariah Courts in Malaysia: Conflict of Jurisdictions." Institute of Islamic Understanding, International Seminar on Islamic Law in the Contemporary World, Malaysia, 24–25 October 2000.

Moosa, Ebrahim. "The Debts and Burdens of Critical Islam," *Progressive Muslims: On Justice, Gender and Pluralism* (ed.) Omid Safi (Oxford: Oneworld, 2003).

Mufti, Mohammad Ali. *Naqd Al-Judhur Al-Fiqriyyah Lil-Dimoqratiyyah Al-Gharbiyyah* (Riyadh: al-Muntada al-Islami and Majallat al-Bayan, 2002).

Mujlisul Ulama of South Africa. "The Concept of Limited Liability—Untenable in Shariah," (n.p.: n.d.), 23. http://www.mohrasharif.com/PDFs/limited-liability.pdf.

Nada, Muhammad Mahmud. *Al-Naskh Fi Al-Qur`an: bayna al-mu'idin wa-al-mu'aridin* (Cairo: Maktabat al-Dar al-Arabiyah lil-Kitab, 1996).

al-Nasa'i, Ahmad ibn 'Ali ibn Shu'ayb. *Sunan al-Nasa'i* (Cairo: al-Matba'a' al-Misriyyah, 1930).

Olson, Roger. *The Mosaic of Christian Beliefs: Twenty Centuries of Unity and Diversity* (Downers Grove: InterVarsity Press; Leicester, UK: Apollos, 2002).

Onsoy, Rifat. "Sened-i Ittifak ve Turk Demokrasi Tarihindeki Yeri," (Ankara: Turkiye'de demokrasi Hareketleri Konferansi 6–8 Kasim 1985 H.U.Edb. Fakultesi Dergisi, c.4, no. 1, 1985).

Ostrorog, Léon. *The Angora Reform: Three Lectures Delivered at the Centenary Celebrations of University College on June 27, 28, & 29, 1927* (London: University of London Press, 1927).

Pew Research Center's Religion & Public Life Project and Pew-Templeton Global Religious Futures Project. *The World's Muslims: Religious, Political and Social Views* (Washington, DC: Pew research Center, 2013).

al-Qaradawi, Yusuf. *Madkhal li-Dirasat al-Shariah al-Islamiyyah* (Cairo: Maktabah Wahbah, 1411/1990).

al-Qaradawi, Yusuf. *Kayfa Nata`amal ma`a Al-Qur'an Al-`Azeem* (Cairo: Dar al-Shorouk, 1999).

al-Qarafi, Ahmad ibn Idris. *Al-Dhakhirah* (Cairo: Matba'at Kuliyat al-Shariah, 1961).

al-Qarafi, Ahmad ibn Idris. *Kitab al-Furuq: anwar al-buruq fi anwa' al-furuq* (Cairo: Dar al-Salam, 2001).

Qureshi, Emran. "Taliban" in *The Oxford Encyclopedia of the Islamic World* (ed.) John Esposito (New York: Oxford University Press, 2009).

al-Rab'ī al-Qazwīnī, Ibn Mājah. *Sunan ibn Majah.*

al-Radi, Muhummad ibn al-Husayn Sharif and Mohammad Askari Jafery (eds) *Peak of Eloquence Nahjul Balagha: Sermons, Letters, and Saying of Imam Ali ibn Abi Talib* (Accra; New York: Islamic Seminary Publications, 1984).

Rahman, Fazlur. *Major Themes of the Qur'an* (Minneapolis, Chicago: Bibliotheca Islamica, 1980).

Raysuni, Ahmad. *Nazariyyat al-Maqasid 'ind al-Imam al-Shatibi* (Rabat, Morocco: Matba'at al-Najah al-Jadidah, 1411/1991).

Raysuni, Ahmed, Muhammad Mustafa Zuhayli, and Muhammad 'Uthman Shubayr. *Huquq al-insan: mihwar maqasid al-shariah* (Doha: Wizarat al-awfaq wa-al-shu'un al-Islamiyah, 2002).

al-Razi, Fahr al-Din. *Al-Tafsir Al-Kabir* (Riyadh: Markaz al-Turath lil-Barmajiyat, 2013).

Rehman, Scheherazade S. and Hossein Askari. "How Islamic are Islamic Countries?," *Global Economy Journal* 10(21) (2010).

Rehman, Scheherazade S. and Hossein Askari. "An Economic Islamicity Index (EI^2)," *Global Economy Journal* 10(3) (2010).

Rida, Mohammad Rasheed. *Al-Wahy Al-Mohammadi: Thubut Al-Nubuwwah Bil-Qur'an* (Cairo: Mu'asasat Izziddin, n.d.).

al-Salam, 'Izz al-Din 'Abd. *Qawa'id al-Ahkam fi masalih al-anam* (Beirut: Dar Ibn Hazm, 2008).

Salih, Mohammed Osman. *"Al-Islam Huwa Nizam Shamil Lihimayat Wa Ta'ziz Huqouq Al-Insan"* (Khartoum: Unpublished paper presented at the International Conference on Islam and Human Rights, 2006).

Sano, Quttub. *Qiraat Ma`rifiyah Fi Al-Fikr Al-Usuli* (Kuala Lumpur: Dar al-Tajdeed, 2005).

al-Sarakhsi, Abi Bkr Muhammad b. Ahmad b Abi Sahl. *Usul al-Sarakhsi* (ed.) Abu al-Wafa al-Afghani (Istanbul: Kahraman yay, 1984).

Şentürk, Recep. "Sociology of Rights: 'I am Therefore I Have Rights': Human Rights in Islam between Universalistic and Communalistic Perspectives," *Muslim World Journal of Human Rights* 2(1) (2005), 1–31.

Şentürk, Recep. "Minority Rights in Islam: From Dhimmi to Citizen" in *Islam and Human Rights* (eds) Shireen T. Hunter and Huma Malik (Washington, DC: Center for Strategic & International Studies, 2005), 67–99.

Şentürk, Recep. "Sociology of Rights: Inviolability of the Other in Islam between Communalism Universalism," in *Contemporary Islam* (eds) Abdul Aziz Said, Mohammed Abu-Nimer, and Meena Sharify-Funk (New York: Routledge, 2006), 24–49.

Şentürk, Recep. *Açik Medenniyet* (Istanbul: Timaş Yay, 2010).

Sertoglu, Midhat. "Tanzimata Dogru," (Bildiriler, Istanbul: Sultan ll. Mahmud ve Reformlari Semineri 28–30 Haziran 1989).

Seyitdanlioglu, Mehmet. "Tanzimatin on hazirliklari ve Meclis-i Vala-yi Ahkam-i Adliye'nin Kurulusu 1838–1840," Bildiriler, Istanbul: Sultan ll. Mahmud ve Reformlari Semineri 28–30 Haziran 1989).

Shahrur, Muhammad. *Nahwa usul jadidah lil-fiqh al-mar'ah: al-wasiyah, al-irth, al-qiwamah, al-ta'uddudiyah, al-libas* (Damascus: al-Ahali lil-Tiba'ah wa-al Nashr wa-al-Tawzi', 2000).

Shamsuddin, Mohhamed Mehdi. *Al-Ijtihad wa-al-tajdid fi al-fiqh al-Islami* (Beirut: al-Muasasah lil-Dirasat wa-al-Nashr, 1999).

Shamsuddin, Mohammad Mehdi. "*Maqasid Al-Shariah*," in *Maqasid Al-Shariah* (ed.) Abduljabar al-Rufa`i (Damascus: Dar al-Fikr, 2001).

al-Sharif, Mohammad Shakir. *Haqiqat Al-Dimuqratiyah* (Riyadh: Dar al-Watan, 1992).

al-Shatibi, Abu Ishaq Ibrahim. *al-Muwafaqat fi Usul al-Shariah* 2 ed. (Beirut: Dar al-Ma'rifa, 1395/1975).

al-Shatibi, Abu Ishaq Ibrahim. *Kitab al-I'tisam* (Makkah al-Mukarramah: al-Maktabah al-Tijariyyah, n.d.).

Shaw, Stanford. *Between Old and New, The Ottoman State Under Sultan Selim 1789–1807* (Cambridge, MA: Harvard University Press, 1971).

al-Shawkani, Muhammad ibn. *Irshad Al-Fuhul ila tahqiq al-haqq min 'ilm al-usul* (Amman: 'A. Hamdan, 2003).

al-Siwasi, Kamaluddin. *Sharh Fath Al-Qadir* 2 ed. (Beirut: Dar al-Fikr, n.d.).

Smith, Wilfred Cantwell. *The Meaning and End of Religion* (Minneapolis, MN: Fortress Press, 1991).

Soroush, Abdul-Karim. "The Evolution and Devolution of Religious Knowledge," in *Liberal Islam: A Source Book* (ed.) Charles Kurzman (New York: Oxford University Press, 1998).

al-Sulami, 'Izz al-Din 'Abd al-Salam. *Qawa'id al-Ahkam fi Masalih al-Anam* (ed.) Taha 'Abd al-Ra'uf Sa'd (Cairo: al-Matba'ah al-Husayniyyah, 1351/1932).

Surowiecki, James. *The Wisdom of Crowds: Why the Many are Smarter than the Few and how Collective Wisdom Shapes Business, Economies, Societies, and Nations* (New York: Doubleday, 2004).

Taylor, Victor and Charles Winquist (eds) *Encyclopedia of Postmodernism* (London: Routledge, 2001).

al-Tubrusi, al-Fadl Ibn al-Hussain. *Majma' Al-Bayan Fi Tafsir Al-Qur'an* (Beirut: Dar al-'ulum, 2005).

al-Tufi, Najm al-Din Sulayman. *Sharh Mukhtasar al-Rawdah* (ed.) Abd Allah al-Turki (Beirut: Mu'assasat al-Risalah, 1407/1987).

al-Turabi, Hassan. *Emancipation of Women: An Islamic Perspective* 2 ed. (London: Muslim Information Centre, 2000).

United Nations High Commission for Human Rights, *Specific Human Rights Issues July, 2003*. Available at http://www.unhchr.cAH/Huridocda/Huridoca.nsf/(Symbol)/E.CN.4.Sub.2.2003.NGO.15.En, accessed on 1 February 2005.

United Nation Development Programme, *Annual Report 2004*. Available at http://www.undp.org/annualreports/2004/english, accessed on 5 February 2005.

University of Toronto Bora Laskin Law Library. *International Protection of Human Rights, 2004*. Available at http://www.law-lib.utoronto.ca/resguide/humrtsgu.htm. accessed on 15 January 2005.

Ibn Warraq, "Apostasy and Human Rights," in *Free Inquiry* (February/March 2006), 53.

Zuraiq, Burhan. *Al-Sahifah: Mithaq Al-Rasoul* (Damascus: Dar al-Numair and Dar Ma'ad, 1996).

Court Cases

Lim Chan Seng v. Pengarah Jabatan Agama Islam Pulau Pinang (1996) 3 CLJ 231.

Latifah Bte Mat Zin v. Rosmawati Binti Sharibun & Anor (2007) 5 MLJ 101.

Index

CPSIA information can be obtained
at www.ICGtesting.com
Printed in the USA
LVOW04s2141050116

469272LV00008B/15/P

9 781137 446817